EVERYTHING YOU WERE TAUGHT ABOUT
AFRICAN-AMERICANS & THE CIVIL WAR IS WRONG

Ask a Southerner!

❧ THE LOCHLAINN SEABROOK COLLECTION ❧

Everything You Were Taught About the Civil War is Wrong, Ask a Southerner!
Everything You Were Taught About American Slavery is Wrong, Ask a Southerner!
Everything You Were Taught About African-Americans and the Civil War is Wrong, Ask a Southerner!
Confederate Flag Facts: What Every American Should Know About Dixie's Southern Cross
Give This Book to a Yankee! A Southern Guide to the Civil War for Northerners
Honest Jeff and Dishonest Abe: A Southern Children's Guide to the Civil War
Confederacy 101: Amazing Facts You Never Knew About America's Oldest Political Tradition
Slavery 101: Amazing Facts You Never Knew About America's "Peculiar Institution"
The Great Yankee Coverup: What the North Doesn't Want You to Know About Lincoln's War!
Confederate Blood and Treasure: An Interview With Lochlainn Seabrook
A Rebel Born: A Defense of Nathan Bedford Forrest - Confederate General, American Legend (winner of the 2011
        Jefferson Davis Historical Gold Medal)
A Rebel Born: The Screenplay
Nathan Bedford Forrest: Southern Hero, American Patriot - Honoring a Confederate Icon and the Old South
The Quotable Nathan Bedford Forrest: Selections From the Writings and Speeches of the Confederacy's Most Brilliant
        Cavalryman
Give 'Em Hell Boys! The Complete Military Correspondence of Nathan Bedford Forrest
Forrest! 99 Reasons to Love Nathan Bedford Forrest
Saddle, Sword, and Gun: A Biography of Nathan Bedford Forrest For Teens
Nathan Bedford Forrest and the Battle of Fort Pillow: Yankee Myth, Confederate Fact
Nathan Bedford Forrest and the Ku Klux Klan: Yankee Myth, Confederate Fact
Nathan Bedford Forrest and African-Americans: Yankee Myth, Confederate Fact
The Quotable Jefferson Davis: Selections From the Writings and Speeches of the Confederacy's First President
The Quotable Alexander H. Stephens: Selections From the Writings and Speeches of the Confederacy's First Vice
        President
The Alexander H. Stephens Reader: Excerpts From the Works of a Confederate Founding Father
The Quotable Robert E. Lee: Selections From the Writings and Speeches of the South's Most Beloved Civil War General
The Old Rebel: Robert E. Lee As He Was Seen By His Contemporaries
The Articles of Confederation Explained: A Clause-by-Clause Study of America's First Constitution
The Constitution of the Confederate States of America Explained: A Clause-by-Clause Study of the South's Magna Carta
The Quotable Stonewall Jackson: Selections From the Writings and Speeches of the South's Most Famous General
Abraham Lincoln: The Southern View - Demythologizing America's Sixteenth President
The Unquotable Abraham Lincoln: The President's Quotes They Don't Want You To Know!
Lincolnology: The Real Abraham Lincoln Revealed in His Own Words - A Study of Lincoln's Suppressed, Misinterpreted,
        and Forgotten Writings and Speeches
The Great Impersonator! 99 Reasons to Dislike Abraham Lincoln
The Quotable Edward A. Pollard: Selections From the Writings of the Confederacy's Greatest Defender
Encyclopedia of the Battle of Franklin - A Comprehensive Guide to the Conflict that Changed the Civil War
Carnton Plantation Ghost Stories: True Tales of the Unexplained from Tennessee's Most Haunted Civil War House!
The McGavocks of Carnton Plantation: A Southern History - Celebrating One of Dixie's Most Noble Confederate Families
        and Their Tennessee Home
Jesus and the Law of Attraction: The Bible-Based Guide to Creating Perfect Health, Wealth, and Happiness Following
        Christ's Simple Formula
The Bible and the Law of Attraction: 99 Teachings of Jesus, the Apostles, and the Prophets
Christ Is All and In All: Rediscovering Your Divine Nature and the Kingdom Within
Jesus and the Gospel of Q: Christ's Pre-Christian Teachings As Recorded in the New Testament
Seabrook's Bible Dictionary of Traditional and Mystical Christian Doctrines
The Way of Holiness: The Story of Religion and Myth From the Cave Bear Cult to Christianity
Christmas Before Christianity: How the Birthday of the "Sun" Became the Birthday of the "Son"
Autobiography of a Non-Yogi: A Scientist's Journey From Hinduism to Christianity (with Amitava Dasgupta)
Britannia Rules: Goddess-Worship in Ancient Anglo-Celtic Society - An Academic Look at the United Kingdom's
        Matricentric Spiritual Past
The Book of Kelle: An Introduction to Goddess-Worship and the Great Celtic Mother-Goddess Kelle, Original Blessed
        Lady of Ireland
The Goddess Dictionary of Words and Phrases: Introducing a New Core Vocabulary for the Women's Spirituality
        Movement
Princess Diana: Modern Day Moon-Goddess - A Psychoanalytical and Mythological Look at Diana Spencer's Life,
        Marriage, and Death (with Dr. Jane Goldberg)
Aphrodite's Trade: The Hidden History of Prostitution Unveiled
UFOs and Aliens: The Complete Guidebook
The Caudills: An Etymological, Ethnological, and Genealogical Study - Exploring the Name and National Origins of a
        European-American Family
The Blakeneys: An Etymological, Ethnological, and Genealogical Study - Uncovering the Mysterious Origins of the
        Blakeney Family and Name

Five-Star Books & Gifts From the Heart of the American South

❧ SeaRavenPress.com ❧

EVERYTHING
YOU WERE TAUGHT ABOUT
African-Americans & the Civil War
IS WRONG, ASK A SOUTHERNER!

LOCHLAINN SEABROOK
JEFFERSON DAVIS HISTORICAL GOLD MEDAL WINNER

Foreword by African-American Educator Gregory Newson

LAVISHLY ILLUSTRATED
EXTENSIVELY RESEARCHED

Sea Raven Press, Nashville, Tennessee, USA

EVERYTHING YOU WERE TAUGHT ABOUT AFRICAN-AMERICANS
AND THE CIVIL WAR IS WRONG, ASK A SOUTHERNER!

Published by
Sea Raven Press, Cassidy Ravensdale, President
The Literary Wing of the Pro-South Movement
PO Box 1484, Spring Hill, Tennessee 37174-1484 USA
SeaRavenPress.com • searavenpress@gmail.com

1ˢᵗ Sea Raven Press paperback edition, 1ˢᵗ printing: June 2016
1ˢᵗ Sea Raven Press hardcover edition, 1ˢᵗ printing: June 2016 (978-1-943737-32-1)

ISBN: 978-1-943737-31-4 (paperback)
Library of Congress Control Number: 2016940907

Everything You Were Taught About African-Americans and the Civil War is Wrong, Ask a Southerner! by Lochlainn
    Seabrook. Foreword by Gregory Newson. Includes an index, endnotes, and bibliographical references.

Front and back cover design, graphic art, book design, layout, and interior art by Lochlainn Seabrook
    All images, graphic design, graphic art, and illustrations copyright © Lochlainn Seabrook
        Cover painting: "The Rescue," copyright © Gregory Newson
        Portions of this book have been adapted from the author's other works

The views on the American "Civil War" documented in this book are those of the publisher.

The paper used in this book is acid-free and lignin-free. It has been certified by the Sustainable Forestry
Initiative and the Forest Stewardship Council and meets all ANSI standards for archival quality paper.

PRINTED & MANUFACTURED IN OCCUPIED TENNESSEE, FORMER CONFEDERATE STATES OF AMERICA

DEDICATION

To the Old South's African-American community and European-American community. During Lincoln's War they displayed a friendship, loyalty, and love toward one another that will forever live as the finest example of American racial unity.

EPIGRAPH

There is neither Jew nor Greek, there is neither slave nor free man, there is neither male nor female; for you are all one in Christ Jesus.

Paul, Galatians 3:28

CONTENTS

℘ ✄☉ PART TWO ☉℘ ℘

AFRICAN-AMERICANS DURING LINCOLN'S WAR

❧ PART THREE ☙

AFRICAN-AMERICANS AFTER LINCOLN'S WAR

Notes To The Reader

THE TWO MAIN POLITICAL PARTIES IN 1860

☛ In any study of America's antebellum, bellum, and postbellum periods, it is vitally important to understand that in 1860 the two major political parties—the Democrats and the newly formed Republicans—were the opposite of what they are today. In other words, the Democrats of the mid 19th Century were Conservatives, akin to the Republican Party of today, while the Republicans of the mid 19th Century were Liberals, akin to the Democratic Party of today.

Thus the Confederacy's Democratic president, Jefferson Davis, was a Conservative (with libertarian leanings); the Union's Republican president, Abraham Lincoln, was a Liberal (with socialistic leanings). This is why, in the mid 1800s, the conservative wing of the Democratic Party was known as "the States' Rights Party."[1]

Hence, the Democrats of the Civil War period referred to themselves as "conservatives," "confederates," "anti-centralists," or "constitutionalists" (the latter because they favored strict adherence to the original Constitution—which tacitly guaranteed states' rights—as created by the Founding Fathers), while the Republicans called themselves "liberals," "nationalists," "centralists," or "consolidationists" (the latter three because they wanted to nationalize the central government and consolidate political power in Washington, D.C.).[2]

The author's cousin, Confederate Vice President and Democrat Alexander H. Stephens: a Southern Conservative.

Since this idea is new to most of my readers, let us further demystify it by viewing it from the perspective of the American Revolutionary War. If Davis and his conservative Southern constituents (the Democrats of 1861) had been alive in 1775, they would have sided with George Washington and the American colonists, who sought to secede from the tyrannical government of Great Britain; if Lincoln and his liberal Northern constituents (the Republicans of 1861) had been alive at that time, they would have sided with King George III and the English monarchy, who sought to maintain the American colonies as possessions of the British Empire. It is due to this very comparison that Southerners often refer to the "Civil War" as the Second American Revolutionary War.

In 1854 Virginia Democrat George Fitzhugh, the epitome of an Antebellum Dixie Conservative, summed up the feelings of traditional Southerners everywhere when he said of our Right-leaning region:

> The South, quiet, contented, satisfied, looks upon all socialists and radical reformers as madmen or knaves. [3]

THE TERM "CIVIL WAR"

☞ As I heartily dislike the phrase "Civil War," its use throughout this book (as well as in my other works) is worthy of an explanation.

Today America's entire literary system refers to the conflict of 1861 using the Northern term the "Civil War," whether we in the South like it or not. Thus, as all book searches by readers, libraries, and retail outlets are now performed online, and as all bookstores categorize works from this period under the heading "Civil War," book publishers and authors who deal with this particular topic have little choice but to use this term themselves. If I were to refuse to use it, as some of my Southern colleagues have suggested, few people would ever find or read my books.

The American "Civil War" was not a true civil war as Webster defines it: "A conflict between opposing groups of citizens of the same country." It was a fight between two individual countries; or to be more specific, two separate and constitutionally formed confederacies: the U.S.A. and the C.S.A.

Add to this the fact that scarcely any non-Southerners have ever heard of the names we in the South use for the conflict, such as the "War for Southern Independence"—or my personal preference, "Lincoln's War." It only makes sense then to use the term "Civil War" in most commercial situations, distasteful though it is.

We should also bear in mind that while today educated persons, particularly educated Southerners, all share an abhorrence for the phrase "Civil War," it was not always so. Confederates who lived through and even fought in the conflict regularly used the term throughout the 1860s, and even long after. Among them were Confederate generals such as Nathan Bedford Forrest, Richard Taylor, and Joseph E. Johnston, not to mention the Confederacy's vice president, Alexander H. Stephens.

In 1895 Confederate General James Longstreet wrote about his military experiences in a work subtitled, *Memoirs of the Civil War in America.* In 1903 Confederate General John B. Gordon penned his wartime recollections under the title, *Reminiscences of the Civil War.* Even the Confederacy's highest leader, President Jefferson Davis, used the term "Civil War,"[4] and in one case at least, as late as 1881—the year he wrote his brilliant exposition, *The Rise and Fall of the Confederate Government.*[5] Well into the early 1900s countless former Rebel soldiers continued to use "Civil War" when describing their military experiences, as can be readily seen by perusing the 20th-Century memoirs of Confederate veterans and their loved ones.[6]

ON THE WORD "RACE"
☛ As with the phrase "Civil War," I use the word "race" only as a concession to popular culture. As genetic studies have repeatedly shown, there is no such thing as a separate or "pure" race of people. In other words, there is no gene that makes one "red" (Indian), "yellow" (Asian), "white" (European), "black" (African), or "brown" (Hispanic). All living humans are simply "varieties" that descend from a single ancestor, belong to a single race, derive their genes from a single source, and form a single species: *Homo sapiens sapiens.*[7]

More scientifically, every member of our species shares the same number of chromosomes, is inter-fertile with all others, and has blood that is constructed of the identical pattern of agglutinins and antigens—which is what makes blood transfusions between *all* humans possible.[8] Even many of our more enlightened ancient predecessors understood this, one of whom was Saint Paul, who said:

> God that made the world and all things therein . . . hath made of one blood all nations of men for to dwell on all the face of the earth.[9]

The widely varied appearances of humans stem not only from heredity (our ancestors), but also from geographic, that is, environmental, conditions. Thus physically speaking we are primarily the products of that part of the world in which our ancestors lived. This means, in turn, that there are no "superior" or "inferior" races, as individuals such as Yankee President Abraham Lincoln and Yankee Generals Ulysses S. Grant and William T. Sherman believed.[10]

Apache Chief Geronimo (pictured here with two of his nieces) is commonly referred to as a "Native-American." Spiritually and genetically speaking, however, there is no such thing, making this term, like all other racial nomenclature, useless and misleading. Not only is the soul race-less (Galatians 3:28), the apparent physical differences between people are nothing more than evolutionary adaptations resulting from where our ancestors once lived. There is only one race: the human race; a great inter-fertile group in which every member shares the same number of chromosomes, identical blood substances, and the same taxonomic family name: *homo sapiens sapiens*. Only racists, whatever their color, would have you believe differently.

For example, prehistoric people who lived in cold dark climates tended to have short stocky bodies, straight hair, small narrow noses, blue eyes, and light skin, all physical adaptations to cool temperatures, low humidity, upper elevations, and decreased sunlight—that is, boreal environments. Prehistoric people who lived in warm sunny climates tended to have tall thin bodies, curly hair, large broad noses, brown eyes, and dark skin, in this case all physical adaptations to hot temperatures, high humidity, low elevations, and increased sunlight—that is, equatorial environments. All humans descend from recent and distant ancestors that were from one or both of these geographical regions (or from regions that lie between them), which explains the immensely diverse physical traits of the human species.

Confounding both popular belief and science, there are exceptions, even reversals, to this rule, such as instances in which white children have been born to black parents with no known Caucasian ancestry, and black children who have been born to white parents with no known African ancestry.[11] And since some whites become quite dark from sun exposure while some do not, and since blacks have dark skin in all environments, we know that it is not just heredity that determines traits like skin color. It is the way an individual reacts to his environment—and it is *this* particular trait that is inherited.[12]

British anthropologist Ashley Montagu has called the idea of race "man's most dangerous myth," for it catalogs people not merely by physically distinguishable populations, but by the common belief that these differences are inherently connected to higher or lower mental capacities, capacities that can allegedly be measured by both cultural achievements and IQ tests.[13] Yet no such measurement can be taken because no such link exists. "Race" then is one of those ideas that lies beyond infallible systemization; it is a nonsensical and thus worthless concept that "deifies all attempts at classification."[14]

In a word, human beings are simply not capable of being arranged into clear-cut categories, for there are far too many variables, from natural selection and environmental adaptation, to genetic mutations and the random modification of hereditary characters. The massive genetic diversity resulting from these sporadic, spontaneous, and often unknowable and untraceable influences makes the very concept of a "pure race" impossible.[15]

Indeed, the "diversity" of the human species is much smaller than popular culture imagines: the female eggs that created the world's present human population would all fit inside a one gallon jar, while the sperm cells that produced us would easily fit into an aspirin tablet. In fact, the hereditary material that formed all living human beings would only take up the space of one large multivitamin.[16]

The word "race" then turns out to be an invented construct, an arbitrary and convenient term that has no relationship to biology (skin color, hair and facial characteristics, body type, etc.), culture, religion, linguistics, or nationality. This, in turn, renders the concept of "racism" pointless (the word was not even coined until 1902),[17] which is why the word race has been slowly disappearing from science books for many decades. Anthropologists, for instance, no longer classify humans by skin color, but rather by biological and genetic variability and the influence of these factors on different populations that are far more accurately called "ethnic groups" or "genogroups," rather than "races."[18] Anything else must be labeled false science and illogical theorizing based on faulty misconceptions about human biology.[19]

In truth what "racist" blacks do not like about non-Africans, what "racist" browns do not like about non-Hispanics, what "racist" yellows do not like about non-Asians, what "racist" reds do not like about non-Indians, and what "racist" whites do not like about non-Europeans, is, in almost all cases, social and cultural, not "racial."

Furthermore, if one is biased toward another due to their appearance, this is lookism, not racism. If one is biased toward another because of their age, this is ageism, not racism. If one is biased toward another due to their gender, this is sexism, not racism. All of these "isms" have, at one time or another, been misinterpreted and mischaracterized as "racism." Hence, I have put forth a replacement word for racism, *socioculturalism*: prejudice toward an individual or group based on their social or cultural background and conditions.

While it is doubtless time to rid our language of the ambiguous, artificial, obsolete, generalized, loaded, stereotyping, imprecise, limited, mystical, and meaningless word "race" and its "built-in confusion,"[20] I continue to use it, in this book because—as there is yet no public consensus agreement on an alternate—my word "socioculturalism" would only confuse my readers.

LANGUAGE
☛ Many Liberals find the use of the terms "reds" (for Native-Americans), "browns" (for Hispanic-Americans), "blacks" (for African-Americans), and "yellows" (for Asian-Americans) "embarrassing." Yet they freely use the term "whites," usually in a disparaging manner, for anyone who is not Indian, Hispanic, African, or Asian. Thus, to be both fair and non-biased, where necessary I use the words reds, browns, blacks, and yellows for the various ethnogroups, including the word whites for European-Americans.

A WORD ON VICTORIAN MATERIAL
☛ In order to preserve the authentic historicity of the Civil War period, I have retained the original spellings, formatting, and punctuation of the 19th-Century individuals I quote. These include such items as British-English spellings, long-running paragraphs, and other literary devices peculiar to the time. Bracketed words within quotes are my additions and clarifications, while italicized words within quotes are

(where indicated) my emphasis.

PRESENTISM

☛ As a historian I view *presentism* (judging the past according to present day ideas) as the enemy of authentic history. And this is precisely why the Left employs it in its ongoing war against traditional American, conservative, and Christian values. By looking at history through the lens of modern day beliefs, they are able to distort, revise, and reshape the past into a false narrative that fits their ideological agenda: the Liberalization *and* Northernization of America, the same agenda that Lincoln had.

This book, *Everything You Were Taught About African-Americans and the Civil War Is Wrong, Ask a Southerner!* thoroughly eschews presentism, and replaces it with what I call *historicalism*: judging our ancestors based on the values of their own time. To get the most from this work the reader is invited to reject presentism as well. In this way—along with casting aside preconceived notions and the erroneous "history" churned out by our left-wing educational system—the truth in this work will be most readily ascertained and absorbed.

LEARN MORE

☛ Lincoln's War on the American people and the Constitution can never be fully understood without a thorough knowledge of the South's perspective. As this book is only meant to be an introductory guide to these topics, one cannot hope to learn the whole truth about them here. For those who are interested in a more in-depth study, please see my comprehensive histories listed on page 2; in particular, *Everything You Were Taught About the Civil War is Wrong, Ask a Southerner!*, and *Everything You Were Taught About American Slavery is Wrong, Ask a Southerner!*

LOCHLAINN SEABROOK
MODERN BOOKS WITH A VINTAGE VIBE

FOREWORD

President Ronald Reagan's quote September 21, 1987, illustrates how quickly we could come together if we shared a common cause.

> In our obsession with antagonisms of the moment, we often forget how much unites all the members of humanity. Perhaps we need some outside, universal threat to make us recognize this common bond. I occasionally think how quickly our differences worldwide would vanish if we were facing an alien threat from outside this world.[21]

My common bond with award-winning author and historian Mr. Lochlainn Seabrook started from a hunger for Civil War knowledge which I

acquired after painting a picture named "The Promotion," depicting a black Confederate soldier. This inspiration culminated from closing down my eight-year old business and publication named, *The New York Minority Business Directory: Black Pages*, a MWBE ("Minority and Women-owned Business Enterprise") profiling business networking directory.

My publication was often praised for being instrumental in helping the government steer contracts to minority owned businesses, but I've always felt like I had sidelined my artistic abilities, which help me think outside the box. As I pondered the black Confederate soldier in my painting, I realized this subject had a therapeutic effect on me, so I began to explore it in more detail.

Author, educator, and artist Gregory Newson, in his Confederate uniform.

I learned that the loyalty of the slave in guarding home and family during his master's absence has been well documented. This Afro-American loyalty extended itself even to service in the Confederate Army. Believing that their land was being invaded by hostile forces, both slaves and freemen were eager to protect their Southern homeland and offered themselves for military service throughout the war. While Afro-Americans were quickly received into the Confederacy's *integrated* fighting force, the North was academically debating the idea of arming blacks, correctly determining that white Yankee soldiers would desert before they would fight next to them.

I became very passionate about the subject, but at the same time I couldn't stop thinking about what I had been taught by Hollywood and by my Grammar and High School teachers: "In the Confederate army," they asserted, "Negroes were used only as cooks, teamsters, construction hands, orderlies and flunkies." This troubled me because I knew now that this was incorrect, and that therefore Abraham Lincoln and his black Union soldiers could not be, and in fact were not, responsible for today's African-American freedoms.

The pursuit of a better understanding of this topic led me to Civil War scholar Mr. Lochlainn Seabrook, a descendant of numerous Confederate soldiers and the author of over forty-five books, most of them on what he calls "Lincoln's War."

Mr. Seabrook's writings rocked my world! The more I read, the more I realized that we have all been force-fed thousands of lies. I used the Internet and other sources to verify his books, and came to the conclusion that his writings are the bomb!

Here is just a little of what I've learned.

When it came to the American Civil War, my Elementary and High School teachers used a Liberally-biased, government-sponsored, cherry-picked form of American history, one that conveniently leaves out the truth in order to promote racial strife and bigotry—part of the Left's deceptive movement to divide and conquer America. On realizing the importance of this finding, as well as how much my country and my community needs to be educated about it, I contacted Mr. Seabrook's people and encouraged him to write a book specifically on this topic. His manager informed me that such a book was already underway, but had been temporarily set aside due to his numerous other literary, film, and music projects. I was happy to learn, however, that he felt the same sense of urgency I did, and agreed to complete the book ASAP. You hold the final product in your hand, complete with my painting, "The Rescue," on the cover of the paperback edition.

In my opinion, *Everything You Were Taught About African-Americans and the Civil War is Wrong, Ask a Southerner!* is a healing book, one meant to foster understanding and unity between the races. For only the truth can cure the deep, centuries-old rift between them. Why? Because this division was built on a lie and is therefore false! I'm speaking of the racial gulf not just between South and North, but between our two communities all across America.

After the end of the Civil War educated Southerners issued a warning that the truth about the conflict, about its actual purpose and its white and black participants, would be buried, replaced by a tall tale designed to make the North look good and the South look bad. They were right! The Federal government paid its historians to conceal the facts and load up our textbooks with their falsehoods. This seems to fulfill the old adage that the victor gets to write the war's history, while the vanquished lose their voice. But it's not true anymore! For a few courageous souls like Lochlainn Seabrook are coming forward to write and preserve the authentic history of the Civil War.

You see, our country, America, needs healing from the racial divide that has existed since before the Civil War. Both Mr. Seabrook and myself agree that it's time to stop thinking in terms of black and white! The people, the issues, the emotions, and the motivations concerning the Civil War are far more complex than simply: "North = good liberators; South = evil slave owners." This type of overly simplistic thinking not only does an injustice to our children, who deserve to know the truth, it polarizes people even further as we confront the racial issues of today. We need to "bind up the nation's wounds," and this can only happen by learning about and understanding what really took place between African-Americans and European-Americans before, during, and after the Civil War. And this can't happen if we rely on the make-believe "history" invented by Northern historians.

But it will by reading Mr. Seabrook's book! In it you'll learn, in most cases probably for the first time, the truth about the birth of African-American slavery in Africa, Africa's 1.5 million white slaves, the creation of both the American slave trade and American slavery in New England, the founding of the American abolition movement in the South, the huge difference between the treatment of slaves in the North and slaves in the South, African-American slave owners, and the Yankee deceptions and myths concerning "slave names," the Underground Railroad, Northern integration, Northern abolition, the cause of the Civil War (it wasn't slavery!), the horrors of being a black Union soldier, the massive Southern black support of the Confederacy during the War, the black Confederate soldier, reparations, the true Great Emancipator Jefferson Davis, white supremacist Abraham Lincoln and his phony Emancipation Proclamation, and much more!

In this artist-writer's opinion, the "aliens" that President Reagan spoke of are those who are enemies of this truth. Sadly, many of them are in government, where they continue to push the educational poison that teachers feed our children. Want to help put a stop to this and be a positive part of the change? Read Mr. Seabrook's work. Because, believe me, racial healing and unification will never come from removing Confederate flags, tearing down Confederate monuments, or moving Confederate graves. As you'll learn from this book, when it came to the black race, the Confederates were the good guys!

Gregory Newson
Newburgh, New York
June 2016

INTRODUCTION

The title I have given this book may sound humorous, but it is not intended to be. For my topic, African-Americans and Lincoln's War, has been used daily over the past 150 years by uninformed and often cruel people to scare, hurt, humiliate, manipulate, and oppress others, using information that not only defies all commonsense, but is patently false and thus historically inaccurate.

For example, most Americans have been taught that white Southern slave owners (they do not want you to know about *black* and *red* Southern slave owners, or even *Northern* slave owners, for that matter) "ritually abused their black chattel on a daily basis." Even someone unfamiliar with authentic American history must, after a moment's reflection, realize the absolute irrationality of this tired old Yankee myth.

The Left has long intentionally misrepresented African-Americans and the American Civil War. It is time to deal with the historical facts: acknowledge them, learn them, embrace them, and once again begin teaching them to our youth. Only in this way can we undertake the Great Healing that is needed between the European-American community and the African-American community. In this case the truth really will set us free.

To begin with, those few white Southerners who actually owned black servants did not view them as a hostile group who could only be controlled by force. This is a Northern stereotype that never existed in the Old South. There were no armed guards on Southern plantations, no fences, no walls or barriers to hold anyone in or keep anyone out. There was complete freedom on the typical Southern farm, and servants could simply walk on and off the property whenever they pleased—and, with but a few exceptions, they did just that.

Second, this informal approach fit the leisurely lifestyle of both Southern whites and Southern blacks perfectly. For, on the whole, nearly all white Southern slaveholders were Conservative Christians possessed of a deep humanitarianism, tender generosity, and an affectionate nature that is peculiar to our region, and which continues to exist to this day under the term "Southern hospitality" (one never hears of "Northern," "Eastern," or "Western hospitality").

Third, this explains why Southern whites had warm and friendly relationships with their black servants, not only legally registering them as family members upon purchase, but treating them as such throughout their entire lives. *All* black Southern servants, for instance, received free food, shelter, clothing, health care, and education from cradle to grave, much to the envy of many free blacks and whites—the poorer who often died from malnutrition or illness, problems virtually unknown among Southern "slaves."

Another popular piece of Yankee folklore pertains to the black Confederate soldier. The typical pro-North, anti-South history book, annually printed in the thousands by history-ignorant Liberal publishers and South-loathing university presses, tells us "there was no such thing." "Why would an African-American ever fight for let alone support the Confederacy?" these pompous provincialists bellow from their insular East Coast offices and their elitist West Coast campuses.

Anyone familiar with genuine Southern history can name dozens of reasons why. Indeed, there is so much evidence for the black Confederate soldier—despite the North's nefarious attempt to suppress and bury it—that I have devoted an entire chapter and an appendix to the subject.

You will learn much more about these particular topics, as well as thousands of others, in this book, including the truth about indigenous African slavery and African-American slavery, the beginnings of American slavery in the North, the beginnings of the American abolition movement in the South, Northern slaves and slave owners, the Northern slave trade, slaves laws in the Old North and the Old South, race relations in the North and South, Northern segregation and Southern integration, so-called "Southern slave abuse," the real cause of Lincoln's War, the Confederate army and blacks, the Union army and blacks, Lincoln's lifelong plans to deport and colonize all African-Americans (or corral them in their own all-black state), what Civil War era blacks really thought of Lincoln, and the epic national disaster and hoax known as the "Emancipation Proclamation."

The Left would rather you not know the truth about blacks, whites, and early America. They would rather you not know that the first blacks to America's shores were not slaves, but regular servants who

were traveling with white servants looking for work; that the first official American slave owner was an African; that the South hated slavery, never wanted it to begin with, and tried to end it long before the North did; that in 1698 there were more white slaves in Virginia than black slaves; that there were more black slaves in the North at the time the U.S. was formed than in the South; that less than 5 percent of Southerners owned slaves; that Lincoln did not like people of color and never tried to hide it; that thousands of Southern blacks supported and assisted the Ku Klux Klan

There is far more that has been hidden from you by misguided progressives than you will ever know. These three individuals, for example, including the white girl on the right, are slaves from New Orleans, Louisiana, photographed some time in the mid 1800s. You are not supposed to know that white slavery was once common across the U.S., and that not only did it exist side by side with black slavery, but that it actually arose prior to it; and that, in fact, European-American slavery paved the way for African-American slavery.

and even formed their own all-black chapter in Nashville; that both Lincoln and Confederate President Jefferson Davis repeatedly asserted that the Civil War was not about slavery; that the Confederacy was planning to initiate complete abolition a year before the Union; that the Emancipation Proclamation did not legally free a single slave, and was never meant to; that Lincoln's poorly planned emancipation (and the subsequent Thirteenth Amendment) killed off at least 25 percent of the African-American population; that emancipation substantially lowered the quality of life for former black slaves and their descendants for the next 100 years. The list goes on.

Why are Liberals, and even some misguided Conservatives, so afraid that you will learn the truth about African-Americans and the Civil War? It is because, as freedom-hating race-baiters who make a living from dividing our country along racial lines, it is in their best financial and political interest. To this end they project their own racism onto non-racist people (like traditional Southerners) and Southern symbols (like the Confederate Battle Flag) in order to stoke the fires of racial discontent. This bogus racial strife is augmented by the creation and use of their fake "race war," an attempt to sow further discord. To reenforce these fairy tales they regularly rewrite, revise, and redact history to reflect their own divisive and sinister

White racist, white supremacist, and white separatist Abraham Lincoln was a big government Liberal who tried to overturn the Constitution and crush states' rights, and who campaigned his entire adult life to have all African-Americans "shipped back to Africa." This is not someone who deserves our adulation. Yet the Left continues to worship him. Why?

agenda: the segregation and alienation of the races. Divided and antagonistic, we are more susceptible to governmental control, the end goal of liberalism, socialism, and communism, the very ideologies that conservative

Southern whites and blacks went to war to stop in 1861—and are still trying to stop in 2016.

It is this false racial history that fills our history books, our libraries, and our schools; it is this false history that your progressive teachers taught you; it is this false history that the leftist media continues to force-feed us. You have become a slave to false history. It is high time to free yourself, and this book is your Emancipation Proclamation!

Mine is not the first literary effort specifically dedicated to African-Americans and the Civil War. In order to maintain what I call "The Great Yankee Coverup" (the North's purposeful concealment of the truth about Lincoln's War), Liberal anti-South authors have been enthusiastically putting out reams of deceptive literature, film, documentaries, and articles on this subject for decades. These works are not just filled with historical inaccuracies and poorly researched misinformation, but with actual disinformation, erroneous fabrications disguised by left-wing academia as "facts"; intentionally planted falsehoods designed to mislead, conceal, and propagandize.

However, this *is* the first book on African-Americans and the War which provides a historically accurate portrait; one without the Yankee distortions, scallywag lies, Northern slander, and anti-South indoctrination that normally accompany such works, authored by enemies of both the South and the Truth.

It is hoped that *Everything You Were Taught About African-Americans and the Civil War is Wrong, Ask a Southerner!* will not only enlighten and educate my readers, but will help to heal the emotional, psychological, racial, and sociopolitical wounds left over by the Liberal North's creation of the American slave trade, American slavery, and the American Civil War. If even one individual is freed from the shackles of false history by reading this book, my work will have been a success and my efforts will have been worthwhile.

Lochlainn Seabrook
Nashville, Tennessee, USA
June 2016

Few topics in American history have been more misunderstood, abused, and controversialized, so wantonly distorted, falsified, and misrepresented, or so heavily imbued with both misinformation and disinformation, than Southern African-Americans, and in particular, the 95 percent who supported and defended the South during the Civil War. Liberals disdain, despise, and deny the black Confederate, while most Conservatives misconstrue, misjudge, and misdeem him. This book completely debunks the dishonest and spurious view of the Old South's beloved African-American, intentionally contrived to misinform and confuse the public and submerge the facts beneath an ocean of malicious fiction, delusion, and sophistry. Mr. Seabrook's *Everything You Were Taught About African-Americans and the Civil War is Wrong, Ask a Southerner!* forever overturns the many demonized myths concerning this unique, talented, valiant, generous, and noble individual, and thoroughly details why traditional Southerners, both white and black, continue to enthusiastically honor him in story, film, and song. With this book the fraud has come to an end.

PART 1

AFRICAN-AMERICANS BEFORE LINCOLN'S WAR

"CONFEDERATE USE OF COLORED PERSONS, 1865"

"A gentleman from Charleston says that everything there betokens active preparations for fight. The thousand negroes busy in building batteries, so far from inclining to insurrection, were grinning from ear to ear at the prospect of shooting the Yankees." — A Washington dispatch to the *Evening Post*, 1861

"We learn that one hundred and fifty able-bodied free colored men of Charleston, yesterday offered their services gratuitously to the Governor to hasten forward the important work of throwing up redoubts wherever needed along our coast." — The *Charleston Mercury* (South Carolina), January 3, 1861

"We learn that about seventy of the most respectable free negroes in this city have enrolled themselves and design tendering their services to the Governor, to act in whatever capacity may be assigned them in defence of the State. Three cheers for the patriotic free negroes of Lynchburg." — The *Lynchburg Republican* (Virginia), April 1861

"The negroes in all this section of the country, slave and free, are as loyal as could be desired. They freely proffer their services to the State, and zealously contend for the privilege of being allowed to work on the batteries. Yesterday [Confederate] Gen. Gwynn declined the services of three hundred [Southern blacks] from Hampton who solicited employment on the batteries, and twice and thrice that number could be obtained in this city and vicinity in a single day, if it was thought advisable to accept them. Indeed, the entire fortifications of this harbor might be constructed by the voluntary labor of negroes, who would claim no higher reward than the privilege of being allowed to contribute their share toward the [Confederate] defence of the State, and the protection of their masters and mistresses, who had always extended a sheltering hand over them." — A letter in the *Petersburg Express* (Virginia), April 23, 1861[22]

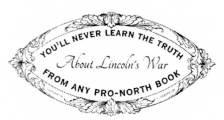

YOU'LL NEVER LEARN THE TRUTH *About Lincoln's War* FROM ANY PRO-NORTH BOOK

1

THE AFRICAN BEGINNINGS OF
AFRICAN-AMERICAN SLAVERY

WHAT YOU WERE TAUGHT: White Americans are totally responsible for American slavery.
THE TRUTH: Africans were practicing slavery on themselves for thousands of years before the arrival of Europeans.[23] For

> negro slavery is not an invention of the white man. As Greeks enslaved Greeks, as Anglo-Saxons dealt in Anglo-Saxons, so *the earliest accounts of the land of the black men bear witness that negro masters held men of their own race as slaves, and sold them to others.* This the oldest Greek historian [Herodotus] commemorates.[24]

In point of fact, "African slavery was coeval with the existence of the African race . . . . [and thus] has existed in Africa since its first [negro] settlement,"[25] predating even the founding of ancient Egypt over 5,000 years ago.[26]

It cannot be stressed enough that, it being a "characteristic part of African tradition" and a truly "universal" aspect of African society, *African slavery was of African origin.* Thus indigenous African slavery is nearly as old as Africa itself. Indeed, not only were slaves an integral part of the commerce of prehistoric and ancient Africa, but just as in early Sudan, as only one example, slave ownership was an accepted sign of wealth, and so was considered no different than owning precious metals or gems. Even the practice of exporting African slaves out of the country can be definitively dated back to at least the 5th Century B.C. It can be truly said then that *early Africa literally revolved around the enslavement of its own people by its own rulers upon its own soil.*[27]

This Fulani woman and Susu man both belong to native African peoples who once vigorously and violently practiced slavery on other Africans.

The native victims of the pre-conquest African slave trade were captured inland or in East Africa by their African brethren, then exported to Persia, Arabia, India, and China.[28] This means that the first European slavers to venture to Africa (Portuguese ship captain Antonio Gonzales arrived in 1434 and purchased several native African boys who he sold in Spain,[29] while Portugal's trade in slaves with the continent began in 1441)[30] only interrupted the booming, "well-developed" slave trade inaugurated by West Africans and various coastal tribes[31]—one that had already been going on there for untold centuries[32] with peoples like the Arabs.[33] It was only much later that Europeans helped stimulate the existing domestic business.[34]

Africa's own slavery system dates back to prehistory, long before written records, and includes some of the most unusual, savage, and shocking forms of human bondage ever chronicled.

2

AFRICA & THE TRANSATLANTIC SLAVE TRADE

The transatlantic slave trade could not have begun or functioned without the participation of Africa, her massive, prehistoric, continent-wide slave system, and her greedy slavery-loving chiefs, kings, and queens.

WHAT YOU WERE TAUGHT: The transatlantic slave trade was forced on an unwilling Africa.

THE TRUTH: Pre-European Africa had been practicing slavery, servitude, vassalage, and serfdom on its own people for thousands of years (in forms far more brutal than anything found in the American South), dating back to before the continent's Iron Age, to the very dawn of African history itself.[35] In fact, Africa is the *only* region that engaged *continually* in the West African-European-American slave trade for its full 424 years, from start to finish.[36]

It was just such facts that made the institution so understandable to many American black civil rights leaders. One of these was African-American educator, intellectual, and author Dr. William E. B. Du Bois, who wrote that he could forgive slavery for it "is a world-old habit."[37]

AFRICA & SELF-RESPONSIBILITY

WHAT YOU WERE TAUGHT: Free native Africans were hunted down in the wilds of Africa by white American slavers before being fettered and loaded aboard slave ships.

THE TRUTH: What Yankee historians, New South professors, and the Liberal media will not tell you is that Africans were never actually hunted down and captured directly by the white crews of foreign slave ships. They were captives who had already been taken during yearly intertribal raids and then enslaved by enterprising African kings, kinglets, chiefs, and subchiefs,[38] who quite eagerly traded them to non-African slavers for rum, guns, gunpowder, textiles,[39] beads, iron, and cloth.[40]

Sometimes these intra-African militaristic style raids and battles were carried on by African slave armies led by African slave officers.[41] Though the attrition rate was extremely high (over the millennia millions upon millions of Africans died during these marauding attacks),[42] greedy African kings would often purposefully start such wars, known as "slave hunts,"[43] in order to obtain slaves, a practice that eventually became "endemic" across large swaths of the continent.[44]

In other words, it was African chiefs who first enslaved other Africans,[45] and it was African slave merchants—slave drivers known as *slattees*[46]—who then forcibly marched them to the coast in chains and sold them to Arabs, Europeans, and eventually Yankees.[47] This means that when it came to African slaves, *all* of the slave hunting, slave capturing, slave abusing, slave torturing, slave marching, slave marketing, slave dealing, and slave selling went on *inside* Africa, perpetuated by Africans on other Africans on African land.[48] In 1908 American historian J. Clarence Stonebraker wrote:

> [Non-African] slave dealers only obtained their slaves by one [African] tribe conquering another and delivering same into the hands of the slave dealers, or by the consent of [African] parents, getting up their children and selling them. The very false stories that a vessel's crew could go into the jungles and drive out as many negroes as they wished is grossly vile, and was hatched along with many others by the unconscionable and incorrigible prejudice of [Northern] partisans, and for an equally vile purpose. Such things are still being taught and believed to an extent in the frigid [Yankee] section of our country . . .[49]

These African slaves were not captured by Europeans or Americans, and they are not destined for either Europe or North America. They were taken near Benguela, a city in western Angola, by fellow Africans and sold by fellow Africans to a European slave ship owner, who is now transporting them by boat to St. Thomas in the Caribbean. Here, they will be sold a second time and put to work on one of the island's many sugar, indigo, coffee, or cotton plantations.

This is why before 1820 no *free* blacks ever came to the U.S. from Africa. All were imported as slaves—that is, they had already been in bondage in their native country.[50]

To put it another way, during the transatlantic slave trade, every one of the Africans brought to America on Yankee slave ships had already been enslaved in their home country by fellow Africans,[51] after which they were marched to the Slave Coast (a 240-mile maritime strip roughly extending between the Volta River and the Akinga River),[52] temporarily held in stockades (wretched slave prisons known as *barracoons*),[53] then sold to white slavers by local African governments.[54]

These early Timbo women filling their gourds at a local water hole in central Guinea had to be on constant guard against stealthy and vicious native African slave hunters, who, at any moment, could rush in and take them captive, then rape, torture, and sell them into slavery. The Timbo, of course, were slavers themselves.

In short, whites only "bought slaves after they had been captured,"[55] and thus played no role in the actual enslaving process that took place in the interior, and had no idea what went on beyond the coastal areas.[56] As one Yankee slave ship owner accurately said in response to an abolitionist in the late 1700s:

> It is true, I have brought these slaves from Africa; but I have only transported them from one master to another.[57]

Before a Congressional committee on abolition another Northerner, Theodore Dwight of Connecticut, repeated the often acknowledged Yankee conviction that

> in importing Africans, we do them no harm; we only transfer them

from a state of slavery at home to a state of slavery attended by fewer calamities here [in America].[58]

Yes, *African slavery was purely an African-on-African business.*

And here is proof: until the first part of the 19th Century, no white man had ever set foot in the interior of tropical Africa.[59] Even the Europeans who first came to Africa's shores in the 1400s had no knowledge of anything "south of the desert."[60] These were the African hinterlands, after all: utterly unnavigable and

During the first half of the transatlantic slave trade, the so-called heart of Africa, the interior of the Dark Continent, was still completely unexplored by the West, and was thus unknown to white slave traders. More evidence that they did not participate in the capture and enslavement of native Africans, as anti-South writers preach. It was the ancient domestic African slave system itself that was fully responsible for this phase of the process; a process in which already enslaved Africans were carried to the coast by other Africans, then auctioned off to white ship owners. As one European slave trader understandably replied to a critic: "I have only transported them from one master to another."

therefore unexplorable, due not just to the ferocity of the native animals, but also because it swarmed with cannibalistic tribes who practiced human sacrifice and other primitive customs.[61]

At one time even radical abolitionists admitted as much. In 1835 Reverend George Bourne—the Briton who inspired fanatical New England abolitionist William Lloyd Garrison[62]—noted that "no ancient and accessible part of the inhabited globe is so completely unknown as the interior of Africa."[63] Thus whites could not have had any knowledge of what went on in the central regions of the continent during most of the Atlantic slave trade.[64]

Truly, without Africa's encouragement, commitment, participation, and collusion there would have been no black slavery in America. It is obvious then that Africa herself must be held accountable for taking part in the enslavement and forced deportation of some 10 to 50 million of her own people during the four hundred years between the 15th and the 19th Centuries.[65]

SLAVERY-OBSESSED AFRICA

WHAT YOU WERE TAUGHT: American enslavement was especially painful for African-born blacks, who in their entire history had been free and had never known slavery or any other kind of bondage or captivity. For early Africa knew nothing of slavery: it never practiced it and had no interest in the slave trade, particularly in enslaving, trading, or purchasing its own inhabitants.

An African chief selecting a prospective slave from a neighboring village, a practice common across the continent for at least 5,000 years before the arrival of the white man.

THE TRUTH: No region on earth has been more dependent on slavery over a longer period of time, practiced slavery more aggressively and widely on its own populace, or allowed slavery to become more entrenched, than Africa. Africa has been so intimately involved with slavery over such an immense duration—with slave majorities thought to be as high as 90 percent of the population in some regions[66]—that its name is today synonymous with the institution. "The great womb of slavery," Yankee abolitionist Charles Sumner correctly called it.[67]

Slavery was so intrinsic to the early African way of life that at one time slaves, revealingly referred to by their own people as "black ivory,"[68] could be found in nearly every African society, where—as in every other country where slavery is found—the minority population dominated and enslaved the majority population.[69] These were not merely "insignificant traces of slavery," as African apologists maintain, but rather true African slave societies, built on and around the bondage of their own people, employing some of the most brutal and sadistic forms of slavery ever recorded.[70]

Slavery's pivotal role in African society certainly explains why not a single organized slave revolt, or even an abolition movement for that matter, ever arose among the African populace during the entire pre-colonial period, and it is why slavery was finally only outlawed by the efforts of non-Africans (mainly Europeans).[71]

It also explains why there has long been a folk belief among the native population that due to Africa's obsession with slavery, "the whole land has been laid under a curse which will never be removed."[72]

An African slave owner at his house in Angola, surrounded by some of his African slaves—originally captured by Africans and sold to other Africans by Africans. It is clear to objective students of history that Africa must accept responsibility for enslaving her own people and for her enormous role in launching and facilitating the 400 year old transatlantic slave trade.

THE MYTH OF
THE MIDDLE PASSAGE

WHAT YOU WERE TAUGHT: The majority of African slaves died during the terrible Middle Passage at sea, en route to the Americas, and thus the full blame for their deaths must be placed on European-Americans.

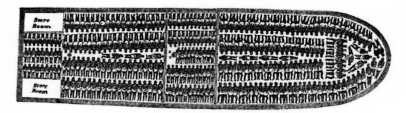

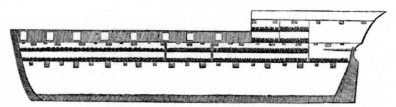

The decks of a slave ship during the infamous Middle Passage, as seen from above and the side. In the captain's effort to increase his profit margin, every square inch of the hold was used to accommodate as many men, women, and children as possible. Despite the obvious horrors that resulted from this barbarous custom, and contrary to Yankee myth, this, the second leg of the Slave Triangle, was not the most dangerous for the African individuals packed inside.

THE TRUTH: While there is no doubt that the oceangoing Middle Passage was indeed horrendous in many ways, it was not the most hazardous or unpleasant leg of an African slave's journey through the notorious Slave Triangle, as pro-North writers insist. It was the harrowing overland Beginning Passage, the land route from Africa's interior to the coast—where *three times as many slaves died as on the Middle Passage.*[73]

This was due not just to the shock of capture, but also to exhaustion, hyperthermia, malnourishment, sleep deprivation, dehydration, illness, animal attacks, and the inevitable physical abuse suffered at the hands of their tyrannical African captors. All of this made the misery and the mortality rates of the Middle Passage—which were after all, as one historian noted, merely part of "the then customary dangers and hardships of the sea" experienced by *all* oceangoing travelers—pale in comparison.[74]

Most importantly, let us note here that the oceangoing Middle Passage was operated by European and American whites, while the overland Beginning Passage, part of the domestic African slavery system, was run and controlled strictly by Africans.[75]

This coffle of African slaves is being driven to the coast by native African slave catchers, who work for native African slave dealers. The adult prisoners and their children were already serving as lifelong slaves of a local African chief when they were purchased from him for sale to Arab and European slave ship owners. It was this phase of the triangular trade, the overland Beginning Passage, not the subsequent seagoing Middle Passage, which proved to be the most hazardous for native African slaves.

THE WORLDWIDE PHENOMENON
OF WHITE SLAVERY

WHAT YOU WERE TAUGHT: As our schools teach only about black slavery, it is obvious that the idea of "white slavery" is a myth, or is at best overemphasized.

THE TRUTH: Our leftist schools focus only on black slavery, completely ignoring the reality of white slavery—and for good reason: America's liberalistic teachers do not want the truth to be known, for it would expose and demolish their false teachings about white racism and capitalism. Here we will correct this imbalance.

Not only did American slavery exist among native peoples—for example, the Aztecs,[76] Incas,[77] Mayans[78]—long before the arrival of Christopher Columbus[79] (the man responsible for starting the European-American slave trade),[80] but Western slavery itself was purely a white man's occupation and had nothing to do with Indians, Africans, or any other people of color, or even racism.

Indeed, historically speaking, *both the earliest known slave traders and the earliest known slaves were Caucasians*: the Babylonians, Assyrians, Sumerians, Akkadians, Mesopotamians, Phoenicians, Egyptians, Mycenaeans, Arameans, East Indians, Chaldeans, Hittites, Scythians, Persians, Arabians, and Hebrews—at some point in their history—all either enslaved other whites or were themselves enslaved by other whites.[81] In India, for example, historic records show that Caucasian slavery was being practiced by 1750 BC, nearly 4,000 years ago,[82] though doubtlessly it arose there thousands of years earlier. Some maintain that white thralldom may have even once been an integral part of Hinduism, one of the world's oldest religions.[83] The Vikings, Celts, Greeks, Italians, British, French, and, in fact, all European peoples, once enslaved other whites.

White slavery existed in Europe and North America long prior to black slavery. This white mother and daughter were kidnaped from their home in France and taken to Cuba, where they are being sold together at auction. They will be put on a slave ship bound for New York City, and sold a second time to a Northern slave merchant, who will in turn sell them, a third time, to a wealthy Yankee family. The reality of white slavery, an institution dating back to ancient Greece and beyond, highlights an inescapable fact: whatever our race, nationality, or skin color, all of our family trees are full of ancestors who were slave owners and slaves.

White slavery was not just a phenomenon of the ancient world, the Middle Ages, or even the 1700s, however. In fact, whites have been continuously and enthusiastically enslaving one another right into the present day. Soviet dictator Joseph Stalin, for example, enslaved an estimated 12 million[84] to 18 million Caucasians during his reign of terror in the 1930s,[85] as many as 14.5 million more white slaves than the American South's 3.5 million black servants. "Harshly treated," and forced to live in labor camps that were located in the northern wilderness of Siberia, Stalin's white slaves were assigned spirit-breaking work in mines and forests.[86]

Between 1941 and 1945, nearly 8 million Caucasians were

enslaved across Europe under Nazi Germany, including children as young as six years of age. This means that the Nazis owned 4.5 million more white slaves than the American South owned black slaves. Under Nazi socialist leader Adolf Hitler and the Third Reich's infamous swastika,[87] white European families were routinely separated and forced to work in factories, fields, and mines, where they were dehumanized, beaten, whipped, and starved by their German overlords.[88]

Though the Nazis' decision to adopt the swastika was based on an error (for it is not "Aryan"), today this archetypal, prehistoric solar symbol continues to be seen by many in the West as a frightening emblem of a dictatorial militaristic organization, one that thought nothing of enslaving, torturing, and murdering millions of fellow Caucasians.

By definition, *all* Nazi concentration camp prisoners were considered slaves, which is why Hitler's right-hand man, Heinrich Himmler, wanted the concentration camps themselves to be turned into modern factories—mainly for the production of German armaments. As sanitary conditions were poor, disease and mortality rates became "extraordinarily high."[89]

Among the millions of whites who were violently coerced into the Nazi Slave Labor Program were Poles, Russians, Slavs, Jews, and Italians. Many of Hitler's white slaves were housed five at a time in dog kennels only three feet tall. Imprisonment could last for as long as six months in camps that lacked water and even rudimentary sanitation. Overworked and underfed, millions of European slaves died at the hands of fellow whites during this period.[90]

White Nazi slavery was the largest revival of the institution in the 20th Century, and one of the fastest and most monumental expansions of slavery in world history.[91] If the Nazis had been victorious, Hitler was planning to operate a massive Caucasian "slave empire" that ran from Europe's Eastern coast on the Atlantic Ocean to the Ural Mountains in Western Russia.[92] All of this occurred a mere 65 years ago, demolishing the Yankee-New South myth that "slavery is a white racist institution focused specifically on blacks."[93]

AFRICA & HER
1.5 MILLION WHITE SLAVES

WHAT YOU WERE TAUGHT: The captivity and subjugation of whites in Africa, particularly in the Barbary States, has been overemphasized. The phenomenon was rare and lasted only a few years, very few whites were ever enslaved, suspiciously no names of the enslaved were ever recorded, and as native Africans are a kind and meek people, their so-called "white slaves" would have been treated graciously and respectfully by their black masters. White slavery in the Barbary States certainly has no connection to American black slavery.

In 1803 American ship Captain William Bainbridge fought bravely in the First Barbary War. He was captured, however, and enslaved by his African adversaries for nearly two years, becoming one of Africa's over 1 million white slaves.

THE TRUTH: Wrong on all counts. In a 1908 travel guide, writer Burton Holmes noted:

A hundred years ago a visit to the Barbary Coast was an experience not to be desired by voyagers from Christian lands, who then came not as tourists with cameras and guidebooks but as *prisoners or slaves in manacles and chains*.[94]

At one time there were so many white slaves in Africa that a series of wars, known as the Barbary Wars, were fought and an abolition society, known as the "Knights Liberators of the White Slaves in Africa," was formed to rescue and emancipate them.[95]

North African slavers specialized in the capture, enslavement, and sale of whites. During the peak years of white slavery in Africa some 1.5 million Caucasians were forced into bondage, under which they were often brutalized and tortured for years before being sold off or killed. The European family shown here has just been kidnaped by African slave dealers, and is being led under the lash to a slave market on the Barbary Coast. Most Liberal book publishers, authors, professors, and teachers completely ignore this dismal and tragic chapter in world history because, according to their leftist agenda, it is politically incorrect, and thus does not fit their idealized sociopolitical views.

The primary period of the enslavement of whites by African peoples lasted some 300 years, roughly from the 16th Century to the 19th Century. It has been conservatively estimated that between the years 1500 and 1800, 1 million to 1.5 million whites—from both Europe and America[96]—were enslaved by the Barbary States,[97] with an average of 5,000 white slaves entering the region each year. At about 14 new whites being imported a day, it was a commonplace occurrence. The city of Algiers, the capital of the African nation of Algeria, alone possessed some 25,000 to 50,000 European bondsmen and women.[98] Over the centuries countless tens of thousands of additional whites were killed during the process of enslavement.[99]

The Barbary Wars were comprised of several full scale U.S. military campaigns, launched in an effort to put a stop to the merciless enslavement of white Christians in Africa: the Tripolitan War (or First Barbary War, 1801-1805) under President Thomas Jefferson,[100] and the Algerian War (or Second Barbary War, 1815) under President James Madison.[101] Shortly thereafter, in 1816, the British, led by Lord Exmouth (Edward Pellew), conducted their own assault on African white slavery in the famed conflict known as the "Battle of Algiers."[102]

One of the many sea battles that took place during the Barbary Wars, a massive Euro-American effort to free Africa's white slaves.

AFRICA'S TREATMENT
OF HER BLACK SLAVES

WHAT YOU WERE TAUGHT: Indigenous African slavery was nothing like slavery elsewhere, for it was based on kinship and family ties. This is why Africans treated their black slaves so well.

THE TRUTH: Though many Africa-sympathetic writers have tried to portray domestic African slavery as a trivial and "harmless institution" that routinely absorbed slaves into families as "quasi-kin," the facts completely refute this. Indeed, in most cases authentic indigenous African slavery was actually "the antithesis of kinship."[103] For one thing, numerous African Kingdoms such as Uganda, Benin, and Dahomey,[104] and slaving peoples such as the Yoruba and the Ashanti, were well-known to ritually sacrifice their personal slaves in great Pagan ceremonials,[105] ranging from funerals and religious rites to political services.[106] The barbaric treatment of slaves is hardly compatible with the idea of kinship.[107] Let us consider the following:

> On the death of a king, or a distinguished [African] chief, hundreds of their courtiers, wives, and slaves are put to death, in order that they may have the benefit of their attendance in the future world. It often happens, that where the sword of the rude warrior is once drawn in such cases, it is not again readily sheathed; whole [African] towns may be depopulated before the thirst for blood is satiated.[108]

African authorities, like this Susu chief and his staff, were responsible for the brutal enslavement of thousands of fellow Africans, a fact now all but ignored by most historians.

Thus in 1800 the funeral of Ashanti King Q u a m i n a w a s accompanied by the ritual murder of 200 African slaves.[109] On another occasion the Ashanti people slaughtered some 2,600 African slaves at a single public sacrifice. In 1873, when the British seized Kumasi, a city in southern central Ghana, they discovered a huge brass bowl five feet in diameter. In it the Ashanti had collected the blood of countless thousands of sacrificed African slaves and used it to wash the footstools of deceased African kings.[110] Once, when the mother of a certain Ashanti king died, 3,000 African slaves were sacrificed at her tomb, and for two months afterward 200 additional slaves were put to death every week "in her honor."[111] Did anything in the American South ever compare to such horrific savagery? Only in the fantasies of Dixie's enemies!

On some occasions and among some African tribes, as Phillips notes, a rare type of kinship did develop between slave and master; but only when slaves were taken from *local* villages:

Slavery . . . was generally prevalent except among the few tribes who gained their chief sustenance from hunting. Along with polygamy, it perhaps originated, if it ever had a distinct beginning, from the desire to lighten and improve the domestic service. Persons became slaves through capture, debt or malfeasance, or through the inheritance of the status. *While the ownership was absolute in the eyes of the law and captives were often treated with great cruelty, slaves born in the locality were generally regarded as members of their owner's family and were shown much consideration.* In the millet zone where there was much work to be done the slaveholdings were in many cases very large and the control relatively stringent; but in the banana districts an easy-going schedule prevailed for all. *. . . The Africans were in general eager traders in slaves as well as other goods, even before the time when the transatlantic trade, by giving excessive stimulus to raiding and trading, transformed the native economy and deranged the social order.*[112]

British journalist Henry Woodd Nevinson explored Angola in the early 1900s, where he discovered the atrocities of the still thriving indigenous African slave industry firsthand.

Domestic slavery was so commonplace on the continent that literally *"all peoples"* of Central Africa later played a role in supporting the European slave trade.[113] Indeed, of the four classes of slavery identified by slavery scholars—1) captives of war; 2) debtors and criminals; 3) individuals who have sold themselves or were sold as children into slavery; and 4) children of slaves—"Negro Africa" is one of the few regions on earth that possesses all four.[114] In the mid 1800s famed Scottish missionary David Livingstone spent 30 years on the continent[115] trying to drain what he called the "open sore of Africa," the African slave trade, in this case with Arabia.[116] He did not succeed.[117]

Blake gives the following example of one British attempt at closing down African slavery, illustrating the virtual impossibility of ever turning the continent into a completely slave-free zone:

When Dr. [Richard Robert] Madden, of England,[118] went to Egypt in 1840, as the bearer of a letter from the Anti-Slavery Convention to Mohammed Ali, the ruler of Egypt, congratulating him upon his having issued an order abolishing the slave hunts, to his great surprise, he found that the order, though issued, had never been enforced, and probably never would be. The truth is, that *Mohammed himself had brought the system of hunting slaves to a high degree of perfection. Nubia was his principal hunting ground, into which he permitted no intruder. His own expeditions were conducted on a grand scale;* and generally took place after the rainy season.[119]

This 1872 illustration shows a meeting between Scottish medical missionary Dr. David Livingstone (right center) and British explorer Henry Morton Stanley (left center) at a village near Lake Tanganyika, in present day Tanzania. Livingstone spent decades in Africa trying to help abolish indigenous slavery, which, like his missionary work to convert the native peoples to Christianity, ended in failure.

Although countless African regions exported African slaves, the chief six were Senegambia, Sierra Leone, Gold Coast, Bight of Benin, Bight of Biafra, and West Central Africa, the last being responsible for some 45 percent of the total trade. Historians describe these areas as existing in a constant state of warfare for the main purpose of slave raiding:[120] neighbors that were captured during battle were immediately enslaved then appropriated for sale and export.[121] Often those incapable of hard labor, such as infants, children, and older women, were mercilessly slaughtered.[122] The rest were shackled and marched to the coast, where bonfires were lit along the beaches as signs to passing slave ships that the natives had slaves for sale.[123]

In the mid 1800s famous French-Italian slaver Theophile

Conneau, better known as Theodore Canot, experienced one of these African slave wars and lived to tell about it. He was visiting a small African town in the area then known as Digby, himself hoping to purchase native slaves from his hosts. Overjoyed to see him in anticipation of profitable sales, he was the focus of a long night of feasting and song. Exhausted from the celebration, all had fallen asleep, when:

> About three in the morning, the sudden screams of women and children aroused me from profound torpor! Shrieks were followed by volleys of musketry. Then came a loud tattoo of knocks at my door, and appeals from the negro chief to rise and fly. "The town was besieged:—the head-men were on the point of escaping:—resistance was vain:—they had been betrayed:—there were no fighters to defend the stockade!"
>
> I was opening the door to comply with this advice, when my Kroomen [members of the Kroo tribe, often hired as African guides by visiting white slavers], who know the country's ways even better than I, dissuaded me from departing, with the confident assurance that our assailants were unquestionably composed of the rival townsfolk, who had only temporarily discharged the bushmen to deceive my entertainer. The Kroos insisted that I had nothing to fear. We might, they said, be seized and even imprisoned; but after a brief detention, the captors would be glad enough to accept our ransom. If we fled, we might be slaughtered by mistake.
>
> I had so much confidence in the sense and fidelity of the band that always accompanied me,—partly as boatmen and partly as body guard,—that I experienced very little personal alarm when I heard the shouts as the savages rushed through the town murdering every one they encountered. In a few moments our own door was battered down by the barbarians, and Jen-ken [the rival chief and head African slaver], torch in hand, made his appearance, claiming us as prisoners.
>
> Of course, we submitted without resistance, for although fully armed, the odds were so great in those ante-revolver days, that we would have been overwhelmed by a single wave of the infuriated crowd. The barbarian chief instantly selected our house for his headquarters, and despatched his followers to complete their task. Prisoner after prisoner was thrust in. At times the heavy mash of a war club and the cry of strangling women, gave notice that the work of death was not yet ended. But the night of horror wore away. The gray dawn crept through our hovel's bars, and all was still save the groans of wounded captives, and the wailing of women and children.

By degrees, the warriors dropped in around their chieftain. A palaver-house, immediately in front of my quarters, was the general rendezvous; and scarcely a bushman appeared without the body of some maimed and bleeding victim. The mangled but living captives were tumbled on a heap in the centre, and soon, every avenue to the square was crowded with exulting savages. Rum was brought forth in abundance for the chiefs. Presently, slowly approaching from a distance, I heard the drums, horns, and war-bells; and, in less than fifteen minutes, a procession of women, whose naked limbs were smeared with chalk and ochre, poured into the palaver-house to join the beastly rites. Each of these devils was armed with a knife, and bore in her hand some cannibal trophy. Jen-ken's wife,—a corpulent wench of forty-five,—dragged along the ground, by a single limb, the slimy corpse of an infant ripped alive from its mother's womb. As her eyes met those of her husband the two fiends yelled forth a shout of mutual joy, while the lifeless babe was tossed in the air and caught as it descended on the point of a spear. Then came the refreshment, in the shape of rum, powder, and blood, which was quaffed by the brutes till they reeled off, with linked hands, in a wild dance around the pile of victims. As the women leaped and sang, the men applauded and encouraged. Soon, the ring was broken, and, with a yell, each female leaped on the body of a wounded prisoner and commenced the final sacrifice with the mockery of lascivious embraces!

In my wanderings in African forests I have often seen the tiger pounce upon its prey, and, with instinctive thirst, satiate its appetite for blood and abandon the drained corpse; but these African negresses were neither as decent nor as merciful as the beast of the wilderness. Their malignant pleasure seemed to consist in the invention of tortures, that would agonize but not slay. There was a devilish spell in the tragic scene that fascinated my eyes to the spot. A slow, lingering, tormenting mutilation was practised on the living, as well as on the dead; and, in every instance, the brutality of the women exceeded that of the men. I cannot picture the hellish joy with which they passed from body to body, digging out eyes, wrenching off lips, tearing the ears, and slicing the flesh from the quivering bones; while the queen of the harpies crept amid the butchery gathering the brains from each severed skull as a *bonne bouche* ["tasty mouthful"] for the approaching feast!

After the last victim yielded his life, it did not require long to kindle a fire, produce the requisite utensils, and fill the air with the odor of human flesh. Yet, before the various messes were half broiled, every mouth was tearing the dainty morsels with shouts of joy, denoting the combined satisfaction of revenge and appetite! In the midst of this appalling scene, I heard a fresh cry of exultation, as a pole was borne into the apartment, on which was impaled the living body of the conquered chieftain's wife. A hole was quickly dug, the stave planted and fagots supplied; but before a fire could be kindled the wretched woman was dead, so that the barbarians were defeated in their hellish scheme of burning her alive.

I do not know how long these brutalities lasted, for I remember very little after this last attempt, except that the bushmen packed in plantain leaves whatever flesh was left from the orgie, to be conveyed to their friends in the forest. This was the first time it had been my lot to behold the most savage development of African nature under the stimulus of war. The butchery made me sick, dizzy, paralyzed. I sank on the earth benumbed with stupor; nor was I aroused till nightfall, when my Kroomen bore me to the conqueror's town, and negotiated our redemption for the value of twenty slaves.[124]

The massacre at Digby (Africa) described in lurid detail by eyewitness Theodore Canot, occurred when a local African tribe attacked another in the middle of the night for the sole purpose of procuring slaves. In the ensuing melee hundreds were tortured and killed in the most brutal manner, such as this baby, who was flung into the air then impaled on a spear as it descended. It could be argued that the dead were the more fortunate of the victims in these types of raids, where the survivors could only look forward to a lifetime of misery, suffering, abuse, and eventually an ignoble death at the hands of their cold-blooded African masters and mistresses. Note the severed heads and limbs being carried by the participants, as well as the assailant inhumanely cutting body parts from a fallen but still living victim.

Africans continued to engage in the internal slave trade (the main pillar of the Afro-Arabic, Afro-European, and Afro-American slave trades) for centuries, despite the fact that it was extremely harmful to Africa's own people in a myriad of ways. The loss of adult males, for example, had a negative impact on African gender ratios, the gender division of labor, and dependency rates, as well as having the effect of intensifying warfare and increasing overall social inequality.[125] Indeed:

> *In Africa [slavery] . . . largely transformed the primitive scheme of life, and for the worse. It created new and often unwholesome wants; it destroyed old industries and it corrupted tribal institutions.* The rum, the guns, the utensils and the gewgaws were irresistible temptations. *Every chief and every tribesman acquired a potential interest in slave getting and slave selling. Charges of witchcraft, adultery, theft and other crimes were trumped up that the number of convicts for sale might be swelled; debtors were pressed that they might be adjudged insolvent and their persons delivered to the creditors; the sufferings of famine were left unrelieved that parents might be forced to sell their children or themselves; kidnapping increased until no man or woman and especially no child was safe outside a village; and wars and raids were multiplied until towns by hundreds were swept from the earth and great zones lay void of their former teeming population.*
>
> The [transatlantic] slave trade has well been called the systematic plunder of a continent. But in the irony of fate those Africans who lent their hands to the looting got nothing but deceptive rewards, while *the victims of the rapine were quite possibly better off on the American plantations than the captors who remained in the African jungle. The only participants who got unquestionable profit were the English, European and Yankee traders and manufacturers.*[126]

These domestic African problems do not mean, however, as some have suggested, that the continent was "forced against her will" to participate in the slave trade with Arabia, Europe, and later America. For since Africa was engaged in indigenous slavery for millennia prior to the Afro-European trade, *the transatlantic slave trade was merely a natural outgrowth of domestic African slavery.*[127]

African countries like Sierra Leone finally freed their *African* slaves in 1927.[128] But many tribes in various parts of the continent continue to engage in both the institution and the trade right into the present,[129] primarily in North,[130] Central, and West Africa, the latter where it has been reported that some 200,000 children alone are still sold into slavery each year.[131] There is evidence of a thriving slavery industry in both Southern Sudan and Mauritania (which, in 1980, banned slavery for the *third* time), while other forms of servitude, such as chattel slavery, forced prostitution, penal slavery, child labor, debt bondage (also known as pawnship), and forced military enlistment, continue unabated across Africa.[132] In 1993 a Mauritanian slave could be purchased for a mere $15. That same year the American Anti-Slavery Group (AASG) was formed for the sole purpose of trying to stop indigenous African slavery.[133] In essence, *intercontinental, large-scale, domestic African slavery is both pervasive and persistent, showing no signs of eradication any time soon.* As you are reading this, thousands of Africans are being enslaved by other Africans somewhere on the continent.

While 19th-Century Americans paid an average of $1,500 for an African servant (the current equivalent of $50,000),[134] as noted, today's Africans sell one another for as little as $15 a person; and they are treated, not as servants, as in America's Old South, but as true slaves: fettered and held at bayonet point, many slaves in modern Africa exist without an income, without civil rights, without proper diet or medical care, and without means or authority to buy their freedom.[135] This is *true* slavery, quite unlike the institution of servitude that was practiced in Victorian Dixie.

During his trek along one of Angola's primary slave trading paths to the coast, Nevinson came across this slave's grave, just one of thousands that dotted the 250-mile trail through the region's notorious Hungry Country. African slaves who were marched through this area never died of natural causes. Their end always came by way of the cruel hand of one of their African captors—just one more example of how native Africans treated their own black slaves.

This reality led many 19th-Century Southerners *and* Northerners to view American slavery as benign in comparison. In 1854 Southern abolitionist and slaveholder George Fitzhugh[136] spoke for many white Americans when he wrote that Africans were far better off being servants in the U.S. than being slaves in their native land, where there existed types of bondage that were infinitely worse.[137]

However much we may condemn slavery today, Fitzhugh was correct. *Indigenous African slavery, a continent in which slavery was both universal and integral to the growth and maintenance of countless kingdoms, was of African origin and often unimaginably savage in nature.*[138]

Prince Abdul Rahman Ibrahim Ibn Sori, commonly known by his nickname the "Prince of Slaves," began life as the son of a Timbo king in his native Africa, a people well-known for their custom of enslaving fellow Africans. One day while "Prince" was out on a slave catching mission, he himself was captured by African slavers, sold into slavery, and eventually transported to Mississippi, where he spent nearly half a century as a plantation overseer before he was freed and able to return to Africa.

EUROPEAN-AMERICAN SLAVERY & AFRICAN-AMERICAN SLAVERY

WHAT YOU WERE TAUGHT: Africans were the only enslaved people in early North America.

THE TRUTH: The well chronicled existence of both African-American slave owners and Native-American slave owners immediately disproves this statement. But there was another type of bondage that also preceded black servitude in North America, and which actually laid the groundwork for African slavery in the U.S.

The vast majority of white immigrants who came to America's original 13 English colonies—at least two-thirds[139]—came as white servants.[140] Made up primarily of English, Germans, Irish, and Scots, some 400,000 whites formed the first non-American servant population in the region's history, working as unskilled laborers on the budding nation's large new plantations.[141]

In fact, *white indentured servitude*, being much preferred over African slavery (Africans were considered "alien" by early white colonialists),[142] *was the institution that paved the way for black slavery in America*;[143] or as Brackett put it, white slavery made "a smoother pathway for the growth of [black] slavery."[144] In 1698, as just one example, not only were there more white servants in Virginia than there were African servants, but white indentured servants were being imported in far greater numbers than black ones at the time.[145]

Victorian legal scholar Roger Brooke Taney, fifth chief justice of the U.S. Supreme Court, descended from ancestors who, in the mid-1600s, emigrated from England to the British colony in Maryland as indentured servants.[146] So many whites arrived in America from Europe as retainers that as writer Hulbert Footner commented in the early 1900s, most of America's earliest European families proudly traced their beginnings to an indentured servant.[147]

Life was not easy for America's early white slaves, many who were sold by slave merchants side-by-side with African slaves.[148] In the colonies, for instance, white indentured servants, of both genders, were

White indentured servants working a colonial plantation in Virginia.

obliged to perform any labor asked of them. Their term lasted for up to five years, after which they were dismissed with nothing but the clothes on their backs—unless they were found guilty of misconduct, for which the length of their indenture could be extended. Maryland's white slaves were given a bonus: fifty acres of land on which to set up their own farms.[149]

Up until the end of the 17th Century, much of the American South's economy was based around, not African slavery, but European slavery; that is, indentured whites.[150] And free whites were not safe either. Across the Northern colonies whites were often sold into slavery as punishment for committing crimes.[151] In addition, many Southern whites lived under another form of servitude, one known as peonage, well into the 1880s.[152]

White slavery was also practiced in the U.S. under the headright system.[153] To accrue property in the American British colonies, wealthy Europeans would pay for the oceanic passage of indentured white servants from England in exchange for land.[154] John Maddison, an ancestor of America's fourth president, James Madison, did just this, acquiring some 2,000 acres of property by 1664.[155] In 1896, of this chapter in American history, Herbert Baxter Adams wrote:

The first slaves that we hear of in North Carolina were white people, and their masters were Indians. [English writer William] Strachey, in his *Travayle into Virginia* [1612], speaks of a story that he had from the Indians of an Indian chief, Eyanoco, who lived at Ritanoe, somewhere in the region to the south of Virginia, and who had seven whites who escaped out of the massacre at Roanoke, and these he used to beat copper. It is not improbable that there is a shadow of truth in the statement, although the details must be fictitious. *That the Indians of the colony later on did enslave the whites whom they could take in their waters, or who were shipwrecked off the coast, we know from the preamble of an act of the Assembly about 1707. This form of white servitude left no trace in the life of the colony.*

The first laborers that the English took to the New World colonies were whites, who during the first years of their residence were obliged to serve the settlers in the capacity of bonded servants. These people were commonly called "servants" or "Christian servants," and as such are to be distinguished from slaves. In regard to them, as well as to the slaves, their history as it related to North Carolina begins in Virginia. There were three sources of the supply of these [white] servants: 1. There were indented [white] servants, people of no means who, being unable to pay for passage to America, agreed to assign themselves for a certain period to some ship-captain on condition that when he reached Virginia he might transfer his right for money to some one who would maintain and work the servant for the given period. 2. Transported [white] felons, who were such criminals, vagabonds, or other obnoxious persons as were sent to the colonies by order of the English courts. 3. Kidnapped [white] persons, usually children, who were stolen by traders or ship-captains in the London or Liverpool streets and taken to America, where they were assigned till of age to such planters as would pay the prices demanded for their passages. *From these three sources many [white] people came to Virginia during the first sixty years of its settlement.* At the time, however, at which North Carolina was being settled, the importation of these people was being checked. This was due to at least three causes: 1. *The British government was actually exerting itself to replace the white servants with negro slaves.* In this the King was interested. In 1661 the Royal African Company was organized. The Duke of York [later known as King James II] was at the head of the enterprise and the King was a large stockholder. 2. The conscience of the English public was awakening to the violations of right which the traders perpetrated on those whom they allured by false promises, or forced by fraud, to go with them. These two causes acted together in 1664 when a commission of inquiry, with the Duke of York at its head, was appointed to report on the condition of such exportation of [white] servants.

At the same time arrangements were provided by which indented servants going to the colonies of their own free will might register their indentures at an office created for that purpose. Public sentiment thus aroused continued to grow until in 1686 an Order of Council was issued, which directed: a) that all contracts between emigrant [white] servants and their masters should be executed before two magistrates and duly registered; b) that no adult should be taken away but by his or her own consent, and no child without the consent of the parent or master; c) that in cases of [white] children under fourteen the consent of the parent as well as the master must be obtained, unless the parents were unknown. The process was supplemented by an order issued in 1671 to stop the transportation of felons to the continental colonies. 3. The incoming of negro slaves, who, when the experimental stage of slavery was past, were seen to be cheaper than white servants, was probably the most powerful of all the causes. The rivalry was between the whites and the blacks. The blacks won.

U.S. Vice President Henry Wilson (under President Ulysses S. Grant) spent eleven years of his youth working as an indentured white servant, after which he became an abolitionist.

It is impossible not to see in this an analogous process to that by which negro slavery supplanted Indian slavery in the West Indies. The abuses connected with Indian slavery touched the conscience of the people, and negroes who could better stand slavery were introduced to replace it. The abuses connected with white servitude touched the hearts of the British people, and again the negro was called in to bear the burden of the necessary labor. In each case it was a survival of the fittest. Both Indian slavery and white servitude were to go down before the black man's superior endurance, docility, and labor capacity.

The checking of the introduction of white servitude just at that time saved the colony of North Carolina for slavery. Whatever [white] servants were now taken thither would be carried into the place in ever decreasing numbers. Another cause operated to deprive the colony of even that number of [white] servants which would under these conditions have been its normal share. This was the poor harbors and the consequent lack of direct trade with Europe. The few ships that came through the inlets of the Currituck, Albemarle, and Pamlico Sounds brought few servants to be indented to the colonists. Furthermore, the poor economic conditions of those early days, when the farms were small and the exports inconsiderable, would have made it an unsafe venture for a trader to have tried to dispose of a shipload of [white] servants.

A few [white] servants very probably came to the colony from the first. In the Concessions of 1665 the Proprietors offered all masters or mistresses already in the colony eighty acres of land for each able-bodied manservant whom they had brought in, armed and victualled for six months, and forty acres for each weaker servant, "as women, children, and slaves." Those who should come in during the next three years were to have sixty and thirty acres respectively instead of eighty and forty acres as just stated. Those who should come later than that should get varying other amounts. This system was continued in its existing form for some time, but toward the end of the century it settled down to the habit of giving each [white] man who came into the colony fifty acres for every person, bond or free, whom he brought in with him. A further inducement was offered to the [white] servants themselves.

The Concessions of 1665 offered to every Christian servant already in the colony forty acres at the expiration of his or her period of servitude. Those coming later were to have smaller amounts. This inducement could not have brought many servants into the government, for two years later they were offered fifty acres on the expiration of their terms of service. Although this offer was not mentioned in the instructions after 1681, it seems to have been allowed as late as 1737, and perhaps later.

The Fundamental Constitutions, whose spirit was entirely feudal, provided for white servitude in that they tried to re-establish the mediaeval leet men and leet women [servants on the manors of lords]. They assumed the existence of such persons and directed that on every manor they should be subject to the lord of the manor without appeal. Such servants should not leave the lord's land without his written permission. Whenever a leet man or leet woman should marry, the lord of each should give the pair ten acres of land, for which he must not take as rent more than one-eighth of the yearly produce. It was also stipulated that "whoever shall voluntarily enter himself a leet man in the registry of the county court shall be a leet man," and " all children of leet men shall be leet men, and so to all generations."[156]

In summary, American white servitude lasted for over two centuries, involved the majority of the nation's first white immigrants,[157] and laid the foundation for American black servitude.[158]

Chief Powhatan, shown here performing a ceremony with his entourage, was a member of the Virginia Algonquians, a group of Native-Americans that regularly enslaved white colonists beginning in the late 1500s. This form of white slavery lasted well into the 1800s.

10

AMERICA'S RACIALLY TOLERANT SOUTHLAND

WHAT YOU WERE TAUGHT: White racism was always far worse in the South than it was in the North, which is why American slavery got its start in the Southern states.

THE TRUTH: Scores of eyewitness accounts, both domestic and foreign, reveal the opposite; namely, that the Old North was far more racist than the Old South. As early as 1831 individuals like French aristocrat Alexis de Tocqueville, who toured the South and the North that year, noticed that Southerners were "much more tolerant and compassionate" toward blacks than Northerners. This is why, while visiting America in the 1850s, Englishman Sir Charles Lyell observed that the Southern states justifiably "make louder professions than the Northerners of democratic principles and love of equality."[159]

The overt racial discrepancy between the South and the North was also remarked on by British journalists, even in the middle of Lincoln's War. In 1862 the *North British Review* noted that in the North, "where slavers are fitted out by scores . . . free Negroes are treated like lepers."[160] This was the same year Lincoln issued his Preliminary Emancipation Proclamation, in which, of course, he called for continued efforts to deport all freed blacks out of the U.S.[161]

After his tour of the states in 1831, Tocqueville summed up his observations this way:

Whosoever has inhabited the United States must have perceived that in those parts of the Union in which the negroes are no longer slaves, they have in no wise drawn nearer to the whites. On the contrary, *the prejudice of the race appears to be stronger in the States which have abolished slavery than in those where it still exists; and nowhere is it so intolerant as in those States where servitude never has been known.*

It is true that in the North of the Union marriages may be legally contracted between negroes and whites; but *public opinion would stigmatize a man who should connect himself with a negress as infamous, and it would be difficult to meet with a single instance of such a union.* The electoral franchise has been conferred upon the negroes in almost all the States in which slavery has been abolished; but if they come forward to vote, *their lives are in danger.* If oppressed, they may bring an action at law, but they will find none but whites among their judges; and although they may legally serve as jurors, *prejudice repulses them from that office. The same schools do not receive the child of the black and of the European. In the theatres, gold can not procure a seat for the servile race beside their former masters; in the hospitals they lie apart; and although they are allowed to invoke the same Divinity as the whites, it must be at a different altar, and in their own churches with their own clergy.* The gates of Heaven are not closed against these unhappy beings; but their inferiority is continued to the very confines of the other world; *when the negro is defunct, his bones are cast aside, and the distinction of condition prevails even in the equality of death. The [Northern] negro is free, but he can share neither the rights, nor the pleasures, nor the labour, nor the afflictions, nor the tomb of him whose equal he has been declared to be; and he can not meet him upon fair terms in life or in death.*

In the South, where slavery still exists, the negroes are less carefully kept apart; they sometimes share the labour and the recreations of the whites; the whites consent to intermix with them to a certain extent, and although the legislation treats them more harshly, *the habits of the [Southern] people are more tolerant and compassionate. In the South the master is not afraid to raise his slave to his own standing,* because he knows that he can in a moment reduce him to the dust at pleasure. *In the North the white no longer distinctly perceives the barrier which separates him from the degraded race, and he shuns the negro with the more pertinacity, since he fears lest they should some day be confounded together.*

Among the Americans of the South, Nature sometimes reasserts her rights, and restores a transient equality between the blacks and the whites; but in the North pride restrains the most imperious of human passions. The American of the Northern States would perhaps allow the negress to share his licentious pleasures if the laws of his country did not declare that she may aspire to be the legitimate partner of his bed; but he recoils with horror from her who might become his wife.

Thus it is, *in the United States, that the prejudice which repels the negroes seems to increase in proportion as they are emancipated, and inequality is sanctioned by the manners while it is effaced from the laws of the country.* But if the relative position of the two races which inhabit the United States is such as I have described, it may be asked why the Americans have abolished slavery in the North of the Union, why they maintain it in the South, and why they aggravate its hardships there? The answer is easily given. It is not for the good of the negroes, but for that of the whites, that measures are taken to abolish slavery in the United States. [162]

What Tocqueville refers to as "those States where servitude never has been known" is a reference to what were then called the Western Territories (today the Western states), at the time an area with the least number of blacks and where slavery had never been practiced. It was here that he found white racism toward blacks the strongest.

To emphasize these facts, the Frenchman goes on to point out that while slaves had been freed in the North and now had so-called "full equal rights," Northern white society continued to strongly discourage blacks, often with the threat of death, from

In the 1830s, decades before the secession of the Southern states and the formation of the Southern Confederacy in 1861, French traveler and historian Alexis de Tocqueville journeyed through what he called "the Confederate States of America" (that is, the United States) and noted that racism was far more serious in the North than in the South. He was only one of many who made this observation during the antebellum era.

voting, sitting on juries, or attending white schools or white churches. According to Tocqueville blacks in the "abolitionist North" were not even permitted to sit next to whites in theaters, take a sick bed next to them in Northern hospitals, or be buried next to them in death. [163]

Englishman Lyell noted that in Louisiana free blacks were allowed to be witnesses in court, while this privilege was denied them in many of the Northern states at the time, such as Indiana[164]—where "there was little hostility to slavery, and bitter hostility to abolitionism."[165] He then goes on to tell this story of a black Yankee, which seems to have taken place in the 1830s or early 1840s:

> Mr. Richard Henry Wilde, formerly senator [representative] for Georgia, told me that he once knew a coloured freeman who had been brought up as a saddler, and was a good workman. To his surprise he found him one day at Saratoga, in the State of New York, acting as servant at a hotel. "Could you not get higher wages," he inquired, "as a saddler?" "Yes," answered he; "but no sooner was I engaged by a 'boss,' than all the other workmen quitted." They did so, not because he was a slave, for he had long been emancipated, but because he was a negro.[166]

In the 1840s English writer James Silk Buckingham wrote that "the prejudice of colour is not nearly so strong in the South as in the North."[167] Here is how Robert Young Hayne, a South Carolina senator, described the treatment of those few Southern blacks who fled to the North:

> . . . there does not exist on the face of the whole earth, a population so poor, so wretched, so vile, so loathsome, so utterly destitute of all the comforts, conveniences, and decencies of life, as the unfortunate blacks of Philadelphia, and New York and Boston. Liberty has been to them the greatest of calamities, the heaviest of curses. Sir, I have had some opportunities of making comparison between the condition of the free negroes of the North, and the slaves of the South, and the comparison has left not only an indelible impression of the superior advantages of the latter, but has gone far to reconcile me to slavery itself. Never have I felt so forcibly that touching description, 'the foxes have holes, and the birds of the air have nests, but the Son of Man hath not where to lay his head,' as when I have seen this unhappy race, naked and houseless, almost starving in the streets, and abandoned by all the world. Sir, I have seen, in the neighborhood of one of the most moral, religious and refined cities of the North, a family of free blacks driven to the caves of the rocks, and there obtaining a precarious subsistence from charity and plunder.[168]

Only a few years later, in 1835, Virginian James Madison met with English author Harriet Martineau at his home, Montpellier, and regaled her with stories of how the Northern states erected numerous barriers in an attempt to thwart Negro emigration. With regard to slavery, Martineau wrote of their celebrated conversation, he was despairing:

> He talked more on the subject of slavery than on any other, acknowledging, without limitation or hesitation, all the evils with which it has ever been charged. . . . [He then] pointed out how the free [Northern] states discourage the settlement of blacks; how Canada disagrees with them; how Hayti shuts them out; so that Africa is their only refuge.[169]

In 1835 English intellectual and writer Harriet Martineau met with former U.S. President James Madison of Virginia, at which time he discussed the problems of white Northern racism with her.

In contrast to this explicit Yankee racism, there was Madison himself, who:

> As long as he was able . . . always superintended his own slaves, and had no overseer, and they were always well cared for. Another [white] visitor at Montpellier had been greatly surprised to see . . . [a group of Madison's female slaves] neatly dressed in bright calicoes, going to church; and when a shower came, to see the

dozen umbrellas that were raised. . . . [So kindly disposed was
Madison toward his slaves that he had recently] parted with some
of his best land [in order] to feed the increasing numbers.[170]

In 1841, after traveling through Philadelphia, an English Quaker,
Joseph Sturge, met with former Illinois Governor Edward Coles. Writes
Sturge:

> In the course of conversation, the Governor spoke of the prejudice against
> colour prevailing here as much stronger than in the slave States [the
> South]. I may add, from my own observation, and much concurring
> testimony, that Philadelphia appears to be the metropolis of this odious
> prejudice, and that there is probably no city in the known world, where
> dislike, amounting to hatred of the coloured population, prevails more than
> in the city of brotherly love![171]

After a visit to New York City, English writer Edward Dicey
recorded his observations concerning Yankee racism and Northern
blacks. In the North, Dicey noted:

> Everywhere and at all seasons the coloured people form a separate
> community. In the public streets you hardly ever see a coloured
> person in company with a white, except in the capacity of servant.
> . . . On board the river steamboats, the commonest and homeliest
> of working [white] men has a right to dine, and does dine, at the
> public meals; but, for coloured passengers, there is always a separate
> table. At the great [Northern] hotels there is, as with us [in
> England], a servants' table, but the coloured servants are not allowed to
> dine in common with the white. At the inns, in the barbers' shops, on
> board the steamers, and in most hotels, the servants are more often
> than not coloured people. . . . White [Northern] servants will not
> associate with black on terms of equality. . . . I hardly ever remember seeing
> a black employed as shopman, or placed in any post of responsibility. As
> a rule, the blacks you meet in the Free [that is, Northern] States are
> shabbily, if not squalidly dressed; and, as far as I could learn, the instances
> of black men having made money by trade in the North, are very few in
> number.[172]

While blacks were "degraded" in the North, they were
"upgraded" in the South, as Englishman Lyell penned in 1855:

> I have heard apologists in the North endeavouring to account for the

degraded position which the negroes hold, socially and politically, in the Free [Northern] States, by saying they belong to a race which is kept in a state of slavery in the South. But, if they really desired to accelerate emancipation, they would begin by setting an example to the Southern States, and treating the black race with more respect and more on a footing of equality. I once heard some Irish workmen complain in New York, "that the niggers shut them out from all the easiest ways of getting a livelihood;" and *many white mechanics, who had emigrated from the North to the Slave [Southern] States, declared to me that every opening in their trades was closed to them, because black artisans were employed by their owners in preference.*[173]

Famed British geologist Sir Charles Lyell, whose ideas influenced Charles Darwin, was impressed by the high level of expertise of the slaves he met on a Georgia plantation in 1846.

Among the many white racist-abolitionist Yankees Lyell came across while visiting the North, there was one whom he felt deserved special mention:

One of the most reasonable advocates of immediate emancipation whom I met with in the North, said to me, "You are like many of our politicians, who can look on one side only of a great question. Grant the possibility of these three millions of coloured people or even twelve millions of them fifty years hence, being capable of amalgamating with the whites, such a result might be to you perhaps, as a philanthropist or physiologist, a very interesting experiment; but *would not the progress of the whites be retarded, and our race deteriorated, nearly in the same proportion as the negroes would gain? Why not consider the interests of the white race by hastening the abolition of slavery.* The whites constitute nearly six-sevenths of our whole population. As a philanthropist, you are bound to look to the greatest good of the two races collectively, or the advantage of the whole population of the Union."[174]

Compare all of this to the South, where whites and blacks worked in close association with one another on a daily basis, creating race relations that, on the whole, were friendlier and warmer than in any other region in America, as the following example illustrates. In his book *The Cotton Kingdom*, Connecticut landscape architect Frederick Law Olmsted, betraying typical Yankee bigotry, wrote of a "scandalous" experience he had during a train ride through the Old Dominion State:[175]

I am struck with the close cohabitation and association of black and white—negro women are carrying black and white babies together in their arms; black and white children are playing together . . .; black and white faces are constantly thrust together out of the doors, to see the train go by. . . . A fine-looking, well-dressed, and well-behaved coloured young man sat, together with a white man, on a seat in the cars. I suppose the man was his master; but he was much the less like a gentleman of the two. The railroad company advertise to take coloured people only in second-class trains; but servants seem to go with their masters everywhere. Once, to-day, seeing a [white] lady entering the car at a way-station, with a family behind her, and that she was looking about to find a place where they could be seated together, I rose, and offered her my seat, which had several vacancies round it. She accepted it, without thanking me, and immediately installed in it a stout negro woman; took the adjoining seat herself, and seated the rest of her party before her. It consisted of a white girl, probably her daughter, and a bright and very pretty mulatto girl. *They all talked and laughed together; and the girls munched confectionary out of the same paper, with a familiarity and closeness of intimacy that would have been noticed with astonishment, if not with manifest displeasure, in almost any chance company at the North.*[176]

This scene, however, would have "astonished" or "displeased" very few white Southerners, nearly all who were accustomed to, and enjoyed, the company of blacks, as this incident clearly shows. Thousands of similar eyewitness accounts could be given.[177]

Victorian Yankee landscape architect, journalist, and author Frederick Law Olmsted visited Dixie in the early 1800s, and was shocked to learn that Southern slavery and black-white relationships were nothing like he had been taught.

Mary Chesnut writes of an incident that too reveals the true state of race relations in the South. One hot August day during the War, she found herself traveling on a river boat in Alabama, one overseen, not by a white deck hand, but by a black one, as was the norm in the South. Writes Mary:

Montgomery, July 30th.—Coming on here from Portland there was no stateroom for me. My mother alone had one. My aunt and I sat nodding in armchairs, for the floors and sofas were covered with sleepers, too. On the floor that night, so hot that even a little covering of clothes could not be borne, lay a motley crew. Black, white, and yellow disported themselves in promiscuous array. Children and their nurses, bared to the view, were wrapped in the profoundest slumber. No caste prejudices were here. Neither [abolitionists] Garrison, John Brown, nor Gerrit Smith ever dreamed of equality more untrammeled.[178]

Naturally such scenes contradict Yankee myth so they are ignored by pro-North historians.

Senator Hiram Rhodes Revels of Mississippi, more evidence of early racial tolerance in the South.

If the North is racially tolerant and the South is racially intolerant (as our historically inaccurate "history" books assert), one must wonder why it was a Southern state, Virginia, that would later vote the first African-American into its highest office: in 1989, Lawrence Douglas Wilder, the grandson of Southern black servants, became the first elected black governor in the U.S. Even the first *non-elected* African-American governor was from a Southern state: as lieutenant governor of Louisiana, Pinckney B. S. Pinchback succeeded to the position in 1872 when Governor Henry Clay Warmoth was impeached and forced to step down.

The first two blacks to serve in the U.S. Congress were also from the South: Hiram Rhodes Revels of Mississippi entered the Senate February 23, 1870; Joseph Hayne Rainey of South Carolina entered the House of Representatives December 12, 1870, and became its first black Speaker.[179]

Contrast all of this with the following: to this day more hate crimes are committed in the North than in the South,[180] and the head of the modern KKK (the National Knights of the Ku Klux Klan)[181] lives, not in the South, but in the North (New York),[182] one of the fastest growing regions for KKK membership in the U.S.[183]

Despite these bold facts, thanks to an anti-South Liberal-run media (which detests all that the traditional South stands for: family values, Christianity, and conservatism), it is the South, not the North, that continues to be unfairly associated with white racism.

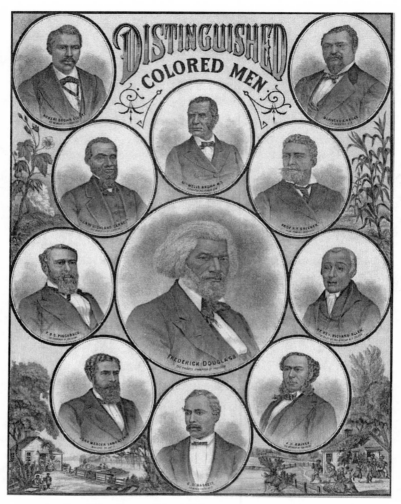

As the title shows, this 1883 illustration highlights various "Distinguished Colored Men" of the period. Top left: Robert Brown Elliott (South Carolina politician); top right: Blanche K. Bruce (Mississippi politician); center: Frederick Douglass (Northern abolitionist). Circle of portraits around Douglass, clockwise from top: William Wells Brown (Southern writer), Richard T. Greener (Northern educator), Richard Allen (Southern politician), Joseph Hayne Rainey (Southern politician), Ebenezer Don Carlos Bassett (Northern educator), John Mercer Langston (Southern politician), Pinckney B. S. Pinchback (Southern politician), Henry Highland Garnet (Northern educator). Note that most of these "distinguished colored men" are from the South, the birthplace of the American abolition movement.

11

THE AMERICAN SLAVE TRADE: BORN IN THE NORTH

WHAT YOU WERE TAUGHT: The American slave trade got its start in the South. Thus, Southerners were "America's slave traders" and Dixie is the region responsible for bringing the first slaves to North American soil.

THE TRUTH: The only slave ships to ever sail from the U.S. left from Northern ports, all were commanded by Northern captains and funded by Northern businessmen, and all operated under the auspices of the U.S. flag.[184]

The South, on the other hand, did not own slave ships and never traded in foreign slaves.[185] Her slavery was strictly domestic, supplied by and purchased from Northerners. This is one of the reasons she banned the foreign slave trade in the Confederacy's new Constitution, penned by the Confederate Founding Fathers in 1861.[186] Thus, while no slave ship ever sailed under the Confederate Flag, it is this very flag that is today still wrongly viewed as a "symbol of slavery"!

Yankee slave ships "generally sailed from place to place peddling their slaves, with notice in advance when practicable."[187] In the mid 1790s, when French nobleman Duke de la Rochefoucauld Liancourt paid a visit to Georgia, he made these observations:

> The law of the land permits the importation of negroes, and this is
> the only state, the ports of which are not yet shut up against this

odious trade. They are not, however, imported in great numbers in Savannah; in the course of last year arrived about six or seven hundred; during the first four months of this year four hundred and fifty have been landed, and two or three thousand more are expected. *Savannah employs no ship in the slave-trade; but it is carried on in ships belonging to New England, and especially to Rhode-Island. The cargo, however, is constantly carried to Savannah . . .*[188]

Yankee slave ships came in a vast assemblage of varieties and sizes. This Yankee clipper from Newport, Rhode Island—where 70 percent of all American slave voyages began—was refitted to serve as a slave ship in New England's lucrative 250 year old Cotton Triangle.

In the early 1830s Northerner Joseph Holt Ingraham visited New Orleans, where he made note of the arrival of *Yankee boats* stocked with goods from Pittsburgh and Cincinnati, "crowded, not infrequently, with slaves for the Southern market."[189] In her 1891 memoir, Elizabeth Buffum Chace of Rhode Island recalled the following experience:

> My grandmother, Sarah Gould, was born near the year 1737, and her father, James Coggeshall, soon after her birth, purchased a little African girl, from a [Yankee] slave-ship just come into port [at Newport, Rhode Island], to serve as nurse-maid to the child. She remained a slave in the household, until the Friends [Quakers] abolished slavery among themselves in 1780. . . .[190]

With these facts in hand we must then ask ourselves: is it the flag of the U.S.A. or the flag of the C.S.A. that deserves to be called

"America's true slavery flag"?   And is it the U.S. capital city (Washington, D.C.) or the C.S. capital city (Richmond, Virginia) that deserves the title of "America's true slavery capital"?[191]

American slave ships sailed under the United States flag, never the Confederate States flag. This 15-star U.S. flag would have been a familiar sight to Yankee slavers operating out of the Northeast in the year 1791.

The answers to these two questions were obvious and well-known until recently, when the pro-North movement took over our educational system and news media, then buried the Truth beneath a mountain of fabricated anti-South propaganda. In 1906, for example, Georgia State Representative William Henry Fleming gave an address before the Alumni of the University of Georgia that included this statement:

> If Charleston, South Carolina, was one of the chief ports of destination for slave-trading vessels, Salem, Massachusetts, was one of the chief ports from whence these vessels sailed.[192]

In his 1910 book *The White Man's Burden,* Southern pastor, editor, and author Benjamin F. Riley writes:

> While the middle of the nineteenth century found the Negroes massed, for the most part, in the states of the South, from Maryland to Texas and Arkansas and Missouri, *they had traveled all the way across the continent from New England. If Southern planters bought the slaves, Northern traders, in the earlier years, sold and supplied them.*[193]

Charleston, South Carolina, the port of entry for thousands of African slaves—all brought from Africa and the West Indies by Yankee ships, commanded by Yankee captains, manned by Yankee crews, funded by Yankee bankers, and sold by Yankee merchants.

Northern politicians were well aware that they could not fool the public about the origins of slavery simply by deflecting the entire issue onto the South. One of these was U.S. Representative Jonathan Ogden Mosely of Connecticut. When, in the late 1700s, the idea of executing slave ship owners by hanging came up before a congressional committee on abolition, the Yankee politician remarked:

> We have been repeatedly told, and told with an air of triumph, by gentlemen from the South, that their citizens have no concern in this infamous traffic; that *people from the North are the importers of negroes, and thereby the seducers of Southern citizens to buy them.* We have a right to presume, then, that the citizens of the South will entertain no particular partiality for these wicked traffickers, but will be ready to subject them to the most exemplary punishment. So far as the people of Connecticut are concerned, I am sure that, should any citizen of the North be convicted under this law, so far from thinking it cruel in their Southern brethren to hang them, such a punishment of such culprits would be acknowledged with gratitude as a favor.[194]

Now we can better understand the words of U.S. Senator Jefferson Davis (who was soon to become the Southern Confederacy's first and, so far, only president), who, in 1848, rightly chastised his Northern brethren on the Senate floor for their abolitionist hypocrisy:

> You were the men who imported these negroes into this country; you enjoyed the benefits resulting from their carriage and sale; and you reaped the largest profit accruing from the introduction of slaves.[195]

Colonial Yankee slave ships flew one of these—or a variation of one of these—early U.S. naval flags from the late 1700s.

This is why, even after slavery had been pushed South by the Yankee,[196] it still mainly served financial interests in the North, as is obvious from 19th-Century records: during the 1850s alone, at least "25,000 slaves were annually sold South from the Northern slave states."[197] These figures do not include the most northern states, where the slave trade was still very active. In 1920 William E. Dodd wrote:

> While agricultural production was concentrated in the comparatively small [Southern] area where cotton could be grown and the returns all seemed to be going to the planters, *the evidence is conclusive that far the greater part of the proceeds was left in the hands of those who supplied the South with its necessaries and its luxuries.* The earnings of the slave plantations were thus consumed by [Northern sponsored] tariffs, freights, commissions, and profits which the Southerners had to pay. Southern towns were only marts of trade, not depositories of the crops of surrounding or distant areas. Thus while the [Southern] planters monopolized the cotton industry, drew to themselves the surplus of slaves, and apparently increased their wealth enormously, *they were really but custodians of these returns, administrators of the wealth of Northern men who really ultimately received the profits of Southern plantations and Southern slavery.*[198]

Hundreds of Yankee slave ships sailed out of New England harbors each year, bound for the Dark Continent. Hundreds more from New York, Pennsylvania, and Maryland annually plied the waters of the transatlantic slave trade. *All* of America's original African slaves arrived on one of these vessels, as Northern ship manifests from the period testify.

Clearly, as will become more evident in subsequent chapters, when it came to American slavery the North was the equivalent of a shrewd and aggressive drug dealer, the South a hapless and reluctant drug addict.

In 1860 alone it has been estimated that 85 vessels—all which had been fitted out in and which had sailed from New York City—brought as many as 60,000 African slaves into the U.S.[199] That same year the overwhelming extent of the nationwide power of the domineering Yankee industrialist and his numerous slaving seaports was described by Southerner Hinton R. Helper:

It is a fact well known to every intelligent Southerner that we are compelled to go to the North for almost every article of utility and adornment, from matches, shoe-pegs and paintings up to cotton-mills, steamships and statuary; that *we have no foreign trade*, no princely merchants, nor respectable artists; that, in comparison with the free [Northern] states, we contribute nothing to the literature, polite arts and inventions of the age; that, for want of profitable employment at home, large numbers of our native population find themselves necessitated to emigrate to the West, whilst the free [Northern] states retain not only the larger proportion of those born within their own limits, but induce, annually, hundreds of thousands of foreigners to settle and remain amongst them; that almost everything produced at the North meets with ready sale, while, at the same time, there is no demand, even among our own citizens, for the productions of Southern industry; that, owing to the absence of a proper system of business amongst us, *the North becomes, in one way or another, the proprietor and dispenser of all our floating wealth, and that we are dependent on Northern capitalists for the means necessary to build our railroads, canals and other public improvements*; that if we want to visit a foreign country, even though it may lie directly south of us, we find no convenient way of getting there except by taking passage through a Northern port; and that nearly all the profits arising from the exchange of commodities, from insurance and shipping offices, and from the thousand and one industrial pursuits of the country, accrue to the North, and are there invested in the erection of those magnificent cities and stupendous works of art which dazzle the eyes of the South, and attest the superiority of free [Northern] institutions!

The North is the Mecca of our merchants, and to it they must and do make two pilgrimages per annum—one in the spring and one in the fall. All our commercial, mechanical, manufactural, and literary supplies come from there. We want Bibles, brooms, buckets and books, and we go to the North; we want pens, ink, paper, wafers and envelopes, and we go to the North; we want shoes, hats, handkerchiefs, umbrellas and pocket knives, and we go to the North; we want furniture, crockery, glassware and pianos, and we go to the North; we want toys, primers, school-books, fashionable apparel, machinery, medicines, tomb-stones, and a thousand other things, and we go to the North for them all. Instead of keeping our money in circulation at home, by patronizing our own mechanics, manufacturers, and laborers, we send it all away to the North, and there it remains; it never falls into our hands again.

In one way or another we are more or less subservient to the North every day of our lives. In infancy we are swaddled in Northern muslin; in childhood we are humored with Northern gewgaws; in youth we are instructed out of Northern books; at the age of maturity we sow our "wild oats" on Northern soil; in middle-life we exhaust our wealth, energies and talents in the dishonorable vocation of entailing our dependence on our children and on our children's children, and, to the neglect of our own interests and the interests of those around us, in giving aid and succor to every department of Northern power; in the decline of life we remedy our eye-sight with Northern spectacles, and support our infirmities with Northern canes; in old age we are drugged with Northern physic; and, finally, when we die, our inanimate bodies, shrouded in Northern cambric, are stretched upon the bier, borne to the grave in a Northern carriage, entombed with a Northern spade, and memorialized with a Northern slab![200]

Phillips gave this description of the average Yankee slave vessel:

The typical New England ship for the slave trade was a sloop, schooner or barkentine of about fifty tons burthen, which when engaged in ordinary freighting would have but a single deck. *For a slaving voyage* a second flooring was laid some three feet below the regular deck, the space between forming the slave quarters. Such a vessel was handled by a captain, two mates, and from three to six men and boys. It is curious that a vessel of this type, with capacity in the hold for from 100 to 120 hogsheads of rum was reckoned by the *Rhode Islanders* to be "full bigg for dispatch," while among the Liverpool slave traders such a ship when offered for sale could not find a purchaser. The reason seems to have been that dry-goods and sundries required much more cargo space for the same value than did rum.[201]

Thousands of wealthy and influential Yankees helped keep Northern slavery alive. One of these was Michigan politician Lewis Cass, who campaigned to keep the Northern slave trade open and unimpeded by countries like Britain.

Despite the fact that slave trading was far more inhumane than slaveholding,[202] vast fortunes were to be made from the barbaric business; which is precisely why Northern slave dealers, Northern bankers, Northern manufacturers, Northern shipbuilders, Northern shipowners, Northern seamen, and Northern merchants kept the slave trade going long after it had been banned in 1808 by then U.S. president and Southerner Thomas Jefferson.[203]

12

AMERICAN SLAVERY: BORN IN THE NORTH

WHAT YOU WERE TAUGHT: American slavery could have only begun in the South, the cradle and home of white racism in the U.S.

THE TRUTH: We have seen that it was not the Old South but the Old North where white racism was most entrenched. Thus no one should be surprised to learn that like the American slave trade (which is integrally connected to but distinct from American slavery), American slavery also got its start as a legal institution in the North. Its birthplace was none other than Massachusetts, the very *first* of the original 13 states (colonies) to legalize it in 1641.[204] In contrast, the *last* of the original 13 colonies to legalize slavery was a Southern one, Georgia, which officially sanctioned it 108 years later, in 1749.[205]

American slavery could only exist, of course, by way of the American slave trade, which fueled it. Thus it was only natural that the former would blossom in the region of the latter: the industrial Northern states. The agricultural Southern states, in contrast, did not trade in slaves, and therefore at that time slavery was not natural to the area.

Before moving forward with this topic, let us look in more detail at the Yankee slave trade, for this will give us better context in which to more fully understand both the business side and the personal side of American slavery.

In 1896 the vociferous pro-slavery policies of the American Northeast and her Yankee slavers led African-American scholar and

Yankee intellectual William E. B. Du Bois to declare what has always been patently obvious to informed Southerners:

> *The American slave-trade finally came to be carried on principally by United States capital, in United States ships, officered by United States citizens, and under the United State flag.* Executive reports repeatedly acknowledged this fact. In 1839 "a careful revision of these laws" is recommended by the President [Martin Van Buren], in order that "the integrity and honor of our flag may be carefully preserved." In June, 1841, the President declares: "There is reason to believe that the traffic is on the increase," and advocates "vigorous efforts." His message in December of the same year acknowledges: "That the American [U.S.] flag is grossly abused by the abandoned and profligate of other nations is but too probable." The special message of 1845 explains at length that "it would seem" that a regular policy of evading the laws is carried on: American vessels with the knowledge of the owners are chartered by notorious slave dealers in Brazil, aided by English capitalists, with this intent. The message of 1849 "earnestly" invites the attention of Congress "to an amendment of our existing laws relating to the African slave-trade, with a view to the effectual suppression of that barbarous traffic. It is not to be denied," continues the message, "that this trade is still, in part, carried on by means of vessels built in the United States, and owned or navigated by some of our citizens." Governor [Thomas] Buchanan of Liberia reported in 1839: *"The chief obstacle to the success of the very active measures pursued by the British government for the suppression of the slave-trade on the coast, is the American [U.S.] flag.* Never was the proud banner of freedom so extensively used by those pirates upon liberty and humanity, as at this season." One well-known

Harvard-educated African-American historian Dr. William E. B. Du Bois of Massachusetts reprimanded the North over its hypocrisy in criticizing so-called "Southern slavery." Citing a slave smuggler, he noted that the American slave trade "is growing more profitable every year, and if you should hang all the Yankee merchants engaged in it, hundreds would fill their places."

American slaver [that is, a ship] was boarded fifteen times and twice taken into port, but always escaped by means of her papers. *Even American officers report that the English are doing all they can, but that the American [U.S.] flag protects the trade.* The evidence which literally poured in from our consuls and ministers at Brazil adds to the story of the guilt of the United States. *It was proven that the participation of United States citizens in the trade was large and systematic.* One of the most notorious slave merchants of Brazil said: "I am worried by the Americans, who insist upon my hiring their vessels for slave-trade." Minister [George H.] Proffit stated, in 1844, that the *"slave-trade is almost entirely carried on under our flag, in American-built vessels."* So, too, in Cuba: the British commissioners affirm that *American citizens were openly engaged in the traffic; vessels arrived undisguised at Havana from the United States, and cleared for Africa as slavers after an alleged sale. The American consul, [Nicholas P.] Trist, was proven to have consciously or unconsciously aided this trade by the issuance of blank clearance papers.*

The presence of American capital in these enterprises, and the connivance of the authorities, were proven in many cases and known in scores. In 1837 the English government informed the United States that from the papers of a captured slaver it appeared that the notorious slave-trading firm, Blanco and Carballo of Havana, who owned the vessel, had correspondents in the United States: "at *Baltimore [Maryland]*, Messrs. Peter Harmony and Co., in *New York*, Robert Barry, Esq." The slaver *Martha* of New York, captured by the *Perry*, contained among her papery curious revelations of the guilt of persons in America who were little suspected. The [Portuguese] slaver *Prova*, which was allowed to lie in the harbor of Charleston, South Carolina, and refit, was afterwards captured with two hundred and twenty-five slaves on board. *The real reason that prevented many belligerent Congressmen from pressing certain search claims against England lay in the fact that the unjustifiable detentions had unfortunately revealed so much American guilt that it was deemed wiser to let the matter end in talk.* For instance, in *1850 Congress demanded information as to illegal searches, and President [Millard] Fillmore's report showed the uncomfortable fact that, of the ten American ships wrongly detained by English men-of-war, nine were proven red-handed slavers.*

The consul at Havana reported, in 1836, that whole cargoes of slaves fresh from Africa were being daily shipped to Texas in American [Yankee] vessels, that 1,000 had been sent within a few months, that the rate was increasing, and that many of these slaves "can scarcely fail to find their way into the United States." Moreover, the consul acknowledged that ships frequently cleared for the United States in ballast, taking on a cargo at some secret point. When with these facts we consider the law facilitating "recovery" of slaves from Texas, the repeated refusals to regulate the Texan trade, and the shelving of a proposed congressional investigation into these matters, conjecture becomes a practical certainty. It was estimated in 1838 that 15,000 Africans were annually taken to Texas, and "there are even grounds for suspicion that there are other places . . . where slaves are introduced." Between 1847 and 1853 the slave smuggler *Drake* had a slave depot in the Gulf, where sometimes as many as 1,600 Negroes were on hand, and the owners were continually importing and shipping. "The joint-stock company," writes this smuggler, "was a very extensive one, and connected with leading

American and Spanish mercantile houses. Our island was visited almost weekly, by [slave purchasing] agents from Cuba, *New York, Baltimore, Philadelphia, Boston,* and New Orleans. . . . The seasoned and instructed slaves were taken to Texas, or Florida, overland, and to Cuba, in sailing-boats. As no squad contained more than half a dozen, no difficulty was found in posting them to the United States, without discovery, and generally without suspicion. . . . The Bay Island plantation sent ventures weekly to the Florida Keys. Slaves were taken into the great American swamps, and there kept till wanted for the market. Hundreds were sold as captured

A slave port at Baltimore, Maryland. Unlike in the South, in the Old Line State—as with the other Northern states—a slave and his or her offspring were made "slaves for life."

runaways from the Florida wilderness. We had agents in every slave State; and *our coasters were built in Maine,* and came out with lumber. *I could tell curious stories . . . of this business of smuggling Bozal [that is, fresh or newly acquired] negroes into the United States. It is growing more profitable every year, and if you should hang all the Yankee merchants engaged in it, hundreds would fill their places."* Inherent probability and concurrent testimony confirm the substantial truth of such confessions. For instance, one traveller discovers on a Southern plantation Negroes who can speak no English. The careful reports of the Quakers "apprehend that many [slaves] are also introduced into the United States." Governor [George B.] Mathew of the Bahama Islands reports that "in more than one instance, Bahama vessels with coloured crews have been purposely wrecked on the coast of Florida, and the crews forcibly sold." This was brought to the notice of the United States authorities, but the district attorney of Florida could furnish no information. Such was the state of the slave-trade in 1850, on the threshold of the critical decade which by a herculean effort was destined finally to suppress it.[206]

Why did American slave ships sail from the North and not the South? The answer is simple. It was the so-called "Cradle of Liberty," the Puritan North,[207] and more specifically intolerant and dogmatic Puritan Massachusetts,[208] that was, from the very beginning, America's first slave trading region:[209] though it had already long been enslaving Native-Americans, to test the waters so to speak, in 1637 Boston, Massachusetts (the city was then only seven years old) had a group of African slaves shipped in from Providence Island, a fellow Puritan colony located off the coast of Central America.[210]

In the early 1600s, prior to purchasing and importing African slaves, white New Englanders regularly attacked and murdered Indians. The survivors were sold as slaves in Massachusetts and Connecticut.

That same year New Englanders fought the Pequot Indians in Connecticut. At least 900 Native-Americans were killed. The surviving males were shipped to the West Indies to be sold off as slaves, while the Indian women and children were retained, enslaved, and sold to white plantation owners and families throughout Massachusetts and

Connecticut. This was the usual New England penalty (particularly in Massachusetts) for any and all Indians known or suspected to have shed colonial English blood.[211]

Both the American slave trade and American slavery got their start in the North, not in the South, as our liberal slanted history books teach. More specifically, the former was launched in Massachusetts in 1638, the latter in Massachusetts in 1641. To this day New England is still known not only for the fine craftsmanship of her 17th- and 18th-Century ships, but for her industrious worldwide maritime trade, which included galleons laden with black human cargo from Africa's Gold Coast.

Finding an enormous Yankee hunger for "sable servants," the next year, 1638, Massachusetts instigated the American slave trade when Boston began importing African slaves commercially for the first time. This occurred when Captain William Pierce brought New England's first remunerative shipload of Africans from the West Indies aboard the 120-ton Salem vessel *Desire*[212] (built at Marblehead, Massachusetts, in 1636).[213]

A few short years later, in 1641, Massachusetts gave birth to American slavery when it became the first colony to legitimatize and monetize the institution.[214] By 1676 Boston slavers were routinely coming home with shiploads of human cargo from East Africa and Madagascar.[215] By 1680 the colony itself possessed 120 black slaves.[216]

After the termination of England's Royal African Company in 1697, New England as a whole took an even more aggressive approach to the African slave trade.[217] By 1708 Boston alone had 400 black slaves,[218] and by 1775 Massachusetts had over 5,000 black slaves and 30,000 bondservants.[219]

But even this was not enough to satiate New England's enormous "retail" demand for African slaves,[220] who were sold on nearly every corner, from taverns and stores to warehouses and slave merchants' homes.[221] Thus the trade carried on, increasing in strength and scope every year for decades thereafter.

So intertwined did the institution become with Massachusetts' state economy that when abolitionists tried to introduce a bill in 1771 to "prevent the importation of negro slaves into this province," Governor Thomas Hutchinson refused to approve it.[222] Even manumission was discouraged, in the case of Massachusetts, by requiring that the owner post a £50 bond in the event that the slave he freed became dependent on the state.[223] All in all, the people of Massachusetts

> took their slave-trading and their slaveholding as part of their day's work and as part of God's goodness to His elect. In practical effect *the policy of colonial Massachusetts toward the backward races* merits neither praise nor censure; *it was merely commonplace.*[224]

Boston, Massachusetts, the birthplace of American slavery. Though New York possessed African slaves as early as the 1620s, Massachusetts earns the title for having launched the institution in the American colonies by being the first to legitimize, monetize, and legalize it in 1641 by way of a series of Yankee laws and statutes.

By 1639 Connecticut had slaves,[225] and in 1650 the institution was formally legalized through the adoption of a code of laws.[226] Though negligible at this time, by 1775 the state owned some 6,500 African bondsmen and women.[227] By 1645 New Hampshire had slaves as well. The largest slave concentrations in New England were in Rockingham County, New Hampshire; Essex, Suffolk, Bristol, and Plymouth Counties, Massachusetts; New London, Hartford, and Fairfield Counties, Connecticut; and Newport and Washington Counties, Rhode Island. Let us bear in mind that most of the Southern states had not even been formed yet.[228]

Providence, Rhode Island, was once one of early America's most active slave ports. Affluent Rhode Islanders, who controlled a large percentage of the transatlantic slave trade, greatly profited from New England's "peculiar institution." Providence merchant and slave trader Nicolas Brown, Sr. cofounded the college that would later be named Brown University in his family's honor.

Not long after it legalized slavery in 1652,[229] there were so many slaves in Rhode Island's Narragansett region that they made up half the population. The slavers of Rhode Island and those of Massachusetts combined to make New England the leading slave trading center in America and slavery "the hub of New England's economy,"[230] a region where eventually even "parish ministers all over New England owned slaves."[231]

At one time Rhode Island's slave traders owned and operated nearly 90 percent of America's slave trade.[232] Though the state's slave ship captains often wrote home from the African coast complaining of the difficulties of trading with the native African slave merchants there,[233] nonetheless by their standards they managed to achieve spectacular monetary success: by 1756 slaves made up at least 16 percent of

Newport's population,[234] and as late as 1770 Rhode Island alone possessed some 150 slave ships,[235] which between 1804 and 1807 brought 20,000 of the 40,000 Africans transported to South Carolina during that period.[236] (The other 20,000 were brought to the Palmetto State by English slave ships.)[237]

Dane Hall in 1832, part of Harvard Law School, built with money made from the Yankee slave trade.

By 1749 Rhode Island had 3,077 blacks, by 1756 at least 4,697, and in 1774, 3,668.[238] "Of this last number Newport contained 1,246, South Kingstown 440, Providence 303, Portsmouth 122, and Bristol 114."[239] By 1775 almost 2 out of every 25 people (6 percent) of Rhode Island's entire population were black slaves,[240] many of them belonging to the white aristocratic planters of the famed fertile Narragansett farming region.[241]

A full two-thirds of Rhode Island's fleets and sailors were devoted to the slave trade. Even the region's state governors participated in it, Yankee politicians such as Jonathan Belcher of Massachusetts and Joseph Wanton of Rhode Island. It was well-known that slavery was so integral to New England's economy that without it she would have collapsed into financial ruin.[242] She was able to achieve this not just by purchasing millions of already enslaved blacks from Africa's shores,[243] but also by categorizing anyone a slave who had "slave blood" on the maternal side of their family. This would have included, of course, scores of Yankees who were considered white not black.[244]

Many notable New England families owe their present-day wealth and celebrity to slavery.[245] Among them: the Cabots (ancestors of Massachusetts Senators Henry Cabot Lodge, Sr. and Henry Cabot Lodge, Jr.), the Belchers, the Waldos (ancestors of Ralph Waldo Emerson), the Faneuils (after whom Boston's Faneuil Hall is named), the Royalls, the Pepperells (after whom the town of Pepperell, Massachusetts, is named), the DeWolfs (at least 500,000 descendants of their slaves are alive today),[246] the Champlains (after whom Lake Champlain is named), the Ellerys, the Gardners (after whom Boston's Isabella Stewart Gardner Museum is named), the Malbones, the Robinsons, the Crowninshields (after whom Crowninshield Island, Massachusetts, is named), and the Browns (after whom Rhode Island's Brown University is named).[247]

The slave trading Royall family, which made millions from their slave plantations in Antigua, donated money and land to what would become the Harvard Law School. The educational center still uses a seal from the Royall family crest.[248] Slavery was so integral to New England's culture, society, and economy that even South-hating Harriet Beecher Stowe, the infamous author of *Uncle Tom's Cabin*, had to acknowledge that:

> The Northern slaveholder traded in men and women whom he never saw, and of whose separations, tears, and miseries he determined never to hear.[249]

Boston, Massachusetts. The founder of both the American slave trade and American slavery, as well as the primary site where hundreds of slave ships were manufactured and launched, Beantown was the epicenter of the Yankee slave system for a century and a half—until this title was taken over by New York City in the mid 1700s.

At least one half of the land in Brookline, Massachusetts, was once in the possession of slave owners, while in the town of Concord, Massachusetts, 50 percent of its government seats were occupied by slave owners.[250] In this quaint New England borough, where slavery continued well into the 1830s (decades after the official "abolition" of slavery there), those blacks fortunate enough to be freed were then, unfortunately, exiled to the woods surrounding Walden Pond, where they struggled for survival in fetid squatter camps.[251]

It was also in Massachusetts that the now wholly disgraced and defunct field of "race science"—or "niggerology," as many Yankees referred to it—got its start, at Harvard University in Cambridge, to be exact. It was this very pseudoscience, one which

Walden Pond, Concord, Massachusetts, where the town's freed blacks were once cruelly banished by its white citizens. At least 50 percent of Concord's politicians were slave owners, just one reason why slavery continued there well into the 1830s, years after so-called "official" state abolition in 1780.

claimed that "blacks are inferior subhumans," that for hundreds of years allowed white Northerners to rationalize the exploitation of people of African descent.[252]

About the same time, the 1830s, the Boston Female Anti-Slavery Society was complaining of the many "obstacles" it continued to encounter around the Bay State. The women pledged to "overcome" resistance to abolition, not just from countless "mobs" and the "judicial courts" of Massachusetts, but also from the state's "ecclesiastical councils."[253]

During the American Revolutionary War, Massachusetts political leader and Continental Army General William Heath (after whom the town of Heath, Massachusetts, is named), complained about the blacks in his regiments. Though thousands had bravely joined to help fellow white colonists fight the British, Heath was unhappy at the mixing of the two races. Fellow officer General Philip Schuyler of New York, who had similar misgivings, did not like the fact that whites were putting their "trust" in black slaves to defend American liberty.[254] In 1819, as other Northern states were passing statutes condemning slavery, it is well-known that "the New England legislatures remained silent."[255]

Former Northern slave Frederick Douglass found white racism so severe in Massachusetts that he could not secure a job there.

Little wonder that when William Lloyd Garrison went to Boston in 1830 to scrounge up support for the launch of his upcoming antislavery newspaper, *The Liberator*, he was turned down by some of the city's most notable men, including William Ellery Channing, Daniel Webster, Jeremiah Evarts, and Jeremiah Mason. His plea was even rejected by Lyman Beecher, the town's most influential Christian leader and the father of the aforementioned abolitionist author Harriet Beecher Stowe. Garrison should not have been surprised: not only were many of Massachusetts' schools and churches segregated, nearly every one of Boston's clergymen—like the leaders of every major protestant denomination in the U.S.[256]—was a member of the American Colonization Society, a Yankee-founded organization devoted to deporting all blacks out of the country.[257] (As we will see, one of its future members and leaders would be the notorious white supremacist Abraham Lincoln, who was to become America's sixteenth president.)[258] Boston itself was once a major center of such black colonization efforts,[259] whose main mission was "to return Negroes to Africa."[260]

In 1788 the state of Massachusetts forbade the emigration of free blacks from outside its boundaries,[261] and well into the early 1800s restrictive Black Codes across New England prohibited African-Americans from voting, testifying in court, intermarrying with whites,[262] or gaining access to jobs, housing, and education. Banned from most restaurants and hotels, New England blacks were also subject to segregation in restaurants, in theaters,[263] on public transportation, and

Famous Faneuil Hall, Boston, Massachusetts, named after noted New England slave merchant Peter Faneuil, who donated profits from the Yankee slave trade to help construct the building in 1742.

in churches and hospitals.[264]

Of course, since all of the Northern colonies (states) possessed slaves[265]—both African and Indian[266]—all of them also passed similar laws, statutes that not only held down the black man and curtailed his rights, but which also reenforced the Yankees' white supremacist ideology. In New York blacks could not own property, in New Jersey they could not own land, and in Pennsylvania any free black who refused to work was automatically enslaved.[267] In the early 1800s, under pressure from abolitionists, Massachusetts, Rhode Island, Maine, New Hampshire, and Vermont began to allow black males to vote, though even this right was often undermined by the white racism that was so endemic to New England.[268]

Freed male blacks traveling to the North after Lincoln's War hoping to find employment were out of luck: though most had numerous skills in a variety of trades, the "fierce racial discrimination" of the Yankee prevented him from securing a job.[269] Not long before, in the late 1830s, famous former Northern slave and black civil rights leader Frederick Douglass, now a freedman, could not get a job as a caulker in New Bedford, Massachusetts, because of the color of his skin. White Yankee caulkers refused to work alongside him.[270]

13

AMERICAN ABOLITION: BORN IN THE SOUTH

WHAT YOU WERE TAUGHT: The American abolition movement started in the North, that thriving center of abolitionist sentiment.

THE TRUTH: The American abolition movement began in the South. While Northern colonies like Massachusetts were busy legalizing slavery and expanding the slave trade, Southern colonies—who considered anything connected to human bondage an "evil"[271]—were busy trying to put a stop to both.

Indeed, the very first American colony to attempt to abolish the entire ugly institution, in particular the slave trade, was a Southern one: Virginia,[272] where the country's first voluntary emancipation took place in 1655,[273] began issuing official statutes as early as 1753 in an attempt to block the importation of slaves.[274] In 1732, when English military officer James Edward Oglethorpe founded the Southern colony of Georgia, it became the first to place a prohibition against commercial trafficking in slaves into her state constitution,[275] calling the institution "unjust and cruel."[276] North Carolina and South Carolina both passed restrictions on the trade in 1787, as did Tennessee in 1805.[277]

In point of fact, at one time or another *all* of the antebellum Southern states tried to stop both the importation of slaves[278] and the kidnaping and selling of slaves within their borders.[279] In other words, the reality is that *up until the year 1800, nearly all Southerners were abolitionists.*[280]

While all of this was going on, the Northern states were busy bringing in as many African slaves as possible through their seaports. In 1776 alone, for example, the year the Declaration of Independence was issued, New Hampshire imported 627 slaves; Massachusetts imported 3,500; Rhode Island, 4,376; Connecticut, 6,000; New Jersey, 7,600; Delaware, 9,000; New York, 15,000; and Maryland, 80,000.[281]

The American abolition movement began in the South, not in the North. This is just one reason why, long prior to the Civil War (as early as 1655), Southern slave owners were emancipating their servants by the thousands, whenever possible. At a financial loss of several million dollars, this wealthy white slaveholder in Georgia is setting all of his slaves free in 1829, a full 34 years before Lincoln issued his fake and illegal Emancipation Proclamation in 1863. While some servants will refuse his offer of freedom (preferring the securities of Southern servitude to the uncertainties of liberation), as was the custom in Dixie, nearly all will stay on with their former master to continue working on his estate, now as independent laborers known as "plantation hands."

In 1835, when Yankee tourist Professor Ethan Allen Andrews told a Virginia slave owner that "the whole public sentiment of the North is decidedly opposed to slavery," the man replied sharply: "So also is that of the South, with but a few exceptions."[282] After visiting the South in the early 1800s, British-American scientist George William Featherstonhaugh wrote:

All Christian men must unite in the wish that slavery was extinguished in every part of the world, and *from my personal knowledge of the sentiments of many of the leading gentlemen in the Southern States, I am persuaded that they look to the ultimate abolition of slavery with satisfaction.*[283]

There were a number of good reasons for the near universal abolitionism across Dixie:

> At the South . . . *humanitarianism* though of positive weight was but one of several factors. The distinctively *Southern considerations against the trade* were that its continuance would lower the prices of slaves already on hand, or at least prevent those prices from rising; that it would so increase the staple exports as to spoil the world's market for them; that it would drain out money and keep the community in debt; that *it would retard the civilization of the negroes already on hand*; and that by raising the proportion of blacks in the population it would intensify the danger of slave insurrections.[284]

These historical facts have forced even the most diehard anti-South historians to acknowledge the bold reality that *Southerners, particularly between 1808 and 1831, played a much greater role in the antislavery movement than Northerners did.*[285]

Among the Virginians who were ardent abolitionists, even advocating "entire emancipation,"[286] was America's first president, George Washington. In 1794, when he began to sell off some of his property, he said that his main motive, "one more powerful than all the rest," was to

> liberate a certain species of property I possess [that is, slaves], very repugnantly to my own feelings, but which imperious necessity compels, until I can substitute some other expedient by which expenses not in my power to avoid, however well disposed I may be to do it, can be defrayed.[287]

Washington was so against the institution that he beseeched God to help bring about emancipation in both the South and the North as soon as possible. Said the celebrated Southern abolitionist:

> Not only do I pray for it on the score of human dignity, but I can clearly foresee that nothing but the rooting out of slavery can perpetuate the existence of our union by consolidating it in a common bond of principle.[288]

As such, he spent much of his adult life trying to come up with a plan "by which slavery may be abolished by slow, sure and imperceptible degrees."[289] It was, Washington asserted to everyone he knew, among his "first wishes to see some plan adopted by which slavery may be abolished by law."[290]

As with the vast majority of Southerners, U.S. President George Washington detested slavery and could not wait to cleanse the country of it. A Virginian, Washington was, in fact, one of America's first abolitionists.

Our fifth president, Southerner James Monroe of Virginia, denounced slavery in the strongest terms, saying:

> We have found that this evil has preyed upon the very vitals of the Union; and has been prejudicial to all the States in which it has existed.[291]

On January 19, 1832, Southern General William H. Brodnax of Dinwiddie, Virginia, uttered the following before the Virginia legislature:

That slavery in Virginia is an evil, and a transcendent evil, it would be more than idle for any human being to doubt or deny. It is a mildew, which has blighted every region it has touched, from the creation of the world. Illustrations from the history of other countries and other times might be instructive; but we have evidence nearer at hand, in the short histories of the different States of this great confederacy [that is, the U.S.], which are impressive in their admonitions, and conclusive in their character.[292]

U.S. President James Monroe, another early Southerner who campaigned for the destruction of slavery.

In 1827, before the legislature of Virginia, Governor William Branch Giles spoke out against the custom of enslaving free blacks accused of crimes:

Slavery must be admitted to be a punishment of the highest order; and according to every just rule for the apportionment of punishment to crimes, it would seem that it ought to be applied only to crimes of the highest order. It seems but an act of justice to this unfortunate, degraded class of persons, to state that the number of convicts among free colored persons, compared with the white population, is extremely small; and would serve to show, that even this description of our population is less demoralized than is generally supposed.[293]

Since the American abolition movement got its start in the South, and more specifically in Virginia,[294] it is little wonder that it was in the Old Dominion State that voluntary emancipation found its greatest success. There was already a large, free black, landowning, black slave owning population in Virginia dating from the early 1600s.[295] But in 1782, at the urging of Thomas Jefferson, this number greatly increased when Virginia legislators passed a law legally permitting the state's slaveholders to emancipate their slaves.[296]

The response was immediate and overwhelming. Between that year and 1790 some 10,000 black servants were voluntarily freed by their white owners, almost always at great financial loss. In contrast, slave owners in the Northern states showed much greater reluctance to give up their black chattel. New Jersey, for example, did not pass its emancipation act until 1804, which is why it still had over 3,500 slaves as late as 1830.[297] There were a number of Northern states, such as Connecticut, that banned manumissions altogether.[298]

After the American Revolutionary War ended in 1783, though the U.S. government had not yet even given citizenship to blacks, numerous Southern states began passing laws allowing African-Americans to own property, testify in court, vote, and travel without restrictions.[299] In addition, many white Southerners were manumitting their slaves as fast as possible. Thus by 1810 the free black population of the Upper South

As stipulated in his father-in-law's will, Confederate General Robert E. Lee, gladly freed his wife's family's slaves in 1862. Lee hated the institution and was one of the first to push for emancipation and black enlistment in the Confederate military.

had risen from 1 percent to 10 percent in less than 30 years.[300] Across the entire South there were 100,000 free blacks by that year, nearly 5 percent of the total free population of the U.S.[301]

By 1860 there were 500,000 free blacks in the South,[302] more than two times as many as were then living in the North. Some 60,000 of these were from Virginia alone, about the same as the number of free blacks living in all of New England and New York.[303] Phillips writes that:

> Manumissions were in fact so common in the deeds and wills of the [Southern] men of 1776 that the number of colored freemen in the South exceeded thirty-five thousand in 1790 and was nearly doubled in each of the next two decades.[304]

Southern emancipations on a large scale were practically an everyday occurrence. Monroe Edwards of Louisiana, for example, set 160 slaves free by deed in 1840; in his will George W. P. Custis of Virginia (Robert E. Lee's father-in-law) liberated some 300 slaves at his death in 1857; and in 1833 Virginian John Randolph manumitted nearly 400 slaves via his will.[305] It was Randolph who famously said:

> Virginia is so impoverished by the system of slavery, that the tables will sooner or later be turned, and the slaves will advertise for runaway masters.[306]

Another noteworthy slaveholder who participated in this early Southern manumission program was Virginian Robert Carter (III) of Nomini Hall, known as America's "First Emancipator" for freeing his 500 slaves in 1791.[307] This was a financial sacrifice of monumental proportions: at approximately $1,000 a piece, these 500 individuals had a value of $15 million in today's currency. By this time, the late 1700s, Virginia herself had "effectively annulled" slavery: blacks could no longer be imported into the state, schools had been established for their education, and numerous Southern societies had sprung up whose sole mission was to legally protect the slaves that still existed.[308] From this same period comes a revealing declaration by a Virginia slaveholder named Paxton. Reflecting the feelings of millions of other Southerners, Paxton went on record as saying that "the best blood in Virginia flows in the veins of slaves!"[309]

In 1807, under another Virginian, President Thomas Jefferson, the Southern states enthusiastically voted to end the slave trade by 1808, the year the Constitution had set as the earliest date Congress could decide on the issue.[310] In fact:

> Jefferson denounced the whole system of slavery, in the most emphatic terms, as fatal to manners and industry, and endangering the very principles on which the liberties of the state were founded—"a perpetual exercise of the most unremitting despotism on the one part, and degrading submission on the other."[311]

Southerner and U.S. President Thomas Jefferson was one of the first and most vociferous enemies of slavery the world has ever known. His fight to destroy the unwanted institution went on for decades, but complete American abolition would not come until 1865—39 years after his death in 1826.

As Beecher noted, the American slave trade could have been brought to a halt in 1787, except for the efforts of Yankees: this was the year a vote was taken at the Constitutional Convention in Philadelphia to close the trade as soon as practicable, or keep it open until 1808. The New England states voted for the latter option.[312]

Vestiges of New England's "peculiar institution" are still obvious to this day, one of the more conspicuous being the pineapple. Though it is now seen as a "welcome" sign across the Northeast, this is a corruption of its original meaning: when New England slave traders returned from their ocean expeditions to the tropics to pick up slaves (mainly in the West Indies),[313] they would skewer a pineapple on their fencepost to let everyone in town know that they were "welcome" to come in and shop for slave products, as well as for slaves themselves.[314] The pineapple motif, that great symbol of Yankee slavery, is still commonly seen all over the U.S., not just in the North, but in the South as well.[315]

Now a symbol of hospitality, the pineapple motif began as an emblem of the Yankee slaver, who impaled one on his gate post as a sign that his slave-laden ships had just returned from tropical Africa, and that the public was "welcome" to come in and shop for slaves and slave products.

14

AMERICA'S FIRST OFFICIAL SLAVE OWNER: AN AFRICAN

WHAT YOU WERE TAUGHT:
America's first slave owner must have been white since whites created black slavery.

THE TRUTH: Africa was the first to create black slavery, a fact which we have already explored in detail. As for the former charge, America's first known official slave owner was Anthony Johnson, an Angolan who came to the colonies as a black African servant.

African-American Anthony Johnson, originally an indentured servant from Angola, was North America's first official slave owner. At his large Virginia plantation he held and worked both black and white slaves.

After his arrival in 1621, he quickly worked off his term of indenture and began purchasing human chattel in Virginia.[316] Later, in the chronicles of Northampton County, there is record of a suit brought by Johnson "for the purpose of recovering his negro servant."[317]

The African slaver from Angola, who owned both black *and* white servants, actually helped launch the American slave trade by forcing authorities to legally define the meaning of "slave ownership."[318] In 1652 his son John Johnson imported and bought eleven white slaves, who worked under him at his Virginia plantation, located on the banks of the Pungoteague River.[319] You never learned any of this in school, and neither will your children or grandchildren.

SLAVERY: COMMON, STANDARD, & UNIVERSAL

WHAT YOU WERE TAUGHT: American slavery was rightly named the "peculiar institution," for as a custom created solely by Europeans it was unusual, uncommon, and an aberration.

THE TRUTH: The uninformed have long referred to American slavery, and more specifically Southern slavery, as the "peculiar institution." Actually, there was nothing "peculiar" about it, and neither was it Southern, for it was once a common worldwide practice.

Indeed, slavery has been embraced by every known civilization, people, race, society, culture, and religion around the globe, from earliest recorded history right into present-day America. Some of the more notable slaving peoples have been the Egyptians, Assyrians, Babylonians, Sumerians, Akkadians, Mesopotamians, Phoenicians, Mycenaeans, Arameans, East Indians, Chaldeans, Hittites, Scythians, Persians, Arabians, Hebrews, Europeans, and Native-Americans, all who have a long history of enslaving their own citizens and their neighbors.[320] In 1886 Yankee historian George Bancroft of Massachusetts wrote:

> Slavery and the slave-trade are older than the records of human society; they are found to have existed wherever the savage hunter began to assume the habits of pastoral or agricultural life; and . . . they have extended to every portion of the globe. The oldest monuments of human labor on the Egyptian soil are the results of slave labor. The founder of the Jewish people was a slave-holder

and a purchaser of slaves. The Hebrews, when they broke from their own thraldom, planted slavery in the promised land. Tyre, the oldest commercial city of Phoenicia, was, like Babylon, a market "for the persons of men."[321]

Slavery was once practiced on every continent, and among all ancient peoples, societies, cultures, and religions. This makes it, not a "peculiar institution," but a common, standard, even universal institution, one upon which human civilization itself was built. We must not allow the distorting lens of presentism to prevent us from acknowledging this important fact of history.

In 1899 North Carolina planter and slave owner William Tasse Alexander penned:

There is no injustice more revolting than slavery, and yet *there is no fact so widespread in history*. In antiquity the system of labor was everywhere slavery. It was found in Rome, in Greece, in Egypt, in Austria, in Gaul, among the Germans, and it is said even among the Scythians. It was recruited by war, by voluntary sale, by captivity for debt, and then by inheritance. It was not everywhere cruel, and in patriarchical life it was scarcely distinguishable from domestic service; in some countries, however, it approached the service of beasts of burden. The brutal insensibility with which Aristotle and [Marcus Terentius] Varro spoke of slaves is revolting; and the manner in which they were treated by the laws is even more so. *These men who were of the same race, who had the same intellect and the same color as their owners*, were declared incapable of holding property, of appealing to the law, of defending themselves; in a word, of conducting themselves like men in any of the circumstances of life. Only the law of the Hebrew people tempered servitude by humanity. Doubtless we might quote certain words of Euripides or Terence, of Epictetus or of Seneca, colored with a more tender pity and evincing some heart. We find also both in Greek and Roman laws, on the monuments, and in the inscriptions and epitaphs which our contemporaries have so carefully studied, the proof that the granting of freedom to slaves, in individual cases, was frequent, and that it was inspired, especially at the moment of death, by religious motives.

But the brutal fact of slavery is incontestable. The evil outweighed the good in an enormous measure; servitude remained from century to century, from country to country, during all antiquity, the universal fact, and the legitimateness of servitude, the universal doctrine.[322]

Northerner George Bancroft was a rare Yankee historian: he acknowledged that slavery was as old as mankind.

In short, slavery is a natural byproduct of human society,[323] placing it alongside our other oldest human social institutions: hunting and gathering, religion, marriage, warfare, puberty rites, funerary rites, and prostitution.[324] Indeed, anthropologists consider slavery not an indication of barbarity, but an early sign of civilization: its emergence meant that humans had begun to enslave rather than kill one another.[325]

Since the master-slave relationship predates human history, American Southern whites were obviously not the inventors of American black slavery. In fact, Southern whites inherited the institution of African servitude very late in the game, many thousands of years after it had been practiced in Europe, the Middle East, Asia, and its ultimate source, of course, Africa.[326]

Indeed, as both the American slave trade[327] *and* American slavery began in New England,[328] the South was actually the *last* region in America to adopt slavery, and it is this fact that has helped contribute to the Yankee myth that she is the one responsible for inventing it. Memories are short and propaganda is long, particularly *Yankee* propaganda.[329]

In summation, an institution that has been found among nearly every people and on every continent since prehistoric times can hardly be considered "peculiar." In fact, as this very section of my book shows, it would be more appropriately and accurately called the universal, standard, ordinary, or everyday institution.[330]

The Native-American Aztecs depended on slaves for every facet of their society, including human sacrifice.

16

WE ALL DESCEND FROM SLAVES & SLAVE OWNERS

The author descends from Vikings who enslaved other Europeans, and who were themselves often enslaved by fellow Vikings.

WHAT YOU WERE TAUGHT: Only people of color have ever been slaves.

THE TRUTH: No one knows who actually invented slavery of course, for it was a worldwide phenomenon that arose simultaneously around the globe. But we do know that it dates from prehistory,[331] was once universally accepted on every part of the planet,[332] and that at one time it was found on every continent, in every single nation, and among every people, race, religion, and ethnic group.[333] Actually, "so far as we can trace back the history of the human race, we discover the existence of slavery."[334]

Slavery was, in fine, the economic system upon which *all* ancient civilizations were built,[335] for "slavery is the precursor to civilization."[336] As such it must certainly be counted as one of humanity's oldest social institutions and an essential feature of both society and economics.[337] It is, as the *Encyclopedia Britannica* puts it, a "universal, useful, indispensable, and inevitable accompaniment of human culture,"[338] one that eventually became so taken for granted that it was seen as a "divinely ordained institution" in every country.[339]

In 1837 America's seventh vice president, South Carolinian John C. Calhoun, rightly noted that

> there has never yet existed a wealthy and civilized society in which one portion of the community did not, in fact, live on the labor of the other.[340]

From its appearance in the prehistoric mists of time, slavery went on to be employed by the Mesopotamians (ancient Iraqis), Indians, Chinese, ancient Egyptians, Hebrews, Greeks, and Romans. In the pre-Columbian Americas slavery became an integral part of such Native-American peoples as the Maya and Inca,[341] who depended on large scale slave labor in warfare and farming.[342]

The reality is that slavery is a worldwide, omnipresent phenomenon, one that stubbornly persists into modern times, and which dates far back into the fog of the Neolithic Period on all continents, and among all races, ethnic groups, religions, societies, and peoples.[343]

Early peoples traditionally enslaved those they captured during war, a usually degraded group that formed the majority of most ancient societies. It is from among these enormous enslaved populations and their masters that you will find many of your own ancestors, whatever your race, creed, or nationality.

All of us then, no matter what our race, color, or nationality, have ancestors who enslaved others and who were themselves enslaved. *We are all descendants of slaves and slave owners.*[344]

SLAVERY:
A BUSINESS, NOT RACISM

WHAT YOU WERE TAUGHT: Slavery is a racist business predominated by whites.

THE TRUTH: Slavery is a business, period, one that has nothing to do with race. As we have seen, Africans, Native-Americans, Europeans, Asians, and Middle-Easterners, all peoples and races, in fact, were enslaving their own kind long before they discovered that there were colors and varieties of humans different than themselves.

Soviet dictator Joseph Stalin (left), seen here with Franklin D. Roosevelt (center) and Winston Churchill (right), enslaved 18 million fellow whites in the 1930s, proving once again that slavery has nothing to do with race or racism.

Let us take an example, Western slavery, which has its roots among Caucasians. Besides the overwhelming evidence of white-on-white slavery across ancient and Medieval Europe, any doubts about its Caucasoid origins vanish when we examine the etymology of the word slave itself: slave derives from the word "Slav," from the name of a European people, the Slavs,[345] today the largest European ethnic and language group inhabiting central and eastern Europe, as well as Siberia. (All 225 million speak one of the Slavonic languages.)[346]

The word Slav became synonymous with slavery due to the enslavement, by other Europeans (mainly Celts),[347] of thousands of Slavic individuals during Europe's early history.[348] As their names indicate, the Slovenes (of *Slove*nia), the Slovaks (of *Slova*kia), and the Yugoslavians (of Yugo*slavia*), are the modern (white) descendants of the ancient Slavs.

German Nazi leader Adolf Hitler presided over one of the fastest growth periods of slavery in world history. The Führer was not concerned with race. All 8 million of his slaves were fellow whites.

Whites were enthusiastically still enslaving one another right into the 20th Century and beyond. Soviet dictator Joseph Stalin, for example, enslaved some 18 million Caucasians during his reign of terror in the 1930s,[349] some 14.5 million more *white* slaves than the American South's 3.5 million *black* slaves.[350] "Harshly treated," and forced to live in labor camps that were located in the northern wilderness of Siberia, Stalin's white slaves were assigned spirit-breaking work in mines and forests.[351]

Between 1941 and 1945, nearly 8 million Caucasians were enslaved across Europe under Nazi Germany, including children as young as six years of age. This means that the Nazis owned 4.5 million more white slaves than the American South owned black slaves. Under Nazi socialist leader Adolf Hitler and the Third Reich's infamous swastika,[352] white European families were routinely separated and forced to work in factories, fields, and mines, where they were dehumanized, beaten, whipped, and starved by their German overlords.[353]

White Nazi slavery was the largest revival of the institution in the 20th Century, and one of the fastest and most monumental expansions of slavery in world history.[354] This appalling event occurred a mere sixty-five years ago, long after the Thirteenth Amendment abolished American slavery, demolishing the Yankee/New South myth that slavery is a white racist institution.[355]

It is true that early Yankees, the founders of American slavery, frequently justified the institution based on their view that Africans were inferior to Europeans. But this does not make American slavery itself racist, for *white* American slavery preceded, and laid the foundation for, *black* American slavery. In the end both were simply businesses striving to produce the greatest profits at the lowest cost.

Slavery in early Africa, as everywhere, was non-racial. Africans have hunted and enslaved their own kind from time immemorial, and they continue to do so to this day.

18

NEW YORK: THE STATE THAT WAS BUILT AROUND SLAVERY

WHAT YOU WERE TAUGHT: New York state had nothing to do with slavery.

A Dutch cottage in New York in 1679. The Empire State was steeped in slavery from its very inception: the colony of New Netherland, as it was then known, was founded in 1624 by the Dutch West India Company for the express purpose of expanding its slavery operations in the New World.

THE TRUTH: Originally known as New Amsterdam, it grew to become the center of the Dutch colony of what was then called New Netherland (later renamed New York by the English), a territory founded in 1624 and governed by the great slave trading corporation, the Dutch West India Company, whose primary goal was to "extend the market for its human merchandise whithersoever its influence reached."[356] Today New York City's official flag still bears the colors of the original flag flown by Netherland's slave ships: blue, orange, and white.

Thus it was that slavery took root in New York at the very beginning, when it was established by the Dutch in 1624. This marked the start of the official recognition of American slavery in the middle colonies, where the institution quickly became a "custom" in the region.[357]

The location of New York state, and more importantly, New York City, was not accidental. The Dutch had carefully and intentionally chosen them, not only for their many protected inlets, but also for their strategic positions, situated midway between the Northern and Southern colonies. From here they hoped to maximize slave sales and further spread their slave trading business throughout the Eastern seaboard.[358]

Both New York and New York City were developed around slavery, the former as a slave trading center, the latter as a slave port.

19

NEW YORK CITY: AMERICA'S SLAVING CAPITAL

WHAT YOU WERE TAUGHT: New Orleans, or some other Southern city, was no doubt America's slave capital.

THE TRUTH: Though the Dutch West India Company brought the first African laborers to New Netherland in 1626[359] (at which time eleven men from Africa's Gold Coast were delivered to the island of Manhattan),[360] it was not until around 1650 that it officially introduced slavery to the colony.[361] Settlers from New England immediately began pouring south into what is now Long Island and Westchester, New York, becoming some of the corporation's "best customers for slaves." In 1651 the inhabitants of Gravesend (now part of Brooklyn) petitioned to have the slave supply increased. To stimulate slave sales the Dutch opened up the slave trade to private ships, hoping to make New Amsterdam (the future New York City) the central slave market for all of the surrounding English colonies.[362] Their desire would soon manifest.

By the time the slavery-obsessed English took over the colony of New Netherland in 1664 and renamed it New York, it "contained more slaves in proportion to its inhabitants than Virginia."[363] From then on the institution only increased in New York. Between 1697 and 1790, for example, Albany's slave population grew from 3 percent to 16 percent. Influential Albany plantation owners, like the Schuyler and Van Rensselaer families, made vast fortunes using black slaves to build up their estates. A number of their well-known homes stand in New York's capital city to this day,[364] including Ten Broeck Manor,[365] Cherry Hill Mansion,[366] and the Schuyler Mansion.[367] In 1665 New York passed Duke's Laws, named after the Duke of York (who later became King James II).[368] A codification of statutes borrowed from the Massachusetts Fundamentals, they allowed Indians and blacks who had not been baptized into the Christian religion to be enslaved.[369]

In the 1600s the New York Harbor area teemed with slaves, slave owners, slave dealers, slave pens, slave yards, slave stockades, slave markets, and slave ships. Early New York was a slaver's paradise.

By the year 1700 New York Harbor was swarming with slave ships and slavery had become the foundation of the state's economy. New Yorkers believed that their "peculiar institution" was so vital to the North's economy that they blocked and delayed emancipation for over 100 years, with so-called "official abolition" not occurring until 1827.[370] New York's slave owners were a brutal lot, engaging in a myriad of cruel practices, from disenfranchisement and the separation of slave families to the whipping and murder of their African chattel.[371]

By the year 1720 New York had become one of the largest slaveholding states in the North, with 4,000 slaves against a white population of only 31,000 (thus that year 13 percent of the state's population were slaves). The situation was unbearable to the North's abolitionist minority, resulting in the nation's first antislavery essay: *The Selling of Joseph*, penned in Massachusetts by the famed Yankee judge who presided at the Salem witch trials, Samuel Sewall.[372] As in ancient Africa, Israel, and Thrace, slaves were such a valuable commodity in the North that they could be used as an insurance policy to cover their master's financial obligations,[373] or be sold to pay off the owner's creditors.[374] This led to the illegal Northern practice of falsely claiming free blacks as "personal property," then selling them to pay off debts.[375]

By the mid 1700s one-sixth of New York City's population was comprised of African slaves.[376] By 1756 New York state possessed some 13,000 adult black slaves, giving it the dubious distinction of having the largest slave force of any Northern colony at the time. That same year slaves accounted for 25 percent of the population in Kings, Queens, Richmond, New York City, and Westchester, making these areas the primary bastion of American slavery throughout the rest of the colonial period.[377] As mentioned, Yankees moving south to Westchester and Long Island were among the most eager slave purchasers, and by 1750 at least one-tenth of the province of New York's householders were slave owners.[378]

A 1656 Dutch map of New York, then called New Netherland. The selection of this specific area on North America's upper East Coast by the Dutch was no accident: the region—with its massive sea frontage and countless natural harbors, bays, ports, and riverways—was strategically situated to expedite and maintain the maritime slave trade between Africa, the American Northeast, and the West Indies.

At New York City's peak, at least one-fifth of the town's population were slaves.[379] Little wonder that in 1785 New York's state legislators rejected a bill advocating gradual emancipation.[380] In 1860 alone it has been estimated that 85 vessels—all which had been fitted out in and which had sailed from New York City—brought as many as 60,000 African slaves into the U.S.[381]

What Northern and New South historians will not tell you is that there is only one reason that New York City is today America's largest and wealthiest municipality: for centuries it served as the literal heart of

North America's slaving industry.[382] A host of the most famous New York names, in fact—names such as the Lehman Brothers, John Jacob Astor, Junius and Pierpont Morgan, Charles Tiffany, Archibald Gracie, and many others—are only known today because of the tremendous riches their families made from the town's "peculiar institution."[383] Many of today's wealthiest New York Jewish families descend from 18th-Century Jewish slave ship owners and slave traders, who eagerly participated with Northern colonial Christians in the Yankee's "peculiar institution."[384]

You will never learn any of this from pro-North mainstream history books, for their anti-South authors and publishers have a deeply vested interest in hiding the truth.[385]

New York City's Federal Hall, Trinity Church, and Wall Street in 1789. Now part of the United States of America, New York's obsession with the slave trade continued to broaden and strengthen. One day she would earn the dubious honor of being the state having the deepest and longest involvement with slavery, far more even than Massachusetts, where both the institution and the trade got their start in the early 1600s. In effect, by this time New York was well on her way to becoming a true slave empire. Her progress was only checked by the passage of the Thirteenth Amendment on December 6, 1865.

20

NEW YORK: AMERICA'S
ONLY TRUE SLAVE REGIME

WHAT YOU WERE TAUGHT: Slavery in New York lasted only a few years, after which the institution was banned.

THE TRUTH: New York City, the center of America's cotton business as early as 1815, was so deeply connected to the Yankee slave trade and to Southern slavery that it opposed all early attempts at abolition within its borders,[386] and, along with New Jersey, was the last Northern state to resist the passage of emancipation laws.[387]

In New York specifically slavery was so firmly fixed that it endured for at least 239 years:

1. Slavery in New York officially began (on the island of Manhattan) under the Dutch, and lasted for 38 years, from 1626 to 1664.
2. New York slavery then fell under the auspices of the English, lasting for 112 years, from 1664 to 1776.
3. After the formation of the U.S., New York slavery was turned over to the new state government, continuing on for another 51 years, from 1776 to 1827, when it was legally "abolished."[388]
4. Slavery in New York then persisted illegally for another 38 years, only being permanently shut down by the ratification of the Thirteenth Amendment in December 1865.[389]

New York's 239-year history of slavery is the longest of any state, and certainly far longer than any Southern state. It is greater even than Massachusetts, where both the American slave trade and American slavery got their start. This makes New York America's premier slave state, our one and only true slavocracy, prompting one early historian to refer to the Empire State as a slave "regime never paralleled in equal volume elsewhere."[390]

In 1664 the English took over the colony of New Netherland, renaming it New York after the Duke of York—who was later to become King James II. Instead of lessening, slavery only intensified under the new British government, which replaced the Dutch West Indian Company with an even more merciless and profit oriented slave trading organization: the Royal African Company. Note the British flag on the galleon to the right, which is bringing a new cargo of African slaves into New York Harbor. After the formation of the U.S.A. in 1776, Northerners and Yankees took over New York, developing it into a true slave regime, one unequaled in slave volume and sales anywhere else in the world.

21

THE NORTHERN
SLAVE POPULATION

WHAT YOU WERE TAUGHT: Since American slavery originated in the South, the North always had far less slaves than Dixie.

A dozen or so slaves in Connecticut holding an indoor religious meeting, part of a much larger *Northern* group that made up the majority of American slaves before 1776. Pro-North historians have labored diligently to suppress the facts about Northern slavery. But plenty of evidence still exists, such as the official name of Rhode Island, "Rhode Island and Providence Plantations," and the countless slave cemeteries and slave farms that are now being excavated by archaeologists across the Northern states.

THE TRUTH: In 1776, at the time of the formation of the *first* Confederate States of America, the U.S.A., of the 500,000 slaves in the 13 colonies, 300,000 (or 60 percent) were possessed by the Northern ones, only 200,000 (or 40 percent) by the Southern ones. It was only later, when Yankee slave traders actively pushed slavery even further south, that Dixie came to possess more slaves than the North. This is the exact procession of events one would expect with American slavery having been launched in the North.[391] At the start of Lincoln's War in 1861, some 500,000 to 1 million slaves were still living and working in the Northern states,[392] compared to 3.5 million in the South.[393]

Two black female slaves serve a white family in Concord, Massachusetts, where freed slaves were later segregated and forced to live in shacks around Walden Pond. As the birthplace of both American slavery and the American slave trade, it is only natural that slaves were once an integral aspect of Northern white society. Indeed, up until the late 1700s, the North possessed far more slaves than the South. It was only when the racist Yankee found slavery unprofitable and the presence of blacks intolerable that he began pushing his slaves on the Southern states. Not in an effort to abolish it in the North, but to foster it in the South, where Yankee businessmen hoped to continue to reap huge profits from selling slaves and buying slave-produced products like cotton.

22

THE PERCENTAGE OF
YANKEE SLAVE OWNERS

WHAT YOU WERE TAUGHT: The percentage of Yankee slave owners was minuscule compared to that of Southern slave owners.

THE TRUTH: By 1690, in Perth Amboy, New Jersey, as just one example, nearly every white inhabitant owned one or more black slaves.[394] This means that nearly 100 percent of the whites in some Northern cities were slaveholders.

Other Northern states shared similar statistics from this time period. Records from the early 1700s reveal that 42 percent of all New York households owned slaves, and that the share of slaves in both New York and New Jersey was larger than that of North Carolina.[395]

Contrast all of this with the Old South, where at no time did white slave owners make up more than 4.8 percent of the total population (only 25 percent of Southern households possessed one or more slaves), the peak number in 1860.[396] *And as one moves further back in time these figures sharply decrease.* In fact, slavery being a rich man's institution, in most Southern towns there were no slave owners.[397]

The conclusion? The percentage of slaveholders in the Old North was always much higher than slaveholders in the Old South. Do not be fooled by anti-South writers who tell you otherwise.[398]

Percentage wise slave ownership was always much higher in the Old North than in the Old South. In fact, at one time nearly every white citizen in some Yankee cities owned black slaves. In Perth Amboy, New Jersey, as just one example, white slave ownership reached 100 percent. In the South, however, individual slaveholding never exceeded 4.8 percent. This illustration shows a white slave owner from Providence, Rhode Island, selling one of his black slaves to a plantation owner from Long Island, New York, necessitating breaking up the slave family—an all too common tragedy in the North, but illegal in Southern states like Louisiana.

23

HOW NORTHERNERS & SOUTHERNERS REGISTERED THEIR SLAVES

WHAT YOU WERE TAUGHT: Northern slave owners treated their slaves much better than Southern ones did.

An old Yankee ad for livestock medicine. Northerners registered their *slaves* as farm animals, quite unlike in the South, where *servants* were registered as family members.

THE TRUTH: From early American records it is quite apparent that Northerners had far less regard for their African-American slaves than Southerners. For instance, the Massachusetts general court evaluated both red and black slaves as "private property" suitable for exportation as "merchandise,"[399] while Rhode Island and New Hampshire more specifically taxed slaves as "livestock." New Jersey and Pennsylvania—the latter state where blacks were present even before William Penn's colony was founded[400]—preferred to see their slaves as "assessable possessions," while New York evaluated its slaves using a poll tax. Everywhere across the North black slaves were registered by Yankee families on the same lists as their horses, cattle, tools, kitchen goods, and other common farm and household items.[401] How different from the South, where a slave owner was legally required to register slaves as literal members of his own family.[402]

24

SLAVE LAWS IN THE NORTHERN STATES

WHAT YOU WERE TAUGHT: The Northern states treated their slaves with utmost respect, and had numerous laws protecting them.

THE TRUTH: Yankee slave owners had complete freedom to discipline their chattel in any manner they saw fit, and various barbarities—from whipping and branding, to public torture and burning slaves at the stake—were legal, routine, and socially accepted.

In New York, for instance, where a liberal 1702 law authorized masters to chastise their human property "at their own discretion,"[403] slaves convicted of heinous crimes, such as murder, were subject to all manner of hideous fates. These included being "burned at the stake," "gibbeted alive," and "broken on the wheel."

This is precisely what occurred in 1712, when New York authorities

Slave auctions, like this one in 17th-Century Boston, Massachusetts, were once an everyday affair in New England: accepted, legal, and well attended. Yankee slaves had few rights and could be punished, even killed, in any manner deemed appropriate by their owners. Infractions suitable for discipline included breaking the nightly curfew or glancing at a white female. Punishments included various and often extreme forms of torture, from the rack and branding, to the wheel and burning at the stake.

hanged 13 slaves, burned four of them alive (one over a "slow fire"), "broke" one on the wheel,[404] and left another to starve to death chained to the floor.[405] In 1741 the Empire State executed 31 blacks:[406] 13 were burned at the stake, 18 were hanged, while another 71 were transported out of state.[407] On another occasion a New York slave named Tom, found guilty of killing two people, was ordered to be "roasted over a slow fire so that he will suffer in torment for at least eight to ten hours."[408]

Such executions were often performed in public, in full view of ordinary New Yorkers. While this was going on, Southern states like South Carolina were banning the public punishment of blacks. The naturally humanitarian Southerner found such scenes "distressing," quite unlike his more thick-skinned Yankee compatriot to the North.[409]

A popular pastime in the Old North was the slave execution, a public spectacle attended by entire families—as can be seen here. This New York slave is being burned at the stake for a minor infraction of the state's strict Black Codes.

This 1863 satirical illustration by Bavarian-American artist Adalbert John Volck reveals the reality for "Free Negroes in the North," who were often reduced to thievery, beggary, and harlotry due to white Yankee racism. Here, in a New York City slum, on the lower left two indigent black men try to sell stolen goods to a passing white. On the lower right a starving homeless black man on the street begs for handouts. In the back right and upper half black female prostitutes ply their trade from a condemned apartment building.

25

SLAVES LAWS IN THE SOUTHERN STATES

Southern "slaves" were not the bedraggled, illiterate, oppressed race that our Yankee biased history books like to portray. This dapper slave couple, for example, George and Susan Page, worked for the Dabney family of Raymond, Mississippi, made famous by Susan Dabney Smedes' 1888 book, *Memorials of a Southern Planter.* When Susan's father, plantation owner Thomas Dabney, passed away in the late 1800s, former body servant George wrote to her, saying: "He was a good master to us all. You are all my children, and I love you all alike."

WHAT YOU WERE TAUGHT:
The Southern states treated their slaves inhumanely, even brutally, and refused to pass laws that would protect them. When they grew ill or too old they were callously discarded to live and die on the street.

THE TRUTH: In the Old South black servants were protected by a literal bible of hundreds of rigorous rules and regulations, crimes against slaves were punishable by law, and cruel slaveholders, though rare, were harshly penalized, even executed, when caught (most were turned in by their neighbors).[410] In truth, as we have seen, Southern servants were legally registered as literal members of the families of their white, black, red, or brown owners, and, in nearly all cases, delicately cared for throughout their entire lives, very much as if they were the adopted children of their owners.[411] Little wonder that many Southern blacks did not welcome emancipation, preferring the "soft life" of servitude instead.[412]

The sight of sociable, cheerful, carefree, polite, healthy, well dressed slaves walking freely about town was a common one in the Old South, much to the consternation and shock of Yankee visitors and Northern transplants.

In 1900 Dr. Henry A. White, history professor at Washington and Lee University, made the following astute comments; words that should be permanently enshrined in granite in the capitol building of every Southern state:

> The [Southern slavery] system produced no paupers and no orphans; food and clothing the negro did not lack; careful attention he received in sickness, and, without a burden [care] the aged servants spent their closing days. The plantation was an industrial school where the negro gradually acquired skill in the use of tools. A bond of affection was woven between Southern masters and servants which proved strong enough in 1861-'65 to keep the negroes at voluntary labour to furnish food for the armies that contended against [Lincoln's] military emancipation.[413] In the planter's home the African learned to set a higher value upon the domestic

virtues which he saw illustrated in the lives of Christian men and women; for, be it remembered, the great body of the slave-holders of the South were devotees of the religious faith handed down through pious ancestors from [John] Knox, [Thomas] Cranmer, [John] Wesley, and [John] Bunyan. *With truth, perhaps, it may be said than no other economic system before or since that time has engendered a bond of personal affection between capital and labour so strong as that established by the institution of [Southern] slavery.*[414]

There was also the fact that it was impossible for a servant to ever experience homelessness or joblessness, or suffer from starvation or neglected health problems. Why? Because their *Southern owners were legally obligated to care for them at all times and through any type of hardship, from the cradle to the grave.*

When a black servant became too old or too ill to work, or if a black child became orphaned, for instance, their masters and mistresses bore the legal responsibility of looking after their welfare until the day of their deaths—or freedom, whichever came first.[415] This means that *at any one time a full one-third of Southern slaves were not working,*[416] and were therefore nonproductive members of their owners' plantations. Yet, they remained under the medical protection and physical guardianship of their masters, who essentially "paid them to do nothing," making this an early form of socialized health care that was unknown in the U.S. until the creation of Medicare in 1965.

Yankee author Joseph Holt Ingraham commented on this unique aspect of Southern "slavery," which he witnessed during his visit to Dixie in the 1830s:

> *Nor are [Southern] planters indifferent to the comfort of their gray-headed slaves. I have been much affected at beholding many exhibitions of their kindly feeling towards them. They always address them in a mild and pleasant manner—as "Uncle," or "Aunty"—titles as peculiar to the old negro and negress, as "boy" and "girl," to all under forty years of age. Some old Africans are allowed to spend their last years in their houses, without doing any kind of labour; these, if not too infirm, cultivate little patches of ground, on which they raise a few vegetables—for vegetables grow nearly all the year round in this climate—and make a little money to purchase a few extra comforts. They are also always receiving presents from their [white] masters and mistresses, [as well as] . . . the [other] negroes on the estate, the latter of whom are extremely desirous of seeing the old people comfortable. A relation of the extra comforts which some planters allow*

their slaves, would hardly obtain credit at the North. But you must recollect that Southern planters are men—and men of feeling—generous and high-minded, and possessing as much of the "milk of human kindness" as the [Yankee] sons of colder climes . . .[417]

In 1912 Southerner Henry Clinton Sydnor wrote of one of his aged family servants, a man who had never been known to work a day in his life:

Another of our negroes was Uncle Americus. No one knew his age, but he was supposed to be about a hundred years old. *Never in my recollection had he performed any work of any kind.* He would tell us children about the Revolutionary War, and they were most remarkable stories. *I looked up to him in awe and admiration.*[418]

During a trip to South Carolina in 1854, Yankee Liberal Dr. Charles Eliot Norton noted—much to his surprise—that there were absolutely no indications of either "negro misery" or "white tyranny."

Here is another example of how Southern slaveholders actually treated their servants, as opposed to the tall tales told in Northern slanted history books. In 1860 there were an estimated 3,427 Southern slaves who were listed in the Census as either "blind," "deaf and dumb," "insane," or "idiotic."[419] All of the needs of these individuals were tended to by their owners; not simply due to legal requirement, but, as mentioned, also from the great Southern philanthropic impulse. This is what Southerners to this day regard as true humanitarianism. Of this legally required but altruistic custom, famed British geologist Sir Charles Lyell offered the following example of a Georgia slave owner whose plantation he visited:

There are 500 negroes on the Hopeton estate, a great many of whom are children, and some old and superannuated [retired]. The latter class, who would be supported in a poor-house in England, enjoy here, to the end of their days, the society of their neighbours and kinsfolk, and live at large in separate houses assigned to them.[420]

26

SOUTHERN SLAVES & QUALITY OF LIFE

WHAT YOU WERE TAUGHT: Southern slave owners worked their slaves all day every day, seven days a week, without pay and without any time off.

THE TRUTH: These are yet more Northern slavery myths. Not only were Southern servants financially compensated, they were also encouraged to own their own businesses. And not only this, the extra money they earned from plying their personal trades—added to their basic daily income—could be quite substantial,[421] and greatly contributed to the thriving "black commerce" that existed across the Old South.[422]

While the average Southern servant's income seems to have been around $48 a year (or about $1,300 in today's currency, a substantial wage at the time), many ambitious blacks earned from $60 to over $300 a year ($1,600 to $8,000 in today's currency, respectively), many drawing "considerably higher wages" than whites doing the same type of labor.[423] The products of home gardens

To this day Yankee authors continue to pretend that the Old South prohibited marriage between slaves. Southern hero, Confederate President Jefferson Davis, rightly called this particular Yankee myth "a gross misrepresentation" of the facts.

(sold at market each Sunday)[424] and work at outside odd jobs also brought in significant extra earnings,[425] some of which were used to buy fancy cloth from which they created "fine clothing" for themselves.[426]

Far from being the "bedraggled, stupid, degraded, indolent slaves" of Northern lore, such commercialism made these Southern servants much more akin to proud peasants and enterprising small town traders.[427] It was not uncommon for a servant to earn enough surplus money that he or she could make a contribution to the collection plate every Sunday at church.[428] Thomson noted that

many of those [Southern slaves] who are hired out make more money than the stipulated wages their owners require. With this [extra income] they are allowed to do as they please.[429]

Under the South's mild African servitude, there were no laws barring black slaves from earning money, owning possessions, or accruing wealth. Thus untold thousands of African-American servants, like these black cattlemen, amassed great fortunes, not only through their own hard work and thriving businesses, but by way of shrewd financial deals. This resulted in a booming internal "black commerce" that helped improve and stabilize the entire Southern economy for centuries.

When German scientist Dr. Johann David Schoepf traveled through South Carolina in the late 1700s, he found that:

The gentlemen in the country have among their negroes, as the Russian nobility among their serfs, the most necessary handicraftsmen, cobblers, tailors, carpenters, smiths, and the like, whose work they command at the smallest possible price, or for nothing almost. There is hardly any trade or craft which has not been learned and is not carried on by negroes, partly free, partly slave; *the latter are hired out by their owners for day's wages.*[430]

In the Old South the slave had hundreds of rights, was well respected and even loved by his "master" and "mistress," and was usually regarded as a member of the owner's family. In this illustration, fun-loving servants attend a weekly shindig on an early Louisiana plantation known as a "slave ball," complete with music, food, dancing, and guests invited from neighboring farms.

As for work days, unlike in the North, not only were Southern slaves paid a weekly salary, they were also given Saturdays, Sundays, rainy days, and holidays off.[431] On such days servants had near complete freedom. They could hunt, fish,[432] nap, rest, play games, garden, spend time with their families, take weekend jaunts into town, almost anything they desired. Visits to family members, friends, and lovers on nearby farms and plantations was a favorite pastime. Servants could also continue working for the plantation and receive extra pay and bonuses, or hire themselves out (or have their owners hire them out) to do odd jobs for additional revenue[433]—a right, by the way, that was denied slaves in many Northern states, such as Pennsylvania.[434]

On Saturdays, the day traditionally set aside for servants to work their own land, they labored either a half day,[435] or had the entire day free. Each year they also had about a week's worth of work free holidays (such as Christmas, Good Friday, Independence Day, and the post harvest period), with odd days off as rewards.[436] On many plantations there was a servant-only party held every Saturday night, complete with whiskey, a barbeque, music (items often contributed by the white owners), and dancing.[437] At slave parties, commonly held in barns or out in the fields, the fiddle and banjo were always present, while bones, stomping feet, and hand-clapping kept the beat as individuals danced various jigs and shuffles.[438]

Southern servants, like this one suffering from an illness (center), received immediate on-site medical care from birth to death, paid for by their owner (far right). This is a right that no true slave could ever expect. Typically, the doctor (kneeling) was the same one used by the owner and his family. In other words, Southern black servants had access to the same high quality health care as wealthy whites—the only difference being that for the former it was free.

As for their daily labor, Southern black servants worked from sunrise to early afternoon (eight hours) five days a week,[439] with one to three hours off for lunch.[440] This made their average work week from 25 to 40 hours long,[441] far below the norm at the time for both free-laboring whites and blacks, who typically put in between 70 and 75 hours a week.[442]

The life of the Southern slave was indeed easy and secure compared to the far more difficult life of the Yankee slave, and even of most free Southern whites and blacks. This is why, when asked, nearly 100 percent of American blacks said they would rather be owned by a Southern slaveholder than a Northern one.[443]

Our Yankee biased history books tell us that Southern slaves were "worked to death" from morning till night, seven days a week, 365 days a year, from the age of five until death. Actually they labored less hours a week than a modern office or factory worker, and had Saturdays, Sundays, sick days, rainy days, and holidays off. And unlike what was found in Europe at the time—where child labor was the norm—Southern slaves were not usually put to work until the age of 15, then were retired in their 60s.

27

ANTILITERACY SLAVE LAWS

WHAT YOU WERE TAUGHT: Antiliteracy laws were a product of the South, where every or nearly every Southern slave owner prohibited his slaves from learning to read and write.

THE TRUTH: To being with, antiliteracy laws, meant to prevent both black slaves and free blacks from learning to read and write, were first invented in the puritanical North, where they were strictly and sometimes violently enforced.[444]

Second, antiliteracy laws were not enacted in all or even most of the Southern states. Actually, only four Southern states ever bothered to officially ratify such regulations: Virginia, Georgia, North Carolina, and South Carolina, and even here the statutes were only loosely obeyed and routinely ignored. Kentucky and Tennessee never issued them,[445] and the rest of the Southern states simply ignored the entire issue since the law was considered archaic, not to mention inhumane and illogical.

The fact is that, just as Mary Chesnut did, millions of Southern slave owners intentionally taught their servants to read and write; or just as often the servants taught themselves.[446] Thus the Northern myth that slave owners prevented their servants from becoming literate for fear of them becoming "too smart," "impudent," and "uppity" is just that, a Northern myth—certainly true of ancient Rome, but completely false when it came to the Victorian American South.[447]

While there were some Southern slave owners who tolerated or even endorsed this counterproductive concept, again, these were the exception rather than the rule. Writing in 1850, Lyell was one of those who discovered this reality first-hand:

I am told that the old colonial statutes against teaching the slaves to read were almost in abeyance, and had become a dead letter, until revived by the reaction against the Abolition agitation [which began in the early 1830s], since which they have been rigorously enforced and made more stringent. Nevertheless, the negroes are often taught to read, and they learn much in Sunday schools, and for the most part are desirous of instruction.[448]

A literate Florida slave. Contrary to Yankee myth, many Southern black slaves were able to read and write, and those who could not displayed an eagerness to learn. While some taught one another and some were taught by their owners' children, many others were instructed in the "three r's" by the owners themselves. Only four Southern states even had antiliteracy laws, and since they were considered silly, they were usually scoffed at, routinely ignored, and almost never enforced.

As noted, the antiliteracy movement began and was strongest in the North. As hard evidence for its widespread existence, not to mention overt white racism, in Yankeedom prior to Lincoln's War, we need look no further than the doleful story of Prudence Crandall.

Crandall was a white New England teacher who founded the "High School for Young Colored Ladies and Misses" in Canterbury, Connecticut, in 1834. One would think that fellow Yanks, had they been true non-racist egalitarians, would have applauded her efforts. Instead, for trying to offer blacks a free education in New England, Crandall, a Quaker and abolitionist, was harassed, persecuted, arrested (three times), imprisoned, and had her home burned down, while Northern white mobs attacked and stoned her school, tore it from its foundations using a team of 100 oxen, then physically drove her out of the state.[449]

None of Connecticut's white population shed a tear for Crandall. Instead, the state, and in particular her politicians, were quite happy to see her, and her school, disappear. Their smug parting comment sums up the North's feelings perfectly during this period: "Once open this door, and New-England will become the Liberia of America," they shrieked as Crandall left Connecticut for the last time.[450] New Hampshire whites followed suit by destroying their state's own black schools.[451]

Prudence Crandall's "School for Colored Girls" being attacked and torched by local townspeople in Canterbury, Connecticut. "Your nigger school shall never be allowed in Canterbury nor in any other town in this State!" the furious Yankee mob shouted. The building was later ripped from its foundation by a team of 100 oxen and destroyed. Crandall was only one of hundreds of Yankee abolitionists who were criticized, harassed, assaulted, and driven from the region for promoting racial equality. Her story highlights the utter disdain the majority of Northerners had for both blacks and abolition at the time.

The headmaster of a public school in New Hampshire blocks the entrance of a black mother trying to bring her two children to class. After launching American slavery, Yankees discovered that they did not particularly like the idea of living in the midst of blacks, as either slaves or as freemen. Thus began a region-wide campaign to prevent African-Americans from entering mainstream white society, and even deport them en masse from the country. One result was the creation of the American Colonization Society in 1816, whose stated mission was to make America "white from coast to coast." The ACS found its greatest patronage in Yankee cities such as Boston, Massachusetts, where men like Harvard University President Jared Sparks gave it their full backing. But the racist organization found massive support in the white Midwest as well. Abraham Lincoln, for instance, was not only a member, but an Illinois chapter leader, one who spent years trying to bar African-Americans from his adopted state.

28

JIM CROW LAWS

WHAT YOU WERE TAUGHT: Jim Crow laws originated in the South but were unknown in the North.

Edward Everett, governor of Massachusetts, was fully aware of the blatant white racism in his region, observing that the lives of so-called "free" Northern blacks were weighted down by "disability, discouragement, and hardship" on all sides.

THE TRUTH: Incorrect. Jim Crow laws were "universal" in all of the Northern states, but were "unusual" in the South.[452] The North's onerous Black Codes, for example, forbade, among many other things, black immigration and black civil rights, and even banned blacks from attending public schools. Little wonder that those blacks who managed to survive in the North were generally less educated and less skilled than Southern blacks. Up to 1855 it was this very type of oppression that prevented blacks from serving as jurors in all but one Northern state: Massachusetts.[453]

Even after Lincoln's admittedly fake and illegal Emancipation Proclamation was issued (on January 1, 1863),[454] literally nothing changed for African-Americans living north of the Mason-Dixon Line. When former slaves managed to make economic progress there, they found themselves blocked at every turn by a hostile racist Northern government, the very body that had "emancipated" them. This blockage was accomplished not only by Black Codes, by also through the implementation of severe Jim Crow laws and public segregation laws,[455] both which were unconditionedly and widely supported by the Yankee populace.[456]

Anti-black sentiment was so strong in the Old North that it was actually life-threatening to be antislavery at the time, which is why Yankee abolitionists like Elijah P. Lovejoy of Maine, were never cordially received by fellow Northerners. As is pictured here, Northern anti-abolition mobs repeatedly broke into his publishing office and destroyed his printing equipment. On November 7, 1837, he was cornered in a warehouse in Alton, Illinois, which mobs attempted to set ablaze. When Lovejoy came out to try and prevent torches from being applied to the wooden roof, he was shot to death. The Yankee abolitionist publisher was 34 years old.

LIFELONG SLAVERY
& SELF-PURCHASE

WHAT YOU WERE TAUGHT: Southerners enslaved blacks for life.
THE TRUTH: This is historically incorrect and impossible, for life enslavement is an aspect of authentic slavery, which was never practiced in the American South. Actually, from the very beginning of American slavery it was Northerners who made their African chattel slaves for life. In 1663, for example, Maryland passed a white racist slavery law whose first section ordered that

The Southern "slave" was not a slave. He was a servant, with all the rights and freedoms of a servant, including self-purchase and self-emancipation.

"all negroes and other slaves within this province, and all negroes and other slaves to be hereafter imported into this province, shall serve during life; and all children born of any negro or other slave, shall be slaves, as their fathers were, for the term of their lives." The second section recites that "divers free-born [white] English women, forgetful of their free condition, and to the disgrace of our nation, do intermarry with negro slaves"; and for deterring from such "shameful matches," it enacts that, *during their husbands' lives, white women so intermarrying*

shall be servants to the masters of their husbands, and that the issue of such marriages shall be slaves for life.[457]

It was only much later that this mandate was vetoed in the North, and slaves were allowed to buy their liberty.

In the South, however, from slavery's very inception slaves could purchase their freedom whenever they wished, and thousands did just that.[458] This is yet just one more proof that authentic slavery never existed in Dixie, for lifelong indenture is an element of true thralldom, and this is something that existed only in the North: the birthplace of, and the only home of, genuine American slavery.[459]

Even when Northern slaves were eventually legally allowed to buy their freedom, Yankees thought nothing of recapturing them and reselling them back into slavery, as was the case with this New York freedman in 1836.

Anti-South writers have fabricated the myth of the "runaway slave" to confuse students of history and denigrate the South. According to this particular fiction, Southern black servitude was so horrendous that slaves took every opportunity to flee for their lives. The truth is that while there were indeed occasional runaways, mainly from the rare cruel Southern master, fugitive slaves were an infrequent peculiarity that never occurred on the typical Southern farm or plantation. The reason for this was simple enough: Southern servitude actually benefitted servants in a myriad of ways by providing safety, stability, and security in the legally sanctioned forms of lifelong free housing, clothing, food, employment, and healthcare. In many Southern communities black servants were actually the envy of free blacks and whites, many who struggled with financial issues that inevitably led to serious housing and health problems, among other things. In truth, runaway slaves were a far more serious problem in the Old North, where the region's rigorous Black Codes often made life unbearable for black servants. Southern blacks who allowed Yankees to talk them into moving North had it especially hard, and usually deeply regretted the decision. While hard at work on the cold stony soil of New England's bleak plantations, it was not uncommon to hear them yearningly singing their favorite Southern tunes. One of those most often heard wafting across the fields of Massachusetts, for example, was the 1859 song, *I Wish I Was in Dixie's Land*: "Oh, I wish I was in the land of cotton, old times there are not forgotten. Look away! Look away! Look away! Dixie Land. Oh, I wish I was in Dixie, hooray! hooray! In Dixie land I'll take my stand, to live and die in Dixie. Away, away, away down south in Dixie. Away, away, away down south in Dixie."

30

THE MYTH OF "SLAVE NAMES"

WHAT YOU WERE TAUGHT: In order to further dehumanize them, Southern slaves were prohibited from giving themselves either first or last names, a right retained by their owners. In rare cases where they were allowed, slaves were forced to the take last names of their owners, the well-known despicable "slave names"—many which, unfortunately, are used to this day.

THE TRUTH: First, there were no laws in the South against black servants naming themselves. Second, they usually chose their own names, and always without the consent or knowledge of their owners.[460] Third, black servants did not refer to these as "slave names," but rather as "entitles," since, as individuals with their own separate identities, they felt they had a right to own a proper first and last name. These were ideas and customs with which nearly all white Southerners agreed.[461]

Fourth, entitles were seldom taken from their owners' names. Typically black servants chose both their first and

A Southern slave auction. There were no laws regarding slave names in the Old South, and first or last names were never forced on African-American servants. Blacks came from Africa already enslaved, and thus often wanted to change their name to reflect their new and improved life in America. Naturally, the surname they chose was sometimes that of their new white or black owner, of whose family they were now a legal member.

last names based on their own parents' names, or just as often on unrelated whites (famous or unknown) whom they trusted or admired, or simply because they liked a particular moniker. Northern slave Frederick Douglass, for example, took his surname from the Douglas family, the powerful, noble Scottish clan featured in Sir Walter Scott's famous 1810 poem, *The Lady of the Lake*.[462]

In many cases Southern blacks simply chose standard occupational surnames (Miller, Butler, Carpenter, Mason, Farmer, Tiler, Baker, Wheelwright), while others preferred native African names and words, such as Phiba, Cudjo, and Juba. Over time such names would usually become anglicized—in these three particular examples as Phoebe, Joe, and Jack respectively.[463]

Contrary to Yankee mythology, there were no hard and fast rules concerning slave names in leisurely Dixie. This young plantation overseer in Kentucky gave himself the first name Odysseus because he liked its classic connotations, and the surname Tinibu, because it was his maternal grandfather's last name.

31

NORTHERN SEGREGATION, SOUTHERN INTEGRATION

WHAT YOU WERE TAUGHT: Anti-black laws and segregation were everywhere in the Old South, but unheard of in the Old North.

THE TRUTH: Those who take the time to study authentic American history rather than the fabricated nonsense put out by pro-North writers will find that the opposite is the case. As Phillips put it, the "antipathy [toward blacks] was palpably more severe at the North in general than in the South."[464] And here is why.

In early South Carolina, French author and traveler Duke de la Rochefoucauld Liancourt, encountered a former black slave who had earned and saved enough money under Southern African servitude to buy his freedom and purchase a large plantation and some 200 black slaves. This would not have been possible under segregation.

As Richard Henry Pratt noted, wherever the various races have the least amount of contact, racism tends to increase—no matter what the skin color of the dominant or majority race.[465] And this is precisely the situation we find in the Old South and the Old North, for in the latter region most whites had little if any interaction with blacks, making racism far more ingrained. This is why both legal and customary segregation was found in nearly all of the Northern states, while it was all but unknown in the Southern ones.[466] Indeed, *during the antebellum period there was no segregation anywhere in Dixie*, yet it was endemic to America's northeastern states right up to, and far beyond, the 1860s.[467]

32

WHITE RACISM IN NEW YORK

President Lincoln's overt bigotry facilitated the nationwide acceptance of white racism, particularly in New York, a state already long plagued with racial intolerance—without question, the most severe and deeply fixed in early America. The last Northern state to relinquish slavery and the country's only true slave regime, the Empire State currently serves as the home of the head of the National Knights of the Ku Klux Klan.

WHAT YOU WERE TAUGHT: New York has always been a liberal non-racist state.

THE TRUTH: Naturally, New York City, America's slavery capital for decades, had its own set of strict Black Codes, all which were considered particularly savage. Offences by black servants could garner punishments ranging from beatings and whippings to deportation and even execution. In 1741 the mere hint of a slave revolt resulted in the public killing of 27 New York slaves, each one who was hanged or burned at the stake.[468]

New York as a whole was arguably the most racially intolerant state, perhaps second only to Illinois and Massachusetts. This is certainly why, for instance, New York City had far less black artisans than Southern towns, such as the far more racially tolerant New Orleans.[469] Between 1702 and 1741 alone the Empire State passed a massive series of statutes that, among other things, allowed blacks convicted of heinous acts to be executed "in such a manner as the enormity of their crimes might be deemed to merit." Along with this law manumissions were restricted, free New York blacks were prohibited from holding real estate, and the state's entire set of Black Codes was strengthened in an effort to gain greater control over both slaves and blacks in general.[470] Well into the 1830s, as just one example, not even free blacks were allowed to drive their own hacks or carts.[471] This same law was also active in Baltimore, Maryland, while in Philadelphia, Pennsylvania, free blacks were not allowed to drive an omnibus.[472]

Hundreds of such illustrations from the racist Old North could be given. No wonder so many African-Americans wanted to get as far away from Yankeedom as they could, requesting that they be sent as far South as possible (to places like New Orleans),[473] or even out of the country.[474]

Illinois Senator Lyman Trumbull spoke for Lincoln, as well as most other white Northerners at the time, when he made this public pronouncement: "There is a great aversion in the [Mid] West—I know it to be so in my state—against having free Negroes come among us. Our people want nothing to do with the Negro."

SLAVERY & SERVITUDE:
A WORLD OF DIFFERENCE

WHAT YOU WERE TAUGHT: The type of black bondage practiced by the Old South was called "slavery."

THE TRUTH: THE TRUTH: This chestnut is perhaps Yankeedom's oldest and most enduring anti-South myth. The only problem is that it happens to be false.

Edward A. Pollard, Virginian, staunch Confederate, and editor of the pro-South Richmond *Examiner* during the War, said it best: there was never such a thing as "slavery" in the Old South. What North and New South writers conveniently and slanderously call Southern "slavery" was actually, Pollard rightly asserts, a "well-guarded and moderate system of negro servitude."[475] As he wrote during Lincoln's War:

> In referring to the condition of the negro in this war, we use the term "*slavery*" . . . under strong protest. For *there is no such thing in the South; it is a term fastened upon us by the exaggeration and conceit of Northern literature, and most improperly acquiesced in by Southern writers. There is a system of African servitude in the South; in which the negro, so far from being under the absolute dominion of his master (which is the true meaning of the vile word "slavery"), has, by law of the land, his personal rights recognized and protected, and his comfort and "right" of "happiness" consulted, and by the practice of the system, has a sum of individual indulgences, which makes him altogether the most striking type in the world of cheerfulness and contentment.* And the system of servitude in the South has this peculiarity over other systems of servitude in the

world: that it does not debase one of God's creatures from the condition of free-citizenship and membership in organized society and [which] thus rest on acts of debasement and disenfranchisement, but [instead it] elevates a savage, and rests on the solid basis of human improvement. *The European mind, adopting the nomenclature of our enemies, has designated as "slavery" what is really the most virtuous system of servitude in the world.*[476]

This iconic piece of Northern propaganda, showing a shackled slave pleading for his life and freedom, was often used as a weapon to try and shame Dixie into abolition. But there was no such thing as authentic slavery in the pro-abolition Old South, making both this fake image and the charge ludicrous.

Let us note that the first blacks brought to British North America (on August 31, 1619)[477] were not regarded as slaves, but as indentured servants, laborers with the same rights as white indentured servants.[478] Indeed, 90 white girls, also indentured servants, were sold at Jamestown, Virginia, at the same time.[479] Though in the case of the Africans this status would eventually change from voluntary servitude to involuntary servitude, most Southerners, unlike Northerners, correctly continued to refer to bonded blacks as "servants" (not "slaves") right up to and after Lincoln's War. As such, Southerners seldom used the phrase "African slavery." Like Jefferson Davis, they used the more correct term "African servitude."[480] To this very day, unlike most Yankees, traditional Southerners still refer to the bonded blacks of 19th-Century America as "servants" rather than "slaves."[481]

What is the difference between slavery and servitude?

Slavery is the state of working under the complete control, ownership, subjugation, or absolute dominion of another, without pay, and usually for life.[482] Additionally, true slaves have no rights of any kind,[483] are generally debased and disenfranchised, and cannot purchase their freedom. In short, a genuine slave is seen by his or her owner as little different than a cow or a horse, just another piece of livestock to be owned and worked until "it" is no longer of value.[484]

Servitude, on the other hand, is for a limited duration, the individual is not "owned" (his boss is not his "owner" or "master," but rather his employer), he is paid a wage, and he may hire himself out to work for others. Servants also possess a wide variety of personal and civil rights that are both recognized and protected by society and tempered by religious sentiment. In this way, under servitude a person's right to comfort and happiness are taken for granted and he or she is treated with common respect and decency.[485] Finally, and most significantly, servants have the right and the power to buy their freedom.[486]

Olaudah Equiano, born in Nigeria around 1745, was a member of the Igbo, one of the thousands of slave owning peoples of Africa. At a young age Equiano was himself enslaved by fellow Africans, then was later sold to a planter in Virginia and renamed Gustavus Vassa. After numerous adventures he ended up in the hands of a Northern slave owner, who allowed Vassa to purchase his freedom, something he would not have been able to do under the authentic slavery system of his own African homeland. Now a freeman, he eventually ended up in England, where he married, bore children, campaigned for abolition, wrote a celebrated memoir of his exploits, and died at the age of 52. Vassa was an example of a black man who lived in bondage on two continents, Africa and America, but who only experienced true slavery on one of them: Africa.

Among the more famous of those black American servants who purchased their liberty (or had it purchased for them) are Northern slave Frederick Douglass,[487] black racist-militant Denmark Vesey,[488] former African slave and later travel adventurer Gustavus Vassa (Olaudah Equiano),[489] and Lincoln's own modiste, Elizabeth Keckley (who purchased her freedom with money she made hiring herself out as a dressmaker).[490] Slightly lesser known are Lott Cary, Hiram Young, Free Frank McWorter, Venture Smith, Amos Fortune, John Parker, Samuel Berry, and Paul Jennings (one of President

James Madison's servants).

Tens of thousands of others could be named. If any of these individuals had lived under authentic slavery (that is, without a single human right)[491] they would have remained in bondage for life, as self-purchase was prohibited. The reality is that by the late antebellum period (1850-1860), most Southern manumissions (the emancipation of specific individuals) were the result of free blacks buying their own enslaved relatives then freeing them.[492]

The use of the injurious and false word "slavery" instead of "servitude" for the type of bondage that was practiced in the Old South has been forced on us by Northern propagandists and by New South Liberals. For this word, like the equally fallacious and deleterious Northern terms "Copperhead," "rebel," "pro-slavery," and "slave state," all help to justify Lincoln's unjust war.

In the North, where black bondsmen were called "slaves," one was more likely to find them working in chains and shackles under the thumb of a racist owner, as can be seen in this early illustration of a New England plantation.

Sadly for Dixie, much of the outside world—misled by anti-South language like this—has never fully understood the true nature of so-called "Southern slavery." But those Southerners who lived through this period, and those today who have researched the institution objectively, understand that it was, in all actuality, a form of servitude not slavery, one not unlike serfdom. This fact is overtly preserved in the Latin words for both serf and servant, each a Western form of "slave": *servus* (male), *serva* (female).[493] So-called Southern "slaves" then were actually serf-like servants, not slaves in the legal, technical, literal, or even in the stereotypical sense.

In fine, there was no such thing as "slavery" or a "slave state" in the Old South. This politicized nomenclature is an invention of enemies of Dixie, whose aim has been to defile the South in the eyes of the world and to excuse Lincoln's unholy war on the Constitution and the American people.

The truth is that Southerners who were labeled "proslavery" and Southern states that were labeled "slave states," were merely pro-states' rights. For, as we have seen, only a tiny minority of white Southerners actually owned servants (less than 4.8 percent in 1860).[494] The South's ultimate goal was always the preservation of the right of self-determination (self-government), not the continuation of black servitude, no matter what the North chooses to believe or what name New South scallywags choose to call the institution. Indeed, this is proven by the fact that the Confederacy began official black enlistment and emancipation several months *before* the War ended.[495]

In point of fact, if one were to take Northern history books and replace every instance of the word "slavery" with the word "servitude," the word "pro-slavery" with "pro-states' rights," the phrase "slave state" with "slavery optional state," and the term "free state" with "slavery prohibited state," one would have a much more accurate and honest portrait of the South-North conflict.[496]

In the South, where black bondsmen were referred to as "servants," one was more likely to find them working in informal conditions, without supervision under the auspices of a tolerant easygoing owner. Note the relaxed strolling "slaves" in this early drawing of a typical Southern tobacco plantation, a Victorian illustration that I used for the cover of my book, *Slavery 101*.

THE MYTH OF
NORTHERN ABOLITION

WHAT YOU WERE TAUGHT: The Northern states legally abolished slavery quickly and completely.

THE TRUTH: First, the Northern states did not end slavery quickly, for it took them over 100 years, and in the case of New York, over 200 years, before they took steps to terminate it. Second, they did not abolish Northern slavery completely, for the institution lingered, in a myriad of forms, until long after the end of Lincoln's War.

From these two facts, in turn, it is obvious that the Northern states never really "abolished" slavery in their region at all. This term, pertaining to Yankee slavery, is, in truth, a misnomer. What they actually did was merely suppress it until, over time, it naturally faded away due to neglect, unprofitability, and ultimately white racist hostility.[497] The Northern states accomplished this through a slow, voluntarily, and gradual process—and, it should be emphasized, *without any interference from the South.*[498]

This exposes the lie that the Northern states literally "abolished slavery" within their borders on a precise date in a specific year, as our Yankee-biased history books claim. For example: "Vermont in 1777," "Pennsylvania in 1780," "Massachusetts in 1780," "Connecticut in 1784," "Rhode Island in 1784," "New Jersey in 1804," and "New York in 1827."[499]

The fact of the matter is that *none* of the Northern states ever truly abolished slavery; they only legislated it into "gradual extinction."[500] This is why a few Yankee states, such as New Hampshire and Delaware, did not fully rid themselves of slavery until the passage of the Thirteenth Amendment, December 6, 1865 (though the U.S. government continued to allow the enslavement of criminals).[501]

In short, while Pennsylvania, Connecticut, Rhode Island, and New Hampshire all intentionally used a *gradual emancipation plan* (wherein freedom was guaranteed to all persons born in their states after the date of so-called "abolition"),[502] the North

The Northern states never "abolished" slavery in the traditional legal sense. While Yankee slave ships continued their trips to Africa and the West Indies right up and into the Civil War, the Northern states from which they sailed had implemented a long, drawn out legislative process known as "gradual emancipation," which allowed for the casual unhurried extinction of the institution. This same right was later cruelly denied the Southern states, but they are still being unfairly punished for the delay nonetheless.

as a whole gave herself over 200 leisurely years to eliminate slavery from within her borders. This is hardly what one would describe as "quick and complete abolition."[503]

If only the Yankee had accorded this same privilege to his Southern compatriots! It would not have prevented Lincoln's War, of course, because the conflict was not about slavery.[504] But it would have greatly eased the constitutional tensions that led Dixie into the War to begin with, and it is much more likely that the South today would be an independent, constitutional, confederate republic[505]—just as our Southern ancestors intended before Lincoln repeatedly violated his oath of office.[506]

THE IMPATIENT,
ARROGANT, MEDDLING NORTH

WHAT YOU WERE TAUGHT: The South had hundreds of years to eliminate slavery, so there was no excuse for them not to do so at the same time the Northern states did.

THE TRUTH: Thanks to meddlesome Yankee, anti-slavery advocate William Lloyd Garrison of Massachusetts, from 1831 on Northern abolitionists began demanding immediate, complete, and uncompensated emancipation across the South—this coming from the very section of the country that gave birth to both the American slave trade and American slavery, and gave itself over 200 years to finally abolish both![507]

No one likes to be ordered around, including Southerners; especially not by self-righteous, liberal do-gooders such as Garrison, who have no respect for the rights, ways, and mannerisms of other people, but only simply want to impose their views on those who do not agree with them.

Though the South had been the center of American abolitionism for a half century by this time, she understood that one could not rush the operation. *Complete* abolition was a complex procedure that had taken other countries years, decades, centuries, to complete, and it would take Dixie just as long, or longer. Time was needed to prepare, from designing laws and rules to regulate the process of readying 3.5 million former slaves for a life of freedom, to finding the capital ($3 billion, or $57 billion in today's currency)[508] to compensate former slave owners and establish housing and jobs for freedmen and women.

Dixie only asked the North for the same amount of time to develop a functional emancipation program that it had given itself. But this the North would not do. The slavery issue came to be used as a Yankee sledge hammer to force Northern ideas on the South. The South resisted, claiming states' rights under the U.S. Constitution. The North ignored her, and as Lincoln disingenuously said, "the war came."[509]

The needless and malevolent abolition agitation stirred up by New England abolitionist busybody William Lloyd Garrison must be counted as one of the main sparks that later ignited the Civil War. This was not due to the slavery issue, as pro-North writers claim, but because of his insinuation that physical force would be needed to end slavery in Dixie—which brought the long simmering states' rights issue to the foreground. This ended 29 years later in the secession of the Southern states with the election of another violent and intolerant, constitutionally ignorant aggressor, Abraham Lincoln.

36

THE MYTH OF
THE "HUMANITARIAN"
YANKEE ABOLITIONIST

WHAT YOU WERE TAUGHT: The North abolished slavery out of concern for the civil and human rights of African-Americans.

THE TRUTH: Although there were a myriad of reasons why slavery was gradually and officially extinguished in the Northern states, not one of them had to do with humanitarian or civil rights concerns about slaves themselves. The worldly Victorian Yankee felt no apprehension, shame, or guilt for engaging in the "sin" of slavery. Thus when it came time to destroy it he was motivated by reasons of an entirely practical nature, all which can be pared down to three primary factors.

The first reason the North wanted to rid itself of slavery was that it eventually became unprofitable (the same reason Europe finally abolished it).[510] And slavery became unprofitable in the American North,[511] in great part, due to the regions's largely rocky sandy soil, hilly terrain, and short cool summers, all which made it unsuitable for large-scale farming.[512]

Second, there was the North's enormous distance from both Africa (where slaves were picked up) and the tropics (where slaves were needed on sugar, coffee, cotton, pineapple, tobacco, and indigo plantations).[513] This made it much more advantageous to sell slaves in, to, and from the American South (which was a shorter distance from both Africa and the Caribbean) than transport them back up to, for example, the slave-trading capital known as Rhode Island.[514]

New England's rocky sandy soil, long cold winters, short cool summers, and hilly terrain made large-scale farming unprofitable and field slavery impractical, just one of the many reasons Yankees pushed their "peculiar institution" southward—onto a largely unwilling populace, it should be added.

Third, along with the North's growing blue-collar demographic (which made Northern slavery more and more redundant) came increasing racial intolerance toward non-whites. As early as the late 1700s white Northerners "were frankly stating an antipathy of their people toward negroes in any capacity whatever."[515] This, of course, now made abolition in the North absolutely essential, especially economically. Yankee John Adams of Massachusetts, who was to become America's second president two years later, wrote the following in a personal letter dated March 21, 1795:

> *Argument might have some weight in the abolition of slavery in the Massachusetts, but the real cause was the multiplication of labouring white people, who would no longer suffer the rich to employ these sable rivals so much to their injury. This principle has kept negro slavery out of France, England, and other parts of Europe. The common people would not suffer the labour, by which alone they could obtain a subsistence, to be done by slaves. . . . The common white people, or rather the labouring people, were the cause of rendering negroes unprofitable servants. Their scoffs and insults, their continual insinuations, filled the negroes with*

discontent, made them lazy, idle, proud, vicious, and at length wholly useless to their masters, to such a degree that the abolition of slavery became a measure of economy.[516]

Here we have the most significant factor leading to the death of Northern slavery: *Northern white racism*. Most 18th- and 19th-Century Yanks simply preferred living in an all-white society,[517] free from the "naturally disgusting" presence of the black man, as Lincoln and other white racist Northerners expressed it.[518]

It was this very sentiment which gave birth to the bigoted American Colonization Society, a popular Yankee black deportation organization founded in 1816 in Washington, D.C., by a Northerner, New Jerseyan Robert

Yankee scandalmonger Harriet Beecher Stowe, the ill-famed author of *Uncle Tom's Cabin*, a purely fictitious novel based on ignorance, slanderous falsehoods, misrepresentations, blatant disinformation, and the fabrications of South-hating abolitionist tracts. Stowe, in fact, had never visited the South and knew absolutely nothing about Southern culture, society, or servitude. U.S. President Woodrow Wilson said that her book was nothing but a product of her imagination, one that would be rejected by true historians as "misleading." Southern belle Mary Chesnut called the book "sickening" and Stowe herself "nasty." Stowe continues to be lauded by uneducated Liberals and misguided Conservatives, despite the fact that she was once a supporter of the racist organization, the American Colonization Society.

Finley—and supported by thousands of liberal Northerners. Among them were Lincoln, Harriet Beecher Stowe (author of *Uncle Tom's Cabin*), Horace Greeley (owner of the New York *Tribune*), William Lloyd Garrison (founder of *The Liberator*), Jared Sparks (president of Harvard University), Henry Rutgers (after whom Rutgers University is named), and Edward Everett (after whom the city of Everett, Massachusetts, is named), as well as many other Yanks of note.[519]

THE SOUTH'S PLANS
TO END SLAVERY

WHAT YOU WERE TAUGHT: The South never wanted to destroy slavery and thus never took any steps toward abolition.

THE TRUTH: Beginning in the 1600s we have numerous records of Southerners seeking the abolition of both the slave trade and slavery. Indeed, as we have discussed, the American abolition movement got its start in the South, in Virginia, to be exact,[520] where, in 1655, the first voluntary emancipation in the American colonies took place.[521] Virginia, of course, is the birthplace of some the South's most famous abolitionists, among them George Washington, Thomas Jefferson, James Madison, and George Mason.

By the early 1800s the American abolition movement was at its peak across Dixie. Of the 130 abolition societies established before 1827 by Northern abolitionist Benjamin Lundy, over 100 (four-fifths of the total membership) were in the South.[522] Southern Quakers too were among the first to come out against the spread of the institution.[523]

Besides North Carolina's noted antislavery leaders, Benjamin Sherwood Hedrick and Daniel Reaves Goodlow,[524] in South Carolina there were the celebrated Quaker sisters Sarah and Angelina Grimké, just two among millions of Southerners fighting for the cause of abolition.[525] The Southern abolition movement involved so many Southerners, so many Southern states, and covered such a large span of time, that the latter Grimké sister wrote an entire book on the subject.[526]

On August 14, 1776, South Carolina rice planter and slave owner Henry Laurens wrote the following to his son John, who was also antislavery:

> You know, my dear son, *I abhor slavery*. I was born in a country in which slavery had been established by British Parliaments and the laws of the country for ages before my existence. I found the Christian religion and slavery growing under the same authority and cultivation. *I nevertheless dislike it*. In former days there was no combating the prejudices of men, supported by interest. *The day I hope is approaching when from principles of gratitude and justice every man will strive to be foremost in complying with the golden rule.* £20,000 sterling [about £2.5 million, or $4 million in today's currency] would my negroes produce if sold at auction tomorrow. I am not the man who enslaved them; they are indebted to Englishmen for that favour. Nevertheless *I am devising means for manumitting many of them and for cutting off the entail of slavery.*[527]

In January 1865, almost a year before the U.S. abolished slavery, Confederate official Judah P. Benjamin announced the C.S. government's pledge to enact total abolition across all of the Southern states.

What our Yankee biased history books do not teach is that from the 1600s on, every year thousands of Southerners simply emancipated their slaves, and at great financial loss—all without any prompting from the North. Among them were slave owners like Nathan Bedford Forrest, who freed his slaves even before Lincoln's War in 1861,[528] and Robert E. Lee, who liberated his wife's servants before the Emancipation Proclamation was issued in 1863.[529] Unlike in the North, there were no laws against manumission in Dixie, so Southerners gave full vent to their humanitarian instincts.

Arguably the South's greatest abolitionist was Thomas Jefferson, who had been working on Southern abolition from his first days as an American statesmen, and who was responsible for prohibiting the

American slave trade after the year 1808 (tragically, Yankee slave traders ignored the ban, continuing to sail to Africa right into the Civil War period). Indeed, it was Jefferson's criticism of Britain for imposing slavery on the 13 original American colonies that helped instigate the American Revolution,[530] which in turn led directly to the first "Confederate States of America"—as the USA was known in the 1700s and 1800s.[531]

The South was still struggling with precisely how to initiate full abolition, or what Jefferson aptly compared to holding "a wolf behind the ears,"[532] when Lincoln tricked the South into firing the first shot of his war at the Battle of Fort Sumter on April 12, 1861.[533]

U.S. President Thomas Jefferson ingeniously compared the dangers of abolishing slavery with holding a wolf by the ears. Unfortunately for the South, Lincoln did not understand this elemental concept—or he did and did not care.

30

THE TRUTH ABOUT SLAVERY & THE AMERICAN SOUTH

Southerner and U.S. Founding Father George Mason felt that slavery always "brings the judgment of heaven upon a country," and deplored the fact that Yankee businessmen had gotten involved in the trade. It was this same Southern hatred of slavery that launched the American abolition movement in Virginia in the 1700s.

WHAT YOU WERE TAUGHT: The American South was the first region in the West to practice slavery and the last to try and abolish it.

THE TRUTH: The opposite is true. In 1749 Georgia became the last of the 13 British-American colonies to legalize slavery.[534] This was long after every Western nation had already adopted the institution. Seventeen years earlier, in 1732, Georgia became the first colony to place a prohibition against commercial trafficking in slaves into her state constitution,[535] making the American South the first Western region to move toward abolition.

Around the same time, dozens of abolition societies began to spring up across Dixie, with Virginia leading the way in white America's tireless attempt to end slavery—which began in the Dominion State with, as noted, the first voluntary emancipation in 1655.[536]

BLACK SLAVE OWNERS

WHAT YOU WERE TAUGHT: There was no such thing as a "black slave owner" in America.

THE TRUTH: Liberal historians have carefully hidden the fact from the general public, but the reality is that there were tens of thousands of black slave owners in early America, most who were not counted in the

U.S. Census (Census takers were prone to vastly underreporting blacks, free and enslaved).[537] Additionally, some black slaveholders abused and whipped their African servants, another fact that you will seldom find in pro-North, anti-South history books.[538]

In 1830 some 3,700 free Southern blacks owned nearly 12,000 black slaves,[539] an average of almost four slaves a piece. That same year in the Deep South alone nearly

These black slaves belong to an African-American, a wealthy freeman in Arkansas. In nearby Louisiana the Metoyers, an affluent African-American family, owned some 400 black slaves, worth the equivalent of $20 million in today's currency.

8,000 slaves were owned by some 1,500 black slave owners (about five slaves apiece). In Charleston, South Carolina, as another example, between the years 1820 and 1840, 75 percent of the city's free blacks owned slaves. Furthermore, *25 percent of all free American blacks owned slaves, South and North.*[540]

It is important to remember that in 1861 the South's 300,000 white slave owners made up only 1 percent of the total U.S. white population of 30 million people.[541] Thus, while only one Southern white out of every 300,000 owned slaves (1 percent), one Southern black out of every four owned slaves (25 percent). In other words, far more blacks owned black (and sometimes white) slaves than whites did: 25 percent compared to 1 percent.

Most Southern black slave owners were not only proslavery, they were also pro-South, supporting the Confederate Cause during Lincoln's War as fervently as any white Southerner did. At church each Sunday thousands of blacks would pray for those blacks, both their own slaves and their free friends, who wore the Rebel uniform. Their supplications were simple: they asked God to help all African-American Confederates kill as many Yankees as possible, then return home safely.[542]

One of America's thousands of moneyed black slave owners. Many possessed white slaves as well.

Wealthy blacks bought, sold, and exploited black slaves for profit, just as white slave owners did. The well-known Anna Kingsley, who began life—as was nearly always the case—as a slave in her native Africa, ended up in what is now Jacksonville, Florida, where she became one of early America's many black plantation owners and slaveholders.[543]

Some, like the African-American Metoyers, an anti-abolition family from Louisiana, owned huge numbers of black slaves; in their case, at least 400.[544] At about $1,500 a piece,[545] their servants were worth a total of $600,000, or $20 million in today's currency.[546] This made the Metoyers among the wealthiest people in the U.S., black or white, then or now. Louisiana's all-black Confederate army unit, the Augustin Guards, was named after the family patriarch, Augustin Metoyer.[547]

These black servants, working a Southern cotton field in the 1840s, were not owned by a white family, but by one of the thousands of affluent black slave owning families that once thrived across the United States. On average black slaveholders owned far more slaves than white slaveholders did, a fact you will never read in any pro-North history book.

We have scores of written records chronicling the existence of black slave owners. Phillips writes:

> The property of colored freemen oftentimes included slaves. Such instances were quite numerous in pre-revolutionary San Domingo; and some in the British West Indies achieved notoriety through the exposure of cruelties. On the continent a negro planter in St. Paul's Parish, South Carolina, was reported before the close of the eighteenth century to have two hundred slaves as well as a white wife and son-in-law, and the returns of the first federal census appear to corroborate it. In Louisiana colored planters on a considerable scale became fairly numerous. Among them were Cyprien Ricard who bought at a sheriff's sale in 1851 an estate in Iberville Parish along with its ninety-one slaves for nearly a quarter of a million dollars; Marie Metoyer of Natchitoches Parish had fifty-eight slaves and

more than two thousand acres of land when she died in 1840; Charles Roques of the same parish died in 1854 leaving forty-seven slaves and a thousand acres; and Martin Donato of St. Landry dying in 1848 bequeathed liberty to his slave wife and her seven children and left them eighty-nine slaves and 4,500 arpents of land as well as notes and mortgages to a value of $46,000 [the equivalent of $1.5 million today]. *In rural Virginia and Maryland also there were free colored slaveholders in considerable numbers.*

Just as there were—and still are—black slave owners in Africa, there were also black slave owners in early America. In fact, 25 percent, or one out of four, of all 17th-, 18th-, and 19th-Century free African-Americans, a largely wealthy class, owned black slaves.

Slaveholdings by colored townsmen were likewise fairly frequent. Among the 360 colored taxpayers in Charleston in 1860, for example, 130, including nine persons described as of Indian descent, were listed as possessing 390 slaves. The abundance of such holdings at New Orleans is evidenced by the multiplicity of applications from colored proprietors for authority to manumit slaves, with exemption from the legal requirement that the new freedmen must leave the state. A striking example of such petitions was that presented in 1832 by Marie Louise Bitaud, free woman of color, which recited that in the preceding year she had bought her daughter and grandchild at a cost of $700; that a lawyer had now told her that in view of her lack of free relatives to inherit her property, in case of death intestate her slaves would revert to the state; that she had become alarmed at this prospect; and she accordingly begged permission to manumit them without their having to leave Louisiana. The magistrates gave their consent on condition that the petitioner furnish a bond of $500 to insure the support and education of the grandson until his coming of age. This was duly done and the formalities completed.

Evidence of slaveholdings by colored freemen occurs also in the bills of sale filed in various public archives. One of these records that a citizen of Charleston sold in 1828 a man slave to the latter's free colored sister at a price of one dollar, "provided he is kindly treated and is never sold, he being an unfortunate individual and requiring much attention." In the same city a free colored man bought a slave sailmaker for $200. At Savannah in 1818 Richard Richardson sold a slave woman and child for $800 to Alex Hunter, guardian of the colored freeman Louis Mirault, in trust for him; and in 1833 Anthony Ordingsell, free colored, having obtained through his guardian an order of court, sold a slave woman to the highest bidder for $385 [$12,000 today].

It is clear that aside from the practice of holding slave relatives as a means of giving them virtual freedom, *an appreciable number of colored proprietors owned slaves purely as a productive investment.* It was doubtless a group of these who sent a joint communication to a New Orleans newspaper when secession and war were impending:

> *"The free colored population (native) of Louisiana .*
> *. . own slaves, and they are dearly attached to their*
> *native land, . . . and they are ready to shed their*
> *blood for her defence. They have no sympathy for*
> *abolitionism; no love for the North, but they have*
> *plenty for Louisiana. . . . They will fight for her in*
> *1861 as they fought in 1814-1815. . . . If they*
> *have made no demonstration it is because they have*
> *no right to meddle with politics, but not because*
> *they are not well disposed [financially]. All they*
> *ask is to have a chance, and they will be worthy sons*
> *of Louisiana."*

Oral testimony gathered by the present writer from old residents in various quarters of the South supports the suggestion of this letter that *many of the well-to-do colored freemen tended to prize their distinctive position so strongly as to deplore any prospect of a general emancipation for fear it would submerge them in the great black mass.*[548]

A Mandingo chief and his enslaved swordbearer. The Mandingo people of Sierra Leone were one of the most aggressive and merciless slavers in the whole of Western Africa, often initiating wars on other villages for the sole purpose of obtaining slaves. The millennia old African custom of slave owning later came, quite naturally, across the Atlantic to America with the African slaves aboard Yankee slave ships, where it flourished among tens of thousands of black slaveholders in both the South and the North. In early Charleston, South Carolina, three out of four, or 75 percent, of all free blacks owned black slaves.

40

RED SLAVE OWNERS

WHAT YOU WERE TAUGHT: American Indians did not own black slaves, or slaves of any other race.

THE TRUTH: Black slavery among Native-Americans began as soon as Yankees began bringing already enslaved Africans into the original 13 colonies, where they bought and sold African chattel right alongside black and white slave owners.[549] In fact, one of the many reasons so many Native-Americans sided with the Southern Confederacy during Lincoln's War was that she promised to enforce the constitutional fugitive slave law in Indian Territory, making it a legal requirement to return runaway slaves to their original Indian owners.[550]

While the average white slave owner owned five or less slaves (often only one or two),[551] the average red slaveholder owned six. One Choctaw slaver owned 227.[552] Once again we see that it was *non-white* slave owners who individually owned the most slaves, not whites.[553]

Slavery was practiced right up until the 1950s by some Native-American tribes, principally the Haida and the Tlingit peoples of the Pacific Northwest.[554] Among the Haida, slaves performed all of the menial labor, ate only food scraps, were refused health care, and could not own property. And since there were no laws of protection, Haida slaves could be purchased, sold, beaten, molested, and even murdered at the whim of their owners.[555] This is true slavery, the exact opposite of the much milder servitude experienced by Africans in the Old American South.[556]

Native-American slave owning did not begin with the

The Apache were just one of thousands of Native-American peoples who engaged in slavery. Most not only enslaved fellow Indians, but later also whites and blacks as well, utilizing crude, appalling, and horrific practices that defy the English language and baffle the modern mind.

introduction of African slaves to the Americas, of course. The institution was known among Indians themselves from as far back as we have records, some, who right into the 1800s, practiced forms of slavery that were notorious for their primitiveness, rapaciousness, and ruthlessness, many which entailed ritual torture and murder.[557]

In the pre-Columbian Americas, for example, slavery was an integral part of such Native-American peoples as the Maya and Inca,[558] who depended on large scale slave labor in warfare and farming.[559] Among the Inca, villages were required by law to supply the king's royal mansions with slaves. One of these leaders, Atahualpa, the last of the Incan kings, was well-known for his cruelty: though it was necessary for certain types of slaves to approach him (such as chefs, cupbearers, and porters), the megalomaniacal potentate ordered that such individuals must afterward be killed for coming into close proximity to his sacred person. Not only were these slaves "pitilessly slaughtered," but Atahualpa had their entire families executed, their houses burned down, and their villages destroyed. All of the peoples in the Cuzco region were oppressed in this manner, with some villages losing 25 percent of their total population.[560]

For the Aztecs slavery was not only vital to their economic, agricultural, and military systems, it also concerned diet: always in need of offerings to propitiate their voracious gods and goddesses, the cannibalistic Aztec people were highly proficient at human sacrifice, the first choice of victim usually being a slave. Spanish Conquistadors reported that Aztec slaves were purposefully fattened up in cages so that the most "succulent cuts" of their bodies (hands and thighs) could later be devoured at mealtime.[561]

Other Indian peoples who once practiced slavery include the Cherokee, Iroquois, Navaho, Seminole, Choctaw, Creek, Chickasaw, Cheyenne, Natchez, Arapaho, Kiowas, Paiute, Chinook, Yuchie, Pima, Papago, Halchidhoma, Guarani, Shasta, and Klamath. Again, some of the forms of slavery employed were particularly brutal, involving torture and cannibalistic rituals. It is said that slavery was as economically important to many Native-American tribes as it was to European-American slavers prior to the Civil War.[562]

Native-Americans with a freshly captured European-American female. Like the fellow Indians they regularly seized in battle, this white woman too will be turned into an Indian slave, as was the custom among most native peoples for thousands of years prior to the arrival of Europeans.

The list of Indian and native peoples who practiced various forms of slavery and servitude also includes such Eskimo tribes as the Aleuts, the Koniagas, the Tlinkits, the Tsimshians, the Nootkas, the Bilballas, the Ahts, and the Puget Sound tribes. There were also the Fish Indians of British Columbia, the Kutchins, the Tacullies, the Atnas, the Koltschanes, the Similkameen people of British Columbia, the Delawares, the Ojibways, the Menomini, the Tuscaroras, the Okanagans, the Atnaks, the Nez Percé, the Shastika, the Shoshones, the Utahs, the Kioways, the Apaches, the Comanches, the Navajos, the

Mojaves, the Cibola Pueblo, Panamanian Indians, Costa Rican Indians, the Caribs of the Antilles, the Continental Caribs, the Arawaks, the Saliva of Columbia, the Goajiro, the Brazilian natives, the Apiacas, the Mundrucus, the Mauhés, the Miranhas, the Guaycurû, the Mbayás, the Chiriguanos, the Záparos, the Conibas, the Yuracarés, the Mocéténès, the Chiquitos, the Moxos, the Enimagas, the Charruas, the Patagons, the Puelches, the Araucanians, and probably the Hurons, the Karayas, the Nishinan, the Flatheads, the Karoks, and the Hupas, among countless others.[563]

In 1900 Nieboer made these comments about black slave owning Indian tribes:

> According to the census of 1860 several Indian tribes had Negro-slaves. Our informant enumerates the *Choctaws, Cherokees, Creeks and Chickasaws. Slavery was carried on to a great extent; some owners had from 50 to 200 slaves.*
>
> . . . The *Creeks* already in Bartram's time (1789) had slaves. He tells us of a chief who kept 15 Negroes; they were slaves until they married Indian women, and then acquired the privileges of the tribe. Schoolcraft informs us that "if an Indian should murder a Negro, the law is satisfied with the value of the Negro being paid to the owner."
>
> The *Seminoles* also had Negro-slaves . . . The Shahnees [Shawnees] . . . also kept a few Negro slaves. Amongst the French *Creoles* the rich possessed slaves, Negroes imported from Africa and Indians overcome and taken in battle.[564]

The full extent of Native-American slave ownership will never be known, but, as is clear from the foregoing, we have proof that—besides the Choctaw, Chickasaw, Cherokee, and Creek—the Seminoles[565] also possessed African-American slaves.[566] The Apaches, among others, not only kept fellow red slaves but white slaves as well,[567] a custom among Native-Americans that began as early as 1527. By the 19th Century, Indians had enslaved tens of thousands of European-Americans,[568] a fact seldom discussed in our liberal-oriented, Northern-slanted history books.

As was the norm among the Great Plains Indians, the Cheyenne were enthusiastic slave owners without racial bias of any kind. Any man, woman, or child—whatever their skin color—who fell into their hands could become a lifelong slave under Cheyenne leaders, like Chief Wolf Robe, seen here in 1904.

41

BROWN SLAVE OWNERS

WHAT YOU WERE TAUGHT: Hispanic-Americans and Latin-Americans never owned black slaves.

THE TRUTH: Neither red, black, or white American slave owners would have ever even had the opportunity to become involved in this occupation had it not been for their brown brethren, Hispanics and Latinos.[569]

Portuguese explorer Henry the Navigator helped open up the African slave trade to the Americas in 1503.

Both the European and the American slave industries got their start with a 15th-Century Portuguese explorer, Henry the Navigator, who, while searching for gold along the West African coast in the early 1400s, happened upon a vast indigenous slave industry run by local African slave owners and slave traders.[570] Henry wasted no time in involving Portugal in the sordid business. This resulted in the first African slaves to be brought to the New World, the black human cargo which was dropped off in Santo Domingo in 1503.[571] The owners, captains, and crews on these ships were all Hispanic-Europeans.[572]

Over the next few centuries African and Hispanic slavers were responsible for the capture, sale, and shipment of literally millions of blacks from Africa to Latin-American colonies and nations, such as Hispaniola and Cuba,[573] the latter being one of the last Western nations to ban slavery, in 1886, 21 years after the Thirteenth Amendment (not Lincoln) outlawed it across the U.S. Between 1580 and 1680 Portugal was responsible for taking 1 million Africans to its Brazilian colony alone.[574]

The very word *negro* is a legacy of those dark days: because Portuguese and Spaniards were the first Europeans to involve themselves in the native African slave business, the word *negro*, Spanish for "black," was later adopted by the English as the logical word for Africans.[575] As a result of the Medieval Portuguese slave trade, today at least one-sixth of the total population of Latin America is negro or mulatto.[576]

Under the auspices of the Spanish government, the Hispanic slave industry persisted with the arrival of Italian explorer Christopher Columbus in the Caribbean islands in 1492, who many historians credit with the founding of European-American slavery itself.[577] Already carrying African slaves on his ships that he had probably purchased from Spain,[578] at Hispaniola Columbus enslaved thousands of the native Indian

Christopher Columbus launched European-American slavery in 1492 when he transported African slaves to the Caribbean, then immediately began enslaving the native Indian population.

inhabitants (whom he referred to as "cannibal pagans"),[579] reducing their free population from 1 million to a mere 60,000, in just 15 years.[580] Contrast this with the black slave population of America's South, which was so well treated, well fed, well housed, and well clothed that far from diminishing in numbers, it rapidly increased by millions from the beginning of the institution in Georgia in 1749 (the Peach State was the first Southern state to start using slaves),[581] to its end in 1865.[582]

It was actually Hispanics who were the first to bring both Africans and African slavery to what is now the United States. This occurred in 1526 when a Spanish Colonial judge named Lucas Vásquez de Ayllón (a man also known to have enslaved Indians),[583] sailed 500 Spaniards and 100 African-Haitian slaves to what may have been present day Virginia, in an attempt to establish a colony. The experiment ended when most of the group perished from local diseases.[584] Had these settlers survived, Hispanics would also have been directly responsible for being the first to introduce black slaves into the Southern states.

Early Spanish explorers brought a particularly gruesome and heartless form of Christian slavery to the Americas, one that had no regard for either the indigenous people or even life itself. Those Indians who resisted enslavement were tortured, gutted, and burned alive, as shown here.

Here is more evidence that American black slavery was not a creation of the South. It was a creation of Europe, and more specifically of Hispanic Europe, which introduced the institution to Latin America long before it was introduced to the American South by Yankees. Neither were these early African slaves first used on cotton plantations in the South, as Northern folklore asserts. They were first sent to work on plantations in such places as Barbados, Curacao, Antigua, and Brazil.

Brown slave trading and brown slave ownership were further augmented with the Spanish Conquest of the Americas by men like Hernán Cortés and their conquistadors. They regarded the Native-Americans they encountered as an "inferior race," a vice-ridden caste whose sole function was to serve as beasts of burden, and who could only be saved from their wretched Paganistic lives by conversion to Christianity. The most efficient way to accomplish this, so they believed, was to enslave them and put them to work in the mines. As such, sometime in the early 1500s the Spanish crown required "the baptism of all pagan slaves upon their disembarkation in the colonial ports."[585]

But this Christianization went only one way. It is said that the Spaniards treated their horses far better than they did their Indian slaves.[586] The result? By 1618 Mexico's native population dropped from 20 million to 1.6 million.[587]

It was in 1517 that a Spanish priest, Bartolomé de Las Casas, recommended to Spain's Queen Isabella that the native Indian slaves of Hispaniola be replaced with African slaves.[588] The Spanish monarch agreed, for it was found that Indians did not do as well under slavery as Africans. Why? Because slavery in the Americas primarily surrounded agriculture, and Native-Americans were mainly nomadic hunter-gatherers, while Africans were mainly farmers, with an agricultural tradition that dated back thousands of years. Spain embarked on the African slave trade, hiring the Portugese to bring back some 4,000 African slaves a year from their "slave factories," that is, European settlements, on the continent's coast.[589] Each slave factory contained a fort, the most remarkable which

> were St. George del Mina, erected by the Portuguese, though it subsequently fell into the hands of the Dutch; Cape Coast Castle, the principal establishment of the English; Fort Louis, at the mouth of the Senegal, generally occupied by the French; and Goree, situated upon an island of the same name, near Cape Verde. Most of these forts mounted from fifty to sixty pieces of cannon, and contained large reservoirs for water, and were not only impregnable to the negroes, but capable of standing a regular siege by a European force.[590]

By 1560 some 100,000 African slaves had been transported to the Americas through this trade system.[591] Thus, though he was only partially correct, U.S. President John Quincy Adams said on April 29, 1819:

> The negro slave trade was the child of humanity [that is, compassion]—the contrivance of Las Casa to mitigate the condition of the American Indians.[592]

As the Indian labor supply proved evermore insufficient,[593] there followed an Hispanic-induced flood of thousands of enslaved Africans to the New World as well, one that both nearly destroyed the Native-American population (due to the "unparalleled cruelty of the Spaniards")[594] and which opened the door to the slave industry across what would one day become the United States of America.[595]

According to de Las Casas' 1656 book *The Tears of the Indians*, during its conquest and enslavement of the Americas, Spain tortured and killed some 20 million natives. At least 4 million of these, including "men, women, youths, and children," he wrote "were by the Spaniards consumed by fire." Note the living Indian baby being tossed into the fire in this 400 year old illustration. The number of those who died "under the intolerable yoke and burdens of their captivity" also numbered in the millions. The Spanish Catholic enslavers referred to their butchery and wholesale massacres as "chastisements."

42

OVER TWO CENTURIES
OF NORTHERN SLAVERY

WHAT YOU WERE TAUGHT: Slavery lasted far longer in the American South than it did in the American North.

THE TRUTH: The reverse is true. Southern slavery lasted from 1749, when Georgia became the first Southern state to legalize slavery,[596] to 1865, the year the Thirteenth Amendment was ratified and American slavery was officially abolished, a mere 116 years.[597]

What I call "The Great Yankee Coverup" is meant to hide the facts about American slavery; a devilish ruse which asserts that slavery did not originate in the North and that Northerners never practiced the institution. To further obfuscate the truth, the blame for the entire business has been pinned on the South. However, not even the most clever and nefarious anti-South historians can suppress antebellum illustrations like this one, which shows entire families of shackled African slaves—having just disembarked from a Yankee slave ship at anchor in the harbor—being marched along in front of the U.S. Capitol Building in Washington, D.C., circa 1836.

In contrast, Northern slavery lasted from 1641, when Massachusetts became the first Northern state to legalize slavery,[598] to 1865, a span of 224 years. This period increases if we count from 1626, the year New York imported the first black slaves into North America, a span of 239 years—ending in 1865.[599]

Either way, the North practiced slavery for over a century longer than the South did, between 108 and 123 years longer.[600]

These Southern servants, "slaves" to Yankees, and their descendants lived under the institution for only 116 years, while in the North black slaves endured it for some 239 years. And yet it is the Confederate flag that is associated with slavery and it is the South that has been labeled the "slave states," while in contrast, the U.S. flag is considered the flag of emancipation and the North has been labeled the "free states." Let us call this duplicitous Northern myth what it is: the overt hypocrisy of anti-South Yankee propaganda, another feeble attempt to hide the Truth about Lincoln's War from the American people.

THE YANKEE SLAVE TRADE & AFRICA

WHAT YOU WERE TAUGHT: The Northern slave trade ended with President Thomas Jefferson's ban in 1808.

THE TRUTH: Yankees were so addicted to slavery that they completely ignored the 1808 suspension law. Instead, they continued plying their trade right into the middle of Lincoln's War, and were only finally stopped by the passage of the Thirteenth Amendment in December 1865. As proof we have the example of Captain Nathaniel Gordon of New York, the only American ever tried, convicted, and executed for slaving. His death occurred on February 21, 1862, at President Lincoln's personal order[601] as his February 4, 1862, letter reveals:

> Respite For Nathaniel Gordon.
> Abraham Lincoln, President Of The United States Of America, To all to whom these presents shall come, greeting: Whereas it appears that at a term of the Circuit Court of the United States of America for the southern district of New York, held in the month of November, A. D. 1861, Nathaniel Gordon was indicted and convicted for being engaged in the slave-trade, and was by the said court sentenced to be put to death by hanging by the neck on Friday the 7th day of February, A.D. 1862; And whereas a large number of respectable citizens have earnestly besought me to commute the said sentence of the said Nathaniel Gordon to a term of imprisonment for life, which application I have felt it to be my duty to refuse; And whereas it has seemed to me probable that the

unsuccessful application made for the commutation of his sentence may have prevented the said Nathaniel Gordon from making the necessary preparation for the awful change which awaits him: Now, therefore, be it known that I, Abraham Lincoln, President of the United States of America, have granted and do hereby grant unto him, the said Nathaniel Gordon, a respite of the above-recited sentence until Friday, the 21st day of February, A.D. 1862, between the hours of twelve o'clock at noon and three o'clock in the afternoon of the said day, when the said sentence shall be executed. In granting this respite it becomes my painful duty to admonish the prisoner that, relinquishing all expectation of pardon by human authority, he refer himself alone to the mercy of the common God and Father of all men. In testimony whereof I have hereunto signed my name and caused the seal of the United States to be affixed.[602]

Furthermore, the last American slave ship to be captured by the U.S. government, a Northern one, of course, was the *Nightingale*, also from New York, confiscated on April 21, 1861. The ship, known fondly to Northerners as the "Prince of Slavers," was built in Maine, fitted out in New Hampshire, sailed from Massachusetts, and had a New York captain. At the time of her seizure, this vessel, from the so-called "abolitionist North," had nearly 1,000 manacled Africans on board.[603] She was doing "business as usual" up until the first few weeks of the Civil War,[604] all the while proudly flying the U.S. flag from her mast.[605]

The notorious U.S. slave ship *Nightingale* had a purely Northern provenance. Constructed in Maine and outfitted in New Hampshire, she sailed from Massachusetts under the command of a New York captain. With some 1,000 African slaves in her hull, in 1861 she became famous for being the last slave ship to be seized by the U.S. government. Note the large U.S. flag flying from her stern.

ANTI-ABOLITIONISM
IN THE AMERICAN NORTH

WHAT YOU WERE TAUGHT: All Northerners were abolitionists who loved and respected people of color.

THE TRUTH: Like Lincoln, the great majority of Northerners, including the Union armies, were anti-abolition and did not support the idea of nationwide emancipation. In fact, abolitionists made up only a tiny but loud and much detested minority in the North,[606] as Lincoln himself was well aware.[607] This is why, after all, abolitionists were given the derogatory nickname "Radicals," for fellow Northerners considered them extremists who held unpopular sociopolitical views.

Proof that the North was not truly an abolitionist area was that while it abolished slavery in its own backyard, the majority of Yankees still did not want to end slavery in the South, for New England's textile mills, and the New York industrialists who owned them, were still making vast fortunes from Southern cotton, picked and ginned by millions of Southern servants. Thus, a full scale Northern effort began to keep Southern slavery alive, and even strengthen and enlarge it.[608]

It was in this way that when the white North grew tired of dealing with blacks and slavery, she pushed the institution southward on a mostly unwilling populace,[609] one that had been trying to abolish it since the early 1700s.[610] For example, when New York slave owner John Bouiness freed one of his black servants in the North, at the same time he also had five other slaves sold in Virginia.[611]

Lincoln with his son Tad. There is good reason why "Honest Abe" won both presidential elections in the anti-abolitionist, slave trade loving North: he was the only candidate who promised *not* to interfere with slavery, a commitment backed by his party, the Republicans (the Liberal Party of the day).

It has been estimated that at least 99 percent of Yankee businessmen were anti-abolitionists who supported the continuation of Southern slavery, for, as mentioned, the cotton that Southern slaves picked was one the North's largest financial assets.[612] Among the most vociferous of this group were New York's "Wall Street Boys,"[613] who had bankrolled Lincoln's first (and later his second) presidential campaign using money they had made primarily from the Yankee slave trade.[614] There was also the Boston elite, who made it known that they were quite willing to make huge concessions to the South in the interest of making money.[615]

Around 1831 Rhode Islander Elizabeth Buffum Chace and her father Arnold Buffum, the first president of the New England Anti-Slavery Society, decided to travel across their region in order to enlist Yankee support for their emancipation plan. In her 1891 memoir Chace made the following somber comments:

> I remember well, how eager we were, in our revived Anti-Slavery zeal, to present the cause of the slave to everybody we met [in New England]; not doubting that, when their attention was called to it, they would be ready, as we were, to demand his immediate emancipation. But, alas! *their commercial relations, their political associations*, and with many, their religious fellowship with the people of the South, so blinded the eyes, hardened the hearts and stifled the consciences of *the North*, that *we found very few people who were ready to give any countenance or support to the new AntiSlavery movement.*[616]

Is it any wonder then that the 1860 Republican (that is, Liberal) Party Platform contained paragraphs promising to leave the "peculiar institution" alone,[617] while declaring that Republicans were only against the extension of slavery, not slavery itself?[618] That in his First Inaugural Address, March 4, 1861, Lincoln pledged not to disturb slavery while lending his full support to the proposed Corwin Amendment—which would have made slavery legal permanently?[619] Or that American slavery did not come to a final end until December 6, 1865 (eight months after Lincoln's death), with the passage of the Thirteenth Amendment?[620]

Here we have more proof, if more is needed, that the Civil War was not a contest over slavery. It was a *Northern* contest over slavery money, a *Southern* contest over constitutional rights (that is, self-determination).[621]

As he states in his First Inaugural Address, Lincoln fully supported the antebellum 1861 Corwin Amendment, named after Yankee Representative Thomas Corwin of Ohio. The measure read: "No amendment shall be made to the Constitution which will authorize or give to Congress the power to abolish or interfere, within any State, with the domestic institutions thereof, including that of persons held to labor or service by the laws of said State." Its meaning is clear. The main reason the amendment was not ratified was because of the start of the Civil War. How different the U.S. would be today if Lincoln's Corwin Amendment had passed!

SLAVERY AS THE "CORNERSTONE OF THE CONFEDERACY"

WHAT YOU WERE TAUGHT: The South believed that slavery was the "cornerstone" of the Confederacy, and their representatives stated so publicly. This makes them racists who are undeserving of our respect.
THE TRUTH: This particular Yankee myth is referring to Confederate Vice President Alexander H. Stephens, whose March 21, 1861, speech at Savannah, Georgia, contained the following statement:

> The corner-stone of our new government rests upon the great truth, that the negro is not equal to the white man; that slavery, subordination to the superior race, is his natural and normal condition.[622]

Let us note that Vice President Stephens does not say that slavery is the cornerstone of the "Union," or even of the "Confederacy," as enemies of the South wrongly assert. Rather, he links the "cornerstone" to the South's "new government," by which he means the Constitution of the Confederate States of America, *which was patterned on the U.S. Constitution.* This is an important distinction, and as we will see momentarily, an intentional one.

Before discussing the facts behind Stephens' words, let us compare them with those of Abraham Lincoln, delivered publicly a few years earlier on July 17, 1858, at Springfield, Illinois:

My declarations upon this subject of negro slavery may be misrepresented, but cannot be misunderstood. I have said that I do not understand the Declaration [of Independence] to mean that all men were created equal in all respects. . . . Certainly the negro is not our equal in color—perhaps not in many other respects . . . [623]

A few months later, on September 18, 1858, at Charleston, Illinois, Lincoln made these comments:

The anti-South movement enjoys excoriating Stephens for his "cornerstone" comments, which they have taken out of context and therefore misinterpret. However, they wholly ignore Lincoln's racist statements, beliefs, and policies, which make Stephens' much tamer racial views pale in comparison.

I will say then that I am not, nor ever have been, in favor of bringing about in any way the social and political equality of the white and black races—that I am not, nor ever have been, in favor of making voters or jurors of negroes, nor of qualifying them to hold office, nor to intermarry with white people; and I will say in addition to this that there is a physical difference between the white and black races which I believe will forever forbid the two races living together on terms of social and political equality. And inasmuch as they cannot so live, while they do remain together there must be the position of superior and inferior, and I as much as any other man am in favor of having the superior position assigned to the white race. [624]

Our point here is that Vice President Stephens' racism was no different than President Lincoln's. Both men were products of a 19th-Century white society that saw blacks as an "inferior race," as Lincoln *always* referred to African-Americans. [625] Thus, if critics of the South wish to avoid being called hypocrites, Northerner Lincoln must be denounced just as heartily as Southerner Stephens. [626] As the "Great Emancipator" Lincoln himself said of "nearly all white people" living in America at the time:

There is a natural disgust in the minds of nearly all white people, to the idea of an indiscriminate amalgamation [mixing] of the white and black races.[627]

While the deeply held lifelong white supremacy in Lincoln's speeches is obvious for all to see, the racism displayed in Stephens' speech turns out to be far less vicious and entrenched, as a closer examination reveals.

First, Stephens in fact was widely known as a true friend of the black man.[628] Second, the Vice President was engaging in hyperbole to get his point across, a common enough practice among politicians.[629]

Third, the speech we read today is not a literal translation of the original, but an "interpretation" by journalists in the audience, who introduced their own biases and mistakes into the final transcription.[630]

Stephens' "Cornerstone Speech" was misunderstood by Northerners at the time he gave it, and it is still being misunderstood by them today. If they care to educate themselves on the matter, they have the vice president's own explanation and rebuttal to help correct their confusion.

Fourth, Stephens himself repeatedly maintained that his words had been misinterpreted, and for good reason.[631] When he made his comment about slavery being the "cornerstone" of American society, he was merely repeating the words of a *Yankee* judge, Associate Justice of the U.S. Supreme Court, Henry Baldwin of Connecticut who, 28 years earlier, in 1833, had said:

> Slavery is the corner-stone of the [U.S.] Constitution. The foundations of the Government are laid and rest on the rights of property in slaves, and the whole structure must fall by disturbing the corner-stone.[632]

As Richard M. Johnston noted later in 1884, all Stephens did during his "Cornerstone Speech" was accurately point out the fact that

> on the subject of slavery there was no essential change in the new [Southern Confederate] Constitution from the old [U.S. Constitution].[633]

In other words, decades before the formation of the Southern Confederacy, Yankees widely regarded slavery as the cornerstone of the Union.[634]

It would be far more accurate to say then that *slavery was indeed the cornerstone of the Union*, for not only would New England, the founder of American slavery, have gone bankrupt without it,[635] it was the North's Wall Street Boys (Yankee financiers, merchants, stock traders, and industrialists) who made the most money from the institution and who were thus the most interested in keeping it alive.[636]

It was this very group, the Wall Street Boys, keen to put anyone into the Oval Office who would maintain the lucrative Northern slave trade and the equally profitable business of Southern slavery, that got Lincoln elected president. For he was the only candidate who promised to do just that.[637] Later, these same backers rewarded "Honest Abe" by donating millions of dollars from their slave profits to fund his War to force the Southern states back into the Union and get him reelected in 1864.[638]

Southerner Stephens spent his entire life around blacks, and treated his own personal servants as family members—and they returned the favor. Here the Confederate vice president poses with an African-American (a servant or attendant), something Northerner Lincoln never did, and never would have done.

As this photo, taken by the author, illustrates, it is nothing but a pernicious Yankee lie that black Southern slaves were forced to live outdoors, or in crude leaky shacks not fit for livestock. This well-built house, part of the "slaves' quarters" at Carnton Plantation in Franklin, Tennessee, shows the high level of design, masonry, and carpentry that went into its construction. Fabricated by some of Tennessee's early black servants to house two families, one on each side, the sturdy brick building is roughly 200 years old, and has withstood both time and the elements—and outlasted Lincoln's War as well. All of the plantation's other outbuildings have long since disappeared. In fact, this is one of the oldest structures in Williamson County, Tennessee, a testament to the expertise of its African-American builders. Not only was it of a higher standard than the homes of many of Franklin's free blacks and whites at the time, to this day it is superior in quality and craftsmanship to many houses across the U.S., South, North, East, and West.

46

THE MYTH OF THE UNDERGROUND RAILROAD

WHAT YOU WERE TAUGHT: Millions of Southern slaves were saved by the Underground Railroad, which allowed them to flee North and escape the horrors of the South's "peculiar institution." Canada was the preferred final destination, since it was an abolitionist nation from the beginning and had never known slavery.

THE TRUTH: Though the Underground Railroad functioned throughout most of the War, only about 2,000 slaves (just 500 servants a year) out of 4.5 million (North and South) availed themselves of it—a mere 0.04 percent of the total.[639] Some reckon there were as many as 4,000 total (1,000 Southern slaves a year).[640] But that would still be only 0.08 percent of the total.[641]

Either way, according to scholarly studies, antebellum Southern slaves did not use the Railroad: the fugitive slaves that passed through New York, for instance, all came from Maryland and Delaware. Black Southern escapees preferred staying in Dixie, simply disappearing into the anonymity of the big Southern cities where they easily merged with the large free black population.[642] (This is not surprising: even after Lincoln's Final Emancipation Proclamation was issued, 95 percent of all Southern slaves voluntarily stayed at home in Dixie, defending both their owners' farms, and the owners themselves, from marauding Yanks.)[643]

There was no actual "Underground Railroad," of course, for it was not literally or even figuratively underground, it was not a railroad, and it was not secret. There were no "hidden tunnels." It was not even organized. There were no set roads, routes, or stopping stations, nor were there "thousands of agents," as Yankee mythologists maintain. The entire so-called "underground system" turns out to be nothing but a few sporadic groups of whites and blacks scattered throughout the North who wanted to help escaped slaves in their bid for freedom—none who came from the Deep South, by the way, but more typically from Maryland and Delaware, as well as the Border States. Here, at a port in Camden, New Jersey, a family of runaway slaves is being secretly deboarded from a steamboat at night, while an assistant blocks the attempts of a passenger trying to interfere. The family will be transported to the next "station" (that is, whoever will take them in temporarily), and from there sent northward to a concealed location in Canada.

It is telling that the definitive early source on the Railroad, William Still's 1872 book, *The Underground Railroad: A Record of Facts, Authentic Narratives, Letters, Etc.*, features not millions, not thousands, not even hundreds, but a mere handful of black slaves who were, as the author phrases it, "plucked from the jaws of slavery" via this particular method. And nearly all of these testimonials are of single individuals, with the exception of a few rare slave groups usually comprising no more than four to six people.[644]

Another 19th-Century authority on the subject, Wilbur H. Siebert, believed that tens of thousands of fugitive slaves had escaped to Canada, but admitted that he had no proof, and that the Census only records 4,669 of such individuals: 2,502 black males and 2,167 black females.[645] But not even these statistics have turned out to be accurate.

As to the comment about Canada, that country did not exist during Lincoln's War: it was founded on July 1, 1867, two years after the conflict's cessation. Up until that year the region had been owned by various countries, including France, Spain, and Britain.

It is true that what is now Canada was free of slavery during our "Civil War," or as we in the American South like to call it, our "Second War for Southern Independence" (1861-1865). However, if those American slaves who traveled north on the Underground Railroad had tried to enter the area just 27 years earlier, they might have found themselves enslaved a second time. This is because slavery was practiced throughout all of Canada for hundreds of years prior to its founding.

In particular was the area known as New France (1534-1763), where Native-Americans were used as slaves, and where Africans had long been imported in order to invigorate the economy. African

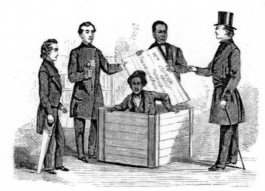

Out of 4.5 million Northern and Southern slaves in 1861, only some 2,000—like this one, who escaped detection in a shipping box sent to Philadelphia, Pennsylvania—ever used the Underground Railroad. Ineffective, disorganized, and inefficient, it served mainly as a psychological crutch for a few Yankee Liberals and abolitionists who wanted to believe that they were helping to end slavery.

slavery came to Nova Scotia in 1749, and it was found in Quebec, New Brunswick, and Prince Edward Island before 1780. What should be called "Canadian slavery" did not end legally until August 1, 1834, the day the British Emancipation Act was implemented.[646]

In any discussion of the Underground Railroad and Canada, we must also consider that many Northern American states possessed laws that sought to prevent slaves from escaping to Canada. One of these was New York, which in 1705 issued a statute providing the death penalty for any slave caught traveling more than 40 miles north of Albany.[647]

In the end, as nearly all enslaved American blacks seeking freedom did so on their own and without any assistance, the so-called "Underground Railroad" was little more than a morale booster for abolitionists as opposed to an actual effective escape system for slaves.[648]

Most American black slaves seeking freedom in Canada made the attempt on their own, not via the Underground Railroad. This runaway slave was in the process of fleeing his owner's plantation in Rhode Island when a New England slave catcher and his dogs caught up with him.

THE STANDARD OF LIVING
FOR BLACK SOUTHERN SLAVES

WHAT YOU WERE TAUGHT: Southern slaves were degraded and exploited, and died young from overwork, harsh conditions, disease, malnutrition, and abuse.

THE TRUTH: Ludicrous. Southern servitude functioned much like a social welfare program with free built-in health and life insurance, operating in many ways like an early form of socialism. Yes, servants helped defray these costs through their work and through monthly percentage payments to their employers. But they earned wages at the same time as well, both via their regular work and also from their personal extracurricular labors. In all, most Southern slaves were so highly indulged and protected by their owners that *being a "slave" came to be an enviable status symbol among many blacks*. Such bold facts have forced even the most South-loathing, biased historians to admit an obvious truth: *servants in the American South were treated far better than servants in any other part of the New World.*[649]

Would servile blacks have given all these benefits up for freedom? Some would have, and some certainly did. But, after contemplating the quasi-freedom of living in the North, where the anti-African Black Codes were strictly enforced and where white racism was more deeply entrenched, many Southern blacks reconsidered. When Lincoln's War came, this group, most of whom were third, fourth, and fifth generation Southern Americans, quite consciously chose to remain in the South, in their own homes, on the plantations with their "white families."[650]

Then, when "Honest Abe" freed them, and he and the North tried to deport them back to Africa, with one voice this group cried "no!" For they quite rightly considered themselves true Americans and true Southerners. After all, by 1860, 99 percent of all blacks were native-born Americans, a larger percentage than for whites.[651] As black educator and former Southern servant Booker T. Washington wrote:

> I was born in the South. I have lived and labored in the South. I wish to be buried in the South.[652]

Thus it was that a majority of Southern blacks would not be removed from their homes, or their home nation, the place of their birth and that of all their known ancestors.[653]

Southern slaves enjoyed numerous rights, protections, and freedoms, including holidays, sick leave, salaries, and lifelong free healthcare, clothing, food, and shelter. The average free white Southern family never even came close to such a secure lifestyle. Is it any wonder that these Tennessee slaves are happy?

Virginia-born Booker T. Washington was a true "son of the South," a concept inexplicable to most non-Southerners, but readily understandable to nearly all Southerners, whatever their race, background, or creed. To this day Washington is held in esteem by traditional Southern whites all across Dixie.

48

WHITE SOUTHERN SLAVE OWNERSHIP

WHAT YOU WERE TAUGHT: While few in the North ever owned slaves, nearly every Southerner was once a slave owner. The Confederacy was a nation of slaveholders.

THE TRUTH: Pro-North writers would have us believe that "every Southerner was once a slave owner." However, the opposite is true. In 1860 the South had reached its highest rate of slave ownership. According to the U.S. Census that year, with a white population of 7,215,525, only 4.8 percent, or 385,000, of all Southerners owned slaves—the exact population of modern day Wichita, Kansas. The other 95.2 percent did not.[654] Of those who did, most owned less than five.[655] Correcting for the mistakes of Census takers—which would include counting slave-hirers as slave owners and counting more than once those thousands of slave owners who annually moved the same slaves back and forth across multiple states—this figure, 4.8 percent, is no doubt too large. Either way, at the time Southerners themselves believed that only about 5 percent of their number owned slaves, which is slightly high, but roughly correct.[656]

Naturally, few white Southerners, America's first abolitionists, were interested in owning or trading in slaves: the average Southerner considered both institutions inhumane, and permanently tainted by having been created by Yankees.

Field hands running a cotton gin on an Alabama plantation. Slave owning was almost solely a rich man's business, which is why, contrary to Yankee myth, at slavery's peak in the antebellum South in 1860, only 4.8 percent of white adult males owned black servants. Southern historian Shelby Foote rightly called the other 95.2 percent "the slaveless majority," a reality never discussed by liberal university professors, never noted by the left-wing media, and never mentioned by pro-North writers.

THE MYTH OF
SOUTHERN SLAVE ABUSE

WHAT YOU WERE TAUGHT: Southern slave owners whipped, beat, and abused their slaves on a daily basis.

THE TRUTH: We have already seen that the Old North had few laws protecting their slaves while the Old South has a myriad of rules and regulations protecting theirs, so obviously this is just another anti-South myth. Indeed, not only were all forms of slave abuse against the law in the Southern states, there was nothing to gain and everything to lose by engaging in it.

Slave owners, most who were experienced, professional, and highly intelligent businessmen, understood this, as did the authors of a variety of Victorian plantation manuals, all which strongly discouraged farm managers from using any kind of corporal punishment on their servants.

Here is what one such work, the popular 19th-Century *Instructions to Managers*, had to say on the subject:

> The most vital ingredient in managing servants is how their superiors act toward them and treat them. It is true that there needs to be a certain amount of discipline on a farm. However, remember that when a servant's work is finished it is only right to *treat him with humanity, sympathy, and even permissiveness.* Kindness and rewards are much more effective than punishment.[657]

These were words that nearly all Southern slave owners, black, white, brown, or red, understood and agreed with. This made whipping and other severe forms of physical discipline on Southern plantations extremely rare—and for good reason. Not only was it bad for morale, it also increased the cost of labor while reducing the value of those slaves it was used on (whip marks, for instance, indicated an unmanageable individual), which is why *all* early plantation manuals strongly advised against the practice.[658]

This illustration of a white Southern slave owner viciously whipping his servant (from the author's book, *Honest Jeff and Dishonest Abe: A Southern Children's Guide to the Civil War*), is a fantasy created by the anti-South movement. In fact, whipping was extremely rare in the Old South. Not only was it considered unmanly, uncivilized, immoral, and un-Christian to hurt one's servants, but it was also both bad business and against Southern law. Those few ignorant owners who violated this statute were reported to the sheriff by concerned neighbors. The criminal was then arrested, tried, and imprisoned. In some cases exceptionally cruel Southern slave owners were hanged and their slaves were confiscated.

Plantation owners themselves encouraged servants to bring them complaints concerning cruel drivers and overseers, or anyone else who hurt or even interfered with them,[659] for everywhere in the South "a bad master was universally execrated."[660] To further discourage cruelty to slaves, in most parts of the South slave owners could not punish their servants without first holding a "plantation trial," the jury of which was made up solely of slave friends of the accused.[661]

Naturally, the majority of Southerners considered those who used the whip to be inhumane,[662] and those who wielded it against their servants were routinely reported by neighbors to the authorities for cruelty.[663] In 1846 Southern historian Matthew Estes noted that

> *this public sentiment is growing stronger and stronger every year: a man now who treats his slaves with any considerable degree of cruelty, is shunned by the community as though he were the veriest monster in existence.*[664]

So-called "Southern slavery" was a largely casual affair. Black servants—like this nonchalant group lounging during one of their daily breaks—were given a wide range of freedoms and were often allowed to come and go as they pleased. On many Southern plantations the rules were so lax that the "slaves" were mistaken for freemen, a situation that sometimes led to social and legal issues. The black Southern bondsman often compared his time as a true slave back home in the barbaric wilds of Africa with his far safer, far healthier, and far more placid life as a true servant in the American South, always favoring the latter. This gave rise to the seldom discussed phenomenon of hundreds of thousands of Southern "slaves" refusing to be emancipated, before, during, and after Lincoln's War.

In the mid 1830s Yankee author Reverend Joseph Holt Ingraham of Maine wrote of the alleged "severity" of the Southern slaveholder:

> It is now popular to treat slaves with kindness; and *those planters who are known to be inhumanly rigorous to their slaves, are scarcely countenanced by the more intelligent and humane portion of the community. Such instances, however, are very rare*; but there are unprincipled men everywhere, who will give vent to their ill feelings and bad passions, not with less good-will upon the back of

an *indented apprentice*, than upon that of a purchased slave.[665]

All Southerners condemned "the barbarous use of slaves" as "bringing on the community, the State and the city the contumely and opprobrium of the civilized world."[666] As President Woodrow Wilson explains,

> *public opinion in the South*, while it recognized the necessity for maintaining the discipline of subordination among the hosts of slaves, *was as intolerant of the graver forms of cruelty as was the opinion of the best people in the North*. . . . It sometimes happened that husbands were sold away from their wives, children away from their parents; *but even this evil was in most instances checked by the wisdom and moral feeling of the slave-owners. Even in the ruder [Southern] communities public opinion demanded that when negroes were sold, families should be kept together, particularly mothers and their children. Slave-dealers were universally detested, and even ostracised; and the domestic slave-trade was tolerated only because it was deemed necessary for the economic distribution of the slave population.*[667]

It was these very reasons (and others) that inhumane practices, such as splitting up slave families, was actually against the law in states such as Louisiana[668]—a fact no Liberal historian would ever want you to know.

As was the norm throughout the South, these Virginia slaves owned their own home, land, outbuildings, livestock, farming equipment, carts, buggies, gardens, products, and supplies. Many Southern slaves owned more land and had a greater net worth than free blacks and whites in the same neighborhood.

Along with the North's ever present "slave police," the "Negro Whipper" was a civil authority figure required by law in every Northern town prior to the Civil War. Handy with the cat-o'-nine-tails and other forms of torture, this one is preparing to lay 39 lashes on the bare back of a white indentured female slave convicted of committing an offence on a Yankee plantation. Pro-North writers never mention the Yankee Negro Whipper, and for obvious reasons. However, he was a central figure in the Old North and therefore we record him here for posterity.

Our liberal anti-South historians like to pretend that whipping was used only by Southern slave owners. The truth is that it was an ordinary form of punishment for lawbreakers—whatever their skin color or gender—throughout all of early America. It was also the standard penalty used by the U.S. military. For instance, while George Washington (seen here entertaining family and friends at home) was serving as general of the Continental Army, he routinely had his wayward soldiers flogged. Though legal and accepted, the severity of his whippings was not, and Congress had to step in to regulate them.

PART 2

AFRICAN-AMERICANS
DURING LINCOLN'S WAR

". . . those champions of Southern Rights, Confederate officers John Hunt Morgan, Braxton Bragg, and Edmund Kirby Smith, are a bold set of fellows. . . The latest intelligence from these fellows is, that *they have armed and equipped one-hundred negroes for [Confederate] military service!* . . . We suppose that nobody will have the hardihood to deny that *the rebels have used the slaves as soldiers wherever they could do it profitably. In Virginia negro sharp-shooters were a strong arm of the rebels,* and many of [U.S. Colonel Hiram] Berdan's Sharp-shooters were killed and wounded by these slaves. Perhaps *the rebels are right in employing whatever instruments promise to be useful in the attainments of their grand purpose: success.* Men who are in earnest look mainly at success. But still *this army of slaves* to overthrow the government, is a bold step. It is an amazingly bold one, we confess."[669]

The *Nashville Daily Union*
(a Southern pro-North newspaper)
September 17, 1862

Edmund Kirby Smith, one of the thousands of Confederate officers who enlisted blacks in the Confederate military as armed soldiers.

THE CIVIL WAR & SLAVERY

WHAT YOU WERE TAUGHT: The American Civil War was fought over slavery.

THE TRUTH: According to pro-North "historians"—most who are blatantly and unapologetically biased against the South—the North fought the South to "preserve the Union" and "destroy slavery," while the South fought the North to "destroy the Union" and "preserve slavery." That this 150 year old belief is nothing but anti-South propaganda, designed to perpetuate what I call "The Great Yankee Coverup,"[670] is easily provable.

It is patently clear to all rational thinking individuals that slavery had nothing to do with the Civil War. For one thing, if slavery had been the cause, the War would have ended on September 22, 1862, when Lincoln issued his Preliminary Emancipation Proclamation, or at least by January 1, 1863, when he issued his Final Emancipation Proclamation. Yet, the bloody, illegal, and unnecessary conflict continued for another two years. If the War was about abolition and America's slaves were now free, why go on fighting?

Furthermore, it would have cost ten times less to simply free America's slaves than to go to war.[671] Not even the megalomaniacal Lincoln, with all of his psychological problems and emotional disabilities, was mentally unbalanced enough to overlook this important fact.

However, the most damning evidence against the Yankee myth that "slavery triggered the Civil War" comes from the top political and military leaders of both the Confederacy and the Union. Here is how

C.S. President Jefferson Davis put it:

> The truth remains intact and incontrovertible, that the existence of
> African servitude was in no wise the cause of the conflict, but only
> an incident. In the later controversies that arose, however, its
> effect in operating as a lever upon the passions, prejudices, or
> sympathies of mankind, was so potent that it has been spread like
> a thick cloud over the whole horizon of historic truth.[672]

Neither Confederate soldiers or Union soldiers believed they were fighting for abolition. The
Southern Cause was always about "preserving the Constitution," the Northern Cause was always
about "preserving the Union"—just as the leaders of both sides repeatedly asserted.

To the last day of his life the Confederacy's celebrated vice
president, Alexander H. Stephens, declared that the South seceded for
one reason and one reason only: to "render our liberties and institutions
more secure" by "rescuing, restoring, and re-establishing the
Constitution."[673] As for the War, the South took up arms, he often
noted, for no other reason than a "desire to preserve constitutional
liberty and perpetuate the government in its purity."[674]

According to the South's highest ranking military officer,
General Robert E. Lee:

All the South has ever desired was that the Union as established by our forefathers should be preserved; and that the government as originally organized should be administered in purity and truth.[675]

From its own point of view, the North held the exact same sentiments. No Northerner was more definitive about the true purpose, and thus the cause, of the "Civil War" than the man who started it: U.S. President Abraham Lincoln. In his Inaugural Address, March 4, 1861, only four weeks before the conflict, he declared:

> I have no purpose, directly or indirectly, to interfere with the institution of slavery in the States where it exists.[676]

In the Summer of 1861, with the War now in full swing, he told Reverend Charles E. Lester:

> I think [Massachusetts Senator Charles] Sumner, and the rest of you [abolitionists], would upset our apple-cart altogether, if you had your way. . . . We didn't go into the war to put down Slavery, but to put the flag back . . .[677]

On August 22, 1862, Lincoln sent this public comment to Horace Greeley, owner of the New York *Tribune*:

> My paramount object in this struggle is to save the Union, and it is not either to save or destroy slavery. If I could save the Union without freeing any slave, I would do it . . .[678]

Impatient over misunderstandings on the topic, on August 15, 1864, Lincoln clarified his position yet again:

> My enemies pretend I am now carrying on this war for the sole purpose of abolition. So long as I am President, it shall be carried on for the sole purpose of restoring the Union.[679]

And let us not forget Lincoln's support of the Corwin Amendment (mentioned in his First Inaugural Address), which would have guaranteed the states the right to practice slavery in perpetuity.[680]

The U.S. Congress also testified that the Civil War had no connection to slavery. On July 22 and 31, 1861, it issued the following resolutions:

> . . . this war is not waged upon our part in any spirit of oppression, nor for any purpose of conquest or subjugation, nor purpose of overthrowing or interfering with the rights or established institutions [that is, slavery] of those States; but to defend and maintain the supremacy of the Constitution and to preserve the Union with all the dignity, equality, and rights of the several States unimpaired; that as soon as these objects are accomplished the war ought to cease. . . . that hostilities against these so-called confederate States shall . . . not be so prosecuted as to . . . interfere with their state governments, or to abolish slavery within their limits.[681]

Like Lincoln, Confederate President Jefferson Davis consistently declared that the War was not related to slavery, abolition, or even African-Americans. In fact, Lincoln's constituents, Northern Liberals, referred to the Civil War as "a white man's war," which completely destroys any pretense that it was over slavery!

The North's most famous general, Ulysses S. Grant, made this comment on the topic of slavery and the cause of the War:

> The sole object of this war is to restore the union. Should I be convinced it has any other object, or that the government designs using its soldiers to execute the wishes of the Abolitionists, I pledge to you my honor as a man and a soldier, I would resign my

commission and carry my sword to the other side.[682]

The majority of Southern citizens themselves, all who were staunch abolitionists, had absolutely no interest in either slavery or its preservation. Why then would they have risked their lives for it? This obvious point was driven home by Confederate General John Brown Gordon in his 1903 memoirs, *Reminiscences of the Civil War*:

> . . . *there would have been no slavery if the South's protests [against it] could have availed when it was first introduced [in the 1600s]* and now that it is gone, although its sudden and violent abolition entailed upon the South directly and incidentally a series of woes which no pen can describe, yet *it is true that in no section would its reestablishment be more strongly and universally resisted. The South steadfastly maintains that responsibility for the presence of this political Pandora's box in this Western world cannot be laid at her door. When the Constitution was adopted and the Union formed, slavery existed in practically all the States; and it is claimed by the Southern people that its disappearance from the Northern and its development in the Southern States is due to climatic conditions and industrial exigencies rather than to the existence or absence of great moral ideas.*
>
> . . . Neither [slavery's] destruction on the one hand, nor its defence on the other, was the energizing force that held the contending armies to four years of bloody work. I apprehend that if all living Union soldiers were summoned to the witness-stand, every one of them would testify that it was the preservation of the American Union and not the destruction of Southern slavery that induced him to volunteer at the call of his country. *As for the South, it is enough to say that perhaps eighty per cent, of her armies were neither slave-holders, nor had the remotest interest in the institution. No other proof, however, is needed than the undeniable fact that at any period of the war from its beginning to near its close the South could have saved slavery by simply laying down its arms and returning to the Union.*[683]

In his invaluable 1881 tome, *The Rise and Fall of the Confederate Government*, the always perspicacious Jefferson Davis summarized the cause of Lincoln's "Civil War" this way:

> . . . the war was, on the part of the United States Government, one of aggression and usurpation, and, on the part of the South, was for the defense of an inherent, unalienable right.[684]

What was that right? The right of state sovereignty and self-determination as laid out in the Declaration of Independence, the Articles of Confederation, the Bill of Rights, and the Constitution itself (see the Ninth and Tenth Amendments in particular).[685] In this same work Davis made the following comment, one that should be enshrined on every state capitol and included in every school history book:

> When the cause was lost, what cause was it? Not that of the South only, but the cause of constitutional government, of the supremacy of law, of the natural rights of man.[686]

Concerning the true cause of the Civil War: case closed.

Midway through the Civil War, when New York newspaper editor and Northern abolitionist Horace Greeley publicly pushed Lincoln to issue an emancipation proclamation, the U.S. president replied sharply: "My paramount object in this struggle is to save the Union, and it is not either to save or destroy slavery."

THE REAL REASON THE
NORTH WENT TO WAR

WHAT YOU WERE TAUGHT: There was only one possible reason the North took up arms against the South: to try and abolish slavery.

THE TRUTH: Based on the words of the highest ranking leaders from both the Confederacy and the Union, we have seen that this is patently false. We have also learned why the South went to war. But why did the North fight if not over slavery?

Lincoln claimed it was to "preserve the Union."[687] But this was just a smokescreen to conceal his true Liberal agenda: to install big government, then known as the "American System," in Washington.[688]

Devised and promoted by Lincoln's political hero, slave owner Henry Clay—a man "Honest Abe" called "my *beau ideal* of a statesman, the man for whom I fought all my humble life"[689]—the American System was a nationalist program in which there was to be a single sovereign authority, the president, who was to assume the role of a kinglike ruler with autocratic powers.[690]

Likewise, the government at Washington, D.C. was to be federated, acting as a consolidated superpower that would eventually control the money supply, offer internal improvements,[691] intervene in foreign affairs, nationalize the banking system,[692] issue soaring tariffs, grant subsidies to corporations, engage in protectionism, and impose an income tax,[693] all hints of Lincoln's coming empire.[694]

In essence, what the American System proposed was a federal

government that was the polar opposite of a confederal government. Under federation, its proponents, the Federalists, Monarchists, or Hamiltonians (named after Alexander Hamilton), as they were variously called,[695] not only sought to create a large, domineering, all-powerful, nationalized government to which all interests (from private to business) were subordinate,[696] but they also proposed that the states be largely stripped of their independence and authority, then placed in an inferior role. Hamilton himself wanted to get rid of the states completely.[697] Jeffersonianism was to be abolished and replaced with the Hamiltonian or American system.[698]

As such, nation-building nationalist Lincoln must be considered nothing less than the "Great Federator": the creator of American big government for big business, with its big spending, Big Brother mind-set.[699] He is also either fully or partially responsible for the following: America's internal revenue program (the IRS), American protectionism, American imperialism, American expansionism, America's bloated military despotism, America's enormous standing army, America's central banking system, America's corporate welfare system (which

Naturally, Lincoln, a Liberal with dictatorial ambitions, has always been revered by dictators, Marxists, communists, and socialists, one of the more famous from the last category being Nazi leader Adolf Hitler, who wrote fondly of Lincoln's anti-states' rights policies in his biography *Mein Kampf* ("My Struggle").

Lincoln called "internal improvements"), America's nation-building agenda, and America's deeply entangled foreign alliances. (Lincoln apparently never read Jefferson's admonition that America's approach to foreign affairs should be: "Peace, commerce, and honest friendship with all nations, entangling alliances with none.")[700]

Is it any wonder that President Lincoln surrounded himself with Marxists;[701] that he was supported by a group of radical socialists called the "Forty-Eighters";[702] that he is still idolized by socialists[703] and communists[704] alike; that in the 1930s American communists formed a military organization called "The Abraham Lincoln Battalion"; that the

1939 U.S. Communist Party Convention in Chicago, Illinois, affectionately displayed an enormous image of Lincoln over the center of its stage, flanked by pictures of Russian communist dictators Vladimir Lenin on one side and Joseph Stalin on the other;[705] or that he has long been adored by nationalists, totalitarians, and bolsheviks from around the world,[706] including socialists such as Francis Bellamy, author of America's *Pledge of Allegiance?*

And here, politically at least, is Lincoln's greatest legacy, for big government opened the door to federal tyranny and its many dangers and horrors: the consolidation of governmental powers, the centralization of executive power, unchecked presidential power, expansion of the military, the growth of the nanny state, unlimited abuses and corruption, and the progressive, intrusive, oppressive, tax-and-spend government that American citizens now labor under, whether they are Lincolnian Liberals themselves, or Independent, Conservative, or Libertarian.[707]

And all of this came at the expense of individual civil liberties and states' rights, the very rights our white and black colonial and Confederate ancestors fought and died for.[708]

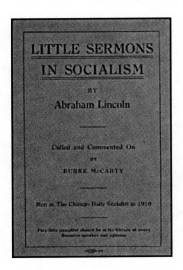

These two books, *Little Sermons in Socialism by Abraham Lincoln* (compiled by Burke McCarty) and *Lincoln and the Communists* (by Earl Browder), reveal what educated Southern conservatives have always known and what Northern liberals do not want you to find out: Lincoln was a big government Liberal with thousands of socialist, Marxist, and communist followers, who desperately wanted to install the anti-Conservative "American System" in Washington. When the Southern states seceded (taking their taxable dollars, natural resources, and slaves with them), Lincoln saw it as a threat to his plans and inaugurated war to force them back into the Union.

52

NORTHERN LIBERALISM VS. SOUTHERN CONSERVATISM

Alexander H. Stephens correctly defined the "Civil War" as a conflict between Conservative Southern "Constitutionalists" and Liberal Northern "Consolidationists."

WHAT YOU WERE TAUGHT: Abraham Lincoln and his supporters were Republicans, and therefore Conservatives, while Jefferson Davis and his supporters were Democrats, and therefore Liberals. So the Civil War was between Northern Conservatives, who wanted to end slavery, and Southern Liberals, who wanted to preserve slavery.

THE TRUTH: This Yankee myth is entirely backwards and upside down! In the 1860s the two main party platforms were reversed, making the Republicans (at the time, mainly Northerners) Liberals and the Democrats (at the time, mainly Southerners) Conservatives. Since we have established that the "Civil War" was not over slavery, it could have only had a political foundation, and indeed it did; and it is the same "war" that began the day the U.S. was founded and it is the same one that has continued into the present: Southern Conservatism versus Northern Liberalism.

As proof we have many of the Civil War's elder statesmen, among them Confederate Vice President Alexander H. Stephens, who declared that the conflict was a battle between what were then called "Consolidationists" or "Centralists" (that is, Liberals who wanted to consolidate all power in the central government) and "Federalists" or "Constitutionalists" (that is, Conservatives who wanted to maintain states' rights and the constitutional separation of powers).[709] Here is how Stephens described the "Late War" in 1870:

> It is a postulate, with many writers of this day, that the late War was the result of two opposing ideas, or principles, upon the subject of African Slavery. Between these, according to their theory, sprung the "irrepressible conflict," in principle, which ended in the terrible conflict of arms. *Those who assume this postulate, and so theorize upon it, are but superficial observers.*
>
> *That the War had its origin in opposing principles, which, in their action upon the conduct of men, produced the ultimate collision of arms, may be assumed as an unquestionable fact. But the opposing principles which produced these results in physical action were of a very different character from those assumed in the postulate.* They lay in the Organic Structure of the Government of the States. *The conflict in principle arose from different and opposing ideas as to the nature of what is known as the General Government. The contest was between those who held it to be strictly Federal in its character [that is, Conservatives], and those who maintained that it was thoroughly National [that is, Liberals]. It was a strife between the [Southern Conservative] principles of Federation, on the one side, and [Northern Liberal] Centralism, or Consolidation, on the other.*
>
> *Slavery, so called, was but the question on which these antagonistic principles, which had been in conflict, from the beginning, on divers other questions, were finally brought into actual and active collision with each other on the field of battle.*[710]

More to the point, the Civil War was a battle between Southern agrarianism and Northern industrialism; between the farming and commerce capitalism of the South and the finance and industry capitalism of the North; between Southern free trade and Northern protective tariffs; between Southern traditionalism and Northern progressivism; between Southern ruralism (the countryman) and Northern urbanism (the townsman); between the South's desire to maintain Thomas Jefferson's "Confederate Republic" and the North's desire to change it into Alexander Hamilton's federate democracy.

Shorn of Northern myth and anti-South propaganda, Lincoln's War was nothing but a conflict that pitted liberal, progressive, Northern industrialists who cared little for the Constitution, against conservative, traditional, Southern agriculturalists who were strict constitutionalists.[711]

This Liberal vs. Conservative conflict rages on today, just as potently as it did in the 1860s.[712] And this explains just one of many reasons why the traditional South continues to wave the Confederate Battle Flag. It represents the cause for which our Southern ancestors fought and died: to preserve the constitutional rights which insure the personal freedoms of every American.[713]

Though a Democrat, C.S. President Jefferson Davis (left) was a Conservative or what was also then known as a "Constitutionalist." Though a Republican, U.S. President Abraham Lincoln (right) was a Liberal or what was also then known as a "Consolidationist." Here the basis for the American Civil War is clearly evident: Southern conservatism versus Northern liberalism.

THE NORTH'S DEPENDENCE
ON THE SLAVE TRADE

WHAT YOU WERE TAUGHT: The American Civil War came about because of the South's dependence on slavery, and her refusal to abolish it.

THE TRUTH: Incorrect on both counts. We have long been taught that the North fought the Confederacy over *Southern* slavery. At the time, however, it was *Northern* slavery that was the principle interest to Yankees. As has been previously pointed out, it was the North's heavy dependence on the Yankee slave trade and on selling its slaves to the South, that both precipitated and helped the Union fund the Civil War.[714]

One Northerner who was well aware of these facts was Yankee abolitionist, individualist, and natural rights advocate Lysander Spooner, who saw right through Lincoln's duplicitous treachery, correctly referring to the president's "Wall Street Boys"—that is, New York City's business establishment (bankers, merchants, manufacturers, and stockjobbers)[715]—as the "lenders of blood money." Wrote Spooner:

> . . . these lenders of blood money had, for a long series of years previous to the war, been the willing accomplices of the slave-holders in perverting the government from the purposes of liberty and justice, to the greatest of crimes. They had been such accomplices for a purely pecuniary consideration, to wit, a control of the markets in the South; in other words, the privilege of holding the slave-holders themselves in industrial and

commercial subjection to the manufacturers and merchants of the North (who afterwards furnished the money for the [Civil] war). And these Northern merchants and manufacturers, these lenders of blood money, were willing to continue to be the accomplices of the slaveholders in the future, for the same pecuniary considerations. But the slaveholders, either doubting the fidelity of their Northern allies, or feeling themselves strong enough to keep their slaves in subjection without Northern assistance, would no longer pay the price these Northern men demanded. And *it was to enforce this price in the future—that is, to monopolize the Southern markets, to maintain their industrial and commercial control over the South—that these Northern manufacturers and merchants lent some of the profits of their former monopolies for the [Civil] war, in order to secure themselves the same, or greater, monopolies in the future. These—and not any love of liberty or justice—were the motives on which the money for the [Civil] war was lent by the North.* [716]

Yankee abolitionist Lysander Spooner of Massachusetts was not fooled by Abraham Lincoln's political chicanery. Instead he accurately attributed the Civil War not to so-called "Southern slavery," but to the North's stubborn support of the Yankee slave trade.

Thus it was the Northern states and their slavery-loving citizens who were responsible for creating the infamous "Cotton Triangle," [717] or "Slave Triangle," as it is also known, [718] a three-way process easily understood by following the money.

1) Yankee slave ships sailed from the North to Africa where rum (made in Northern distilleries) [719] was traded for African slaves (already enslaved by other Africans). [720] The going rate was 115 gallons of rum for a healthy African male slave, 95 gallons for a healthy African female slave. [721] 2) These individuals were brought back to America and auctioned off at Southern ports, sold a second time as laborers in the cotton growing industry on Dixie's expansive plantations. The harvested cotton was then sold to New England's textile mills, whose products were peddled worldwide at huge profits. 3) These profits were then used to fund new Northern slave expeditions

to Africa, completing the Triangle,[722] each time accruing evermore vast fortunes for Yankee slavers.[723]

In contrast to the Northern obsession with slavery, in March 1861 the newly constitutionally formed Confederate States of America adopted its Constitution, which included a clause banning slave trading with foreign nations.[724] "Foreign nations," of course, now included the United States of America. The North panicked, deciding it was better to beat the South into submission than allow her to cut off one of her primary revenue streams: the transatlantic Yankee slave trade and its many associated businesses.[725]

Big government Liberal Abraham Lincoln, the only 1860 presidential candidate who promised *not* to interfere with slavery,[726] and who was put into office by Northern industrialists using profits from the Northern slave trade,[727] launched the War of Northern Aggression in April, just a few weeks later.[728]

An old illustration of the misnamed 703 ton clipper *Sunny South*, the only sailing ship ever built by Northerner George Steers (designer of the famous racing yacht *America*). Known as "one of the prettiest clippers ever launched at New York," in 1860 the *Sunny South* was seized by the British ship *Brisk*, with a cargo of 850 slaves on board. Though there was now one less Yankee slave ship on the prowl, her capture had no impact on the Yankee slave trade—which continued until it was forcibly shut down by the U.S. government during the Civil War.

THE CONFEDERATE MILITARY: MULTIRACIAL & MULTICULTURAL

WHAT YOU WERE TAUGHT: The Confederate army was 100 percent white.

THE TRUTH: We have been taught that the Confederate armies were "100 percent white," this due to the "boundless white racism" that existed across the Old South. We have already seen that the integrated South was far less racist than the segregated North, so it is obvious that this charge cannot be true. The South's army and navy, in fact, reflected the region's citizenship, which was made up of every race, creed, and nationality. Though—thanks to the vicious Yankee custom of burning down Southern courthouses[729] and the purposeful exclusion of countless Confederate records dealing with Southern blacks from the official U.S. archives[730]—exact statistics are impossible to come by, Southern historians have determined that the following numbers are roughly accurate. In descending numerical order the Confederate army and navy was composed of about 1 million European-Americans,[731] 300,000 to 1 million African-Americans,[732] 70,000 Native-Americans, 60,000 Latin-Americans,[733] 50,000 foreigners,[734] 12,000 Jewish-Americans,[735] and 10,000 Asian-Americans.[736] True Southerners, of all races, continue to be proud of our region's multiracial history, and of the many contributions made to Dixie by individuals of all colors, religions, and nations.[737] As for the black Confederate soldier, we will have much more to say about him in the following chapters.

These black Confederate soldiers are on picket duty near Houma, Louisiana, just two of the 1 million African-Americans who gallantly served, in one capacity or another, under the Confederate Battle Flag in an effort to preserve the Constitution.

THE BLACK CONFEDERATE SOLDIER

WHAT YOU WERE TAUGHT: There was no such as a "black Confederate soldier." The phrase is an oxymoron.

THE TRUTH: Why do we never hear about the black Confederate soldier? It is because he (and in some cases she) has been cleverly concealed by enemies of the South. Yet, thankfully, they have not been able to hide or destroy all of the evidence.

There is still plenty of proof for their existence, beginning with both the eyewitness testimonies of white Confederate soldiers—many who took their African-American servants into the War with them (men like General Nathan Bedford Forrest)—and the accounts of numerous black Confederate soldiers themselves. As Yankees had the malicious habit of illegally and unnecessarily torching Southern courthouses (where thousands of records were kept), a great deal of this evidence has literally gone up in smoke.[738] Nonetheless, much remains.

"Uncle" Mack Dabney of Cornersville, Tennessee, black Confederate soldier.

One of the better known African-American Rebel soldiers was "Uncle" Mack Dabney,[739] who served for the entire War with "one of the best of the Tennessee regiments": the Third Tennessee Regiment under General John C. Brown. In 1913, nearly 50 years later, Uncle Mack could still vividly remember fighting in such battles as

Vicksburg, Missionary Ridge, Chickamauga, and Franklin II. Surrendering on May 10, 1865, at Gainesville, Alabama, he was one of the last Confederate soldiers to lay down his arms. Known to white Southerners as a "faithful servant and negro soldier," of him Confederate Captain Andrew P. Gordon wrote:

> "Old Uncle" Mack Dabney was born and reared three miles south of this place (Cornersville, Tenn). His old master, the late J. O. Dabney, one of Giles County's best citizens, *sent five noble boys to the Confederate army and also Uncle Mack to cook and wait upon them, which he did well and faithfully to the end.* He was with us in all the marches from Fort Donelson to Atlanta and on to Gainesville, Ala., where we all surrendered. [After the War he] . . . came home with us and went to work to try to make an honest living for himself and family, and in all these long fifty years just passed I have never heard one single thing against Uncle Mack Dabney. *He is true and faithful to his family and the old [Confederate] soldier.* He is now, and has been for years, sexton at the Methodist church. All the young masters that he went out with have passed away, except one, Sam D. Dabney, who lives here.[740]

Two other black Confederates of note were William Johnson and "Uncle Ned" Hawkins, both who were written up in the September 1900 issue of *Confederate Veteran* magazine in a special section called "Tributes to Faithful Servants":

> While the race problem creates serious concern for the welfare of both races and for the country, *it behooves the [white] Southern people, who are, and ever have been, their best friends [i.e., blacks], to be on the alert for opportunities to influence all classes for the general good. The* Veteran *improves its opportunities to pay tribute to faithful slaves, and it bespeaks the cooperation of our people in sending concise contributions to the honor of those who have ever been faithful.* Two illustrations are here given.
>
> William Johnson (colored) lives by Nolensville, Tenn., near his birthplace. He was a slave, and the property of Mr. Ben Johnson, as was also his mother.
>
> In 1862 a part of the army commanded by Gen. [Nathan Bedford] Forrest was stationed at Nolensville, and young William Johnson (fifteen years old) drove one of the wagons with provisions for the army. Capt. B. F. White, who had been assistant adjutant general on the staff of Gen. Forrest, had been detached, and was in

command of a battery of artillery captured at Murfreesboro. Seeing the boy William, he liked him, and proposed to buy him. Mr. Johnson sold him to Capt. White for $1,200, and *he went with Capt. White in the regular field service.*

William Johnson of Nolensville, Tennessee, black Confederate soldier.

Soon after his purchase of William, the great battle of Murfreesboro was fought; and while on the battlefield, during the battle, Capt. White was attacked suddenly with inflammatory rheumatism. His servant William was with the wagon train, and did not reach him until the next day. The day following, the Confederates retreated, and the Federals, who also had been falling back, retraced their movements and occupied the area in which Capt White was left in that painful and awful predicament, attended only by his servant William. For three months Capt. White was guarded by the Federals in a house on Thomas Butler's plantation, near the village of Salem. One bitter cold night the [Yankee] guard went to his camp some distance away, when the Captain asked William if he couldn't get him away from there. It was soon arranged for him to take a spring wagon and a broken-down army horse on the Butler farm. He put his charge in the wagon, and by a circuitous route got away without apprehension. Late in the night the horse so nearly gave out that William walked in water and ice over his boots, and would lift the wheels of the vehicle out of the mire, and moved on until they were safe in the Confederate lines. A better horse was procured, and the afflicted officer was taken to Shelbyville, and from there he was permitted to visit Mobile, where he recuperated, William of course going with him. This faithful servant remained with Capt.

Enemies of the South have been trying to hide all traces of the black Confederate since the War itself. Fortunately, they have not been able to suppress this photo, which shows Andrew Martin Chandler (left) and one of his family's servants, Silas Chandler (right), wearing official Confederate uniforms—full fledged soldiers in the 44th Mississippi Infantry. Armed to the teeth in preparation for the fight against the illicit Northern invaders, such brave young men, white and black, were prepared to face death side-by-side if need be. This type of interracial pairing was repeated hundreds of thousands of times across the South during Lincoln's War. While Dixie's black servants were sometimes ordered to go into battle to accompany white loved ones, just as often they went of their own accord, anxious to put on Confederate gray or butternut, and show "Marse Linkum" who was boss.

White, who went back into field service, but his health failed, and when his constitution gave down he was put on post duty, and at the end of the war he was paroled at Albany, Ga. He brought William back to Nashville, leaving him with an uncle when he left to reside in Memphis. He afterwards moved to California. They never met again.

When the notice of Capt. White's death appeared in the December *Veteran* for 1899, *William saw it, and asked to pay tribute to his memory. That desire becomes the occasion for the Veteran to pay just and well-merited tribute to William Johnson.*

. . . William has lived all these years in the neighborhood of his birthplace, and *has maintained a reputation as an honest, upright man—such as will ever have the devoted friendship of the white people, and who will prove it if later in life misfortunes should render him unable to support himself.*

During the time of Capt. White's confinement in the Federal lines he allowed William to carry three young ladies through the lines to Shelbyville. They were Misses Sallie J. McLean and Lizzie and Julia Lillard. After his return from that trip, Capt. White gave him [William] permission to visit his mother, at Nolensville, before *they escaped to the South.*[741]

The second "faithful" Confederate servant mentioned in this article, "Uncle Ned" Hawkins, is described like this:

Comrade C. L. Kalmbach, of Cobb's Legion (Ga), procured through Samuel L. Richards, a nephew of Uncle Ned's mistress, a sketch of his labors in the [eighteen] sixties. The scouts generally of the Northern Virginia army knew him, and will gladly recognize his kindly face after these many years. The data furnished is as follows:

Living on the banks of the Rappahannock, in the county of Culpeper, is a venerable old colored man, known by all near him as "Uncle Ned." *His fidelity to his old [white] mistress, his loyalty to the Confederacy, and his devotion to our soldiers were truly remarkable. He risked his liberty and his life more than once for the safety of our citizens and soldiers.* On one occasion some of our scouts called at the house of his mistress—*knowing they were always welcome there*—and while she and her sister, assisted, of course, by "Uncle Ned," were busily engaged in preparing for them a much-needed breakfast, the dreaded cry was heard: "The Yankees are coming!" They were guided by *the ever-faithful* "Uncle Ned" to the pines near by, and he returned to the house. After the Yankees left, he took the breakfast in an old haversack, with a few ears of corn on top, and told our [Confederate] scouts if all was right when approaching them he would raise his hat and scratch his head, and if not, his hat would remain on his head: and should he meet the Yanks, with those ears of corn, his excuse would be that he was hunting his sheep. *Many, many such acts he did for the safety of our soldiers, and now he and*

"Uncle Ned" Hawkins of Culpepper County, Virginia, black Confederate soldier.

his aged companion are struggling hard for a living; and—O that some brave Confederate could assist them in their good old age! He is certainly worthy of notice.[742]

As I am a Tennessean let us continue with a few more examples of notable African-American Confederate soldiers from the Volunteer State. The obituary of Bill King, of the Twentieth Tennessee Infantry, was written up in the June 1910 issue of *Confederate Veteran*:

BILL KING, A BLACK CONFEDERATE—Bill King is dead. Members of the 20th Tennessee (Battle's) Regiment will remember him. *No more faithful negro ever served a cause than did Bill King serve the boys of the old 20th. He went into the war as the body servant of the sons of Mr. Jack King, of Nolensville, Tenn., but he became the faithful servant of every member of this regiment. He went with the brave boys into the heat of battle, he nursed and cared for them in sickness, and assisted in burying the dead on the battlefields. He was as true to the cause of the*

Liberals (and uninformed Conservatives) who accept the Yankee lie that "there was no such thing as a black Confederate soldier," will be baffled by this old photo of several dozen African-American men. But here in the traditional South we know exactly who they are. A group of aging but still very patriotic black Confederate veterans attending a Confederate Reunion in 1910, many still proudly wearing their medals and tattered war gear. At their own request, and as was the custom among black Confederates, most were later buried in their Rebel uniforms inside Confederate Flag-draped coffins.

South as any member of that gallant band under the intrepid leadership of Col. Joel A. Battle. In Shiloh's bloody affray Colonel Battle was captured, and the leadership fell to young Col. Thomas Benton Smith.

When one of his young masters was killed in battle, *Bill was one of the escort which tenderly bore the body back to his mother and father.*

Since the war Bill King had been classed as an unreconstructed Rebel. He was a true and loyal Confederate until his death. He affiliated with old soldiers, attending every gathering within his reach. He was a member of Troop A, Confederate Veterans, Nashville. He lived on his old master's farm, near Nolensville; but he died in Nashville at Vanderbilt Medical College, where he underwent a serious surgical operation.

Mr. William Waller, an undertaker, took the body back to Nolensville for burial. *The body was clad in the Confederate uniform which he had during the past few years worn on all reunion occasions, according to his request.* The funeral service was conducted in Mount Olivet Methodist Church (white) by the pastor, Rev. H. W. Carter.

Bill King was seventy-three years old, and leaves a wife and ten or eleven children. He was a Baptist; but as there is no church of this denomination near his home, his friends decided to have the funeral in the Methodist church. He was buried in the Nolensville Cemetery.[743]

Another black Confederate Tennessee soldier was "Uncle" Jerry Perkins of the Thirty-First Tennessee Infantry. The September 1903 issue of *Confederate Veteran* provides the following information on him:

Charles Perkins enlisted at Brownsville, Tenn., under Capt. H. S. Bradford, who was afterwards Col. Bradford, of the 31st Tennessee Infantry. He was killed in the battle near Atlanta July 22, 1864. The boy Jerry went with him as a body servant. Before leaving, Charley's mother told Jerry that he must bring his "Marse Charley" back to her, and he promised that he would do it; that he would take him back alive or dead.

On that fateful July 22 young Perkins was killed; and when the regiment fell back to bivouac for the night, Jerry was alarmed not to see Marse Charley, and, upon being told that he was dead, said, "Here's your supper. I'm going to find Marse Charley," and away in the darkness he went.

In a short while he returned, carrying the dead body of his young master on his back. He carried it a mile or so farther to a farmhouse, got some plank, borrowed a saw, hatchet, and nails, made a box, dug a grave, and buried him in the farmer's yard. He walked from Atlanta to Brownsville, Tenn., and reported the sad news. He was supplied with a farm wagon and a metallic coffin, went back to Georgia, disinterred the body of Charley Perkins, and hauled it home to Brownsville.

Jerry is a favorite with the Hiram S. Bradford Bivouac, and attends all of their [Confederate] Reunions. The foregoing data comes from J. W. McClish, of Brownsville.[744]

"Uncle" Jerry Perkins of Tennessee, black Confederate soldier.

From the same issue comes this next story of a black boy named Jim Battery, whose time with the Confederate army is as revealing as it is educational. The attitude of the typical Southern black toward both the Confederates and the Yankees is made apparent:

CASE OF A NEGRO BOY DURING THE WAR. By W. H. Strange. Gift, Tenn., June 23, 1900: "While at Holly Springs [Earl] Vandorn's [Van Dorn] Cavalry went to the enemy's rear and captured that place one morning about daybreak. A negro boy was making his way out, and, being dressed in blue and in the early twilight, I took him to be a Federal and halted him. After finding that he was only a negro boy, *I would have let him go on, but he wanted to go with me for protection [from Union soldiers]* and, picking up an old mule, I put him on it and let him go with us. He said he was thirteen years old and was waiting on an artillery officer, Maj. Mudd, I think. The boy said he lived near Huntsville, Ala., and went with the Federals from there to Memphis.

"After taking Holly Springs, our command continued to go north, and, crossing Little Hatchie at Davis's Bridge, we had quite a skirmish with the enemy in getting across the river. The lame horse crowd being in the rear and one of my neighbor friends being in the crowd, I let the little negro stay with him. They got cut off from the command and went home, in Tipton County, Tenn., and the boy went with him. After getting home, the boy went to my father's and remained there during the war. *Although the Federals were frequently at my father's after that, he never wanted to go with them, but stayed at home and would help to hide the [live] stock. On one occasion he got one horse back from them after they had it in their possession. After I got home from the war, he lived with me for several years.*

"He was a bright boy, and *I taught him to read and write.* He took a great interest in learning and progressed rapidly, finally *becoming a Methodist preacher.* He got a country circuit, and after three or four years was made presiding elder. Since that time I have not known much of him, but think he has quit preaching and *is running a large farm in Arkansas. He was always Democratic [the Conservative Party of that day] in politics, and would sometimes take an active part in trying to get the negroes to vote for some of his white friends.* He has always gone by the name of Jim Battery. I do not remember who he belonged to before emancipation."[745]

One of the more illuminating stories of a black Confederate concerns Jerry W. May:

An interesting figure at the Louisville reunion was Jerry W. May, colored. Jerry is a mail carrier at Macon, and has been in the service for over twenty years. *Each year when the time for the Confederate Reunion rolls around Jerry asks for his vacation and accompanies Camp Smith to the rendezvous of the old Confederates. This is the fourteenth reunion he has attended.*

During the war Jerry was the body servant of William Wynn, of Georgia, who enlisted and served throughout the long contest as a private. His master [Wynn] was a member of the 7th Georgia Regiment of Harrison's Brigade. After the war, his master, who had lost everything by the ravages of the Federal army, moved to Prescott, Ark, leaving Jerry in Macon. A few years later he died, and his widow was left alone with nothing on which she might rely for a support. *Jerry began the task of securing a pension for her, and after several years of hard work he was successful. Through his efforts she was enabled to live comfortably.*

The *Veteran* wrote to Jerry in regard to the above, and he responded promptly, stating:

"My old master, William Wynn, was born and reared in Monroe County, Ga. He enlisted in the 7th Georgia Regiment, as stated, Company D. He took me as body servant; and after the war, everything was lost to him—even I myself came near being lost to him, but not quite. After the war, he moved to Prescott, Ark, and began farming; but he was quite old and feeble, so he could do but little at it. Later he wrote me that he could get a pension under the Arkansas laws, but he was too feeble mentally and physically, and he wanted me to do it for him. *I replied that I would do anything in my power on earth for him and his wife as long as they lived. I went at once to [U.S.] Gen. C. M. Wyley, the Ordinary for Bibb County, got application blanks, took one to every member of the old company that I could find, got them signed with affidavits before proper officers, made oath myself, and had seals put on where seals could be found. Sad but true, he died just before I got the papers ready. I then went back and got other blanks, and did the same work for his widow. I paid every cent of money necessary without any cost to her. I sent all the papers for him and her both, and the committee put her on the pension list. She wrote me her sincere thanks for what I did, and said she was all the more grateful because I had been one of her slaves.*"[746]

Jerry W. May of Macon, Georgia, black Confederate soldier.

The warm Civil War relations between Confederate whites and blacks has carried down into the present day. These two buddies, photographed by the author, recently attended an event honoring Confederate General Nathan Bedford Forrest at Chapel Hill, Tennessee. Dressed in period style Rebel uniforms, they are posing in front of an original outbuilding that still stands on the grounds of the Nathan Bedford Forrest Boyhood Home. Can we have any doubt that, had they lived at the time, these two young men would have wanted to join the Confederate army and fight alongside their fathers, brothers, and friends?

Such dedication and courage was profoundly appreciated by all Southerners, whatever their race. Stone memorials were often erected across the South by whites in honor of "faithful servants." In 1899 one such Confederate monument was described in the following manner:

> Four steps of masonry support a marble pedestal, on which is a square shaft for inscriptions.
> On the south side is inscribed:

1860
Dedicated to
the faithful Slaves
who, loyal to a sacred trust,
toiled for the support
of the army with matchless
devotion, and with sterling
fidelity guarded our defenseless
homes, women, and children during
the struggle for the principles
of our Confederate States of America.
1865

> On the east side, in a receding panel, appears a log under a shade tree, whereon rests one of the faithful slaves, his hat on the ground, shirt open in front, with a scythe and at rest. Before him are shocks of grain.
> On the north side is the following:

> "1895. Erected by Samuel E. White, in grateful memory of earlier days, with the approval of the Jefferson Davis Memorial Association."

> There are added names of some faithful slaves.
> On the west side, in a receding panel, appears a farmer's mansion, and on the front steps sits an "old black mammy" with a white child in her arms, both of whom are in loving embrace, while in the foreground are the baby's wagon and other playthings. Above this square shaft is a tall obelisk of pure white marble.[747]

A Confederate reunion of the men of General Nathan Bedford Forrest's Escort, about 1890. One of the most dangerous and successful military outfits ever organized, this specialized, hard-charging, lightning fast, racially integrated cavalry unit was both respected and feared by Yankee troops—who were racially segregated under Lincoln's bigoted military rules. Near the center a woman is holding up a large Confederate Third National Flag with the words "Forrest's Escort" on it. Three of Forrest's 65 black Confederate soldiers are in attendance. No signs of racism here. Just a band of color-blind brothers honoring one another and the Confederate Cause.

The truth is that despite the North's effort to destroy, suppress, and expunge them, thousands of records of black Confederate soldiers have been preserved. These include courageous African-American servicemen like Joe Warren, Fielding Rennolds, Henry Love, Hiram Kendall, and Dan Humphreys, all of the Fifth Tennessee Infantry.

Then there was Monroe Gooch of Davidson County, Tennessee, who served in the Forty-Fifth Tennessee Infantry under Confederate Captain William Sykes. On one occasion during the War Gooch was given a pass to go home, where he could have remained had he so desired. But being true to the Confederate Cause, he returned to his infantry until the final surrender in 1865. After the conflict it is said that Gooch was proud to be a Confederate veteran.

I have a personal connection to one black Rebel soldier: Private Louis Napoleon Nelson, whose grandson, African-American educator Nelson W. Winbush, M.Ed., wrote the foreword to my bestselling book, *Everything You Were Taught About the Civil War is Wrong, Ask a Southerner!* Private Nelson was born March 15, 1847, and served with Company

Monroe Gooch of Davidson County, Tennessee, black Confederate soldier.

M, Seventh Cavalry, Tennessee, for the entire duration of the War. He worked in various capacities, from body guard and cook, to forager and armed soldier. He fought in some of the War's most momentous battles, including Shiloh, Lookout Mountain, Brice's Cross Roads, and Vicksburg.[748]

Like nearly all Southern "slaves," Nelson returned to live with his former white owners (in his case, the Oldhams in Lauderdale County, Tennessee) after the War. The only known official black chaplain in the C.S. army, he belonged to the John Sutherland Camp, United Confederate Veterans, and attended 39 postwar Confederate reunions proudly dressed in his uniform and medals. He died on August 25, 1934, at the age of 87, a true unreconstructed Confederate-American patriot to the end.[749]

Along with an abundance of military records and photos of black Confederates dating back to the War itself, entire books have been written on this subject. Do we really need to continually go over this ground just to placate South-haters? At this point only mean-spiritedness and ignorance can account for individuals who are unaware of the reality of the Confederacy's 1 million African-American soldiers.[750]

Confederate Private Louis Napoleon Nelson, the only known black chaplain in the Rebel army, fought in numerous battles and attended 39 Confederate reunions after the War. At his funeral in 1934 his coffin was draped with a Confederate Battle Flag. His memory and legacy are still being honored by Confederate descendants to this day.

A photo of a section of the famous Confederate Memorial at Arlington National Cemetery that has been banished from our mainstream history books. Why? Because it shows an armed black Confederate soldier (center rear) proudly marching off to war, side by side with his white Southern brothers. Proof in stone of the African-American Confederate!

AFRICAN-AMERICAN SUPPORT
OF THE CONFEDERACY

WHAT YOU WERE TAUGHT: No black man or woman ever aided the Confederate Cause.

THE TRUTH: Actually, nearly all of them did. Let us look at the authentic records.

Of the South's 3.5 million black servants,[751] the "vast majority,"[752] 95 percent (19 out of 20), stayed in the South during the War, all the while maintaining their loyalty to Dixie.[753] Ignoring Lincoln's fake proclamation of freedom, they instead pledged their allegiance to their home states, to the South, and to their white families.[754] Remaining at home they ran their owner's farms, grew food, produced provisions for the Confederate military, and protected their master's family and property while he was away on the battlefield.[755] In 1910 Pastor Benjamin F. Riley noted that the Southern black servant

sustained the armies of the Confederacy during the great Civil War; he was the guardian of the helpless women and children of the South while the husbands and sons were at the distant front doing battle . . .; against him was not a whisper of unfaithfulness or of disloyalty during all this trying and bloody period; when the land was invaded by the [Northern] armies . . . he remained faithful still, and often at great personal risk of life, secreted from the invader [his owner's] . . . horses and mules, and buried the treasures of the family that they might not fall into the hands of the enemies of the whites . . .; in many thousands of instances he declined to accept freedom when it was offered by the invading army, preferring to remain loyal and steadfast to the charge committed to him by the absent master, all this and more the Negro slave did. There was not a day during the trying period of the Civil War when he might not have disbanded the Southern armies. An outbreak on his part against the defenseless homes of the South would have occasioned the utter dissolution of the Southern armies, and turned the anxious faces of the veterans in gray toward their homes. But no Southern soldier ever dreamed of the possibility of a condition like this. So far as his home was concerned, it was not any apprehension of the unfaithfulness of the slaves which occasioned the slightest alarm.[756]

This romanticized illustration shows grateful blacks thanking John Brown (center) one last time before he ascends the steps to his death on the gallows. Actually, African-Americans did not thank Brown for anything, none joined his cause, and most, like former Northern slave Frederick Douglass, pronounced him insane. Lincoln, however, using the Emancipation Proclamation, later adopted parts of Brown's monstrous plan to destroy the South through invasion, violence, destabilization, and attempts to foment slave rebellions. Both plots failed. There was not a single slave insurrection across Dixie between 1859 (when Brown attacked Harpers Ferry) and 1865 (the end of the Civil War), and Brown's life ended in the hangman's noose, while Lincoln's came to a close with an assassin's bullet.

In an effort to raise money for the Southern war effort many Southern slaves and freemen bought Confederate bonds.[757] Others held bake sales and auctions, while still others donated clothing and other goods in an effort to help support Confederate soldiers.[758] Those untold thousands of African-Americans who marched off to resist Lincoln and his illegal invaders, proudly stood up for "ole Jeff Davis," wearing placards on their hats that read: "We will die by the South."[759] Among them were tens of thousands who served the Confederacy as teamsters, bridge and road builders, musicians, nurses, carpenters, smithies, couriers, lookouts, and cooks[760]—many from among the last occupation who had been trained by the best culinary schools in Paris.[761]

Sometimes black support for the South and the Confederacy was not so obvious. In 1895 the following article, entitled "Chattanooga Negroes Compliment a Confederate," appeared in *Confederate Veteran* magazine:

> *W. P. McClatchy, Commander N. B. Forrest Camp, Chattanooga, Tenn., has been honored by the negro men of that city. They presented him with a gold-headed cane. Addresses were made by J. W. White and J. G. Burge, negro lawyers there.* Comrade McClatchy held the office of City Recorder (Judge of the City Court) last year, and at the expiration of his term he was greatly surprised when these men presented it as a token of their friendship and esteem, and for *the just and impartial manner in which he had dealt with their race.* He asked them why they had "U.C.V. 1861—65," engraved on it, and they replied that they wished to emphasize that while he was a Southern man, and a Confederate soldier, he had administered the law justly and impartially. *The N. B. Forrest Camp hearing of this compliment to its commander, by a rising vote thanked the donors for their expression of confidence in and esteem for a Confederate soldier, and a Southern Democrat* [then the Conservative Party] who had "administered the law, in wisdom, justice and moderation."
>
> The inscription reads: "U.C.V., 1861—1865, J. W. and J. G. to W. P. McC., 1895." Which stands for United Confederate Veteran 1861 to 1865, J. B. White and J. G. Burge to W. P. McClatchy, 1895.
>
> In a note the comrade [a white Confederate veteran] says: "I never had a present in my life that I appreciated anymore than this. Every true Southerner understands and appreciates a good negro, while *the negro understands that the Southern man is the best friend he has. But for the meddling of people [that is, Yankees] who really care nothing for the negro, but who are prejudiced against the South, there would be no friction between the races.*"[762]

An 1896 article by a former white Confederate soldier relates the following tribute to "faithful George," a loyal Confederate African-American during Lincoln's War. Reminiscing, the author writes,

> revives the memory of a faithful man in black who followed me through from First Manassas. Leesburg, where he assisted in

capturing the guns we took from Baker, to the Peninsular, the Seven Days before Richmond, Fredericksburg, the bombardment of the city December 11, and the battle, two days after, at Marye's Heights; to Chancellorsville, the storming of Harper's Ferry, and the terrible struggle at Sharpsburg (Antietam now), and last, Gettysburg. Here *he lost his life by his fidelity to me—his "young marster" and companion.* We were reared together on "de ole plantation" in "Massippi."

I was wounded in the Peach Orchard at Gettysburg on the second day. The fourth day found us retreating in a cold, drizzling rain. George had found an ambulance, in which I, Sergeant Major of the Seventeenth Mississippi, and Col. Holder of that regiment (still on this side of the river), and an officer of the Twenty-first Mississippi, whose name escapes me, embarked for the happy land of Dixie. All day long we moved slower than any funeral train over the pike, only getting eight miles—to Cashtown. When night came I had to dismount from loss of blood and became a prisoner in a strange land. On the next day about sundown faithful George, who still clung to me, told me that the Yankees were coming down the road from Gettysburg and were separating the "black folks from dar marsters"; that *he didn't want to be separated from me* and for me to go on to prison and he'd slip over the mountains and join the regiment in retreat, and we'd meet again "ober de ribber," meaning the Potomac. We had crossed at Williamsport.

I insisted on George accepting his freedom and joining a settlement of free negroes in the vicinity of Gettysburg, which we had passed through in going up to the battle. But he would have none of it; he wanted to stay with me always. I had him hide my sword, break it off at the hilt and stick it in a crack of the barn (that yet stands in the village) to the left of the road going away from Gettysburg, where I, with about thirty other wounded, lay. I can yet see that faithful black face and the glint of the blade as the dying rays of that day's sun flashed upon them. A canteen of water and some hard tack was the last token of his kindly care for me.

In the spring of 1865, I saw a messmate from whom I was separated on that battlefield, and he told me the fate of poor, faithful George. He had gotten through the lines safely and was marching in the rear of our retreating command, when met by a Northern lady, who had a son in our command, whom George, by chance, happened to know. He was telling her of her son, who was safe as a prisoner, when some men in blue came up. George ran and they shot and killed him. He was dressed in gray and they took him for a combatant. The lady had him buried and then joined her son in prison. She told my messmate of this and he told to the boys in camp the fate of *the truest and best friend I ever had*. George's prediction will come true—I feel we will meet again "over the river."[763]

These 17th-Century British galleons, sailing under the auspices of England's Royal African Company, were specifically outfitted for the transatlantic slave trade, and were responsible for bringing tens of thousands of African slaves into North America and the West Indies (the Caribbean). Ships sailing under Britain's sister organization, the East India Company, busied themselves transporting slaves from Madagascar to India and the East Indies (Asia). Britain's deep interest in the slave trade was later imposed on the American colonies against the wishes of Southerners like George Washington, Thomas Jefferson, and George Mason. This additional affliction on the already over-taxed colonies helped inspire both the American Revolutionary War in 1775 and the Declaration of Independence in 1776.

The following 1915 article by Joseph A. Mudd is entitled "The Confederate Negro":

The Confederate negro is the proudest being on earth. A few weeks ago I was standing at the counter of the water office, Municipal Building, in Washington, when in came a negro who, standing near by, began his business with one of the clerks. He was rather shabbily dressed, but evidently one of the "old stock," as black as ink . . . eyes beaming with intelligence and a great depth of human sympathy, a countenance one loves to rest one's gaze upon, and with a bearing of modest and courteous dignity. His business over, I said to him: "How long have you been in Washington?" "Since 1870, suh." "Where did you come from?" I could see his chest swelling, and I knew the answer before it was spoken. "From Ferginny, suh." *"Were your people in the war?"* "Yes, suh," *with a smile of enthusiasm and a bow that bespoke reverence for the memories of the olden days.* "They tell me you people 'fit' [fought] some." I could almost see the lightning dart from his eyes as he straightened himself up. *"'Fit?' Why, dey outfit [outfought] de world, suh; never did whip us, suh. If dey hadn't starved us out, we'd been fightin' yit."* As he *passed me going out of the office he said: "I was wid 'em foh [four] years, suh. I cahd [carried] my young master off de field once when I din't think he'd live till I got him to de doctor; but he's living yit."* I did not tell him I was a Confederate soldier, and he didn't seem to care. He knew what he was, and that was enough.

I have never seen a Confederate negro that was not full of pride in his record. I believe this sentiment is an evidence of his patriotism as well as a testimony of his love and loyalty to his white folks. During the last year of the war I was on duty as assistant surgeon at Howard's Grove Hospital, Richmond. There were about seventy-five young negro men and about the same number of young women employed as laborers in the three divisions of the hospital. *In our division there was a bright young [black] fellow whose avowals of patriotism were so frequent and intense that we suspected his sincerity. When the proposition came to enlist the slaves,* we accidentally heard that a meeting was to be held at night outside the hospital grounds to consider the matter and that this young fellow would make a speech. Taking care that no white person attended, two or three of us sneaked up in the darkness to where we could hear without being seen. *He was speaking, and for a half hour we listened to a most eloquent and earnest plea for every [black] man to enlist in our glorious cause and help to drive the ruthless [Yankee] invader from the sacred soil of Virginia.*[764]

The following three articles appeared in a 1912 edition of *Confederate Veteran.* The first is entitled "Master and His Faithful Slave," by Samuel Coleman, Sixth Alabama Cavalry:

This contribution records a deed done during the war by one in the humblest walks of life, *as heroic in character as any ever performed by the men who to-day proudly wear the victor's cross of honor.* The facts were brought more vividly to mind by an accidental meeting with one of the actors recently. In the lobby of a hotel in Houston I noticed a tall, heavily built man wearing the cross of honor. I spoke to him as a comrade, and learned that he was a member of the staff of Brig. Gen. James H. Clanton, of Alabama. I then recognized him as Baxter Smith, ordnance officer of the command, now a practicing physician of Bay City, Tex.

Well, to the story. On the morning of July 14, 1864, a detachment of the 6th Alabama Cavalry, about one hundred and fifteen men, under the command of General Clanton, encountered a largely superior force of the Rousseau raiders at Greensport Ferry, on the Coosa River. Colonel Livingstone, with about two hundred and fifty men, was holding back the enemy's main body at Ten Island Ford. It was imperative for us to hold the road until reenforcements could reach us; otherwise the Oxford Iron Works, upon which the Confederate foundries at Selma, Ala., depended, would be destroyed.

The men had been well posted behind trees and rocks on the slope of a thickly wooded hill, and the road extended along the river bluff. The firing on both sides was spirited. The enemy, in spite of superior numbers, could not drive our boys from their position; but they seemed determined to gain possession of the road, and they formed a heavy column with which they could pass our thin line and clear the road before them. General Clanton and two of his staff officers, Capt. R. A. Abercrombie and "Bat" Smith, also Tommy Judkins, were standing in the middle of the road dismounted. A few feet away on the side of the road were five or six young fellows attached to headquarters and eight or ten boys of the 6th Alabama Cavalry, also dismounted. I was behind a large tree, a few feet in advance of the General, and had a good view of everything in front. A heavy column of the enemy on foot was coming around the curve of the road, about two hundred yards distant. Suddenly just behind me I heard a loud, fierce yell, and the two staff officers, followed by the headquarters' boys and the small squad of the 6th Alabama Cavalry, dashed at the enemy, who quickly poured a deadly fire upon them and then halted.

Abercrombie and Tommy Judkins were killed. Bat Smith and the handful of boys close behind him kept on. In a few seconds Smith fell headlong upon his face and then turned over on his back. The effect of the enemy's fire was appalling. Not one of that gallant little band was left standing. *The charge was reckless in the extreme, but it illustrated the spirit and high courage of our soldiers. That feat of daring was followed by another of the lowliest and humblest man there present. A tall, strapping, young negro named Griffin approached General Clanton and asked: "General, where is Marse Bat?" The General pointed down the road and said: "There near the enemy's line dead." Griffin at once started down the road. He was called back, but did not heed. He sped on in the face of that heavy fire, took up the wounded young officer, and carried him in his arms from the field. He came up the road for a few yards, then stepped into the woods and came out again on the road just where the General was standing. "Is he dead, Griffin?" asked General Clanton. "I don't know, sir," he replied. "Mammy was his nurse, and I am the older. I promised mammy to take care of him and to bring him back to her, and I am going to carry him home."*

Simple words, but how much do they convey! An untutored

negro slave carrying out his mother's commands in behalf of her nurseling at the risk of his own life! I have often thought of that day, and the scene is vivid. I can see the deathly pale face of the unconscious and sorely wounded young officer as he was being carried to safety in the arms of his faithful slave.

If some of our Northern neighbors could have witnessed this scene, they might form some conception of the devotion existing in the old days South between master and servant.[765]

Just as there was no such thing as a "Northern abolition ship," there was no such thing as a "Southern slave ship." All legal, and nearly all illegal, shipments of African slaves came to the U.S. aboard Yankee slave vessels, designed by Yankee engineers, constructed by Yankee shipbuilders, fitted out by Yankee riggers, piloted by Yankee ship captains, manned by Yankee crews, launched from Yankee marine ports, funded by Yankee businessmen, and supported by the Yankee population. It is now time to put the responsibility for American slavery where it belongs, instead of on a Southern scapegoat!

This article is entitled "Gratitude of a Faithful Servant," and was penned by "Black Hawk," a former slave and black Confederate soldier from Woodstock, Virginia:

I thank you for putting my picture in your magazine. *I am proud of my war record.* I was given when a young man by my old master, Samuel C. Williams, who was a member of the Virginia Secession Convention, to his oldest son, who was then Lieut. James H. Williams, of Chew's Battery, and *I stood by him and his brothers until the close of the war. I was taken prisoner twice, captured once with the watches and money of our boys and others of the Williams mess upon my person, given into my care when the battle began. I escaped and returned with watches and money all safe.*

The picture you published was taken while Dr. Averitt was on a visit to Mrs. James H. Williams at Woodstock, Va. I was not Dr. Averitt's camp servant, nor was he ever a member of the Williams mess. As far as I know, Dr. William McGuire, of Winchester, Va., L. B. Morel, of Florida, and myself are the only living members of that mess. Rev. Dr. Averitt was often our guest.

Like the rest of the veterans, I am growing old; but I am with my people in Woodstock, where I was born. [766]

The courage, strength, hard work, fidelity, and friendship of the African-American Southerner inspired Dixie's European-American community to memorialize him in stone. The following 1912 article is entitled "Honor for the Old-Time Negro," by John Paulette:

The time is not far distant when a monument will be erected in Montgomery, Ala., or Richmond, Va., as a tribute to the memory of the old-time Southern negro. The loyal devotion of the men and women who were slaves has had no equal in all history. They took care of the women and children whose natural protectors were with Lee and Jackson, Forrest and Joe Johnston, and were faithful to the trust.

Women during the great war did not fear to ride alone through large plantations to give directions as to the crops. These women were protected and never outraged. It was the coming of the carpetbagger, with his social equality teachings, that caused many negroes to become brutes. The old-time negro will soon be but a memory, and while a remnant survive an imposing monument should be erected as a tribute to their faithfulness. It should be a monument worth fifty thousand dollars. This money could be easily raised if the religious and secular papers in the South would take up the matter in the spirit that the cause merits. [767]

In 1913 Mrs. Edward Carter of Warrenton, Virginia, penned this brief article entitled "Build Monument to Faithful Slaves":

I see in the September *Confederate Veteran* the suggestion of a monument being erected in memory of the old-time Southern negroes. *I hope very much that such a monument will be erected.* I believe *there would be a liberal response throughout the entire South* to such an appeal. *No people could be more faithful and more deserving of appreciation.* I have the *deepest veneration* for their memory. Of all the monuments erected in the South, none would appeal to my heart more feelingly. Such a monument would also show to the world the devotion which existed in the South between master and servant. [768]

In 1904 Mrs. C. Gilliland Aston of Asheville, North Carolina, wrote this article entitled "A Monument to the Faithful Old Slaves":

My Dear Sisters: Will not every one of you raise your voice with mine in making amends for a long-neglected duty in rearing a monument to our faithful old slaves? *Of all people that dwell upon the earth, I think these deserve the grandest monument.* Soon all this generation will have passed away. Let us hasten with the work while some of us still survive. Confederate veterans have for some time been speaking of raising a monument to the Southern women. We appreciate this, and thank them for their remembrance of our self-denials and hardships which tried women's souls; but what else could have been expected of us when our dear ones were at the front? While this was the case we felt we were enduring this for sacred ties of kindred and country.

How different with the faithful slaves! They did it for love of masters, mistresses, and their children. How nobly did they perform their tasks! Their devotion to their owners, their faithfulness in performing their labors and caring for us during these terribly disastrous years, and their kindness at the surrender, while we were powerless and helpless, have never been surpassed or equaled. At the time of the surrender we were entirely defenseless.

Our noble, famished, ragged patriots were still away from their homes, and among us was a band of robbers [Union soldiers] who were bad counselors to our slaves. Their kindness and their devotion to us was the most beautiful this earth has ever witnessed. From the Mason and Dixon line to the Gulf and from the Atlantic to the Gulf there was not a massacre, house-burning, or one of those unmentionable crimes which are now so common in the whole country. Think of this; 'tis wonderful. Our gratitude to God and love for the old-time servants should be boundless. Who will say they do not deserve the greatest monument that has ever been erected?

This acknowledgment from us to them of our appreciation of kindness and devotion shown by them to their

The whip! Where would Yankee mythology be without the whip? It is one of the mainstays of the entire artificial structure, and once it is removed the unstable edifice falls like the house of cards that it is. American society has been so indoctrinated by Northern anti-South propaganda that most people will assume that this early illustration depicts a white Southern slave owner whipping a Southern black slave. In fact, slave whipping was rare and strongly discouraged across the Old South, and was even illegal in most areas. Here we have the true "Lord of the Lash"; not a Southern slaveholder, but a Northern one. For the tormentor in this image is a white Bostonian and his naked victim—bound by cordage to a tree—is a black Yankee slave from Massachusetts. Such a scene should surprise no one. American slavery got its start in the Bay State, and it is the Northeastern U.S. where blacks had the least legal protection, and where they suffered under the nation's toughest and most inhumane Black Codes. Indeed, contrary to Yankee myth, America's Black Codes were invented, developed, and first implemented in the Northeast.

former owners would be in their last days a beautiful thought. *To those of their race of the present generation it would verify the character of the Southern people, their former owners, and also show the true relation that existed between master and servant.* Would it not be an act of justice for the women of the South to ask our noble men if we may not be permitted to turn this monument over to those who, if not more deserving, are equally so with our Southern sisters? I would suggest that when it is erected a tablet might be inserted bearing this inscription: "Given by the Confederate Veterans as a memorial to the women of the South, and given by them in memory of the faithfulness of our former servants."[769]

In 1894 C. M. Douglas of Columbia, South Carolina, wrote this article called "A Notable Colored Man":

One of the best-known freedmen in Columbia, S. C., is old William Rose, who has been messenger for the Governor's office under every Democratic administration since 1876. . . . He is now eighty years of age, but is still active and vigorous enough to be at his post of duty every day, and *nothing delights him more than to take part in any Confederate demonstration.*

William Rose was born in Charleston in 1813, and was a slave of the Barrett family of that city. He was brought to Columbia when only twelve years old, and was taught the trades of carpenter and tinner. In his younger days he went out to the Florida War as a drummer in Capt. Elmore's company, the Richland Volunteers, an organization which is still in existence, and which has made a proud record for itself in three wars. Subsequently he went through the Mexican War as a servant for Capt. (afterwards Col.) Butler, of the famous Palmetto Regiment. But *the service in which he takes the greatest pride was that in the days of the Confederacy.* He was the body servant of that distinguished Carolinian, Gen. Maxey Gregg, and *as soon as he heard that his beloved master had fallen on the field at Fredricksburg he rushed to his side as fast as a horse could take him, and remained with him until the end came.* His description of the death of Gen. Gregg, of his reconciliation with Stonewall Jackson, and his heroic last message to the Governor of South Carolina are pathetic in the extreme and are never related by the old man without emotion. William saw [Grover] Cleveland inaugurated, and was present at the unveiling of the soldiers' monument at Richmond, and at *the recent grand Confederate reunion at Birmingham. From the latter he returned laden with badges which he cherishes as souvenirs of the occasion. For sixty years he has been identified with the Richland Volunteers, and they never parade without him.* About two years ago he presented a gold medal to the company, which is now shot for as an annual prize. He never forgets Memorial Day, and no 10th of May has passed by since the close of the war without some tribute from him placed on the Gregg monument at Elmwood. *Recently he has been given a small pension by the United States for services in the Florida War.*

Old "Uncle" William is of a class fast passing away. They will not have successors, but all the world may witness benefactors in Southern whites until the last of them crosses the "dark river."[770]

New South proponent Henry Woodfin Grady of Georgia spoke the following words during an address delivered at the Dallas, Texas, State Fair on October 26, 1887. Though not a friend of the Old South, still he could say:

History has no parallel to the faith kept by the negro in the South during the war. Often five hundred negroes to a single white man, and yet through these dusky throngs the [white] women and children walked in safety, and the unprotected homes rested in peace. Unmarshaled, the black [Southern] battalions moved patiently to the fields in the morning to feed the [Confederate] armies their idleness would have starved, and at night gathered anxiously at the big house to "hear the news from marster" . . . Everywhere humble and kindly, the bodyguard of the helpless, the rough companion of the little ones, the observant friend, the silent sentry in his lowly cabin, the shrewd counselor, and, when the dead came home, a mourner at the open grave.

A thousand [slave] torches would have disbanded every Southern army, but not one was lighted. When the master, going to . . . war . . . said to his slave, "I leave my home and loved ones in your charge," the tenderness between man and master stood disclosed. And when the slave held that charge sacred through storm and temptation, he gave new meaning to faith and loyalty. I rejoice that when freedom came to him after years of waiting, it was all the sweeter because the black hands from which the shackles fell were stainless of a single crime against the helpless ones confided to his care.[771]

In response to Grady's comments Charles Morris writes:

These few words speak volumes for the relations of amity which existed between the [Southern] whites and blacks before the war, and go far to prove that the stories of [rare] ill treatment of the slaves had to do only with local instances. In the annals of the manufacturing industries of the

North it is highly probable that examples of cruel treatment of the laboring class were much more common than on the plantations of the South, though it did not take the same form.

The feeling which the blacks entertained toward their master's family was reciprocated, the relation between them being largely a patriarchal one, with much warm affection between the ruling and the serving races.[772]

The Southern "Aristocratic Planter"—one of whom is shown here with his wife and daughter visiting the servants' quarters on his plantation in the 1700s—was the rarest of all slave owners in Dixie, comprising a mere 0.03 percent of the total white Southern population in 1860. In order to besmirch the South, however, pro-North historians paint him as the "typical" Southern slave owner.

In regard to the sentiments of North and South in this particular, A. K. McClure writes:

The prejudice of race is five-fold stronger in the North than in the South. The Northern people have no love for the black man, and even those who battled for his freedom and enfranchisement, as a rule, cherish vastly more profound prejudice of race than do the Southern people. While the North maintains its deep prejudice of race, the people of the South have a general and strong sympathy for the negro. Nearly all of them have played with the negro in childhood, have been nursed by the black "mammy" and have grown up with more or less affection for them.

Classify it in what type of affection you may, it is none the less *an affection that tempers the hard, unyielding prejudice of race that prevails in the North.*[773]

In her 1892 book *Life in Dixie During the War*, white authoress Mary A. H. Gay revealed the tender respect and friendship that existed between the races across the South, as well the devotion of the typical Southern African-American to the Southern Cause—even among black children. In the following anecdote she describes the death of Toby, one of her family's young house servants, who had been ill for several days:

I sat there alone by that dying boy. Not a movement on his part betrayed pain. His breathing was hard and at intervals spasmodic. With tender hand I changed the position of his head, and for a little while he seemed to breathe easier. But it was only for a little while, and then it was evident that soon he would cease to breathe at all. I went to my mother and waked her gently and told her I thought the end was near with Toby, and hurried back to him. I thought him dead even then, but after an interval he breathed again and again, and all was over. The life had gone back to the God who gave it, and I doubt not but that it will live with Him forever.

The pathos of the scene can never be understood by those who have not witnessed one similar to it in all its details, and I will not attempt to describe it. No time-piece marked the hour, but it was about midnight, I ween, when death set the spirit of that youthful negro free. Not a kindred being nor a member of his own race was near to lay loving hand upon him, or to prepare his little body for burial. *We stood and gazed upon him as he lay in death in that desolated house, and thought of his fidelity and loving interest in our cause and its defenders, and of his faithful service in our efforts to save something from vandal [Yankee] hands, and the fountain of tears was broken up and we wept with a peculiar grief over that lifeless form.*

My mother was the first to become calm, and she came very near me and said, as if afraid to trust her voice: "Wouldn't it be well to ask Eliza Williams [a neighbor's trusted black servant] and others to come and 'lay him out?'" Before acting on this suggestion I went into another room and waked Telitha [the family's young black servant girl] and took her into the chamber of death. A dim and glimmering light prevented her from taking in the full import of the scene at first; but I took her near the couch, and, pointing to him, I said: "Dead! – Dead!!"

She repeated interrogatively, and when she fully realized that such was the case, her cries were pitiable, oh, so pitiable.

I sank down upon the floor and waited for the paroxysm of grief to subside, and then went to her and made her understand that I was going out and that she must stay with her mistress until I returned. An hour later, under the skillful manipulation of good "Eliza Williams"—known throughout Decatur as Mrs. Ami Williams' faithful servant—and one or two others whom she brought with her, Toby was robed in a nice white suit of clothes prepared for the occasion by the faithful hands of his "Miss Polly," whom he had loved well and who had cared for him in his orphanage.

We had had intimation that the Federals would again occupy Decatur [Georgia], and as soon as day dawned I went to see Mr. Robert Jones, Sen., and got him to make a coffin for Toby, and I then asked [servants] "Uncle Mack" and "Henry"—now known as Decatur's Henry Oliver—to dig the grave. Indeed, these two men agreed to attend to the matter of his burial. After consultation with my mother, it was agreed that that should take place as soon as all things were in readiness. Mr. Jones made a pretty, well-shaped coffin out of good heart pine, and the two faithful negro men already mentioned prepared with care the grave. When all was in readiness, the dead boy was placed in the coffin and borne to the grave by very gentle hands.

Next to the pall-bearers my mother and myself and Telitha fell in line, and then followed the few negroes yet remaining in the town, and that funeral cortege was complete.

At the grave an unexpected and most welcome stranger appeared. "Uncle Mack" told me he was a minister, and would perform the funeral service— and grandly did he do it. The very soul of prayer seemed embodied in this negro preacher's invocation; nor did he forget Toby's "nurses," and every consolation and blessing was besought for them. And thus our Toby received a Christian burial.[774]

The following article, entitled "A Black Skin, But White Soul," must be read without the Liberal-biased presentism that is ubiquitous in our modern historically inaccurate, politically correct textbooks. Written by W. T. Gass in 1904, it concerns one of his black servants, a "loyal old Southern plantation negro," "Uncle" Jim Gass of Bonham, Texas:

The announcement of the sudden death of this faithful and honest old man was a cause for tears and sorrow to the writer. The faithful negro carried us around in his arms and on his sturdy back and shoulders in infancy, and as we grew older taught us to swim, to fish, to hunt, and to ride. He was black, but he had a whiter soul and purer life than hundreds of boys and men we have known with white skins. When the war clouds of 1861 came, although but a boy of fifteen, I enlisted in the Confederate service. *Jim came to me and said: "Marse Will, I want to go wid you to de war. I'll stay wid you and never leave you."* My mother was a widow, father having died a short time before, and I explained to Jim that we both couldn't leave home at once; that one of us would have to stay to care for her and four brothers and sisters younger than myself. The argument was unanswerable. "Dat's a fact, Marse Will; I specks I'm de one to stay."

Looking back through the mist and tears of forty-one years, *it is a melancholy pleasure to testify to the faithfulness of our trusty old slave and companion of boyhood, for he was as true to his trust as was any Confederate soldier true to his flag during all those four years of war, blood, fire, and blockade. And when, in May, 1865, I returned home, I found Jim still at his post of duty. With two horses and a wagon he had been making numerous trips to Shreveport, taking down flour and trading it for sugar and molasses, helping my widowed mother to keep the wolf from the door, Jim being her mainstay and chief purveyor of the commissary department. Peace to his ashes!*[775]

In his 1900 book *Up From Slavery,* former Virginia slave Booker T. Washington provides the following facts about Southern African-Americans and their behavior and attitudes during Lincoln's War:

One may get the idea, from what I have said, that there was bitter feeling toward the white people on the part of my race, because of the fact that most of the white population was away fighting in a war which would result in keeping the Negro in slavery if the South was successful.[776] *In the case of the slaves on our place this was not true, and it was not true of any large portion of the slave population in the South where the Negro was treated with anything like decency.* During the Civil War one of my young [white] masters was killed, and two were severely wounded. I recall the feeling of sorrow which existed among the slaves when they heard of the death of "Mars' Billy." *It was no sham sorrow, but real.* Some of the slaves had nursed "Mars' Billy"; others had played with him when he was a child. "Mars' Billy" had begged for mercy in the case of others when the overseer or master was thrashing them.

The sorrow in the slave quarter was only second to that in the "big house." When the two young masters were brought home wounded, the sympathy of the slaves was shown in many ways. *They were just as anxious to assist in the nursing as the family relatives of* the wounded. *Some of the slaves would even beg for the privilege of sitting up at night to nurse their wounded masters. This tenderness and sympathy on the part of those held in bondage was a result of their kindly and generous nature. In order to defend and protect the women and children who were left on the plantations when the white males went to war, the slaves would have laid down their lives.*

Booker T. Washington statue, Tuskegee University, Tuskegee, Alabama. The stone inscription on the memorial reads: "Booker T. Washington: 1856 to 1915. He lifted the veil of ignorance from his people and pointed the way to progress through education and industry."

The slave who was selected to sleep in the "big house" during the absence of the males was considered to have the place of honour. *Any one attempting to harm "young Mistress" or "old Mistress" during the night would have had to cross the dead body of the slave to do so.* I do not know how many have noticed it, but I think that it will be found to be true that *there are few instances, either in slavery or freedom, in which a member of my race has been known to betray a specific trust.*

As a rule, not only did the members of my race entertain no feelings of bitterness against the whites before and during the war, but there are many instances of Negroes tenderly caring for their former masters and mistresses who for some reason have become poor and dependent since the war. I know of instances where the former masters of slaves have for years been supplied with money by their former slaves to keep them from suffering. I have known of still other cases in which the former slaves have assisted in the education of the descendants of their former owners. I know of a case on a large plantation in the South in which a young white man, the son of the former owner of the estate, has become so reduced in purse and self-control by reason of drink that he is a pitiable creature; and yet, notwithstanding the poverty of the coloured people themselves on this plantation, they have for years supplied this young white man with the necessities of life. One sends him a little coffee or sugar, another a little meat, and so on. Nothing that the coloured people possess is too good for the son of "old Mars' Tom," who will perhaps never be permitted to suffer while any remain on the place who knew directly or indirectly of "old Mars' Tom."

I have said that there are few instances of a member of my race betraying a specific trust. One of the best illustrations of this which I know of is in the case of an ex-slave from Virginia whom I met not long ago in a little town in the state of Ohio. I found that this man had made a contract with his master, two or three years previous to the Emancipation Proclamation, to the effect that the slave was to be permitted to buy himself, by paying so much per year for his body; and while he was paying for himself, he was to be permitted to labour where and for whom he pleased. Finding that he could secure better wages in Ohio, he went there. When freedom came, he was still in debt to his master some three hundred dollars. Notwithstanding that the Emancipation Proclamation freed him from any obligation to his master, this black man walked the greater portion of the distance back to where his old master lived in Virginia, and placed the last dollar, with interest, in his hands. In talking to me about this, the man told me that he knew that he did not have to pay the debt, but that he had given his word to his master, and his word he had never broken. He felt that he could not enjoy his freedom till he had fulfilled his promise.[777]

The following obituary of black Southern servant Albert Peete appeared in *Confederate Veteran* magazine in June 1912:

Albert Peete was buried on March 6, 1912, from the Colored Baptist Church of Nashville, Tenn. *He was [Confederate] Gen. William B. Bate's cook for forty-five years. He was true and honest.*
When the Second Tennessee Regiment [CSA] was in

Huntsville, Ala., the [Confederate] soldiers gave all their money to General Bate to take care of for them. He took Albert with him one night and buried half of the money, placing the other half under the floor at Martin's store.

Albert ripped up the floor and placed it back [with the other buried half]. Every cent of the money was returned to the soldiers after the war. The Yankees dug deep all over the yard looking for hidden treasure; and when they came near the crape myrtle tree at the front porch, it was feared they would find the money, but they missed it.[778]

Albert Peete, a faithful Southern servant and loyal Confederate soldier, he was known to all as "true and honest."

The following tribute to black Southern servant Aleck Kean of Virginia, written by Judge George L. Christian of Richmond, appeared in the same issue of *Confederate Veteran*:

Early in November, 1911, three of us, ex-members of the second company of Richmond Howitzers during the war of the sixties, honored ourselves by attending the funeral services of Aleck Kean, which took place near Green Springs, in Louisa County. *The career of Aleck as an honest, upright, faithful servant and man was so conspicuous and unique that it deserves this public notice.*

When the war broke out, John Henry Vest, a son of the late James M. Vest, of Louisa, entered the Confederate army as a private in the second company of Richmond Howitzers, and took Aleck along as his body servant and cook, as was customary in those days. The "Renfrew" mess was soon formed with Aleck as the cook, and without hesitation I affirm that *he was the most faithful and efficient man in the performance of every duty pertaining to his sphere that I have ever known. His whole mind and soul seemed bent on trying to get and prepare something for his mess to eat; and if there was anything to be gotten honestly, Aleck always got the share which was coming to his mess, and he always had that share prepared in the shortest time possible and in the most delicious way in which it could have been prepared in camp. The comfort of having such a man as Aleck around us in those trying times can scarcely be described and certainly cannot be exaggerated.*

Young Mr. Vest (Aleck's young master) died in the fall of 1863, and after that Aleck, although he had offers to go to others or to return to his home, had become so attached to the members of the "Renfrew" mess that he refused to leave them, and, with his master's consent, remained with that mess up to the very last, when he surrendered with them near Appomattox. He was always loyal, true, brave, honest, and faithful not only to the members of his mess but to every man in the 2nd and 3rd Howitzers, all of whom knew, respected, and admired his fidelity and efficiency.

When the war ended, he went back to his old home. His old master, Mr. James M. Vest, gave him a little home a very short distance from his own dwelling, and it was there within hearing of his own people and always ready and willing to do their bidding that he spent the rest of his life. There was scarcely any one in all that community who was more respected by all the people, white and colored, than Aleck, and certainly no other deserved that respect and confidence more than he did. His funeral was largely attended both by white and colored, all of whom seemed anxious to attest by their presence the high regard in which he was held both as a man and a Christian.

Such a career of fidelity, loyalty, and devotion is worthy of being published to the world and ought to stimulate others, both white and black, to strive to follow his example. Nearly every year since the formation of the Howitzer Association an invitation to its annual banquet has been sent to Aleck, and whenever he was able to do so he attended. Every member of the association knew and respected him, and was glad to extend to him the cordial greeting which he received at these annual gatherings.[779]

In 1912, looking back to Lincoln's War, Henry Clinton Sydnor wrote about his experiences in the Old Dominion State as well. His story included the following revealing description of white/black relationships in the South, along with the latter's feeling about the Confederacy:

> After our [Confederate] soldiers left, [our servant] Uncle Tom
> came running in and said: "Marse . . ., dey is cum for sure. My
> God, Marster, de woods is full of dem Yankees! Well. Marster,
> I wants to tell you right now . . . *you is been a good marster to me, an'*
> *you can count on dis nigger stayin' with you till dis war am over."* And
> *how proud we all felt of Uncle Tom!*
>
> He was one of the most aristocratic of negroes. He
> seldom worked in the field, just attended to the carriage team and
> occasionally went to market. He had a consequential air, dressed
> well, and bossed it over the other darkies, who looked up to him
> with reverence and respect. I never knew him to open a gate or
> shut one when a negro boy was in sight. The negroes always rated
> their standing from the amount of slaves and money their masters
> possessed. *He always occupied the front seat in the gallery at the church;*
> *and when the carriage arrived at church, all the small boys stood around*
> *and watched him as he drove up.* He would open the carriage door, let
> down the steps, and help my mother and the children out, and with
> a wave of the hand fold up the steps, close the door, turn his team
> over to the footman and go in to church.[780]

Such Southern African-American sentiments extended to the battlefield. As we have seen, by most objective estimates at least 300,000 Southern blacks donned Rebel uniforms (when they were available), marched unhesitatingly onto the field of action, and fought fearlessly for the Southern Cause.[781] Those who were crack shots served as sharpshooters, helping to bring down thousands of Yankee interlopers.[782] But if we use Yankee General August Valentine Kautz's definition of a "private soldier,"[783] then as many as 1 million Southern blacks served in one capacity or another in the Confederate military. This means that 50 percent of the South's soldiers were black,[784] and that five times, or 500 percent, more blacks fought for the Confederacy than for the Union.[785]

Here too Lincoln once again failed in his goal of trying to launch massive slave rebellions in the South by issuing the Emancipation Proclamation. For far from initiating even a tiny revolt, his overt racism and selfish political scheming only turned most Southern blacks further against him, while renewing their love for Dixie.[786] Of this situation Derry writes:

> *The conduct of the slaves during the war gives strong proof of the kind*
> *feeling that existed between them and their masters.* The great majority

of them remained on the plantations and by their labor supplied the armies in the field. Many negro men went with their young masters to war, faithfully waited on them, nursed them when sick, and, if they died in camp or in battle, returned with the lifeless bodies to lay them beside their kindred dead in the family burying-ground.[787]

You would never know it from reading our Yankee-authored, mainstream American history books, but hundreds of thousands of Southern blacks fought for the Confederacy. In this illustration black and white Confederate scouts surveil a Union camp in Virginia in preparation for an attack. Note the Rebel uniform, rifle, belted cartridge box, and hat (taken off to help avoid detection by the enemy) of the black Confederate soldier in the foreground.

Postwar Southern whites credited Southern blacks with literally saving the Confederacy from complete and utter destruction. In fact, Southern blacks were more important to the Confederate Cause during Lincoln's War than they were before it. Their talents, intelligence, experience, and labor were absolutely vital to the South's survival, and Dixie would have lost the War much sooner without their assistance.

Distinguished African-American historian Benjamin Quarles maintains that the Southern black's contributions to the Confederate Cause were beyond counting,[788] and with good reason. The support of countless Southern slaves (and also free Southern blacks) who served in the Confederate Army as teamsters, construction workers, drivers, cooks, nurses, body servants, and orderlies,[789] not to mention the hundreds of thousands who served as soldiers,[790] helped prolong the South's military efforts against Lincoln and his Yankee invaders.[791]

As noted, just as importantly, with the bulk of young and middle-aged white males away on the battlefield, it was primarily the bravery, strength, strong work ethic, and ingeniousness of Southern African-American servants—who remained at home and kept the farms going, provided food and supplies for the Confederate armies, and protected white females and their children against the ravages of Lincoln's violent blue-coated meddlers—that ultimately spared Dixie from utter annihilation.[792]

Yankee commanders on the battlefield frequently complained of this very reality, which is one of the reasons they suggested "emancipating" Southern black slaves. Not to give blacks freedom and equal rights with whites, but to eliminate the Confederacy's primary support system: millions of loyal Southern blacks who refused to leave their homes, farms, and plantations. For by remaining in the South they helped maintain Southern resolve, supported Confederate troops, and protected Southern families, whatever their race or skin color.

After the War, white Confederate soldier Luther W. Hopkins made the following comments about Southern blacks and their relationship to white Southerners:

> Now I want to say that I shall ever have a tender spot in my breast for the colored people, owing to what I know of the race, judged from my association with them from early childhood up to and including the years of the Civil War, and, indeed, some years after.
>
> My home in Loudoun county [Virginia], on the border line between the North and South, gave me an unusual opportunity of judging how far the negro could be trusted in caring for and protecting the homes of the men who were in the Southern armies. Scattered all through the South, and especially in the border States, there were white men who were not in sympathy with the South, and some of them acted as spies and guides for the Northern troops

as they marched and counter-marched through the land. *But I never knew of negroes being guilty of like conduct. They not only watched over and protected the women and children in their homes, but were equally as faithful and careful to protect the Southern soldier from capture when he returned home to see his loved ones.*

No soldier in Loudoun or Fauquier counties ever feared that his or his neighbor's servants would betray him to the enemy. The negro always said, in speaking of the Southern soldiers, "our soldiers," although he well knew that the success of the North meant his freedom, while the success of the South meant the [temporary] continuation of slavery.

Another remarkable thing. No one ever heard of a negro slave, or, so far as I know, a free negro of the South, offering an insult or an indignity to a white woman. They were frequently commissioned to escort the daughters of the family to church or to school, or on any expedition taking them from home. Sometimes the distance was long and across fields and through lonely woods, but the . . . colored man always delivered his charge safely, and would have died in his footsteps to do it if the occasion required. Freedom, education, or both, or something else, has developed in the negro a trait that no one ever dreamed he possessed until after the close of the Civil War. Hence, *I have a great respect for the race.*[793]

Many blacks, though they did not wear Confederate uniforms, served the Confederate armies in a myriad of clever and dangerous ways. This next account, of the Union's Kilpatrick-Dahlgren Raid (February 28–March 3, 1864), illustrates just such an example. Related by Confederate Brigadier Generals Armistead L. Long and Marcus J. Wright, it is the story of a Southern servant named Martin Robinson, who had been captured by Union soldiers. Known to Yankees by the derogatory term "contraband," the courageous African-American paid the ultimate price for remaining loyal to the Southland that he loved:

[Union General Hugh Judson] Kilpatrick, having failed to meet [Union Colonel Ulric] Dahlgren at the appointed time before Richmond, determined not to wait, but to attack [the Rebels] at once. He crossed the outer line of defences without resistance, but on reaching the second line he was so warmly [that is, violently] received that he was obliged to retire, and with difficulty made good his retreat through the Confederate lines. This lack of co-operation in the Federal forces was due to the fact that Dahlgren put in the responsible position of guide *a [negro] contraband [Robinson] who showed his fidelity to the Southern cause by misleading him from his proposed line of march,* and thus created a delay which prevented his forming a junction with Kilpatrick. We are told that *the negro was executed on the alleged charge of treachery [Dahlgren cruelly hanged Robinson on the spot using the reins of his horse].* When Dahlgren approached the neighborhood of Richmond he was met by a Confederate force and signally defeated; he himself was killed, and only a remnant of his command escaped destruction. [794]

Truly, the citizens of Richmond, Virginia, should immortalize Robinson in marble for his devotion and sacrifice to the South!

Yankee war criminal Union Colonel Ulric Dahlgren, who illegally murdered a loyal black Confederate, Martin Robinson, in Virginia in early 1864. Dahlgren was never charged and died in battle soon afterward.

Stories of the heroism, courage, tenacity, and superb fighting skills of black Confederate soldiers and servants are legendary, and appear in countless early memoirs and recollections of Confederates of all colors. These include everything from retrieving a dead master's body from a live battlefield to themselves bravely fighting on the front lines.[795] Such chronicles demonstrate the immense devotion black Southerners had toward Dixie and the cause for which she fought: freedom from Liberal Yankee tyranny.

In 1905 Gilbert Moxley Sorrel, a Lieutenant-Colonel under Confederate General James Longstreet, related the following eyewitness account, which took place at the Battle of Williamsburg, May 5, 1862:

> It was a stubborn, all-day fight, with serious losses on both sides, but the enemy was beaten off and we resumed the march that night, the Federals having enough of it. We were not again molested. This was our first severe fight, and the steadiness and order of officers and men appeared to be very satisfactory. I was promoted to be major soon afterwards, the commission dating May 5, the day of the action. There was a gruesome but affecting sight during the battle. Colonel Mott, of high reputation, had brought from his State the Nineteenth Mississippi Infantry. *It was hotly engaged in a long, fierce fight, and Mott fell. His black servant in the rear immediately took a horse and went to the firing line for his master's body. I met the two coming out of the fire and smoke. The devoted negro had straddled the stiffened limbs of his master on the saddle before him, covered his face with a handkerchief, and thus rescued his beloved master's body for interment with his fathers on the old Mississippi estate.*[796]

Thousands of similar stories have come down to us from wartime observers. Even Lincoln recognized the immense contribution of Southern black soldiers to the Confederacy, as he stated on March 17, 1865:

> There is one thing about *the negro's fighting for the rebels* which we can know as well as they can, and that is that they cannot at the same time fight in their armies and stay at home and make bread for them.[797]

Yankee Quartermaster-General Montgomery C. Meigs had the same complaint, as he grumbled in an official report on November 18, 1862:

> The labor of the colored man supports the rebel soldier, enables him to leave his plantation to meet our armies, builds his fortifications, cooks his food, and *sometimes aids him on picket by rare skill with the rifle.*[798]

Actually, the shooting skill of Southern blacks was not "rare," it was common. Only the racist Yankee, who had little or no knowledge of Dixie's African-American population, would think otherwise.

Meigs goes on to recommend liberating Southern blacks; again, not for the purpose of civil rights. He, like Lincoln, merely wanted to employ them in the Northern army, and then only if segregated and "put under strict military control." As the Union officer wrote:

> In all these modes it [that is, the labor of Southern blacks] is *available to assist our Army*, and it is probable that there will be less outrage, less loss of life, *by freeing these people, if put under strict military control*, than if left to learn slowly that war has removed the white men who have heretofore held them in check, and to yield at last to the temptation to insurrection and massacre.[799]

Like Lincoln and the majority of other Yankees, Union General Montgomery C. Meigs only wanted to emancipate the South's black slave force because the U.S. army was in need of more soldiers. He also assumed black enlistment would prevent slave riots and the widespread "massacre" of whites in Dixie by their former black servants—showing just how little Meigs knew about Dixie and her white and black inhabitants.

Like Lincoln's, Meigs' wish for a Southern black "insurrection and massacre" also failed to materialize, and millions of Dixie's African-Americans remained at home where they continued to support the Confederate Cause in whatever way they could. This is how the Southern tradition of sharecropping began: after the War planters subdivided their land into small plots known as "fragmented plantations," that were then tilled by millions of former black servants. Pro-North historians, of course, never mention where these men and women came from, but I will: they never left the South to begin with! When Lincoln illegally invaded the Confederacy in 1861 they refused to forsake their homeland, families, friends, farms, and businesses.[800]

Still, many Southern blacks preferred being in the midst of the fight than staying on the farm. In 1879, looking back on the War, former Confederate General Richard Taylor gave the following account:

> The Confederate Congress had enacted that negro troops, captured, should be restored to their owners. We had several hundreds of such, taken by [Confederate General Nathan Bedford] Forrest in Tennessee, whose owners could not be reached; and they were put to work on the fortifications at Mobile, rather for the purpose of giving them healthy employment than for the value of the work. I made it a point to visit their camps and inspect the quantity and quality of their food, always found to be satisfactory. On one occasion while so engaged, a fine-looking negro, who seemed to be leader among his comrades, approached me and said, "Thank you, Massa General, they give us plenty of good victuals; but how you like our work?" I replied that they had worked very well. *"If you will give us guns we will fight for these works too. We would rather fight for our own white folks than for strangers."* And, doubtless, this was true. In their dealings with the negro, the white men of the South should ever remember that no instance of outrage occurred during the war. Their wives and little ones remained safe at home, surrounded by thousands of faithful slaves, who worked quietly in the fields until removed by the Federals. This is the highest testimony to the kindness of the master and the gentleness of the servant; and all the dramatic talent prostituted to the dissemination of falsehood in [Harriet Beecher Stowe's] Uncle Tom's Cabin, and similar productions, cannot rebut it.[801]

Hopkins gives us the following wartime story, yet another example showing the undying fidelity that Dixie's blacks had for both whites and for their Southern homeland:

. . . there was not a day that we [Confederate soldiers] were not in danger of being surrounded and captured. The bluecoats were scouting through the country almost continuously in search of Mosby's "gang," as they called it. We had to keep on guard and watch the roads and hilltops every hour of the day. We had the advantage of knowing the country and the hiding places and the short cuts, and then *we had our loyal servants, always willing to aid us to escape "them Yankees."*

For instance, I made a visit to Sunny Bank, the home of my brother-in-law, E. C. Broun. My horse was hitched to the rack, and I was inside enjoying the hospitalities of an old Virginia home, when one of the little darkies rushed in and said, "Yankees." They were soon all around the house, but, before they got there, *one of the servants took the saddle and bridle off my steed, hid them, and turned him loose in the garden, where he posed as the old family driving nag,* while I went to the back porch, climbed a ladder, and lifting a trap-door, got in between the ceiling and the roof. The trapdoor was so adjusted that it did not show an opening. The ladder was taken away, and there I stayed until the enemy departed. I got back home safely, eight miles off, and had other close calls, but *owing to the fidelity of the colored people, who were always on the watch, and whose loyalty to the Confederate soldiers, whether they belonged to the family in which they lived or not, was touching and beautiful beyond comprehension. They always called the Confederates "Our Soldiers," and the other side "Them Yankees."*[802]

In May 1865, one month after War's end, South Carolina diarist Mary Chesnut remarked that in her region there was not a single case of a servant betraying their master or mistress, and that on most plantations "things looked unchanged." Blacks, now free laborers known as "plantation hands," were still working in the fields of their original white families, as if not one of them had ever seen a Yankee or even knew they existed.[803]

Thus it could truly be said that while white Southern soldiers lost on the battlefield, Southern black servants won the War on the home front by helping to preserve both white and black families and their agricultural holdings across Dixie. Except for the many Southern lives themselves that were expended in the fight against the North, no single greater contribution to the South's War effort can be named.[804]

Slave rebellions, like this one in early 19th-Century Pennsylvania, were extremely rare in the South. Northerners ignorantly assumed that the South's 3.5 million black servants were miserable, starving, abused, fettered wretches, pining away for freedom on military prison-like plantations, run by rich, sadistic, racist white planters. Nothing could have been further from the truth, of course, which is why all Yankee attempts at provoking slave revolts in Dixie ended in failure. The most celebrated of these was Lincoln's Emancipation Proclamation, which stirred not a single Southern servant to rebel against his master. The edict, in fact, was widely criticized in both the South and the North, and even around the world, as nothing more than a desperate, disreputable last ditch attempt by a weakening army and an ineffectual commander-in-chief, to wreck the South by freeing her slaves. As proof we have the words of Ulysses S. Grant who, in his postwar memoirs, admitted that if the Confederacy had continued fighting for just one more year, the North would have given up and the South would have gone free.

THE BLACK UNION SOLDIER

WHAT YOU WERE TAUGHT: The North, under President Lincoln, enlisted blacks long before the South did under President Davis.
THE TRUTH: The opposite is true. Southern black enlistment came even before the War's first major conflict, the Battle of First Manassas (First Bull Run to Yanks) on July 18, 1861.[805] In June 1861, one year and three months before the Union officially sanctioned the recruitment of blacks in August 1862,[806] and almost two years before Lincoln began arming blacks in March 1863, the Tennessee legislature passed a statute allowing Governor Isham G. Harris to receive into military service "all male free persons of color, between the ages of 15 and 50 . . ."[807]

On February 4, 1862, the Virginia legislature passed a bill to enroll all of the state's free Negroes for service in the Confederate army. Earlier, on November 23, 1861, a seven-mile long line of Confederate soldiers was marched through the streets of New Orleans. Among them was a regiment of 1,400 free black volunteers.[808] Hundreds of other such examples could be given. We have already seen that five times as many blacks fought for the Confederacy than for the Union.[809]

Anti-South proponents have carefully suppressed such facts, making our already Northern-slanted history books even more incomplete, inaccurate, and misleading than they should be.

WHAT YOU WERE TAUGHT: The Union formed all-black troops before the Confederacy did.
THE TRUTH: The South's first all-black militia was officially formed

on April 23, 1861, only nine days after the first battle of the War at Fort Sumter, South Carolina. The unit, known as the "Native Guards (colored)," was "duly and legally enrolled as a part of the militia of the State, its officers being commissioned by Thomas O. Moore, Governor and Commander-in-Chief of the State of Louisiana . . ."[810]

In contrast, the North's first all-black militia, the First South Carolina Volunteers, was not commissioned until over a year and a half later (on November 7, 1862), under Yankee Colonel Thomas Wentworth Higginson.[811]

Early in the conflict, under Lincoln's orders, Yankee Secretary of War Simon Cameron declared that the U.S. had "no intention" of enlisting either "coloreds" (African-Americans) or "savages" (Native-Americans).

Indeed, Lincoln did not allow *official* black enlistment until January 1, 1863, with the issuance of his Final Emancipation Proclamation, as that document tacitly states.[812] Up until then he had strictly barred both blacks and Native-Americans (whom he and his administration referred to as "savages") from joining the Union military as armed soldiers.[813]

Since blacks had served officially, legally, and courageously as soldiers in *all* of America's conflicts up until the Civil War, Lincoln must be named as the one who injected white racism and racial segregation into the U.S. military for the first time, an unfortunate situation that lasted well into the late 1940s.[814]

WHAT YOU WERE TAUGHT: All of the 180,000 blacks who fought for Lincoln and the Union were freed slaves from the South.
THE TRUTH: Just half, or 90,000, of the 180,000 blacks who

eventually fought for Lincoln were "emancipated" Southern blacks. It is important to note, however, that a large percentage of these men did not enroll voluntarily. They were forced to join up at gunpoint—or risk physical assault, a whipping, or even being murdered.[815]

The other 50 percent of Lincoln's African-American soldiers were "free" Northern blacks,[816] many who were probably "emancipated" from the pool of 500,000 to 1 million black slaves who were still enslaved in the "abolitionist" North in 1860.[817]

During the first two years of the War, when Northern blacks tried to join the Union army, they were quickly turned away at Federal recruiting stations by Lincoln's orders. Those who managed to sneak into service were soon discovered, honorably discharged, and sent home. Neither Lincoln, his officers, or his soldiers wanted blacks in Union trenches. "We don't want to fight side and side with the nigger," said Yankee Corporal Felix Brannigan of the Seventy-fourth New York Regiment, a sentiment echoed by most white U.S. soldiers.

Many of these men only enrolled because they had been lured into it by the false promises of Union enlistment officers, who assured the would-be "sable soldiers" that for their service they would receive "forty acres and a mule" and the knowledge that they had helped "preserve the Union." But as with most of the North's other pledges to blacks, these too turned out to be lies.[818] To begin with, there were no mules or land giveaways for African-Americans.[819] Only deprivation, starvation, and vagrancy.[820]

Lincoln's racist prohibition against black enlistment was in stark contrast to America's history of negro soldiery. African-Americans, like the man above on the far left, fought, for example, at many of the Revolutionary War's most important engagements, including the Battles of Lexington, Concord, Ticonderoga, Brandywine, Saratoga, and Yorktown, to name but a few.

As for "preserving the Union," Lincoln, of course, did no such thing. What he did do was destroy it,[821] for the republic created by the Founding Fathers was meant to be voluntary. By using physical force, however, Lincoln turned it into an involuntary union, making his title, "the Savior of Our Country," darkly ironic indeed.[822] For a union, by definition, is a *voluntary* association between groups, whether they are groups of people or groups of states.[823]

In an 1870 essay, Yankee abolitionist Lysander Spooner wrote of Lincoln's idea of "union," and how the president and his partners in crime, his Wall Street Boys, had perverted its authentic meaning:

> Their pretenses that they have "Saved the Country," and "preserved the Glorious Union," are frauds like all the rest of the pretenses. By them they mean simply that they have subjugated, and maintained their power over, an unwilling people. This they call "Saving the Country"; as if an enslaved and subjugated people—or as if any people kept in subjugation by the sword (as it is intended that all of us shall be hereafter)—could be said to have any country.

This, too, they call "preserving our Glorious Union"; as if there could be said to be any Union, glorious or inglorious, that was not voluntary. Or as if there could be said to be any union between masters and slaves; between those who conquer, and those who are subjugated.[824]

Spooner is correct. A "union" held together by force is *not* truly a union. It is a dictatorship, an empire. This is why Lincoln was, and still is, often rightly referred to in the South not only as the "American Caesar,"[825] but as the "Tyrant," "Czar," "King," "Cambyses," "Charles IX," "Philip II," the "Northern Nero," "King John," "George II," and the "American Nebuchadnezzar."[826] Jefferson Davis referred to Lincoln as "His Majesty Abraham the First."[827]

Like Lincoln, Union General William Tecumseh Sherman held that blacks, or "niggers," as the two often referred to them, were inferior to whites and that the two races should be kept apart. Naturally he was also against black enlistment in the U.S. army. "I would prefer to have this a white man's war," Sherman declared during the conflict.

WHAT YOU WERE TAUGHT: Southern blacks could not wait for the arrival of the Northern armies and greeted them with open arms.

THE TRUTH: Those few Southern blacks who welcomed the sight of the invading Yankee troops only did so because their heads had been filled with anti-South, pro-North propaganda from Union sympathizers, or other equally misinformed African-Americans.

The reality is that most Southern blacks wanted nothing to do with Lincoln, the North, the U.S. government, or Federal soldiers. The more typical response to the arrival of the Union armies is illustrated in the following account. It was recorded shortly after the War by a white former Confederate soldier who witnessed the scene firsthand:

> In a raid by the Federals, on the Mississippi river, they [Union soldiers] took off [with] the son of [Jenkins,] a negro man belonging to Senator Henry. The boy was about ten years old; and *when Jenkins ascertained that his son was on board the Yankee boat, he immediately repaired to the boat, foaming at the mouth, like an enraged tiger.* He went on board, knife in hand, and demanded his boy. "Give me back my boy!" exclaimed he, in those terrible, fierce tones that electrify with fear all who hear them, "or I will make the deck of this boat slippery with your blood. You are nothing but a set of vile robbers and plunderers, and I will spill the last drop of my blood but I will have my child. Give him to me, or I will plunge my knife into the heart of the first man I reach." The captain of the boat seeing the desperate determination of Jenkins, told the soldiers they had better give him up, or some of them would be killed, and he was given up. Hurrah for Jenkins! *He had previously resisted all appeals to him [by Yankee soldiers] to desert his [white Southern] master, and he took his boy back to his contented home in triumph. He is one amongst a thousand [Southern blacks who did the same thing].*[828]

Confederate General Robert E. Lee's son, Robert, Jr., wrote of the following story concerning a Yankee raid on their property in the Summer of 1863. One of the family's servants, captured by U.S. soldiers, hazarded life and limb to not only return to the home and people he loved, but to protect the Lees' horses:

> The next day I found out that all the horses but one had been saved by the faithfulness of our servants. The one lost, my brother's favourite and best horse, was [accidently] ridden straight into the

[Union] column [of troops] by Scott, a negro servant, who had him out for exercise. Before he knew our enemies [were there], he and the horse were prisoners. Scott watched his opportunity, and, not being guarded, soon got away. By crawling through a culvert, under the road, while the cavalry was passing along, he made his way into a deep ditch in the adjoining field, thence succeeded in reaching the farm where the rest of the horses were, and hurried them off to a safe place in the woods, just as the Federal cavalry rode up to get them.[829]

Countless such examples could be provided.

If Southern slaves were treated so terribly, and if they detested their white owners and the South so vehemently—as anti-South writers enjoy telling us *ad infinitum*, why did nearly all of Dixie's black servants resist Yankee capture? And why did those who were taken prisoner or "freed" always try to return home, at great risk, at the first opportunity? Why do we never read about any of these brave, intelligent, and faithful African-Americans in pro-North histories?

It is because their stories would expose the truth, revealing Lincoln's War for what it really was: not a battle to "preserve the Union" or "abolish slavery," but an unconstitutional and unnecessary liberal assault on the conservative, Christian, traditional, Southern people and their inalienable natural rights.

African-Americans who made it through Lincoln's barbaric military enlistment program were treated very differently than his European-American soldiers. These black recruits, who are being subjected to medical examinations, will be consigned to slave-like labor and paid half that of white U.S. soldiers.

Untold numbers of blacks deserted Lincoln's armies. But why would they if, as pro-North writers claim, Union soldiers were egalitarian abolitionists coming to rescue them from the horrors of so-called "Southern slavery"? The truth is that blacks serving in the U.S. military suffered extreme persecution, from racist slander and unequal pay to slave labor conditions and even physical beatings. The black man suspended from this particular Union army noose, Private William Johnson, was one of the unlucky ones: a member of the First New York Cavalry, Twenty-Third U.S. Colored Troops, after he was caught trying to desert, in June 1864 he was marched up the scaffold, had his wrists and ankles tied, and was hanged—taking the record of his personal sufferings at Union hands to the grave. The realities of black U.S. military abuse and desertion have been wholly ignored by anti-South partisans, another futile attempt to prevent the facts from coming out.

BLACK CONFEDERATES:
THE REAL NUMBERS

WHAT YOU WERE TAUGHT: Very few if any blacks fought for the Confederacy. Why would they?

THE TRUTH: The truth that you will never read in pro-North Civil War histories is that far more blacks fought for the Confederacy than for the Union. The Union possessed about 3 million soldiers. Of these about 200,000 were black, 6 percent of the total. The Confederacy had about 1 million soldiers. Of these an estimated 300,000 were black, 30 percent of the total.[830] Simply put: 30 percent of Davis' army was black, but only 6 percent of Lincoln's army was black.

And these numbers are conservative if we use the definition of a "private soldier" as determined by German-American Union General August Valentine Kautz in 1864:

> In the fullest sense, *any man in the military service who receives pay, whether sworn in or not, is a soldier*, because he is subject to military law. Under this general head, laborers, teamsters, sutlers, chaplains, etc., are soldiers.[831]

By Kautz's definition of a "private soldier," some 2 million Southerners fought for the Confederacy: 1 million whites and perhaps as many as 1 million blacks.

As most of the 4 million blacks (3.5 million servants, 500,000 free) living in the South at the time of Lincoln's War remained loyal to the Confederacy,[832] and as at least 1 million of these either worked in or fought in the Rebel army and navy in some capacity, Kautz' definition raises the percentage of Southern blacks who defended the Confederacy as real soldiers to as much as 50 percent of the total Confederate soldier population[833]—five times more than fought for the Union.[834]

Indeed, there were so many black Rebels on the battlefield that Northern soldiers, most who were overtly racist,[835] were dumbstruck at

the sight. And their fear was justified: Confederate blacks were known to be ferocious fighters, fearless soldiers, and crack shots. Indeed, the first Northerner killed in the War, Major Theodore Winthrop of the 7th Regiment, New York State Militia, was brought down by a black Confederate sharpshooter at the Battle of Bethel Church, June 10, 1861.[836]

General Stonewall Jackson's army alone contained some 3,000 black soldiers.[837] Clad "in all kinds of uniforms," and armed with "rifles, muskets, sabres, bowie-knives, dirks, etc.," to the shocked Yankee soldiers they were "manifestly an integral portion of the Southern Confederacy."[838] "They were

Compared to their black counterparts in the Union armies, black Confederate soldiers had it good. Not only did they fight in racially integrated troops, they were treated as equals, paid the same as whites, given pensions, assigned important military positions, and honored at postwar reunions. Here a group of white and black Confederate infantrymen enjoy a campfire story told by a black sharpshooter.

seen riding," wrote Dr. Lewis H. Steiner, a U.S. Sanitary Commission inspector then living in Maryland, "on horses and mules, driving wagons, riding on caissons, in ambulances, with the staff of generals and promiscuously mixed up with all the Rebel horde."[839] Among the Rebel prisoners that were marched through Gettysburg after the famous battle there in early July 1863, one eyewitness reported seeing seven fully armed, uniformed black Confederate soldiers.[840]

Dr. Alexander T. Augusta, a free born African-American from Virginia, was a distinguished physician who made the mistake of joining the Union army during the Civil War. The breveted lieutenant colonel and chief surgeon of the Seventh U.S. Colored Troops withstood years of harassment and even physical abuse from white U.S. soldiers due to his skin color. At one Yankee military camp, after the white medical staff complained of Augusta's presence, Lincoln had him removed and put on "detached service"—at half the pay of a white U.S. private.

On March 1, 1865, Union Colonel John G. Parkhurst sent a battlefield dispatch to Union General William D. Whipple, reporting that:

> The rebel authorities are enrolling negroes in Mississippi preparatory to putting them into service.[841]

If more proof of Southern black support for the Confederacy is needed we need look no further than a letter written by former Northern slave Frederick Douglass to Lincoln in 1862. In it the black civil rights leader uses the example of the overwhelming number of blacks in the Confederate army to urge the president to allow blacks to officially enlist in the Union army (Lincoln had steadfastly refused up until that time).[842] Wrote Douglass:

> There are at the present moment, many colored men in the Confederate Army doing duty not only as cooks, servants and laborers, but as real soldiers, having muskets on their shoulders and bullets in their pockets, ready to shoot down loyal [Yankee] troops, and do all that soldiers may do to destroy the Federal government and build up that of the traitors and rebels. There were such soldiers at Manassas, and they are probably there still. There is a negro in the [Confederate] army as well as in the fence, and our Government is likely to find it out before the war comes to an end. That the negroes are numerous in the rebel army, and do for that army its heaviest work, is beyond question.[843]

Unfortunately, the reality of the black Confederate soldier does not conform to Northern and New South myths about Southern blacks and slavery, and so it has been disregarded and suppressed. But the South is bringing it back into the light of day for all to see.

Confederate President Jefferson Davis was one of thousands who witnessed Lincoln's savage Southern black recruitment process firsthand. Wrote Davis: "Wherever the enemy have been able to gain access, they have forced into the ranks of their army every able-bodied [black] man that they could seize, and have either left the aged, the women, and the children to perish by starvation, or have gathered them into camps, where they have been wasted by a frightful mortality."

CONFEDERATE INTEGRATION, UNION SEGREGATION

WHAT YOU WERE TAUGHT: The Union army was integrated, the Southern army was segregated.

THE TRUTH: The opposite was true. Lincoln, a dyed-in-the-wool white separatist, was literally obsessed with the idea of American apartheid (the geographical segregation of the races), which is one reason why, when he was a member of the Illinois legislature, he asked for funds to expel all free blacks from the state. This was also the reason he became a manager of the Illinois chapter of the American Colonization Society (ACS), eventually headed by his *"beau ideal,"* slaver Henry Clay.[844] Moreover, just two years before he was elected president of the U.S., he was publicly supporting the idea of corralling all African-Americans in their own all-black state—but only if mass deportation proved unworkable.[845] His goal? To make the entire U.S. "as white as New England."[846]

Not surprisingly, after finally allowing official black enlistment in 1863, Lincoln ordered all of his black troops to be racially segregated[847] and led by white officers.[848] Furthermore, after earlier promising equal pay,[849] his order (via the Militia Act of July 17, 1862)[850] that black soldiers receive half the pay of white soldiers,[851] infuriated both blacks and abolitionists.[852] This was a "necessary concession" to white Northern racism,[853] Lincoln explained to a stunned and disappointed Frederick Douglass in the summer of 1863.[854] Many of

Lincoln's black soldiers were *never* paid. Former slave Susie King Taylor wrote:

> I was the wife of one of those [black] men who did not get a penny for eighteen months for their services [in the Union army], only their rations and clothing.[855]

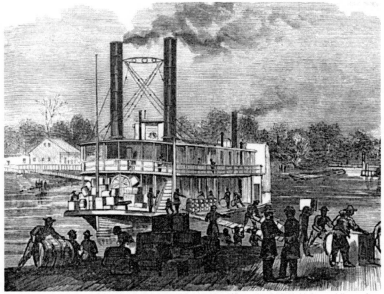

Eyewitnesses of the interaction between white Union officers and black Union soldiers often described a variety of abuses, such as disrespectful language and assault. Though this white racism was endemic to Yankee culture, it was further fueled by the U.S. military's own commander-in-chief. It was Lincoln, after all, who once said: "What I would most desire is the separation of the white and black races." Should we be surprised then that he segregated his troops and assigned blacks to do slave-like tasks that whites refused to do? The black U.S. soldiers in this illustration are unloading government stores from a Yankee river boat near Richmond, Virginia, as their white superiors stand nearby conversing.

There was also the issue of white recruitment: Lincoln and his cabinet feared that granting equal pay to black soldiers would discourage Northern whites from enlisting,[856] most who did not want to fight next to blacks anyway, however noble the Union cause.[857]

Adding fuel to the fire, black Yankee officers, those rare few that existed,[858] were paid the same as white Yankee privates.[859] Yet when the Confederacy also finally officially enlisted blacks, March 23, 1863, they were immediately integrated and given equal pay and equal treatment with white soldiers.[860]

Naturally, in the far more racially tolerant South, birthplace of the American abolition movement, President Davis simply incorporated blacks directly into his army and navy. As in Southern society itself, there was no desire for segregation among the South's military forces. For unlike in the racist North, Southern troops neither wanted segregation or needed it.[861]

Born a free man in the South, when war came Martin R. Delany switched allegiances, becoming one of the few black officers in the Union military, and the only one to achieve the rank of major. The sight of an African-American commander was so upsetting to Lincoln's white troops that eventually most of them had to be replaced with European-American officers.

WHITE RACISM
IN THE UNION ARMY

WHAT YOU WERE TAUGHT: The Confederacy was racist towards her black soldiers, and treated them unfairly and abused them. The Union was not racist toward hers, and treated them equally with white soldiers.

THE TRUTH: There was certainly white racism in Old Dixie, and our people have never tried to hide this fact as the North has tried to conceal its own wartime white racism. But because, as Tocqueville and others have pointed out, white racism was far less severe here in the South,[862] the Confederacy treated its black soldiers far more equitably than the Union did its black soldiers. In fact, the Rebel military was ordered to do so by the Confederate government.[863]

Lincoln, on the other hand, who frequently referred to blacks as "niggers,"[864] who wanted to put African-Americans in their own all-black state,[865] and who postponed both the emancipation of slaves and the enlistment of blacks into the Union army for as long as possible, possessed an entrenched white racism that was all too typical of Liberal Yankees at the time. Just as a fish rots from the head down, it is not surprising that the president's publicly avowed distaste for people of color was seen as an endorsement of bigotry by the branches of government under him, including the military.[866]

Indeed, white Yankee soldiers were well-known for their racial intolerance generally and their utter dislike of blacks specifically.[867] This is just one of the many reasons Dishonest Abe would not permit blacks to serve as active combatants in the U.S. military during the first half of his War.[868] As a hesitant Lincoln put it to a group of abolitionist clergyman on September 13, 1862, a few days prior to issuing his racist Preliminary Emancipation Proclamation:

> . . . I am not so sure we could do much with the blacks. If we were to arm them, I fear that in a few weeks the arms would be in the hands of the rebels; and, indeed, thus far we have not had arms enough to equip our white troops.[869]

The racial abuse of black U.S. soldiers became so severe throughout Lincoln's armies that Union General Lorenzo Thomas was forced to issue a warning of dismissal for violators. The admonition was roundly ignored and Thomas ended up ejecting a number of his more racist white Federal officers.

Lincoln's hesitation was warranted, but not for the reason he states: when he finally allowed full-fledged black recruitment, white soldiers hissed and booed, desertions increased, and a general "demoralization" set in across the entire Federal military.[870]

The mere mention of the idea of "black enlistment" brought many white regiments close to insurrection.[871] A white Yankee soldier with the 90th Illinois reported on the general feeling among his fellow Union compatriots at the time: "Not one of our boys wants to give guns to the negroes. This is a white man's war and that's the way we want to keep it. Besides we have no desire to fight next to blacks on the battlefield!"[872]

Northern white outrage at the idea of enlisting blacks was somewhat mitigated when Lincoln ordered the U.S. army and navy to be racially segregated, but newly recruited blacks were not happy with the president's command that all colored troops were to be officered by whites.[873] Even pro-North historians have had to concede that most white Northern soldiers were "bitterly hostile . . . to Negro troops."[874]

White Yankee racism continued well into the War. During inclement weather, for example, white Yankee soldiers were known to beat black Yankee soldiers, then push them out into the freezing night air in order to have the tents all to themselves.[875]

Most white Union officers never completely accepted commanding black troops, as there was "no prestige" in it. In fact so few white officers could be found who were willing to "lower" themselves to leading blacks that white privates, induced with the promise of promotion,[876] finally had to be virtually coerced into taking the positions.[877]

The situation got so out of hand that Federal officers had to be ordered to "treat black soldiers as soldiers," and the word "nigger," along with degrading disciplinary action and routine offensive language aimed at blacks, had to be banned with harsh punishments.[878] Meanwhile white Union soldiers continued to put on minstrel shows that satirized and humiliated African-Americans, a not uncommon form of Yankee entertainment, particularly on U.S. warships.[879]

But Northern white racism in the Union army often manifested in far more serious and diabolical ways. Southern diaries, letters, and journals are replete with reports of incredible Yankee brutality against not only white Southern women they came across, but black Southern women as well, even against those that had at first naively cheered them on as liberators. Yankee soldiers' crimes against black females included robbery, pillage, beatings, torture, rape, and even murder.[880]

Southern black males were often treated even worse by their Northern "emancipators." Those who survived such crimes were taken, against their will at gunpoint, from their relatively peaceful, healthy, and safe lives of service and domesticity on the plantation, to the filth, hardships, and dangers of life on the battlefield, where at least 50 percent of them died alone in muddy ditches fighting under compulsion for bigoted Yanks against their own native land: the South.[881]

Those blacks who resisted "involuntary enlistment" into

Lincoln's army were sometimes shot or bayoneted on the spot. When black soldiers rebelled against the abuse of white Yankee soldiers, they were whipped.[882] Both white and black Union soldiers were known to abuse Southern slaves who remained loyal to Dixie, entering their homes, shooting bullets through the walls, overturning furniture, and stealing various personal items.[883]

This unhappy group of captured Southern slaves, "contraband" to Yankees, have been Unionized (that is, inculcated with fictitious anti-South propaganda), and are now ready to be put into service. Most will end up doing slave labor for the U.S. military. The rest will be used as shock troops, forced onto the front lines to take the brunt of the initial attack, sparing the lives of white Federal soldiers.

Is this shocking? Not when we realize that this was all merely a continuation of Lincoln's policy of coercion, the same one he had used to invade the South in an attempt to destroy states' rights to begin with.[884]

Many newly "freed" black males were used as Yankee shock troops, sent first into battle in conflicts usually known beforehand to be hopeless, where they would draw fire and take the brunt of the violence, sparing the lives of Northern whites.[885] This is almost certainly what Lincoln was intimating in his letter to James C. Conkling on August 26, 1863, when he wrote:

> . . . whatever negroes can be got to do as soldiers, leaves just so much less for white soldiers to do in saving the Union.[886]

This included, of course, receiving cold Confederate lead and steel, and countless thousands of African-Americans in Lincoln's army died doing just that.[887]

After years of pleading, blacks who were finally allowed to enlist in the Union army by their reluctant president, however, were in for a rude surprise if they expected to don a fancy new uniform and fight next to whites on the battlefield. For at the beginning of black Federal enlistment, Lincoln turned nearly all freed black males into common workers who performed what can only be described as "forced labor";[888] in other words, slavery. Their work, in fact, was identical to the drudgery they had experienced as slaves. Black military duties under Lincoln included construction, serving officers (known in the South as "body servants"), cooking, washing clothes and dishes, tending livestock, and cleaning stables.[889]

Actually, the first black soldiers in the U.S. military were not allowed to serve as active combatants in any form; rather they were signed up specifically to work as ordinary grunts: teamsters, blacksmiths, carpenters, masons, scouts, longshoremen, pioneers, wheelwrights, medical assistants, orderlies, laundry workers, spies, and of course, "slaves,"[890] almost anything but armed fighters.[891] Most were to be used merely for monotonous guard duty, or as Lincoln put it in his Final Emancipation Proclamation,

> to garrison forts, positions, stations, and other places, and to man vessels of all sorts in said service.[892]

This so-called "Freedmen's labor system," authorized by Lincoln and overseen by Yankee General Nathaniel Prentiss Banks, was so blatantly racist that Banks was even roundly criticized by other Northerners, who accused him of "forcing negroes back into slavery." The brutal U.S. government program was also rife with corruption and fraud: freed blacks were regularly whipped, while their already paltry wages were often "withheld" by unscrupulous and inhumane white Northerners who pocketed the money then disappeared.[893]

The fact that one of Lincoln's top officers, the cross-eyed General Benjamin "the Beast" Butler, insisted on referring to freed Southern blacks as "contraband" (that is, illegal goods) certainly did not help the cause of black civil rights.[894] Instead, it revealed that the North still regarded blacks as inferior to whites[895] and as the legitimate property of whites—even after so-called "emancipation."[896]

But Lincoln never objected to the dehumanizing title. In fact he approved it. The name stuck and continued to be widely used in the North, even after the War.[897] This was only natural, as the North's commander-in-chief, Abraham Lincoln, who led the North by example, always referred to whites as the "superior race"[898] and blacks (and all non-whites) as an "inferior race."[899]

Southern blacks were far from being truly free after Lincoln's Emancipation Proclamation. Indeed, this is why Lincoln and the rest of the North referred to them as "freedmen" rather than as "freemen": they had been freed from the "shackles of slavery," but they were not yet free from the shackles of Northern racism.

Lincoln's own personal racism seemed boundless, and it is a tragedy that he allowed it to permeate his role as U.S. commander-in-chief. Along with the bigoted policies already mentioned, he also refused to grant black Union soldiers equal treatment in any way.[900] For example, he gave them half the pay of white soldiers:[901] white U.S. privates were paid thirteen dollars per month, while black U.S. privates were paid just seven dollars per month.[902]

U.S. black soldiers hard at work on river obstructions. This is not what they had signed up for.

Contrast this with the Confederacy: in some Southern states blacks were actually paid up to three times the rate of whites for military service.[903]

Three of the seven dollars of the black Union soldiers' monthly pay was a deduction for clothing, a deduction not imposed on white Union soldiers. Often even this small amount was withheld from black recruits by Yank officers, who sometimes simply "skimmed" the money for themselves, only one of dozens of ways the U.S. government

The glum look on the faces of these freshly "enlisted" black Union soldiers speaks volumes to those who know the truth about African-Americans and Lincoln's War.

defrauded African-Americans during the War.[904]

Lincoln also refused to give his black soldiers bonuses, pensions, or support for dependents, all which were routinely accorded to white soldiers.[905] He would not even allow black soldiers equal medical treatment. Medicines and emergency care were to go to whites first, blacks second.[906]

To add to the insult, blacks in Lincoln's army could not officially be promoted beyond the level of noncommissioned officer.[907] And in those rare cases when they were, black officers were paid the same as white privates. At least eighteen blacks who protested Lincoln's inequitable wages were charged with "mutiny" and executed by hanging or firing squad.[908] These executions went on even after Lincoln's death and the War had ended. As late as December 1, 1865, six black Union privates accused of "mutiny" (that is, for protesting Lincoln's racist pay scale) were rounded up and killed by musketry at Fernandina, Florida. This was a full year-and-a-half after the U.S. Congress authorized retroactive equal pay for black soldiers in June 1864.[909]

During his life, Lincoln, an avowed atheist and anti-Christian,[910] had not been the forgiving type, and neither were many of those who followed in his footsteps. As one Yankee newspaper journalist at the time observed:

> Many, very many of the [Federal] soldiers and not a few of the officers have habitually treated the [Southern and Northern] negroes [in their ranks] with the coarsest and most brutal insolence and inhumanity; never speaking to them but to curse and revile them.[911]

An eyewitness living on Hilton Head Island, South Carolina, in 1862, reported that the occupying white Yankee soldiers there repeatedly talked down to blacks using the foulest and most disrespectful language imaginable, while in Norfolk, Virginia, a freed black woman wrote of seeing other blacks being continually abused psychologically, verbally, and physically by Union troops.[912] These Yankee crimes included the destruction of property, pillage, assault and battery, and even rape, against naive Southern blacks who had fled to them, believing them to be "emancipators." (This is all the more appalling since the War was not over slavery, as Lincoln himself stated repeatedly.) This same

African-American woman forlornly penned: "I'm nothing more than one of Master Lincoln's slaves now."[913]

It is obvious that even after reluctantly allowing blacks into the Union army and navy, Lincoln and his military men continued to see them as little more than servile laborers and cannon-fodder.[914]

Contrary to Yankee myth, just 90,000, or only half, of Lincoln's roughly 180,000 black troops were from the South. The other 50 percent were from the North, culled from the *purposefully uncounted* and *undocumented* 500,000 to 1 million black slaves still living in the Union in the 1860s.

In comparison to the Yankees' grossly unjust treatment of her black soldiers, the Southern Confederacy's approach was the epitome of equality. Not only were blacks paid equal with whites and integrated into all military units under President Davis' General Order No. 14, issued March 23, 1865, but:

> All officers . . . are enjoined to a provident, considerate, and humane attention to whatever concerns the health, comfort, instruction, and discipline of those [black] troops, and to the uniform observance of kindness, forbearance, and indulgence in their treatment of them, and especially that they will protect them from injustice and oppression.[915]

In sharp contrast to the equal rights accorded to African-American combatants in the Confederacy, Lincoln's prejudices against his own "sable soldiery" continued throughout the War. Black civil rights leaders, like Sojourner Truth, complained to the U.S. president about his pitiful treatment of black soldiers, but to no avail.[916] Another, celebrated African-American orator Frederick Douglass, expressed his displeasure with Lincoln's long-time reluctance to allow blacks to enroll in the Union military. "Mr. President," he asked, "if blacks were good enough to serve under U.S. General George Washington, why are they not now good enough to serve under U.S. General George B. McClellan?"[917]

Most black men who eventually joined Lincoln's army probably did not want to serve under McClellan anyway. Like so many other Northern officers, he spent much of his time enforcing the Fugitive Slave Law of 1850, which required runaway servants to be returned to their owners. This was the same law that Lincoln promised to strengthen in his First Inaugural Address,[918] despite the fact that overturning it, or even ignoring it, would have helped bring slavery to an end much sooner.[919]

Southern female servants and their children, meanwhile, could expect little better in the way of treatment from their "Northern liberators." Driven from their homes in cattle-like droves, they were set to work on "U.S. government plantations," so-called "abandoned" Southern farms.[920] In reality these were Confederate plantations whose original owners had been chased off or killed, replaced by Yankee bosses who often withheld food, clothing, bedding, and medicine from their new black charges, resulting in an atrocious death toll.[921] Though their numbers were never recorded, eyewitnesses testify that the vast majority of blacks rounded up and put in Yankee "contraband camps" did indeed die, the U.S. government apparently placing little importance on their survival.[922]

Southern blacks were so frightened of Lincoln's soldiers that they went to almost any length to avoid being taken away by them, for they knew that they would very likely be tortured, forced into labor camps, or even killed. Some simply wanted to avoid hearing the Yanks' horrible un-Christian language or having to gaze upon what they had heard were their "hideous looking" faces. One of the most ingenious methods Southern blacks came up with to escape being "freed" by Yankees was to feign illness. Many a Southern black, for instance, was spared "a fate worse than death" by faking a limp, wearing a perfectly good arm in a sling, or taking to bed with a host of alarming moaning sounds.[923]

The dread of Northern racism was great enough in Dixie that during the War whites "refugeed" their servants by sending them further South for protection.[924] But almost none had to be coerced, for no Southern black wanted to be "freed," then re-enslaved by the invading Union army, only to end up fighting against their own homeland and people. Thus most went further South voluntarily, requested to be moved, or simply moved "down yonder" on their own.[925]

The reality of this fact was brought to life by Southern belle Mary Chesnut. In 1862 she noted in her journal that after Confederate General Richard Taylor's home had been attacked and (typically) looted by foraying Yanks, his black servants then deliberately moved themselves southward to the city of Algiers, not far from New Orleans. Apparently the white Yankee penchant for intimidating and abusing Southern blacks was contagious. According to Chesnut, *black* Union soldiers treated Southern blacks even worse than *white* Union soldiers did.[926]

In this early illustration the U.S. provost guard (Federal military police) is implementing Lincoln's dishonorable and illegal plan to physically coerce blacks into Union military service. Awakened in the middle of the night when they are least likely to resist, these African-Americans will be marched to the nearest Union camp and prepared to serve as menial laborers on various army projects. Those who resist "enlistment" will be threatened. That failing they will be beaten, whipped, or killed.

Yanks viewed Southern blacks no better after the War than they did during the conflict. We have record of an incident in South Carolina, for instance, of a black man running up to thank a white Federal officer for Lincoln's emancipation. The grateful former servant threw his arms around the Union general, embracing him affectionately. But the Union soldier violently pulled himself away, quickly drew a pistol, and shot the innocent man dead. "I want nothing to do with such ridiculous falderal!" he yelled sternly, and walked calmly away.[927]

It was not just Southern blacks who feared white Yankees, of course. Tens of thousands of Northern blacks, as well, experienced the horrors of "Yankee rule" between 1641—the year slavery was first legalized in an American colony (Massachusetts),[928] and 1862—the year the North officially, and finally, ceased trading in slaves.[929]

As the innocent victims of the instigators of the American slave trade, Northern blacks certainly had much to fear from their Yankee masters. This is why former Northern slave Sojourner Truth often referred to the U.S. flag, not as the "Stars and Stripes," but as the "Scars and Stripes."[930] Her attitude is not surprising considering the facts that: Lincoln used slave labor to build many of Washington D.C.'s most important Federal structures (including the White House and the U.S. Capitol);[931] the District once possessed America's largest slave mart;[932] and slavery continued to be practiced within sight of these same buildings well after Lincoln issued his Final Emancipation Proclamation.[933]

This racist late 1861 Yankee cartoon, entitled "Dark Artillery," pokes fun at the dehumanizing manner in which Lincoln used captured Southern blacks.

The fears of Northern blacks were particularly understandable when we consider that it was Lincoln (the man leading the Northern government) who repeatedly, as noted, referred to blacks using the word "nigger"[934] and described them as a base and primitive type of human,[935] while it was Ulysses S. Grant (the future U.S. president who led the Northern military) who disliked Jews,[936] bought, owned, and sold slaves,[937] and refused to fight for abolition.[938] And let us not forget that it was William T. Sherman, to this day still one of the North's most idolized war heroes, who said:

> A nigger as such is a most excellent fellow, but he is not fit to marry, associate, or vote with me or mine.[939]

With such information at hand, can there be any doubt that white Southerners saved thousands of black lives during Lincoln's War by refugeeing them further South?[940]

African-Americans joining Lincoln's armies could not expect to be treated like official soldiers. Like this "negro work crew" of the U.S. Quarter Master's Department, at Belle Plain, Virginia, nearly all were put to work doing whatever white soldiers would not do; in other words, they were employed as slave laborers.

The Southern Confederacy took its name from the original name of the United States of America: "The Confederate States of America." This proves that by seceding the South was not trying to destroy the Union, as Lincoln absurdly complained. Rather she was trying to recapture and preserve the original one, which she knew was about to be torn asunder by Lincoln's Constitution-loathing, dictatorial, left-wing politics. This old illustration shows some of the Confederacy's most important military officers. Clockwise from upper right: Stonewall Jackson, John Bell Hood, James Longstreet, Braxton Bragg, and Joseph E. Johnston. Center: Robert E. Lee.

61

CONFEDERATE GENERALS: SLAVERY & ABOLITION

WHAT YOU WERE TAUGHT: All or most Confederate generals were slave owners and anti-abolitionists.

THE TRUTH: The vast majority of Southerners, as well as Confederate militiamen and politicians, were longtime advocates of not only abolition, but of black enlistment as well. One of these was General Robert E. Lee, across the South still one of the most beloved and highly regarded Confederate officers.

On December 27, 1856, five years before Lincoln's War, Lee—who unlike General Grant and many other Northern officers, never owned slaves in the literal or technical sense, and who had always been opposed to slavery—wrote a letter to his

Long before Lincoln's War, Robert E. Lee referred to slavery as a "moral and political evil," and during the conflict he called for abolition and black enlistment.

wife Mary Anna in which he stated that slavery is a "moral and political evil," worse even for the white race than for the black race.[941]

Lee's sentiment is just what one would expect from a Virginian, the state where the American abolition movement began,[942] and whose native sons, most notably U.S. Presidents George Washington[943] and Thomas Jefferson,[944] struggled for so long to rid America of the institution; and this while the North was sending hundreds of slave ships to Africa, and whose main port cities, like New York, Providence, Philadelphia, Baltimore, and Boston, were functioning as the literal epicenters of slave trading in the Western hemisphere.[945]

But Lee was far from being the first prominent Confederate to advocate emancipation and the recruitment of Southern blacks. Another example was my cousin Confederate General Pierre G. T. Beauregard, the "Hero of Fort Sumter," and the Rebel official who gave the final approval for the design of the Confederate Battle Flag.[946]

Yet another important Southerner was Louisiana governor and commander-in-chief Thomas O. Moore, who, on March 24, 1862, commissioned the first black militia in the Confederacy (the Native Guards of Louisiana). Moore called on the all-black unit, one that had already been protecting New Orleans for several months, to "maintain their organization, and . . . hold themselves prepared for such orders as may be transmitted to them." Their purpose? To guard homes, property, and Southern rights against "the pollution of a ruthless [Northern] invader."[947]

In 1890 Joseph Thomas Wilson made note of this landmark decision in his book, *The Black Phalanx*:

> The leaders at the South in preparing for hostilities showed the people of the North, and the authorities at Washington, that they intended to carry on the war with no want of spirit; that every energy, every nerve, was to be taxed to its utmost tension, *and that not only every white man, but, if necessary, every black man should be made to contribute to the success of the cause for which the war was inaugurated. Consequently, with the enrollment of the whites began the employment of the blacks.*
>
> *Prejudice against the negro at the North was so strong that it required the arm of public authority to protect him from assault, though he declared in favor of the Union. Not so at the South, for as early as April, 1861, the free negroes of New Orleans, La., held a public meeting and*

began the organization of a battalion, with officers of their own race, with the approval of the State government, which commissioned their negro officers. When the Louisiana militia was reviewed, the Native Guards (negro) made up, in part, the first division of the State troops. Elated at the success of being first to place [Confederate] negroes in the field together with [Confederate] white troops, the commanding general sent the news over the wires to the jubilant confederacy:

"New Orleans, Nov. 23rd, 1861. Over 28,000 troops were reviewed to-day by Governor Moore, Major-General [Mansfield] Lovell and Brigadier-General [Daniel] Ruggles. The line was over seven miles long; one regiment comprised 1,400 free colored men."[948]

Confederate General Patrick R. Cleburne died from Yankee fire (at the Battle of Franklin II) before seeing his dream of official full black enlistment realized.

Another noteworthy pro-black white Confederate officer was General Patrick R. Cleburne, known as the "Stonewall Jackson of the West" for his bold tactics on the battlefield.[949] A native of Ireland and a division commander in the Army of Tennessee, at an officers' meeting on January 2, 1864, the beloved Irishman disclosed a written proposal that would soon become known as the "Cleburne Memorial." Calling for the immediate enlistment and training of black soldiers, it promised complete emancipation for all Southern slaves at the end of the War.[950] This was one year before Lincoln issued what he called his "military emancipation,"[951] the Emancipation Proclamation—one of whose main purposes was to recruit freed blacks.

In early 1865 Southern Congressman Ethelbert Barksdale stated before the House that every Confederate soldier, whatever his rank, wanted and supported black enlistment. This sentiment was backed up by such establishments as the renowned Virginia Military Institute, which agreed, if called upon, to train Southern blacks in the art of soldiering.[952]

UNION GENERALS:
SLAVERY & ABOLITION

WHAT YOU WERE TAUGHT: Union officers did not own slaves and they fought for abolition.

THE TRUTH: Thousands of Yankees are known to have owned slaves right up to and through Lincoln's War, and many of them swore they would never fight for abolition. Among them were the families of Union General George H. Thomas, Union Admiral David G. Farragut, Union General Winfield Scott, and the family of Lincoln's wife, Mary Todd.[953]

Arguably the most famous Yankee anti-abolitionist and slaveholder was Union General Ulysses S. Grant, an Ohioan who evinced no sympathy for the situation of American blacks, never discussed the Underground Railroad, and as an officer in the Mexican War, was waited on by servants—one, a Mexican man named Gregorio, whom he took home with him after the War to entertain his family. Grant never showed any personal interest in his colored servants—except perhaps those who attended him while he was slowly dying in New York in 1885.[954]

Upon his marriage to Julia Boggs Dent in 1848, Grant inherited a small army of 30 black Maryland slaves that belonged to her family.[955] Later, in 1858, he was known to still own "three or four slaves, given to his wife by her father," Colonel Frederick Dent.[956] Grant leased several additional slaves and personally purchased at least one, a 35 year old black man named William Jones. Never once did he reveal a desire to free either his own slaves or Julia's.[957]   Instead, like his wife, and most other Northerners at the time, Grant assumed that the white race was superior to non-white races, and that this was simply the natural order of things.

On the eve of Lincoln's War in early 1861, Grant grew increasingly excited over the possibility that a conflict with the South would greatly depreciate black labor, then, he happily exclaimed, "the nigger will never disturb this country again."[958]   In an 1862 letter to his father Jesse Root Grant, General Grant wrote honestly:

> I have no hobby of my own with regard to the negro, either to effect his freedom or to continue his bondage.[959]

This apathy for the black man continued throughout Lincoln's War. In 1863 Grant penned: "I never was an abolitionist, not even what could be called anti-slavery."[960]   Even after the issuance of Lincoln's

Emancipation Proclamation Grant maintained the same sentiment, noting sourly that white Americans were now still "just as free to avoid the social intimacy with the blacks as ever they were . . ."[961]

Since Lincoln's bogus and illicit Emancipation Proclamation on January 1, 1863, did not liberate slaves in the North (or anywhere else, for that matter),[962]   Grant was permitted to keep his black chattel—which is precisely what he did. In fact, he did not free them

Union General Ulysses S. Grant was an authentic Northern anti-abolitionist and slave owner, one who leased, purchased, and sold slaves before, during, and even after the War had ended. His obsessive slaving proclivities were only put to a stop by the Thirteenth Amendment in December 1865.

until he was forced to by the passage of the Thirteenth Amendment on December 6, 1865,[963] which occurred eight months *after* the War was over.[964]

And what or who was behind the Thirteenth Amendment? It was not Grant, Lincoln, Greeley, Garrison, or any other Northerner. It was proposed by a *Southern* man, John Henderson of Missouri.[965]

But the amendment seemed to have little meaning to Grant or his wife Julia, the latter, who as late as 1876, still looked upon all blacks as slaves.[966] We should not be shocked by any of this. It was the celebrated Yankee General Grant who, in the midst of Lincoln's War, said that the only purpose of the conflict was to "restore the union," and if he ever found out it was for abolition he would immediately defect to the other side and join the Confederacy.[967]

Upon his marriage to Julia Boggs Dent, Grant inherited some 30 black slaves from her family. It is said that the couple continued to view blacks as slaves even after the end of the Civil War and the ratification of the Thirteenth Amendment.

63

THE NORTH: AMERICA'S ONLY TRUE SLAVOCRACY

WHAT YOU WERE TAUGHT: The Old South was America's slavocracy.

THE TRUTH: The Confederate States of America was not a "slavocracy," as anti-South partisans have maliciously and incorrectly labeled it. As discussed, in 1860 only 4.8 percent of the total white male population of the South owned black servants, and this in the same region where the American abolition movement was born. That same year 95.2 percent of white Southern men did not own slaves.[968] This is

The North was America's only true slavocracy, and New York was its only true capital: a 239 year long slave regime without parallel in the annals of Western history.

hardly what could be called a "slavocracy," which is defined as a government or region "ruled and dominated by slave owners."

Early America did indeed have its slavocracies, but they were not in the South.

Our first slavocracies existed among Native-Americans, who enslaved one another as a routine aspect of Indian society, using some of the most brutal and sadistic forms of slavery ever chronicled. After European colonization, Native-Americans began enslaving untold thousands of whites, blacks, and browns as well.[969]

America's greatest slavocracy, however, emerged among the white colonists of the Northeast, where both the American slave trade and American slavery were born in the early 1600s. Of these states, New York came to be "America's Slave Capital," a true slave regime that imported and sold millions of (previously enslaved) Africans over a period of 239 years, far longer than any other state, North or South.[970]

During the late 1700s and early 1800s Captain James DeWolf of Bristol, Rhode Island, also a U.S. senator, was the richest man in America. Why? Because of his involvement in the lucrative Yankee slave trade. Known for his cruel treatment of black slaves (such as amputations and drownings), his New England family—the largest slave-trading dynasty in U.S. history—was responsible for launching nearly 100 slave voyages, whose profits they protected using their own slavery bank and slave trading insurance company. The anti-abolitionist patriarch himself died in 1837 in New York City, by then the slave capital of North America. Some 500,000 direct descendants of the DeWolf family slaves are alive today.

64

THE MYTH OF THE CONFEDERACY & THE SLAVE TRADE

A Southern mammy with one of her white children.

WHAT YOU WERE TAUGHT: The South was America's slave trading region.

THE TRUTH: The only American slave ships to ever sail from the U.S. left from Northern ports aboard Northern slave vessels, that were designed by Northern engineers, constructed by Northern shipbuilders, fitted out by Northern riggers, piloted by Northern ship captains, manned by Northern crews, launched from Northern marine ports, funded by Northern businessmen, all which was supported by the vast majority of the anti-abolitionist Northern population.[971]

In other words, the American slave trade was a purely Yankee business, one that operated under the auspices of, not the Confederate Flag, but the U.S. Flag. Yet it is the Confederate Flag that is now associated with slavery. Such has been the overwhelming power of the North's revisionist version of American history that lies, slander, and disinformation concerning the Southern Confederacy have come to be regarded as fact.[972] This is just one aspect of what I call "The Great Yankee Coverup," and I have devoted an entire book to it.[973]

A Dutch slave ship off-loading African slaves (who had already been enslaved by fellow tribesmen in Africa) at a slave market in New York Harbor. There was no such thing as a Confederate or even a Southern slave ship, Southern slave ship captain, or Southern slave port. All American slaves entered the country aboard either foreign ships or Northern owned vessels operating under the U.S. flag.

65

CONFEDERATE ABOLITION PLANS

WHAT YOU WERE TAUGHT: The North abolished slavery in its region long before the South.

Southern emancipation, the "Day of Jubilee," certainly called for celebration. But not all of Dixie's black servants were happy about it—and for good reason.

THE TRUTH: In January 1865 Confederate Secretary of State Judah P. Benjamin ordered Confederate commissioner Duncan F. Kenner to England to announce the C.S.'s commitment to full emancipation.[974] This was nearly a year before the U.S. issued the Thirteenth Amendment (on December 6) banning slavery throughout the nation.

Let us bear in mind that, contrary to Yankee mythology, the Northern states *never* officially abolished slavery. Instead they slowly and methodically destroyed the institution through a long drawn out process known as "gradual emancipation," taking over 100 years to complete the process.[975] Tragically, the North refused to grant the South the same privilege, and instead demanded "immediate, complete, and uncompensated abolition," an impossibility at the time.[976]

The Confederacy's motion to abolish slavery across the South had the full support of the Southern populace, of course, the very people who had inaugurated the American abolition movement in the early 1700s.[977] As noted, one of the better known of the great Southern abolitionists was the celebrated antislavery Virginian, Robert E. Lee, who, on December 27, 1856—five years before Lincoln's War—made this comment about the "peculiar institution":

> There are few, I believe, in this enlightened age, but what will acknowledge that slavery as an institution is a moral and political evil in any country.[978]

Later, during the War, like *all* Southern civilians and Confederate soldiers and officers,[979] Lee supported the idea of immediate abolition and black enlistment, a fact you will never read in any pro-North history book.[980]

Southern abolition, as well as black enlistment, had the full support of the Confederate military. The Southern people as a whole also backed the idea. And why would they not? Humanitarian Dixie, where slave owners had been eagerly manumitting their chattel since the mid 1600s, was the birthplace of the American abolition movement. This is why President Davis instituted official Southern-wide black enlistment and abolition in March 1865, nine months before the North's Thirteenth Amendment. Unfortunately, the move was too late to make any real impact on the War, which ended only a few weeks later with Lee's surrender on April 9.

66

THE WORST DAY IN THE HISTORY OF THE WHITE HOUSE

WHAT YOU WERE TAUGHT: Lincoln showed his deep humanitarian concern for African-Americans by constantly inviting them to the White House, so he could discuss civil rights and other important black issues with them.

THE TRUTH: Since Lincoln never showed an ounce of interest in black civil rights, this Yankee myth is already half submerged. And it will sink completely after we review what I call "The Worst Day in the History of the White House."

Lincoln loyalists like to pretend that his racism softened, and even disappeared, as time passed, particularly during his War. But this is not true.

On August 14, 1862, almost a year-and-a-half into the conflict, Lincoln requested that a group of blacks meet with him at the White House. They were the first free African-Americans to ever enter those hallowed halls. (Up until then, under Lincoln's "no negroes allowed" policy, only black slaves had been permitted entrance to clean and wait on government staffers.)

But the event was not something that many would want recorded in the pages of American history.[981] The fact that the five black men were hand-picked by Reverend James Mitchell, Lincoln's commissioner of emigration, hints at the enormous social fiasco Lincoln was about to create, surely the worst to ever occur inside the Executive

Mansion.

None of the Negroes who were hurriedly ushered into the president's office that day were well-known. In fact, four of them were "lowly contrabands" (captured Southern slaves). The awe-struck, passive group had been selected purposefully to avoid a "scene." For as it turns out, Lincoln wanted a captive, uneducated audience who would sit and listen to a racist monologue on the advantages of black deportation (known then as "colonization"), not engage him in an intellectual debate about slavery.[982]

As the colored delegation sat in reverential silence, Lincoln removed a crumbled up piece of paper from inside his large stovepipe hat. On it was a speech, written in hastily scrawled words. In his thin alto voice, Lincoln began to read aloud the following:

On August 14, 1862, big government Liberal Lincoln initiated the greatest social debacle that has ever taken place in the White House: he invited a group of free blacks into his office to ask them if he could deport them, along with their families and friends, to foreign colonies in order to make life easier for Northern whites. Naturally, the incident caused an uproar among abolitionists and educated blacks, who forcefully denounced the president for his stupidity and racial insensitivity—then asked him to mind his own business. Lincoln, of course, completely ignored the colossal backlash, and continued his hopeless campaign to ship negroes "back to their native land," as he put it.

> . . . many [white] men engaged on either side [of the Civil War] do not care for you one way or the other. . . . It is better for us both, therefore, to be separated. . . .
>
> There is an unwillingness on the part of our people [the white race], harsh as it may be, for you free colored people to remain with us. . . . The [African] colony of Liberia has been in existence a long time [since 1821]. In a certain sense it is a success. . . . The question is, if the colored people are persuaded to go anywhere, why not there? . . .
>
> The place I am thinking about for a colony is in Central America. . . . The country is a very excellent one for any people . . . and especially because of the similarity of climate with your native [African] soil, thus being suited to your physical condition. . . . this particular place has all the advantages for a colony. . . .
>
> The practical thing I want to ascertain is, whether I can get a number of able-bodied [black] men, with their wives and children, who are willing to go when I present evidence of encouragement and protection. . . . I want you to let me know

whether this can be done or not.[983]

Those blacks, if there were any, who wanted to help Lincoln with his insane plan, would not be allowed to think for themselves, however. Instead, as the president told the group:

> It is exceedingly important that we have [black] men at the beginning capable of thinking as white men . . .[984]

As a final affront to common sense and social propriety, Lincoln added that any blacks who refused to leave the United States were taking "an extremely selfish view of the case."[985] "For the sake of your race," he told the disquieted black committee in closing,

> you should sacrifice something of your present comfort for the purpose of being as grand in that respect as the white people.[986]

Lincoln waited, but did not receive an immediate answer to his question concerning how many African-Americans would allow themselves to be shipped to Central America, or "back to Africa." Unbeknownst to the "Great Emancipator," there was good reason for this: the five black delegates were in a state of humiliation, confusion, anger, and shock, and needed time to formulate a response.

A few days later, their reply arrived at the White House. The missive was brief and to the point. Furious, the black committee members scolded Lincoln for campaigning for the deportation of America's colored population, then asked him to please mind his own business.[987]

Lincoln must have scratched his head in bewilderment. He never grasped what every black and nearly every white Southerner understood instinctively: if America was ever to rid herself of color prejudice, Lincoln's black colonization plans were certainly not the "solution." In fact, it was obvious to nearly everyone that the deportation of blacks would only aggravate the problem;[988] obvious to everyone, that is, except Lincoln. But then again, he was never truly interested in working toward a racist-free society. For him it was either deportation or ongoing racism.

After President Lincoln's disastrous meeting with the black delegation at the White House, abolitionists and black civil rights leaders were enraged. "You may hate us," one African-American activist wrote to Lincoln in an open letter later that year, "but we don't hate you." Revealingly there was no reply.

When educated black leaders heard about the White House conference they were infuriated. Easily seeing through the charade, Frederick Douglass, the prominent abolitionist, former Northern slave, and Lincoln's confidant, publicly denounced the president for his white racial pride, disdain for blacks, and rank dishonesty.[989] Furthermore, wrote a fuming Douglass in his newspaper:

> The tone of frankness and benevolence which Mr. Lincoln assumes in his speech to the colored committee is too thin a mask not to be seen through. *The genuine spark of humanity is missing in it. It expresses merely the desire to get rid of them* . . .[990]

A New Jersey newspaper printed the response of an exasperated black citizen. In lambasting the "meddlesome, impudent" president, he asked Lincoln to remember that in God's eyes there is only one race on earth: the human race.[991] But being an anti-Christian "infidel," Lincoln never understood, or believed, this simple but powerful divine truth.

Black people across the country were indeed disgusted after learning what Lincoln had told the five-man committee, for by 1862 nearly all blacks in both the U.S. and the C.S. were native-born Americans. Most were fourth and fifth generation Americans[992]—some were as much as sixth and seventh generation Americans, or more (we will recall that blacks were in the area now known as Virginia by 1526).[993] A great many whites, however, were not more than first, second, or third generation Americans. In light of this, which race was more American, the white or the black one, blacks rightly asked? After all, by 1860, 99 percent of all blacks were native born Americans, a larger percentage than for whites.[994]

Colonizationist Lincoln's response to the criticisms he received over his White House debacle was predictable: he ignored them or laughed them off. Yet the fact remained that the vast majority of African-Americans had no intention of taking the president up on his offer to be shipped to a foreign land, for it meant leaving behind their loved ones (both black and white), their homes and farms, and their family cemeteries, filled with ancestors dating back to the early 1600s, and in some cases, even beyond.

Angered about Lincoln's endless and insensitive promotion of colonization, blacks from Long Island, New York, put their foot down, declaring:

> This is our native country; we have as strong attachment naturally to our native hills, valleys, plains, luxuriant forests, flowing streams, mighty rivers and lofty mountains, as any other people.[995]

Taking a spiritual approach, a group of black men from Pennsylvania wrote up "An Appeal From the Colored Men of Philadelphia to the President of the United States." It read in part:

> We can find nothing in the religion of our Lord and Master [Jesus] teaching us that color is the standard by which He judges His creatures, either in this life or in the life to come. . . . We ask, that by the standard of justice and humanity we may be weighed, and that men shall not longer be measured by their stature or color.[996]

On August 28, 1862, just two weeks after the catastrophe at the White House, African-American Robert Purvis spoke for nearly all American blacks in an open letter to the president:

> The children of the black man have enriched the [American] soil by their tears, and sweat, and blood. *Sir, we were born here, and here we*

choose to remain. For twenty years we were goaded and harassed by systematic efforts to make us colonize [abroad]. We were coaxed and mobbed, and mobbed and coaxed, but we refused to budge. We planted ourselves upon our inalienable rights, and were proof against all the efforts that were made to expatriate us. For the last fifteen years we have enjoyed comparative quiet. Now again the malign project [of black deportation] is broached, and again, as before, in the name of humanity are we invited to leave.

In God's name what good do you expect to accomplish by such a course? If you will not let our brethren in bonds go free, if you will not let us, as did our fathers, share in the privileges of the government, if you will not let us even help fight the battles of the country, in Heaven's name, at least, let us alone. Is that too great a boon to ask of your magnanimity?

I elect to stay on the soil on which I was born, and on the plot of ground which I have fairly bought and honestly paid for. Don't advise me to leave, and don't add insult to injury by telling me it's for my own good; of that I am to be the judge. It is in vain that you talk to me about the "two races," and their "mutual antagonism." In the matter of rights there is but one race, and that is the *human* race. "God has made of one blood all nations to dwell on all the face of the earth" [Acts 17:26]. *And it is not true that there is a mutual antagonism between the white and colored people of this community. You may antagonize us, but we do not antagonize you. You may hate us, but we do not hate you.*[997]

All of these "appeals" were forwarded directly to the president. If he ever read any of them, no one would have known. For despite them, he continued to pursue his plan to deport all blacks out of the U.S. as vigorously as ever.

The five African-Americans Lincoln invited to the White House in order to ask them to leave the country were not the first to be disappointed in their visit with the bigoted president. Still they were fortunate to get in. During Lincoln's entire administration, right up until his final months of life, while black slaves worked on finishing the White House (its construction had not yet been completed when he took office), free blacks, like Frederick Douglass, were barred from the premises.[998]

JEFFERSON DAVIS:
THE TRUE GREAT EMANCIPATOR

WHAT YOU WERE TAUGHT: Lincoln was rightfully called the Great Emancipator. That racist Southern President Jefferson Davis couldn't hold a candle to him.

THE TRUTH: As far as Lincoln being the "Great Emancipator," suffice it to say that this idea is absurd in the extreme. For Lincoln was what we would today consider a white racist, a white supremacist, and a white separatist.[999] Furthermore, he did not legally or officially free a single American slave during his lifetime[1000]: it was eight months after Lincoln's death, in December 1865, that the Thirteenth Amendment finally freed all American slaves.[1001]

In truth, it was Davis who was the true Great Emancipator, which is why he is known as such by all enlightened Southerners. For it was Davis who began the official, *and* legal, emancipation of slaves over a year earlier, on November 7, 1864,[1002] with the recruitment of Southern blacks into the Confederate military;[1003] and it was Davis who, in early 1865, was busy designing plans for full and complete abolition across the South[1004]—nearly a year before the ratification of the Thirteenth Amendment in the North.[1005]

As for Davis being a "racist," consider the following. While Lincoln was blocking emancipation, black enlistment, and black civil rights, and working day and night on his colonization plan to deport all blacks out of the U.S., our Confederate president was busy trying to figure out a way to end Southern slavery, enlist blacks, initiate black civil rights, and incorporate blacks into mainstream American society.

In the meantime, during the War Davis and his wife Varina (Howell) adopted a young black boy, Jim Limber, who they raised as their own in the Confederate White House—and who was later cruelly torn from them after the family's illegal capture on May 10, 1865, near Irwinsville, Georgia.[1006]

For his respectful attitude toward African-Americans, his adoption of a black child during the War, and his desire to abolish slavery before the U.S., Confederate President Jefferson Davis earns the title of the *true* Great Emancipator.

Furthermore, the Davises were widely known as a family who always treated their black servants equitably and with the greatest respect, as part of their family in fact, as was the Southern custom.[1007] Not surprisingly, President Davis' first Confederate states marshal was a black man.[1008] Lincoln never appointed a black man to any position, let alone U.S. states marshal, and unquestionably he would have never adopted a black child. He would not even let blacks enter the White House without special permission,[1009] said if there was ever a race war he would side with fellow whites,[1010] declared that he would never marry a woman who was not Caucasian,[1011] and at his funeral, acquiescing to his distaste for African-Americans, people of color were barred from the services.[1012]

After Lee's surrender, during the Davis family's escape southward, their coachman was a "faithful" free African-American.[1013] Later, after the War, the one-time Southern leader and his wife sold their plantation, Brierfield, to a former slave.[1014] Davis even spoke once of a time when he led a unit of "negroes against a lawless body of armed white men . . .,"[1015] something we can be sure that white separatist Lincoln never did.

In light of these facts, and many others that could be discussed, it is time for America to completely reevaluate its views of both Presidents Davis and Lincoln. Here in the South we are quite confidant that the great Southern leader, who stood for conservative, Christian, family values, and who only reluctantly accepted secession to help preserve the Constitution, will ultimately be judged far superior.[1016]

When it came to America's multiracial society, Liberal Indiana Senator Albert Smith White held the typical progressive Yankee views: blacks are inferior to whites, the two races should not intermix, the black race "degrades" the white one, the U.S. should be an all-white nation, and black colonization was the only feasible solution to the "racial problem." "There are irreconcilable differences between the two races which separate them, as with a wall of fire," White assured his left-wing constituents in an 1862 report to the U.S. Congress.

With the final ratification of the Thirteenth Amendment on December 6, 1865, eight months after Lincoln's death, the United States became one of the last civilized countries in the world to abolish slavery, thanks in great part to the anti-abolitionist shenanigans of Lincoln himself. Throughout his entire presidential tenure he used various clever stall tactics to delay abolition and derail black civil rights. Such racist-based procrastination did not go unnoticed by fellow Northern politicians, who began referring to him sneeringly as "the slow coach at Washington." Even Lincoln's Emancipation Proclamation had only been issued under ongoing pressure from radical abolitionists, dire military needs, and political expediency—and that three years *after* he became chief executive. In contrast to the U.S., as this illustration commemorates, slavery in the West Indies was officially abolished on August 1, 1838, and, as was the case everywhere in the world—except the United States—*without war or bloodshed.* Indeed, few countries eradicated slavery after the U.S. One of them was Brazil, which did not end the institution within its borders until 1888.

PART 3

AFRICAN-AMERICANS
AFTER LINCOLN'S WAR

In the Fall of 1855 thirty-one year old Thomas Jackson, soon to be known as the beloved Confederate General "Stonewall" Jackson, opened up a Sunday school for some 100 African-Americans in Lexington, Virginia. He gave lessons and sermons himself, and donated money to the small church, which he and his local white staff successfully maintained for many years. After Jackson's death, grateful members of the General's African-American church donated money toward erecting a monument to him in Lexington. Though known as a "slave owner" by the uneducated, this is not accurate, for all of his black servants were either given to him or had asked to be placed with him due to his charitable Christian nature.[1017] Jackson was only one of millions of white Southerners who loved, respected, admired, and cared for blacks in countless ways. But the Left would rather you not know this. Wrote Jackson to his aunt in the 1850s:

> "My Heavenly Father has condescended to use me as an instrument in getting up a large Sabbath-school for the negroes here. He has greatly blessed it, and, I trust, all who are connected with it."[1018]

The eccentric, indomitable, conservative, and universally idolized Confederate General Thomas "Stonewall" Jackson, treated his black servants as literal family members. Tragically wounded by friendly fire at the Battle of Chancellorsville, Virginia, May 2, 1863, his premature death was mourned by the entire South, both white and black.

ABRAHAM LINCOLN'S BLACK COLONIZATION PLAN

Note: Though the Final Emancipation Proclamation was issued on January 1, 1863, it had no real impact on abolition or the War, because, as discussed in the previous chapters, the War was not fought over slavery. What did occur after the War ended (on April 9, 1865) and Lincoln's death (on April 15, 1865), however, was the disastrous fallout from the Emancipation Proclamation and the subsequent ratification, eight months later (on December 6, 1865), of the anti-South Thirteenth Amendment. Thus I have included material in this, the postbellum section, pertaining to Lincoln's views on slavery, black colonization, and emancipation.

WHAT YOU WERE TAUGHT: Lincoln loved African-Americans and wanted to make them permanent citizens of the U.S., with full civil rights.

THE TRUTH: From the earliest known records we find Lincoln supporting the idea of what was then known as "black colonization," the racist plan to deport all people of African descent to colonies in foreign countries, such as Liberia. The pro-North movement would rather you not know this. But even if you do, they would like you to believe that Lincoln gave up on the idea before he became president.

As I have thoroughly covered this aspect of Lincoln's life in my other books, I will merely touch on it here. First, let us examine the Yankee claim that Lincoln stopped endorsing black colonization prior to entering the White House.

What historians call the Emancipation Proclamation was actually the final version of a document that underwent several minor and major revisions in draft form.[1019] As such, it would be more accurate to call the last one, issued January 1, 1863, the Final Emancipation Proclamation.

Northern blacks who would not leave the U.S. voluntarily were often forced to under the threat of violence. Here a group of African-Americans at one of New York City's ship ports is being coerced, at the tip of a whip, to board a waiting clipper bound for Liberia.

The document that is of most interest to us in regards to this particular Northern myth, however, is known as the Preliminary Emancipation Proclamation, and what an interesting article it is. If only it was studied as closely as the Final Emancipation Proclamation, our sixteenth chief executive would never have been wrongly apotheosized as the "Great Emancipator"!

The Preliminary Emancipation Proclamation, which Lincoln said he "fixed up a little" over the previous weekend,[1020] then read to his cabinet on September 22, 1862—just four months before issuing the Final Emancipation Proclamation—contained the following remarkable statement:

> It is my purpose . . . to again recommend . . . that the effort to colonize [that is, deport] persons of African descent with their consent upon this continent or elsewhere . . . will be continued.[1021]

Why did this sensational clause, directed at the U.S. Congress, not make it into the Final Emancipation Proclamation? Against his wishes Lincoln's own cabinet members talked him out of including it because it might further alienate abolitionists, a group that was already bitterly disappointed with Lincoln's refusal to abolish slavery after being in the White House for over two years. Lincoln would need their votes in his upcoming bid for reelection in 1864. Promising to deport newly freed blacks out of the country was hardly the way to win the hearts, minds, and votes of the small but vociferous Yankee antislavery crowd. And so the item on black colonization, one of Lincoln's most ardent lifelong aspirations, was struck from the Final Emancipation Proclamation.[1022]

Southern icon Confederate General Nathan Bedford Forrest is widely criticized by the uninformed for being a "racist." But it was Forrest, a Conservative, who, after the War, repeatedly called for *importing* blacks into the country. It was Lincoln, a Liberal, who repeatedly called for *deporting* blacks out of the country. Yet it is Lincoln, not Forrest, who anti-South advocates consider a "friend of the black man." The pro-North version of the Civil War simply does not stand up to the facts. Revisionist history never does.

Thus this version, the only one known by the public today, is *not* the Emancipation Proclamation Lincoln wanted. It was the one forced on him by his cabinet and by political expediency.

But this did nothing to slow down his personal campaign to expel all African-Americans from the country. Indeed, shortly thereafter, just one month before issuing the Final Emancipation Proclamation, he reemphasized his position on the issue, lest anyone should forget. In his Second Annual Message to Congress on December 1, 1862, Lincoln stated unambiguously:

> I cannot make it better known than it already is, that I strongly favor colonization.[1023]

In this same speech he once again asks Congress to set aside funding for black deportation,[1024] even suggesting that it be added as an amendment to the Constitution in order to expedite it.[1025] According to Lincoln:

> Congress may appropriate money and otherwise provide for colonizing free colored persons, with their own consent, at any place or places without the United States.[1026]

While Congress continued to allocate money for Lincoln's bizarre deportation scheme, by this time few politicians besides the president actually believed it was feasible.[1027]

When it came to the Northern populace, however, Lincoln was far from being alone in his desire to rid America of blacks. At the time, all across the North, white racism was deeply entrenched, far more so than in the much more racially tolerant South.[1028] Even Thaddeus Stevens, one of the North's most infamous and fervent South-hating abolitionists, had founded a colonization society devoted to freeing and deporting blacks.[1029]

Why were Lincoln and thousands of other white Northern Liberals so keen to "cleanse" the U.S. of African-Americans?

It was the common Yankee belief, even among most Northern abolitionists, that people of African descent were inferior to those of European descent, inferior in intellect, morality, psychology, emotionality, creativity, and physicality. They were a kind of "bridge," or even a separate species, between apes and man, many white Northerners staunchly maintained.

Respected Yankee historian James Ford Rhodes, for instance, described slaves as "indolent and filthy," "stupid" and "duplicitous," with "brute-like countenances."[1030] Esteemed New York physician and Union officer Robert Wilson Shufeldt, who wrote a book called, *The Negro: A Menace to American Society*, came to the anthropological conclusion that blacks were an inferior race whose presence could only degrade the European-American community. As such, like Lincoln, Shufeldt spent much of his life developing ideas and methods by which to rid the United States of its African population. By way of deportation and colonization, wrote the Cornell University alumnus,

> we have it in our power to render the negro race extinct in the United States in very short order.[1031]

In 19th-Century Massachusetts blacks were widely regarded by whites as a cross between a juvenile, a lunatic, and a "retard."[1032] Other Northerners were even less charitable. Famed Harvard scientist Louis Agassiz declared that "the negro race groped in barbarism and never originated a regular organization among themselves."[1033] Agassiz, like his English associate Charles Darwin (who originated the idea of natural selection, or "survival of the fittest"),[1034] believed that blacks were so evolutionarily feeble that once freed from slavery they would eventually "die out" in the U.S.[1035] Thus no Northerners blinked, except a few authentic abolitionists,[1036] when on September 16, 1858, Lincoln made the following remarks during a senatorial debate with rival Stephen A. Douglas at Columbus, Ohio:

Author of the lyrics of the U.S. National Anthem, *The Star-Spangled Banner*, Francis Scott Key of Maryland, supporter of the American Colonization Society.

> . . . this is the true complexion of all I have ever said in regard to the institution of slavery and the black race. This is the whole of it, and *anything that argues me into his idea of perfect social and political equality with the negro is but a specious and fantastic arrangement of words,* by which a man can prove a horse-chestnut to be a chestnut horse. I will say here, while upon this subject, that *I have no purpose either directly or indirectly to interfere with the institution of slavery in the States where it exists.* I believe *I have no lawful right to do so,* and I have no inclination to do so. *I have no purpose to introduce political and social equality between the white and the black races.* There is a physical difference between the two which, in my judgment, will probably forever forbid their living together upon the footing of perfect equality, and *inasmuch as it becomes a necessity that there must be a difference, I, as well as Judge Douglas, am in favor of the race to which I belong having the superior position. I have never said anything to the*

contrary . . . I agree with Judge Douglas, he [the black man] is not my equal in many respects—certainly not in color, perhaps not in moral or intellectual endowments.[1037]

Lincoln preferred the idea of living in a black-free America, and his own words prove it.

The motivating idea behind black deportation was that the freed negro "should be sent where he would never provoke friction with the whites," with Africa being "considered the most desirable place for the realization of this object."[1038] In 1819 the Board of Managers of the American Colonization Society issued a statement declaring that their goal was "the happiness of the free people of colour and the reduction of the number of slaves in America."[1039] The actual charter of the ACS states that its object is

Union General Benjamin F. Butler testified that Lincoln met with him just days before his assassination to discuss the deportation of blacks to Europe, Latin America, the Caribbean, and particularly Africa, home of the president's favorite black colony: Liberia.

to promote and execute a plan for colonizing, with their consent, the free people of color residing in our country, either in Africa, or such other places as Congress shall deem expedient.[1040]

ACS supporter Samuel J. Mills of Connecticut put it more honestly: "We must save the negroes [through deportation], or the negroes will ruin us,"[1041] a sentiment then widely held across Yankeedom.

Our leftist pro-North historians would like us to believe that Lincoln's preoccupation with making all of America "as white as New England" simply vanished before he even became president. Obviously this is false because, as we have just seen, he was still vigorously promoting the idea after his election in November 1860. Indeed, contrary to Yankee myth, Lincoln not only continued his campaign to free the U.S. of its black citizens throughout his entire presidency,[1042] he never abandoned the weird obsession. In fact, he lobbied feverishly for colonization right up to the day he died, two years after issuing the Emancipation Proclamation, as Yankee General Benjamin "the Beast" Butler attests.

According to Butler, in April 1865, just days before Lincoln was assassinated by Northerner John Wilkes Booth, the president called the general to the White House to discuss the practicalities of black expatriation.[1043] Of the meeting Butler writes:

> A conversation was held between us after the [peace] negotiations [with the Confederacy] had failed at Hampton Roads [February 3, 1865], and in the course of the conversation he [Lincoln] said to me: —"But what shall we do with the negroes after they are free? *I can hardly believe that the South and North can live in peace, unless we can get rid of the negroes.* Certainly they cannot if we don't get rid of the negroes whom we have armed and disciplined and who have fought with us, to the amount, I believe of some one hundred and fifty thousand men. *I believe that it would be better to export them all to some fertile country with a good climate, which they could have to themselves.* You have been a staunch friend of the race from the time you first advised me to enlist them at New Orleans. You have had a good deal of experience in moving bodies of men by water,—your movement up the James was a magnificent one. Now we shall have no use for our very large navy; *what, then, are our difficulties in sending all the blacks away?*"[1044]

Butler responded by discussing his own idea of how to "send all the blacks away." The solution was simple: settle a colony for them in the Isthmus of Darien (modern Panama). To this Lincoln agreed, replying: "There is meat in that, General Butler; there is meat in that."[1045] Days later Lincoln was dead.

In 1922 historian J. G. de Roulhac Hamilton put it like this:

> *Lincoln's belief in colonization of the negro as a practical solution of the question never faltered. It was a major policy of his during the war in connection with emancipation.*[1046]

Of this distasteful aspect of Lincoln's political career, in 1919 Charles H. Wesley wrote:

> From the earliest period of his public life it is easily discernable that Abraham Lincoln was an ardent believer and supporter of the colonization idea. It was his plan not only to emancipate the Negro, but to colonize him in some foreign land. His views were presented not only to interested men of the white race, but to persons of color as well. As may have been expected, the plan for colonization failed, both because in principle such a plan would have been a great injustice to the newly emancipated race, and in practice it would have proved an impracticable and unsuccessful solution of the so-called race problem. [1047]

"I cannot make it better known than it already is, that I strongly favor colonization." U.S. President Abraham Lincoln, December 1, 1862, from his Second Annual Message to Congress.

Emancipation first. Colonization second. This was Lincoln's plan for blacks from the beginning to the very end of his life. Had he survived Booth's attack, there is no question that he would have done everything in his power to fulfill the second half of his program. Thus it was, in great part, Booth who finally freed American blacks, not Abraham Lincoln. For the stark reality is that African-Americans, whether enslaved or free, would have never been completely liberated while Lincoln was alive—and indeed they were not.[1048] Booth's bullet was the true "Great Emancipator."[1049]

The American Colonization Society issued this one cent token in 1833 for use in its African colony Liberia. The back of the coin (shown here) displays the organization's name and founding year. The development of Liberia delighted President Lincoln, who was himself not only a devoted benefactor of the colony, but who was at one time an ACS official in Illinois. His ongoing efforts in the cause of black deportation prompted one of his party's liberal members, Massachusetts-born Samuel Clarke Pomeroy, to kindly suggest naming a freedmen's colony in Latin America, "Linconia."

THIRTY-SIXTH

ANNUAL REPORT...

OF THE

AMERICAN COLONIZATION SOCIETY,

WITH THE PROCEEDINGS OF THE

BOARD OF DIRECTORS AND OF THE SOCIETY;

AND THE ADDRESSES

DELIVERED AT THE ANNUAL MEETING,

January 18, 1853.

WASHINGTON:
C. ALEXANDER, PRINTER.
F ST., NEAR NAVY DEPARTMENT.
1853.

The cover of the American Colonization Society's 36th Annual Report, dated January 18, 1853, Washington, D.C. It includes proceedings from the Board of Directors of the ACS. ACS supporter, member, and leader Lincoln no doubt read this report with great interest.

69

THE MYTH OF
LINCOLN & SLAVERY

WHAT YOU WERE TAUGHT: Abraham
Lincoln was the most anti-slavery
abolitionist who ever lived. He wanted to
abolish slavery in every part of the U.S.

THE TRUTH: Lincoln always did what
was most politically expedient at the
moment,[1050] a trait for which he was
roundly criticized, even by members of his
own party and constituency.[1051] However,
there was one topic on which he never
wavered: slavery. But contrary to Yankee
myth, Lincoln's number one goal when it
came to slavery was never to totally
eliminate it. It was merely to *limit* its
growth, as he himself said on numerous
occasions. He only later acquiesced to the
idea of complete abolition due to pressure
from party radicals and political
self-interest.

On December 22, 1860, in a letter
to Southerner and soon-to-be Confederate
Vice President Alexander H. Stephens,

In the beginning Lincoln only wanted
to contain slavery in the South, not
completely abolish it. And this was
only because he and his white Liberal
constituents did not want blacks
moving North, not because he cared
about black civil rights.

Lincoln wrote: "You think slavery . . . ought to be extended; while we think it . . . ought to be restricted." "Honest Abe," for once being completely honest, ended his letter to Stephens with this sensational statement: This is the "only substantial difference between us."[1052]

Just a few months later, on March 4, 1861, he would repeat the same sentiment almost word for word in his First Inaugural Address:

> One section of our country believes slavery . . . ought to be extended, while the other believes it . . . ought not . . . be extended. This is the only substantial dispute.[1053]

Thus, just prior to the War, Lincoln held that the only real difference between the South's view of slavery and the North's was that the former wanted to allow it to spread (mainly into the new Western Territories, eventually to become America's Western states), while the latter wanted to contain it where it already existed (that is, mainly in the South). No mention of emancipation or abolition. Just limitation.

Six years earlier, during his debate with Stephen A. Douglas on October 16, 1854, at Peoria, Illinois, Lincoln outlined his reasons for wanting to restrict, not end, slavery:

> Whether slavery shall go into Nebraska, or other new Territories, is not a matter of exclusive concern to the people who may go there. The whole nation is interested that the best use shall be made of these Territories. *We want them for homes of free white people. This they cannot be, to any considerable extent, if slavery shall be planted within them. Slave States are places for poor white people to remove from, not to remove to. New free States are the places for poor people to go to, and better their condition. For this use the nation needs these Territories.*[1054]

Four years later, on October 15, 1858, at Alton, Illinois, in his seventh and final joint debate with Douglas, Lincoln reasserted his views on the matter, this time even more vigorously:

> Now, irrespective of the moral aspect of this question as to whether there is a right or wrong in enslaving a negro, *I am still in favor of our new Territories being in such a condition that white men may find a home—may find some spot where they can better their condition—where they can settle upon new soil, and better their condition in life. I am in*

favor of this not merely (I must say it here as I have elsewhere) for our own people [that is, whites] who are born amongst us, but as an outlet for free white people everywhere, the world over—in which Hans, and Baptiste, and Patrick, and all other men from all the world, may find new homes and better their condition in life.[1055]

Besides limiting the spread of slavery, Lincoln believed, another way to "better the condition" of white Americans was to separate the races through black deportation—preferably by sending negroes back "to their own native land," as he publicly suggested at Peoria, Illinois, in 1854.[1056] But, as he declared later on June 26, 1857,

as an *immediate* separation is impossible the next best thing is to *keep them apart where they are not already together.*[1057]

Limiting the spread of slavery into the North was important to

Liberal Illinois Senator Lyman Trumbull of Connecticut fully agreed with Lincoln that it was more important to contain slavery than abolish it. To this end the newly named Liberal Party, the "Republican Party," was convinced that the still largely undeveloped Western Territories should remain "as white as New England." Trumbull left no doubt as to where Lincoln and the Republicans stood on the matter: Ours is "the white man's party," he announced. His boss concurred. "If there was a necessary conflict between the white man and the negro, I should be for the white man," Lincoln once proudly stated.

Lincoln and other Yankee racists for a number of reasons, some of which we have already discussed. Here is another. By forcing slavery to stay in the South they believed that it would also serve as an ideal method of "race control": keeping blacks in bondage in Dixie meant that Northerners need not worry about a "flood of darkies" coming over the Mason-Dixon Line any time soon, with whites "tied down and helpless, and run over like sheep," as Lincoln bluntly put it.[1058] With slavery confined to the South, Yanks could continue to promote antislavery views without fear of having to actually deal with the "unthinkable horror" of how to handle 3.5 million newly freed, hungry, homeless, and jobless blacks, many of them illiterate, armed, and angry.

This is why for Lincoln the issue was never about permanent and total emancipation. Rather it was about containing the spread of slavery so that racist whites like himself would not have to intermingle with blacks.[1059] "If we do not let them [blacks] get together in the [Western] Territories," he said publicly on July 10, 1858, "they won't mix [with whites] there."[1060]

U.S. President Woodrow Wilson noted that in Lincoln's mind it was not a question of slavery continuing in the South or anywhere else. It was a question of keeping it out of the newly developing Western Territories.[1061] On this issue in particular Lincoln had the "almost unanimous" support of the North, nearly all of whose inhabitants agreed with the

Congressman David Wilmot of Pennsylvania, the author of the 1846 Wilmot Proviso (which sought to keep slavery from spreading West) and later a member of Lincoln's Liberal Party, considered it his special mission to resist Yankee abolitionists. Like Lincoln, Wilmot believed that America was meant for whites only, and that slavery was a barrier to that goal. On the debate over whether the "peculiar institution" should be abolished or simply contained in the South, Wilmot said: "I have no squeamish sensitiveness upon the subject of slavery, no morbid sympathy for the slave. I plead the cause and the rights of white freemen. I would preserve to free white labor a fair country, a rich inheritance, where the sons of toil, of my own race and own color, can live without the disgrace which association with negro slavery brings upon free labor."

president that the territories should remain "as white as New England."[1062] One of Lincoln's own senators, Lyman Trumbull, summed up the president's feelings on the matter perfectly when he referred to their political party as "the white man's party."[1063]

President Lincoln revealed his *true* views on blacks and slavery countless times. On February 1, 1861, for example, he told his secretary of state, William H. Seward:

As to fugitive slaves, . . . slave-trade among the slave States, and whatever springs of necessity from the fact that the institution is amongst us, I care but little . . . [1064]

The man who uttered these words was America's sixteenth president, the same man who, one month later, openly supported the Corwin Amendment, which would have allowed slavery to continue indefinitely throughout all the states, both North and South. [1065]

Four years on, at the Hampton Roads Conference on February 3, 1865, just two months before his death, Lincoln told a group of Confederate diplomats (which included Vice President Alexander H. Stephens) that since the Emancipation Proclamation was nothing more than a "war measure," it would end when the conflict did. After that, for all he cared, the South would be free to continue slavery if it wished. [1066]

Confederate statesman and Virginia Senator Robert M. T. Hunter was present at the Hampton Roads Peace Conference in February 1865, when Lincoln told the group that since the Emancipation Proclamation was a "war measure," it would cease to be active when the War ended. After that, he promised the Confederate delegation, the South could go back to practicing slavery if it chose.

70

THE MYTH OF THE EMANCIPATION PROCLAMATION

WHAT YOU WERE TAUGHT: The Emancipation Proclamation freed *all* of America's slaves, just as Lincoln intended.

THE TRUTH: It is well-known to most Southerners today that the Final Emancipation Proclamation, issued January 1, 1863, only "freed" slaves in the South, and even then, only in specific areas of the South. Lincoln's edict purposefully excluded Tennessee, for example (the entire state had been under Yankee control since the fall of Nashville, February 25, 1862),[1067] all of the Border States,[1068] and numerous Northern-occupied parishes in Louisiana and several counties in Virginia.[1069]

The Final Emancipation Proclamation, in fact, was issued only in areas of the South *not* under Union control; that is, it only "freed" *Southern* slaves who had sided with the Confederacy.[1070] It did not ban slavery anywhere in the North, where thousands of Yankees still practiced it, including Union officers like General Ulysses S. Grant and his family.[1071] As Lincoln states in the proclamation itself, the North and those places exempted "are for the present left precisely as if this proclamation were not issued."[1072] Lincoln could not have made the meaning of this sentence more clear: *slavery was to be allowed to continue in the U.S. (that is, the North) and in any areas of the C.S. (that is, the South) controlled by the U.S. (that is, by the Union armies).*

The question Southerners have been asking Northerners for the past century and a half is why, if Lincoln was so interested in black equality, did he only abolish slavery in the South where he had no jurisdiction but not in the North where he had full control?

The answer is obvious to most Southerners today, just as it was to a majority of them in 1863: the Emancipation Proclamation was nothing more than a clever political illusion, for he did not free slaves where he legally could (in the North and in the Border States), yet he sought to free them (in the South) where he had no legal right to do so.[1073] If Northerners had asked themselves this same question at the time, they would have never created the myth of Lincoln the "Great Emancipator" to begin with!

In truth our sixteenth chief executive did not issue the Emancipation Proclamation for the specific purpose of trying to establish black civil rights across the U.S. If that had indeed been his intention he would have also banned slavery in the North and in non-Union occupied areas of the South.

Being the penultimate politician, halfway through his war Lincoln decided that it would be politically expedient to shift the character of the conflict from "preserving the Union" to

Abraham Lincoln's Emancipation Proclamation was a sham, and an illegal and toothless one at that. The truth behind it was revealed by the Mephistophelian Union president himself when he referred to it as both a "military emancipation" and a "war measure."

"abolishing slavery." Both were rank falsehoods, however, carefully calculated to procure Northern and abolitionist votes in the upcoming 1864 presidential election. Part of this devilish ruse was the issuance of the Final Emancipation Proclamation on January 1, 1863, which, revealingly, he publicly referred to not as a "civil rights measure," but as a "*war* measure"; not as a "civil rights emancipation," but as a "*military* emancipation."[1074] Thus according to Lincoln himself, the edict did not have anything to do with black equality or even true abolition.

Yet, what a dastardly brilliant idea it was. For no one could argue against emancipation—not even the most pro-South Northerners (Copperheads) or pro-North Southerners (scallywags)—if Lincoln could prove that freeing the slaves was vital to winning the War.[1075] Assuming that he would reap untold benefits from this shift in the character of the conflict from a political basis to a moral one, it did not matter whether or not any Southern slaves were actually freed to not. And thus legally none were.[1076]

Lincoln showing his cabinet the *Final* Emancipation Proclamation. At a previous meeting they had discussed the president's September 22, 1862, *Preliminary* Emancipation Proclamation, at which time they talked him into removing his infamous black colonization clause because it would offend abolitionists in his party. The redacted material included Lincoln's request of Congress that it apportion funds for his black colonization plan, which would deport freed slaves to foreign lands. The secretly deleted clause read: "It is my purpose . . . to again recommend . . . that the effort to colonize persons of African descent with their consent upon this continent or elsewhere . . . will be continued." Thus, the Final Emancipation Proclamation—*the only one known to the public*—is not the document President Lincoln had originally wanted. It was the one that was forced on him by political expediency.

WHAT YOU WERE TAUGHT: Lincoln loved African-Americans so much and hated slavery so much, issuing the Emancipation Proclamation was only natural to him.

THE TRUTH: Despite his cynical backroom conniving, President Lincoln did hope that his Emancipation Proclamation would yield results beyond merely garnering public support. But why did he wait nearly three years before issuing the document? If he was concerned about black civil rights, as pro-North advocates claim, why did he wait so long, only succumbing after years of pressure and harassment?[1077]

The fact is that, being the penultimate politician, Lincoln had five primary goals in mind when he wrote out the edict, not a single one of them concerning authentic emancipation:

1) He hoped the Emancipation Proclamation would secure Europe's support.
2) He hoped it would instigate slave rebellions across the South.
3) He hoped to procure new troops to compensate for his drastically declining white soldiery.
4) He hoped to get new voters for the upcoming 1864 election.
5) He needed to free black slaves before he could legally deport them.

Unfortunately for him, all five motives were utter failures, for he was widely known among Southern blacks as a white racist[1078] who detested the abolition movement[1079] and said that abolition was worse than slavery;[1080] stalled the Emancipation Proclamation for as long as possible[1081]—and then only issued it for military, political, and deportation purposes;[1082] was a leader in the American Colonization Society;[1083] forced slaves to complete the construction of the Capitol dome in Washington, D.C.;[1084] implemented extreme racist military policies;[1085] used profits from Northern slavery to fund his War;[1086] often referred to blacks as "niggers";[1087] said he was willing to allow slavery to continue in perpetuity if the Southern states would come back into the Union;[1088] pushed nonstop right up to the last day of his life for the deportation of all American blacks;[1089] as a lawyer defended slave owners in court;[1090] backed the proslavery Corwin Amendment to the Constitution in 1861;[1091] and continually blocked black enlistment, black suffrage, and black citizenship.[1092] All of this is, in great part, why Northern Radicals were still demanding various black civil rights, such as negro suffrage and citizenship, long after the War ended.[1093]

This is also why Frederick Douglass said that Lincoln's attitude toward blacks lacked "the genuine spark of humanity."[1094] And it is why, as noted, Lincoln referred to his Emancipation Proclamation, not as a "*civil rights* emancipation," but as a "*military* emancipation."[1095]

71

LINCOLN COMPARED FREED
SLAVES TO WILD HOGS

WHAT YOU WERE TAUGHT: Lincoln felt nothing but compassion for his freed slaves, which is why he wrote out a detailed post-emancipation plan designed to help them in every way.

THE TRUTH: Lincoln had absolutely no formal plan for dealing with the millions of Southern slaves he pretended he was going to suddenly liberate in January 1863. If he truly cared about African-Americans, as we are asked to believe, this makes no sense whatsoever.

The reality is that he cared little for blacks, and he seldom tried to hide the fact. Once, when asked what was to become of liberated blacks after they were "freed" by his planless

When questioned about his plans for freed slaves, President Lincoln compared them to wild hogs, and joked: "Let 'em root, pig, or perish!"

Emancipation Proclamation, grinning, he likened them to wild hogs and said: "Let 'em root, pig, or perish!" And that is exactly what occurred, as our next entry shows.[1096]

LINCOLN'S "ROOT, PIG, OR PERISH" EMANCIPATION PLAN

WHAT YOU WERE TAUGHT: The Emancipation Proclamation not only freed the slaves from their horrible lives in the South, it improved their lives on every level.

THE TRUTH: After the issuance of the Final Emancipation Proclamation on January 1, 1863, only three things happened immediately: Union recruitment plummeted, Union desertion skyrocketed, and the quality of life for blacks sank to an all time low, remaining far beneath even slavery levels for the next 100 years.[1097]

After the War, and in particular after the ratification of the Thirteenth Amendment, for instance, black life span dropped 10 percent, diets and health deteriorated, disease and sickness rates went up 20 percent, the number of skilled blacks declined, and the gap between white and black wages widened, trends that did not even begin to reverse until the onset of World War II, 75 years later, in 1939.[1098] At least one out of four "freed" blacks died in a number of Southern communities.[1099]

Of life after January 1, 1863, Adeline Grey, a black South Carolina servant, wrote that when "liberation" came she could still vividly remember it, while slavery was but a dim memory. Why? Because "life was much more difficult and painful after emancipation than before."[1100]

The "pain" of emancipation was due, in great part, to the fact that Lincoln never pushed through any kind of organized, gradual, or compensated emancipation plan, as nearly every other Western nation had done when it abolished slavery.[1101] His proclamation, for example, contained no program of any kind for freed black slaves, no provisions for housing, food, clothing, employment, or healthcare.

Within months after it was issued it was already plain that Lincoln's Emancipation Proclamation was going to be a failure and a disaster of nationwide proportions, and he admitted as much when he called it "the greatest folly of my life." However, the true folly was that the North voted an unqualified, big government Liberal into the White House to begin with; one who himself stated that he was "not fit to be president." That these facts have for so long been concealed by the anti-South movement is surely a blight on the North's reputation, a travesty against the American people, and an insult to the countless thousands who gave their lives in Lincoln's War—both Confederate and Union. If there were no other reason for exposing what I call "The Great Yankee Coverup," this alone would suffice.

Freed slaves were merely "turned loose" to fend for themselves; literally cast out into the streets with no education, no jobs, no shelter, no job training, no grants or loans. The more unfortunate ended up on so-called "government plantations," odiferous squatter camps that bred little but despair, disease, crime, starvation, and harlotry.[1102]

And Lincoln's promise to freedmen of "forty acres and a mule" was little more than a carrot on the end of a stick, used to lure blacks into a false sense of governmental protection after emancipation. After all, his so-called "black land giveaways" were never meant to be permanent, and what little of these were dispersed went primarily to wealthy white Northerners.[1103]

Under Lincoln's "root, pig, or perish" emancipation plan, blacks who as servants had lived quality lives equal to and often superior to many whites and free blacks, now found themselves living out in the open or in makeshift tents, begging for food and work. There was now less labor available to them under freedom than there had been under servitude, and thus the once booming Southern black economic system plunged.[1104]

Disease, homelessness, starvation, and beggary now became the lot of untold thousands of former black servants. Even many of those who managed to become sharecroppers eventually found themselves in a state of peonage (a debt that tied them to the land), living in crude filthy shacks, suffering from illiteracy, ill health, and malnutrition.[1105] All of this was a far cry from the excellent quality of life experienced by Southern blacks when they had lived as "slaves." By 1867, just four years after the Emancipation Proclamation was issued, 1 million, or 25 percent, of all Southern blacks had perished from everything from starvation and neglect to infanticide, corruption, and disease.[1106]

Black civil rights leader William E. B. Du Bois of Massachusetts summed up Lincoln's emancipation "plan" this way: "Former slaves are now free to do whatever they want with the nothing they never had to begin with."[1107]

This ridiculous and misleading piece of pro-North propaganda portrays Lincoln as "The Great Emancipator." He was anything but. Not only did he delay abolition for as long as possible and block black advancement at every turn, he also supported the Corwin Amendment, campaigned to have all blacks deported, and refused to issue the Emancipation Proclamation until he was forced to by political expediency: he was running out of white soldiers and needed the abolitionist vote for his reelection in 1864. And still the unenlightened continue to call him "The Great Emancipator"! As Lincoln was the ultimate demagogue, a more appropriate title would be "The Great Impersonator," which is how I refer to him in the title of my book of the same name.

Of the Yankee president's "root, pig, or perish" emancipation program, former slave Thomas Hall later spoke for millions of Southern blacks:

> Lincoln got the praise for freeing us, but did he do it? He give us freedom without giving us any chance to live to ourselves and we still had to depend on the Southern white man for work, food, and clothing, and he held us through our necessity and want in a state of servitude but little better than slavery. *Lincoln done but little for the negro race and from a living standpoint nothing.*[1108]

In 1868 Lincoln's wartime modiste, former slave Elizabeth Keckley, left this description of life after emancipation and the

Thirteenth Amendment:

> Well, the emancipated slaves, in coming North, left old associations behind them, and the love for the past was so strong that they could not find much beauty in the new life so suddenly opened to them. Thousands of *the disappointed*, huddled together in camps, fretted and pined like children for the "good old times." In visiting them in the interests of the Relief Society of which I was president, they would crowd around me with pitiful stories of distress. *Often I heard them declare that they would rather go back to slavery in the South, and be with their old masters, than to enjoy the freedom of the North. I believe they were sincere in these declarations.*[1109]

Due to how it was handled, the Emancipation Proclamation was truly a national disaster on an epic scale, as Lincoln himself admitted. It was "the greatest folly of my life," he later opined. And we in the South agree.[1110]

If pro-North historians are correct, Lincoln gave all "emancipated" Southern slaves "forty acres and a mule" to start their "wonderful new lives of liberty." In reality, he had most removed onto "government plantations," like this one. These were Southern farms whose inoffensive and nonaggressive white owners had been driven off or murdered. Here so-called "freed" black men, women, and children, were put to work doing ordinary labor, like laundry (above), the same drudgery they had often performed previously as slaves, and from which Lincoln was allegedly trying to free them. A ten-hour work day, 26 days a month, was mandatory. The pay was $10 a month ($0.26 a day, or 2.6 cents an hour). "Insubordination" was punishable by "imprisonment in darkness on bread and water." This was a harsh aspect of the real emancipation behind Lincoln's Emancipation Proclamation, one that you will never hear about from any unenlightened Liberal, anti-South proponent, New South scallywag, or pro-Lincolnite.

73

WHAT FREDERICK DOUGLASS REALLY THOUGHT OF LINCOLN

WHAT YOU WERE TAUGHT: Lincoln was a humanitarian and a nonracist, and in particular was an admirer and respecter of African-Americans—which is why 19th-Century blacks loved him.

Like other educated Victorian African-Americans, Frederick Douglass was both disappointed and angered by Lincoln's apathy toward the black race.

THE TRUTH: This may be how he is seen by most people today, but this is not how he was perceived during his life. Though Lincoln's own words refute this Yankee myth,[1111] let us allow one of Lincoln's so-called black "friends," former *Northern* slave Frederick Douglass, reveal the facts.

When it came to people of color Lincoln's words often lacked "the genuine spark of humanity," Douglass once observed acidly.[1112] As for his supposed "love of the black man," Douglass set the record straight for all those willing to read his words: "Lincoln was a hypocrite who was only proud of his own race and nationality. Though voted into office as an antislavery Liberal, he was actually a prejudiced, black colonizationist, with nothing but contempt and even hatred for the Negro," the black orator stated.[1113]

Years later, on April 14, 1876, Douglass elaborated on his feelings about Lincoln in a speech he gave at Washington, D.C. Former Union general, now U.S. President Ulysses S. Grant (today still known in the South, like Lincoln, as a war criminal), was in attendance. The old Yankee warhorse must have cringed as he listened to Douglass utter the following words to his primarily black audience:

> It must be admitted, truth compels me to admit, even here in the presence of the monument we have erected to his memory, *Abraham Lincoln was not, in the fullest sense of the word, either our man or our model. In his interests, in his associations, in his habits of thought, and in his prejudices, he was a white man.*
>
> *He was preeminently the white man's President, entirely devoted to the welfare of white men. He was ready and willing at any time during the first years of his administration to deny, postpone, and sacrifice the rights of humanity in the coloured people to promote the welfare of the white people of this country. . . . He came into the Presidential chair upon one principle alone, namely, opposition to the extension of slavery. His arguments in furtherance of this policy had then motive and mainspring in his patriotic devotion to the interests of his own race. To protect, defend, and perpetuate slavery in the States where it existed, Abraham Lincoln was not less ready than any other President to draw the sword of the nation. He was ready to execute all the supposed constitutional guarantees of the United States Constitution in favour of the slave system anywhere inside the slave States. He was willing to pursue, recapture, and send back the fugitive slave to his master, and to suppress a slave rising for liberty, though his guilty master were already in arms against the Government. The race to which we belong were not the special objects of his consideration.*[1114]

Contrary to so-called Northern "history," it is clear that "Honest Abe's" attitude toward African-Americans was nothing like we have been taught.[1115]

SOJOURNER TRUTH
& ABRAHAM LINCOLN

WHAT YOU WERE TAUGHT: Sojourner Truth and President Lincoln were wonderful friends, and she had nothing but the highest regard for him, and he for her.

THE TRUTH: Abolitionist, former Northern slave, and black separatist, Sojourner Truth, held the same generally low opinion of Lincoln that other educated African-Americans did in the 1860s. And here are a few of the reasons why.

Ever since Lincoln's election abolitionists had been pleading with him to abolish slavery in America's capital city, Washington D.C., and on every occasion he refused. As he himself put it just a few months prior to his inauguration:

> I have no thought of recommending the abolition of slavery in the District of Columbia, nor the slave-trade among the slave States.[1116]

Lincoln's delay tactics in ridding not only the District but America of slavery earned him a number of unflattering titles from fellow Republicans, such as "the tortoise president" and "the slow coach at Washington."[1117] One of his least praiseworthy nicknames was "America's biggest slave owner." An angry Charles Sumner wrote:

Do you know who, at this moment, is the largest slaveholder in this country? It is Abraham Lincoln; for he holds all of the three thousand slaves of the District, which is more than any other person in the country holds. [1118]

Former Northern slave and abolitionist leader Sojourner Truth was often barred from entering the White House because she was African-American. Even when she was allowed in, it was said that President Lincoln treated her like a "washerwoman."

On April 14, 1862, while Lincoln was still refusing to free Washington, D.C.'s slaves, noted black bishop, Daniel A. Payne, head of the African Methodist Episcopal Church, decided to pay him a visit. "Do you intend to sign a bill of emancipation or not?" he asked the president impatiently. Lincoln obfuscated, told stories and jokes. Forty-five minutes later, he still had not answered Payne's question, and the frustrated clergyman politely got up and left. [1119]

Political expediency and constant pressure over the past year, including his meeting with Bishop Payne, finally forced Lincoln's hand, and two days later, on April 16, 1862, the country witnessed the passage of the District of Columbia Emancipation Act. Because of the president, it had not come easily. [1120] In fact, the entire process, from bondage to emancipation, had taken hundreds of years! But finally, to the great relief of the North's handful of vociferous abolitionists, slavery had at last been banned in Washington, D.C. [1121]

This "humanitarian" act was tainted, however, by several things. One was the fact that Lincoln's emancipation proclamation in

Washington, D.C. turned out to be for the benefit of black colonizationists like himself, not for the benefit of the slaves. For he had included a clause in the bill insinuating a request for their immediate deportation upon liberation.[1122] The day the bill was signed into law (April 16, 1862) the president even wrote a letter to the House and Senate applauding them for recognizing his call for the deportation of the city's newly freed blacks and for setting aside funds for their colonization.[1123]

There was also the anger of the District's whites, most who had no taste for abolition to begin with.[1124] At the same time, antislavery advocates fumed over Lincoln's concomitant demand of Congress that it appropriate funding to deport, to Liberia and Haiti, the very blacks he had just freed. (Though the crafty president finally liberated the city's slaves, cleverly he had never promised that he would not attempt to colonize them outside the U.S.)[1125]

Lincoln's half-hearted attempt at ending slavery in the nation's capital, of course, had little effect on the endemic Yankee trade there. In 1864, some two years after the District of Columbia Emancipation Act had been issued, former Northern slave Sojourner Truth discovered, to her horror, that white Yankees near Washington, D.C. were kidnaping the black children of freed Southern servants and forcing them back into Northern slavery.

The small community the freed blacks lived in, ironically called "Freedman's Village," had been set up by the U.S. army to help newly emancipated African-Americans adjust to living in free white society. Truth used the court system to have the children released and returned to their parents; but not before her own life was threatened by the violent and unrepentant Yankee slavers. Lincoln, whose offices were not far away, must have been aware of these crimes, yet he did nothing. As we have seen, it was Lincoln's overt complicity in the institution of slavery that often prompted Truth to refer to the U.S. flag, not as the "Stars and Stripes," but as the "Scars and Stripes."[1126]

But Miss Sojourner's direct experiences with Lincoln were, if anything, even less pleasant.

On February 25, 1862, a year into Lincoln's presidency, Truth was denied admission to the White House on account of her skin color. On other occasions she was able to make her way inside. But according

This obvious piece of pro-North propaganda, depicting President Lincoln showing a Bible to Sojourner Truth, would have us believe that the two were on cordial terms, that she was always warmly welcomed at the White House, and that Lincoln himself was a Bible-believing Christian. All of these assumptions are demonstrably false. Like Frederick Douglass and most other blacks at the time, Truth, who was rarely admitted into the White House due to the color of her skin, saw Lincoln as a serious impediment to black civil, legal, and social progress. As for the president's alleged "religiosity," he had none! From his earliest days as a politician, he was a publicly avowed "infidel" who opposed organized religion (particularly Christianity), told impious stories, denounced his wife's spiritualism, never prayed, never attended church, never joined any religious faith or denomination, never opened a Bible, and never spoke of Jesus. He was also well-known for his lack of belief in the divinity of Christ, Christian salvation, the sanctity of the Bible, and even in God Himself. According to his associates, Lincoln once wrote a "little book" declaring that the Bible was "uninspired" and historically inaccurate, that its miracles went against the laws of Nature, and that Jesus was a "bastard." This devilish volume was later burned by one of Lincoln's friends to protect his future reputation. It worked.

to her own testimony, even then she was seldom made to feel welcome, had to wait longer than whites, and was never received with any "reverence." An eyewitness at one of the rare meetings between the two said that Lincoln kept referring to Truth pejoratively as "aunty," just "as he would his washerwoman."[1127]

Though calling black women "aunt" or "aunty" was considered a harmless pet-name by Lincoln and other racist white Yankees, most Northern African-Americans saw it for what it really was: a term of derision meant to "keep blacks in their place."[1128] Nonetheless, before she left, the always racially insensitive Lincoln autographed his black "friend's" scrapbook with the following words: "For Aunty Sojourner Truth, A. Lincoln, October 29, 1864."[1129]

Certainly blacks, like Truth, who lived through Lincoln's War, would be aghast to hear him referred to today as the "Great Emancipator," for this is one of the North's more recent and most pernicious myths. As mentioned, not only did Lincoln never officially require permanent emancipation, his proclamation never legally freed a single slave. In fact, as I have repeatedly noted, servitude was only finally officially abolished and outlawed "forever" in all states across the entire U.S. on December 6, 1865, with the ratification of the Thirteenth Amendment—eight months *after* Lincoln died.[1130]

While today Lincoln masquerades as the liberator of black people, many 19th-Century African-Americans saw him for what he really was: a white racist, a white supremacist, and a white separatist;[1131] a bigoted Yankee Liberal who opposed slavery, not because it violated the God-given civil rights of fellow human beings, but because it brought the two races into close contact with one another. This, he feared, would result in what he referred to as "amalgamation," the creation of "half-breeds" or mulattos. "There is," Lincoln opined publicly on June 26, 1857,

> a natural disgust in the minds of nearly all white people, at the idea of an indiscriminate amalgamation of the white and black races.[1132]

To avoid confusion on the part of his listeners, white separatist Lincoln, who had long been calling for American apartheid, added this clarifying statement:

A separation of the races is the only perfect preventive of amalgamation; but as an immediate separation is impossible the next best thing is to keep them apart where they are not already together. If white and black people never get together in Kansas, they will never mix blood in Kansas. That is at least one self-evident truth.[1133]

Informed 20th- and 21st-Century blacks have agreed with the black Victorian assessment of Lincoln as a dangerous racist in abolitionist clothing. Black activist Malcolm X, for example, thought that Lincoln did more to hurt and deceive blacks than anyone else, before or since,[1134]

Lincoln was nothing like our history books teach. Well informed blacks have known the truth about our sixteenth president from the time of the Civil War to the present.

while Southern professor and author Julius Lester maintained that blacks should feel anger not gratitude toward Lincoln.[1135]

One of the more recent and objective African-American examinations of Lincoln comes from former *Ebony* magazine editor, historian, and scholar Lerone Bennett Jr., who holds that Lincoln was the very embodiment of the white supremacist, though one with good intentions. But, Bennett asserts, his good intentions only went so far, for as we have seen, Lincoln was not opposed to slavery itself.[1136]

As Frederick Douglass and scores of other 19th-Century black leaders pointed out, Lincoln was only opposed to the *extension* and *spread* of slavery, a view substantiated by thousands of others, including no less an authority than America's twenty-eighth president, Woodrow Wilson.[1137] In 1854, Lincoln himself said: "I now do no more than oppose the extension of slavery,"[1138] an opinion he held all the way into his presidency.[1139]

Is it any wonder that Sojourner Truth and her 19th-Century African-American compatriots viewed the so-called "Great Emancipator" with doubt, skepticism, and at times even loathing?

75

THE REAL ORIGINAL
KU KLUX KLAN

Pro-North advocates do not want you to know that Southern blacks, like this former female "slave," supported and often aided the Reconstruction KKK.

WHAT YOU WERE TAUGHT: The original Southern KKK was a racist, anti-black organization.

THE TRUTH: Actually it was a *Conservative, anti-Liberal, pro-Constitution* organization, one that quite correctly described itself as an institution of "chivalry, humanity, mercy, and patriotism."[1140] In fact, during the first two years of its existence this social aid organization[1141] was comprised of thousands of white *and* black members,[1142] as well as countless Conservative Northerners (including many of Lincoln's own soldiers).[1143] For its sole mission was to enforce the Constitution in the South after the War, as well as protect and care for the weak, the disenfranchised, and the innocent, *whatever their race.* This explains why there was an all-black Ku Klux Klan that operated for several years in the Nashville area,[1144] and it is why thousands of Southern blacks both supported it and even assisted it.[1145]

The KKK's other primary goal was to help maintain law and

order across the South. Though Lincoln's Reconstruction program had called for military rule, its implementation had the opposite effect. Under Liberal Lincoln's anti-Constitution administration, lawlessness and vicious criminal behavior became commonplace, problems exacerbated by the appearance of thick-skinned, greedy carpetbaggers (Northerners) and treasonous, unscrupulous scallywags (Northernized Southerners), both groups which sought to prey on and exploit the long-suffering Southern survivors of Lincoln's War.[1146]

The original Reconstruction KKK was founded as a form of entertainment after the War ended. But this quickly changed when the Liberal North began to discuss passing a series of repressive, brutal, and unconstitutional "reconstruction" acts in the Conservative South. It was at this time that the Reconstruction KKK transformed into a Dixie-wide social aid and protective society, employing fear as its primary weapon. The aim of this mounted Klansman out of Tennessee, for example, was neither racism or violence, but rather simple intimidation of anti-South partisans (whatever their skin color) using strange costumes, bizarre language, and odd behavior. This approach worked brilliantly, helping end Yankee rule in much of the South in just three short years. By 1877 Reconstruction, the "Second Civil War," was dead, one of the greatest sociopolitical failures in U.S. history.

In 1869 the social atmosphere in the South changed dramatically. By this time the government-sponsored black Loyal Leagues and the Freedmen's Bureau had been formed, organizations supposedly created to aid Southern blacks dispossessed by Lincoln's cruel, illegal, and unplanned emancipation (note that no U.S. government leagues were ever formed to aid dispossessed Southern whites specifically). Instead, Yankee Liberals, carpetbaggers, and scallywags used the Leagues to inculcate freed slaves in pro-North, anti-South propaganda,[1147] training them to use weapons and military tactics to taunt, punish, and even murder their former employers ("owners").[1148]

This illustration, from 1868, reveals the true enemy of the Reconstruction KKK: it was not blacks, but *carpetbaggers* (hanging on right), treacherous Northern whites who came South after the War in order to prey on the ravaged region, and *scallywags* (hanging on left), turncoat Southerners brainwashed by Yankee myth and who sided with the Liberal North.

As part of their counter-Reconstruction efforts, KKK members responded by carrying coffins through the streets with the names of prominent Bureau leaders on them. Underneath their names were the words: "Dead, Damned, and Delivered!"[1149] The left-wing U.S. Bureau, as it turned out, was not only unnecessary, as traditional Southerners had long maintained, but it was an absolute hindrance to any kind of racial harmony in the South—one of the reasons progressive Northerners created it to begin with. This is why Conservative former Confederates saw it as nothing less than the imposition of an alien government, reinforced by an occupying army with progressive ambitions—ambitions that included Northernizing the South.[1150] After all, de-Southernizing agricultural Dixie and turning it into a replica of the industrial Northern had always been one of Lincoln's chief goals. As the culturally intolerant Yankee president told Interior Department official T. J. Barnett during the War: "The entire South needs to be obliterated and replaced with new businessmen and new ideas."[1151]

The Bureau's overt political efforts to create a fake "race war" in Dixie (by attempting to make former black servants hate their former white owners) were intended to further divide the Southern people by breaking down their morale in order to make them more easily controllable (a standard ploy that continues to be used by the Left today). Ultimately, to the great remorse of Northern Radicals (that is, Yankee abolitionists), it did not work—for, as we have seen, white racism was almost nonexistent in the traditional Old South. But various white elements in the KKK began to understandably turn their attention, some of it violent, toward African-Americans, particularly those who were committing hate crimes against white families under the directives of the U.S. government's Black Leagues. Again, these particular white groups were acting out of self-preservation, not racism.[1152]

Proof of this is that when carpetbag rule ended that year, in 1869, this, the original KKK, immediately came to an end as well all across the "Invisible Empire" (that is, the Southern states). For when Southerners were allowed to begin to take back political control of their own region, there was no longer any need for a self-protective social welfare organization like the KKK. This is why former Confederate officer and Southern hero General Nathan Bedford Forrest, the Klan's most famous and influential supporter, called in its members and shut the entire fraternity down in March of that year.[1153] By the end of 1871 the

Like many other Liberal Yanks, Richard Yates, governor of Illinois, wanted the North to continue its war on the Conservative South even after Lee's surrender. It was just such Yankee arrogance that gave birth to the Reconstruction Ku Klux Klan.

KKK had disappeared from most areas of the South.[1154]

Still, now inaccurately associated with bigotry, the damage had been done, and to this day what I call the *Reconstruction KKK* has been branded, unfairly and unhistorically, with the racist label.

We will note here for the record that the KKK of today, which emerged in 1915,[1155] is in no way similar or even connected to the original Reconstruction KKK of the Southern postbellum period, which was only meant to be temporary in the first place. This is why it only lasted a mere three years and four months: December 1865 to March 1869. Indeed, there are indications that the modern KKK is far more popular in the North than in the South, with flourishing clans in Indiana, New York, California, Oregon, and Connecticut, just to name a few.[1156] Illinois, Lincoln's adopted home state, has also seen a recent resurgence of Klan activity.[1157]

Criminals sometimes impersonated Reconstruction KKK members in order to hide their immoral deeds against minorities and others. This practice wreaked havoc within the real Klan—which thoroughly repudiated violence and racism—and tainted its image and reputation with the public. Even worse, it is the illegal and violent legacy left behind by these imposters which modern day Liberals have pinned on Forrest and the Reconstruction KKK. The facts are that the General severely denounced such acts and the Klan itself issued the death penalty for anyone violating its strict rules of conduct.

WHAT YOU WERE TAUGHT: The Old Southern KKK was a violent organization that preyed on blacks.

THE TRUTH: In the previous entry we learned that the Reconstruction KKK was an anti-Liberal, pro-Constitution, aid-and-welfare organization, with thousands of black members, assistants, and supporters. The "racist" myth then has been thoroughly destroyed. As for violence within the group, physical force, like racism, was against the official constitution of the Reconstruction KKK. Those who did not agree with this regulation were quickly expelled, and the death penalty was issued against anyone caught committing such crimes.[1158]

But the real problem was imposters, non-KKK individuals who

hid behind the masks and robes of the Reconstruction KKK to hurt and kill non-whites.

These Reconstruction Klansmen from Alabama are not what they appear to be to modern day Liberals: "ruthless thugs and racist mercenaries." In reality, beneath the frightening costumes were average conservative white and black Southern men, most former Confederate soldiers, who used fear not violence as their primary weapon.

Their deception worked, and the many problems they caused were one of the reasons Forrest shut down the Reconstruction KKK in early 1869. Unfortunately for the South, to this day South-hating Yanks and Liberals still associate and confuse the crimes of these disreputable imposters with the noble organization, which was initiated and operated by law-abiding, conservative Southern "gentlemen of education and refined tastes."[1159] Historian Mrs. S. E. F. Rose (neé Laura Martin) comments on this particular problem:

> Many outrages were committed in the name of the [Reconstruction] Ku Klux, by parties who did not belong to the Klan; reckless firebrands, with private hatreds to appease, and

having the audacity to call themselves Ku Klux. Thus the impression was made that the [Reconstruction] Ku Klux were a set of vicious men with no regard for law and order; but these outrages were committed by bands of thieving Scalawags, who used the name as a cloak for their evil deeds. *No genuine Ku Klux would have been guilty of a deed or an act that would bring the blush of shame to any brave or honorable man. They belonged to the best class of citizens, once soldiers of the Confederacy, who had only the best interests of society in view, and would scorn to do a mean or cowardly act. . . . It would be very unjust and unfair to place upon the real [Reconstruction] Ku Klux the odium of these evil deeds, which were deeply regretted by them, but impossible to control.*[1160]

The anti-South movement has, of course, used the accounts of these nefarious impersonators to its advantage in its war on Dixie and her traditional family, religious, and political values. But this is to be expected from a group that cannot abide reality, shuns facts for fantasy, and thinks nothing of rewriting authentic history to suit its leftist views and progressive ideologies.[1161]

Our twenty-sixth president, Liberal-leaning New Yorker Theodore Roosevelt, publicly praised the Western vigilantes, a group that was nearly identical in origins and purpose to the Reconstruction KKK. Why then does the latter continue to be excoriated by the Left?

WHAT YOU WERE TAUGHT: The KKK was a purely Southern invention.

THE TRUTH: While the founding of the original KKK in 1865 did indeed occur in the South (as mentioned, at Pulaski, Tennessee),[1162] it was not a purely Southern entity. This is because it borrowed heavily from numerous similar secret *Northern* organizations that long preceded it.

One of these was the anti-Catholic, anti-immigrant group known as The Order of the Star Spangled Banner, founded in Boston, Massachusetts, in 1849. The original Southern KKK adopted many of the Order's traditions, such as its esoteric signals, handclasps, rituals, and codes, and later, it seems, even some of it strong arm tactics, including nighttime terrorist attacks, and general deception, fraud, and hocus-pocus antics (known as "dark lantern tactics").[1163]

In 1854 The Order of the Star Spangled Banner evolved into the Know-Nothing or American Party, a rabid anti-immigration, anti-Catholic, anti-foreigner movement that got its start in New York.[1164] When this too dissolved in 1856, the organization's racially intolerant members cast about for a political group to join. By 1860 there was only one logical choice: the party of white supremacy, white racism, and white separatism. The Liberal party of Abraham Lincoln.[1165]

U.S. President Abraham Lincoln, who had long cruelly campaigned to have the South subdued, industrialized, and Northernized, perished before he could see his harsh Reconstruction plans go into effect. Unfortunately for Dixie, the Radical South-haters who succeeded him initiated even stricter, far more savage Reconstruction policies after his death, sparking the formation of the original Ku Klux Klan in late 1865.

Of all those responsible for Reconstruction and its many evils, none was more responsible than history-ignorant busybody and Yankee supremacist Thaddeus Stevens of Vermont. This ethnomasochist (one who hates his own race) did more to injure the South and her people than anyone else except Lincoln. From creating the malevolent and dangerous anti-white Union Leagues to unlawfully wiping out the South's state governments, Stevens was behind it all. His goal? To "put the white South under the heel of the black South." Only his death from health problems in 1868, shortly after the start of Reconstruction, prevented him from doing more damage, and only the Reconstruction KKK (whose founding he helped inspire) saved the South from the disastrous fallout that came later. How many Southerners were tortured, raped, and murdered as a result of his sinister actions will never be known. The New Englander's Radical Reconstruction plans included a full scale Northernization of Dixie, right down to eliminating Southern accents! "The whole fabric of Southern society must be changed," he argued, and, according to him, only *his* revolutionary plan would "work *a radical reorganization in Southern institutions, habits and manners.*" Obsessed with destroying "Southern slavery," like Liberals today he never acknowledged that the "peculiar institution" got its start in his own backyard (Massachusetts), that the American abolition movement was born in the South (Virginia), and that the South was (and always has been) more racially tolerant than the North. Understandably, we traditional Southerners still cringe at Steven's name, maintaining that there is an especially hot place in Hell where he is roasting still.

76

NATHAN BEDFORD FORREST: TRUE FRIEND OF THE NEGRO

WHAT YOU WERE TAUGHT: Because he was a slaveholder, racist Confederate General Nathan Bedford Forrest was a criminal; one who should also be repudiated for founding the KKK and being its first grand wizard. He was without question one of the worst enemies of African-Americans.

THE TRUTH: We have seen that the Reconstruction KKK, which lasted for only a little over three years (late 1865-early 1869), had nothing to do with racism or even violence, and that its chief function was to act as a protective pro-Constitution organization in the South, as well as a relief and aid society for any Southerner (of any race) who had been dispossessed by the War. Thus, even if Forrest had been its founder or leader, this could not be counted against him.

The well respected, physically impressive, 6 foot, two inch Nathan Bedford Forrest, seen here as he appeared during Reconstruction. Of him, one of his greatest former adversaries, Union General William T. Sherman, later said: "I think Forrest was the most remarkable man our Civil War produced on either side." Thousands of black Southerners agreed, decimating the many ridiculous and slanderous anti-Forrest myths put out by the pro-North movement.

In all actuality the names of the six men who founded the Reconstruction KKK on Christmas Eve 1865 in a haunted house in Pulaski, Tennessee, are well-known.[1166] They are: J. Calvin Jones, Captain John C. Lester, Richard R. Reed, Captain James R. Crowe, Frank O. McCord, and Captain John B. Kennedy.[1167] Forrest did not begin to associate with the organization until two years later, in 1867.[1168] Obviously then he could not have been either the founder or the first grand wizard.[1169]

The members of the original "Civil War" KKK never wrote anything down or saved anything (on penalty of death),[1170] so there is no hard physical evidence stating who the first grand wizard was. Where then did South-haters come up

Union General Ulysses S. Grant owned slaves before, during, and after the Civil War, while in the midst of the conflict he declared: "The sole object of this war is to restore the union. Should I be convinced it has any other object, or that the government designs using its soldiers to execute the wishes of the Abolitionists, I pledge to you my honor as a man and a soldier, I would resign my commission and carry my sword to the other side." The fact that Liberals and South-haters call Forrest a racist and not Grant only further exposes their hypocrisy.

with the name Forrest? They fabricated it. The mysterious man's true identity was eventually revealed by Ora Susan Paine, the widow of my cousin George W. Gordon.[1171] According to Ora's sworn testimony, Gordon served as the organization's first and only grand wizard, from 1865 to 1869.[1172]

As for Forrest being a "racist slaveholder," here are the facts; facts that have been rigorously suppressed by enemies of the South for the past 150 years—but which you have a right to know.

Anti-South writers disingenuously promote the idea that slavery was illegal in the 1800s, and that therefore slave-owning Forrest was a criminal. But under the Constitution slavery was legal in every state both North and South at the time. Forrest was not a criminal because he owned slaves.[1173]

Pro-North historians tell us that Forrest was a racist because he owned slaves. If this is true, then the millions of Northerners, like Ulysses S. Grant, who also owned slaves, must also be considered racists,[1174] as would America's thousands of early black and Indian slaveholders. Forrest was not a racist because he owned slaves.[1175]

Anti-South writers claim Forrest was a slave trader his entire life. False. The General was only involved in the slave trade for seven short years, from 1852 to 1859, and was a slave owner for only 11 years, from 1852 to 1863. (Again, this is in stark contrast to Yankees like Grant, who bought, leased, kept, and sold slaves for decades, and only finally emancipated their black chattel when they were forced to under the Thirteenth Amendment.) Recognizing that slavery was coming to an end, Forrest wisely and compassionately closed up his trading company and emancipated his last slaves two years before the start of Lincoln's War (1861), five years before Lincoln's phony and illegal Emancipation Proclamation (1863), and seven years before the Thirteenth Amendment finally officially abolished slavery across the U.S. (1865).[1176]

Confederate Colonel George W. Adair, founder in 1860 of the daily journal *Southern Confederacy*, was a volunteer aid on Forrest's staff. According to Adair the General was "kind, humane, and extremely considerate of his slaves . . . who were proud of belonging to him," African-American men and women with whom Forrest shared a "strong personal attachment." Yankee myths die hard. But die they must.

What many do not realize is that Forrest got out of the slave trading business in great part because of his slaves themselves. While the North finally abolished its slave trade gradually over a span of many years—and then, only when it became unprofitable—Forrest abolished his immediately and at the height of its profitability in 1859. Why? In large part because his servants had come to him "in a body" with the idea of closing his slave trading business and opening up a plantation, where they could continue to work for him without fear of being sold to someone else.[1177]

One of the North's favorite Forrest myths pertains to the manner in which he treated the slaves he sold. According to these fairy tales Forrest abused and even tortured his slaves, beating many of them to death with chains. As the abuse of slaves was illegal and punishable by fines—and, in extreme cases, even execution—in the South, as only psychopaths engage in the violent mistreatment of others, and since slaves were worth the equivalent of $50,000 a piece in today's currency, this accusation is illogical to say the least.[1178]

As for the former charge, first-hand accounts from those who purchased slaves from Forrest reveal that he was an exemplary master whose servants were regularly bathed and well-groomed, and daily dressed in

Forrest never had a problem with runaway servants, one common in the North. Indeed, at auction not only did black Southern slaves ask to be purchased by the General, after emancipation nearly all of them enthusiastically came back to work for the man they fondly called "Marse Befud."

clean, freshly starched, stiff clothing. One of Forrest's own slave sale advertisements noted that his rules regarding "cleanliness, neatness and comfort . . . [are] strictly observed and enforced."[1179]

Along with these obviously fabricated myths we are told that Forrest refused to allow his servants to learn to read and write, that he treated them with contempt, and that he regularly and cruelly divided up his slave families purely for financial gain.

More left-wing bunkum. Forrest encouraged his servants to learn to read and write (quite unlike typical slave treatment in the North), always handled them with respect and dignity, and went out of his way to make sure he did not divide families—even though there was no law against this in Mississippi or Tennessee at the time. Indeed, it was his routine practice to purchase all the members of a slave household if need be, in order to keep husbands, wives, and children together.[1180]

In cases where the male heads of slave families had been sold away from their wives and children, Forrest would go in search of them, no matter how widely scattered they happened to be, then purchase them on the spot. Thus in countless instances he was instrumental in reuniting servant families who had been separated. As his biographers Jordan and Pryor write, he was a slaver of "admitted probity and humanity" who never split slave families up, even if he had to take a loss.[1181]

Along with Confederate President Jefferson Davis, thousands of African-Americans attended Forrest's funeral in the Fall of 1877, while hundreds officially walked in his funeral procession. Such facts sharply contradict the Yankee myth that the General was a racist who was universally detested by blacks.

Another misconception we must do away with is that Forrest, being a "barbaric slave trader," preferred doing business with the same sort of unsavory individuals. The truth is that he refused to do trade with inhumane slavers, and, according to journalist Lafcadio Hearn, Forrest possessed a list of especially vicious Memphis slave traders that he refused to sell to.[1182]

All in all, Forrest turns out to be the epitome of an honest, genteel, and humanitarian slave trader who made sure that his servants were well housed, well clothed, and well fed, and were sold to reputable, altruistic, kindly owners. Little wonder that Forrest's black servants were "strongly attached to him," or that when he attended slave auctions, blacks would line up and plead for him to buy them.[1183]

Confederate Colonel George W. Adair, an intimate friend of the General and a member of his staff, summed up Forrest the slave trader this way:

> *Forrest was kind, humane, and extremely considerate of his slaves. He was overwhelmed with applications from a great many of this class, who begged him to purchase them.* He seemed to exercise the same influence over these creatures that in a greater degree he exercised over the soldiers who in later years served him as devotedly as if *there was between them a strong personal attachment.* When a slave was purchased for him his first act was to turn him over to his negro valet, Jerry, with instructions to wash him thoroughly and put clean clothes on him from head to foot. *Forrest applied the rule of cleanliness and neatness to the slaves which he practised for himself.* In his appearance, in those ante-bellum days, he was extremely neat and scrupulously clean. In fact, so particular was he in regard to his personal appearance that some were almost inclined to call him foppish. *The slaves who were thus transformed were proud of belonging to him. He was always very careful when he purchased a married slave to use every effort to secure also the husband or wife, as the case might be, and unite them, and in handling children he would not permit the separation of a family.*[1184]

If Forrest was truly the "racist monster" portrayed in Yankee folklore, one must wonder why he enlisted sixty-five slaves in his cavalry, forty-five of them belonging to the dashing officer himself.[1185] Of these particular individuals the General later remarked that at the start of Lincoln's War

> I said to forty-five colored fellows on my plantation that . . . I was going into the army; that if they would go with me, if we got whipped they would be free anyhow, and that *if we succeeded and slavery was perpetuated, if they would act faithfully with me to the end of the war, I would set them free.* Eighteen months before the war closed I was satisfied that we were going to be defeated, and I gave these

forty-five men, or forty-four of them, their free papers.[1186]

Forrest enlisted 65 blacks in his cavalry, impressed seven of them into service as his personal armed guards, and after the War referred to the whole group as "great Confederates"—hardly the actions of a white racist.

Revealingly, during the War none of Forrest's black soldiers ever tried to flee or join the enemy, and as promised, he granted all of the heroic survivors their liberty. However, as we just saw, he did not wait until the end of the War as he had previously pledged. He abolished slavery in his own cavalry in September 1863 (shortly after the Battle of Chickamauga).[1187] As noted earlier, this was over two years prior to the ratification of the Thirteenth Amendment (on December 6, 1865), which finally halted slavery all across the U.S. He also hand selected seven well-armed *African-American soldiers* to serve as his personal guards.[1188]

The following story, from a 1901 edition of *Confederate Veteran*, concerns two of Forrest's black soldiers:

With the batteries of Capt. John W. Morton, Gen. Forrest's chief of artillery, there were two negroes, Bob Morton, a cook, and Ed Patterson, the hostler for the captain, both of whom served with the artillery throughout the war. *Ed Patterson, whose fidelity and loyalty stoutly withstood the test of battle and even of capture, still survives. He is a respected householder and property owner, near Nashville, and delights to recall the time when he wore the gray in Morton's Battery. Everybody in the artillery service of Forrest knew and liked Ed. He took good care of the horses, and performed his duties with unflagging good humor.*

On one occasion it was feared that Ed was lost to the battery. In the terrific fight at Parker's Cross Roads, when Morton's men, behind the guns, were almost overwhelmed by superior numbers of the enemy in a sudden charge, about twenty members of the battery were run over and captured. Ed was among them. He was missed, notwithstanding the confusion of the disaster, and the temporary reverse of the almost invariably successful artillerists was regarded by them as aggravated by the loss of their diligent hostler. Capt. Morton particularly mourned his absence. One morning, a few days after the battle, he rode into the camp of the battery, mounted upon a superb horse, whose caparison denoted it the property of an officer of no mean rank.

"Hallo, Ed! Where did you come from?" was the artillery chief's greeting.

"I des come f'om de Yankees." responded Ed complacently, as he dismounted and stood proudly eying his steed.

"How did you get away, and where did you get that horse?"

"Wall sah; dey taken us all along. When we got out o' sight o' y'all, I notice dat dey didn't 'pear to notice me, an' when dey got to whar dey was gwine into camp, I sort o' got away. De Yankees des seed me ridin' 'roun', an' I 'spec' maybe dey thought I was waitin' on some o' de officers. I des went on th'ough de woods. I seed a heap o'dead men wid blue coats on, an' heap of 'em was 'live, too.

"D'rectly I come to a big road. I seed one o' our boys walkin' what 'ad done los' his horse. I axed him which erway Marse John went. He knowed me, an' said de artillery done gone down dis road.

"I kep' on, an' passed a heap o' our men walkin'. I axed 'em which er way de artillery done gone, an' dey said, 'Down dis road.' I kep' on an' kep' on 'til I got here; an' dat's why I'm here, Marse John. Dey took yo' horse away f'om me, but I done got you a better one, sho. No, sah; dey didn't 'pear to notice me at all. When I was comin' on I seed some mighty nice-lookin' hosses tied in de bushes, en' ez dey wan' nobody noticin' I tuck 'n' pick me out one, an' des got on dis 'n' and rid him to hunt y'all. I seed a blue overcoat layin' on de groun', an' I took'n' put it on. An' it's a good one too, Marse John."[1189]

For decades after the conflict ended, the black survivors of Forrest's unit eagerly attended Confederate reunions, dressed in their old battered uniforms, where they were always welcomed as loyal patriots and courageous heroes. Of the stalwart "negroes" who served under him, General Forrest later commented:

These boys stayed with me, drove my teams, and better Confederates did not live.[1190]

To one of them, J. W. Carter, an "old negro ex-Confederate soldier," Forrest gave a gold watch for his services and loyalty.[1191]

Forrest's magnificent equestrian statue in Memphis, Tennessee, is regularly attacked, vandalized, and defaced by the ignorant, uninformed, and uneducated. If the truth about the great Confederate general and Lincoln's War were more widely known, these same individuals would be erecting more monuments to Forrest rather than having them torn down.

As it turns out, "Ol' Bedford" was not a lifelong slave trader, a cruel slaveholder, a racist, a white supremacist, a criminal, or the founder or first leader of the KKK as you have been taught. To the contrary, here in the South, the man I like to refer to as the "John Wayne of Dixie,"[1192] is considered one of our greatest military heroes; a true American patriot who was willing to sacrifice his life to defend the traditions of the conservative South and the U.S. Founding Fathers.[1193]

Since I have covered Forrest's life extensively in my other works, let us bring this brief chapter to a close with a look at the real man as he was in the last few years of his life, for when it comes to African-Americans and Forrest, no topic has ever been so savagely distorted and grossly revised by foes of the traditional Christian South. It is time to set the record straight.

What follows is a speech that Forrest gave at Memphis, Tennessee, on July 4, 1875. His audience was the Independent Order of Pole Bearers, a sociopolitical group of black Southerners and the forerunner of the modern NAACP. As reported by the unreconstructed Memphis *Daily Avalanche*, July 6, 1875, an African-American woman named Miss Lou Lewis, handed Forrest a bouquet of flowers, "as a token, of reconciliation, an offering of peace and good will." Bowing to the crowd, Forrest said:

> Miss Lewis, ladies and gentlemen—I accept these flowers as a token of reconciliation between the white and colored races of the South. I accept them more particularly, since they come from a lady, for if there is any one on God's great earth who loves the ladies, it is myself.
>
> *This is a proud day for me. Having occupied the position I have for thirteen years, and being misunderstood by the colored race, I take this occasion to say that I am your friend. I am here as the representative of the Southern people—one that has been more maligned than any other. I assure you that everyman who was in the Confederate army is your friend. We were born on the same soil, breathe the same air, live in the same land, and why should we not be brothers and sisters.*
>
> When the war broke out I believed it to be my duty to fight for my country, and I did so. I came here with the jeers and sneers of a few white people, who did not think it right. *I think it is right, and will do all I can to bring about harmony, peace and unity. I want to elevate every man, and to see you take your places in your shops, stores and offices. I don't propose to say anything about politics, but I want*

you to do as I do—go to the polls and select the best men to vote for. I feel that you are free men, I am a free man, and we can do as we please.

I came here as a friend, and whenever I can serve any of you I will do so. We have one Union, one flag, one country, therefore let us stand together. Although we differ in color, we should not differ in sentiment.

Many things have been said in regard to myself, and many reports circulated, which may perhaps be believed by some of you, but there are many around me who can contradict them. *I have been many times in the heat of battle—oftener, perhaps, than any within the sound of my voice. Men have come to me to ask for quarter, both black and white, and I have shielded them. Do your duty as citizens, and if any are oppressed, I will be your friend. I thank you for the flowers, and assure you that I am with you in heart and hand.*[1194]

Here Forrest calls African-Americans "brothers and sisters," assuring them that he is their friend—as is every former white Confederate soldier.

During Lincoln's War, besides the 65 blacks Forrest personally impressed into service, countless thousands more, from other Confederate units, fell under his command throughout the conflict. None deserted, but instead remained with their fearless leader until the final surrender of his cavalry in May 1865. Where is the racism?

Around this same time Forrest began campaigning for racial equality, coming up with a method to help revitalize the "prostrate South." Noting that it was not necessary for there to be a battle between people of different colors, he declared:

Let us all work together. In that way our entire nation will flourish.[1195]

As he told the Louisville *Courier-Journal*, in an effort to rebuild Dixie he wanted to repopulate the region with both freedmen and new immigrant blacks from Africa.[1196] How different this was from Lincoln who, as we have seen, right up until his death, campaigned incessantly to rid the country of blacks altogether, as one of his own generals (Benjamin F. "the Beast" Butler) later detailed in his memoirs.[1197]

African-Americans played a large and positive role in Forrest's life, as he did in theirs. Here, Forrest's wife Mary Ann teaches some of the family's house servants how to read and write.

But Southerner Forrest was cut from a very different cloth than the typical Northerner. For example, he often remarked on the warm feelings he felt toward blacks, and even had a plan on how to procure new U.S. laborers, not just from Africa, but also from China.[1198]

One last glimpse of the real Forrest was offered to the world after his death on October 29, 1877. During the ensuing funeral services (wake, march, and burial) at Memphis, Tennessee, over the next few days, some 20,000 individuals attended in order to pay their respects to the beloved Southern hero. Among them were President Jefferson Davis, *along with thousands of grieving African-Americans, who comprised one-third of the total mourners.*[1199]

The question is not, "Was Forrest a racist?" The question is, "Why were African-Americans not only allowed but encouraged to attend Forrest's funeral, but were strictly prohibited from attending Lincoln's?" The answer is in this book.

According to the Memphis *Appeal*, untold numbers of "negroes" (of all ages) "flocked" to Forrest's funeral, demonstrating not only their fascination with the General, but "genuine sorrow" over the demise of the celebrated military man. On the morning of October 31 alone, over 500 blacks walked solemnly past Forrest's casket, and hundreds more asked or were invited to walk in his funeral procession. From them not a single denigrating word was heard. Only adulation and admiration for Nathan Bedford Forrest, the "true friend of the negro."[1200]

Unlike in the North, blacks and whites in the South enjoyed one another's company, and typically developed powerful friendships that lasted a lifetime. This is one reason so many of Forrest's former black servants stayed with him throughout and after the War.

APOLOGIES & REPARATIONS

WHAT YOU WERE TAUGHT: The South should be ashamed of itself for practicing slavery, and owes an apology to the world for doing so.
THE TRUTH: The white South does feel shame for its involvement in slavery, and it has apologized for it repeatedly over the years—and continues to do so, at every opportunity.[1201]

The Northern states were responsible for both the American slave trade and American slavery, yet they have never issued a formal apology, or even acknowledged their culpability in the matter. The blame has all gone South.

What the South wants to know is why the North has not also apologized for its role in the "peculiar institution"? After all, it was Northerners (in Massachusetts) who first introduced the slave trade to the American colonies in 1638;[1202] it was Northern ship builders who constructed America's first slave ships; it was Northern businessmen who financed these ships; it was these Northern slave ships which first sailed to Africa; it was Northern ports that harbored the first American slave ships;[1203] it was a Northern state (the colony of Massachusetts) that first legalized slavery in 1641;[1204] it was Yankee businessmen who owned and operated the entire American slave trading business; it was New England slavers who transported African slaves to every port in the Americas;[1205] it was the North that first prospered from slavery; and finally, it was the North that sold its slaves to the South when it finally found them to be both disagreeable and unprofitable.[1206]

New Englander Henry Ward Beecher publicly criticized his region for its "responsibility for the existence of slavery," something few Yankees did then or now.

Thus when New England abolitionist William Lloyd Garrison campaigned for the secession of the Northern states from the Union, so that they could break their association with the "horrid slave states" to the South, another Yankee "antislavery reformer,"[1207] Henry Ward Beecher, disagreed, saying:

> . . . Union with slaveholders was not a sound principle of political action [on which to secede]. Secession from the Union was neither right nor expedient. It was not right, because the North as well as the South was responsible for the existence of slavery; the North as well as the South had entertained and maintained it; *the importation of slaves was carried on by New England shipping merchants and defended*

by New England representatives; and when the proposition came before the Constitutional Convention [in 1787] for the prohibition of the slave-trade, New England voted for the clause that it should not be abolished until 1808. Thus the North shared with the South in the responsibility for the sin and shame of slavery, and it had no right, Pilate-like, to wash its hands and say, "We are guiltless of this matter." It was under sacred obligation to remain in the partnership and work for the renovation of the nation. As it was not right, so neither was it expedient.[1208]

An Ibo family from southern Nigeria. The Ibo were once one of the great slave owning peoples of Africa. Neither the Ibo or any of the other thousands of African tribes, people, and ethnic groups who once practiced slavery on fellow Africans, and who aided in the development and maintenance of the transatlantic slave trade, have ever given an official apology for either their participation in or their contribution to American slavery.

An apology for African slavery in America is also due not only from England (which imposed slavery on the American colonies), but also from the thousands of descendants of early slave owning African-Americans, Native-Americans, and Latin-Americans, as well as from Africa herself: as we saw in Part 1, Africa not only practiced domestic slavery long prior to the arrival of Europeans, but greatly expedited and even encouraged Europeans in developing the Atlantic slave trade.[1209]

WHAT YOU WERE TAUGHT: The American South owes modern day blacks reparations for slavery, which should be paid out by the living descendants of early slave masters.

THE TRUTH: While today's New South Southerner may be receptive to this proposal, traditional Southerners understand that it would be difficult if not impossible to fulfill it for the following reasons.

The Dutch were the first to successfully transport blacks to North America in 1619 (an earlier attempt by Spain failed in 1526). In 1624 they founded the colony of New Netherland (later to become the state of New York) for the express purpose of opening up the slave trade to America's British colonies, dominating the sordid business for decades afterward. If reparations are to be paid American blacks for slavery, should not the Netherlands be the first in line?

A white female being sold on the auction block at a slave market in downtown Boston, Massachusetts. At one time hundreds of thousands of European-Americans also served as slaves and indentured servants across the U.S. Are not the descendants of these individuals owed reparations as well?

First, slavery was legal across the entire U.S. from 1776 to 1865,[1210] and was practiced by both by Southerners *and* Northerners. The North was itself the instigator of North American slavery[1211] and the epicenter of the American slave trade for decades.[1212] Because of this the North would also have to contribute. But why would it after spreading the falsehood, for the last 150 years, that "the South is totally responsible for American slavery"? By doing so it would be admitting its role in inaugurating and maintaining slavery for several hundred years, something it clearly does not want to do.

Second, European-Americans, as we have seen, were not the only ones who bought, sold, and owned blacks slaves. Tens of thousands of African-Americans, as well as untold scores of Native-Americans, Asian-Americans, and Latin-Americans, were also slave traders and slaveholders.[1213] Additionally, most Southern whites did not own slaves.[1214]

Third, reparations for American blacks would, allegedly, be paid by Americans. But it was not Americans who were responsible for the founding of the American slave trade in the Western hemisphere. It was an Italian, one by the name of Cristoforo Colombo, or Christopher Columbus, as we know him in English.[1215] If recompense is to be awarded American blacks, should it not then be paid by Italy, his birthplace, and by Spain, the nation that financed his expeditions to the Americas?

Scores of Native-American peoples, such as this member of the Nez Percé tribe, enslaved hundreds of thousands of other Indians, as well as whites, blacks, and browns. Such facts underscore the complications involved in paying reparations to American blacks for the "sin" of slavery.

Fourth, in 1619 the Dutch were the first to successfully bring blacks (as indentured servants)[1216] to North America.[1217] Thus the Netherlands would also need to help pay reparations. Great Britain and Portugal too, like Spain, were deeply involved in opening up slave trade routes between Africa and the New World.[1218]

Queen Isabella of Spain bids farewell to Columbus as he prepares for his first voyage to the New World on August 3, 1492. Columbus, who brought Africans to the Caribbean, eventually enslaved millions of Native-Americans, making him the founder of European-American slavery. Spain in turn funded the expedition, making her partly responsible for helping launch African slavery in the Americas.

Lastly, other racial and ethnic groups in early America besides blacks were also held in various types of bondage, from slavery to servitude, from indenture to involuntary apprenticeship. Among these were European-Americans themselves, the great majority who, like one of Lincoln's ancestors (an early relation who was part of the Massachusetts Bay Colony), came to America as indentured servants.[1219]

With these facts in mind, who would decide—and *how* would they decide—which European nations, and which European-Americans, African-Americans, Native-Americans, Asian-Americans, and Latin-Americans are obligated to pay reparations for slavery and who are not?

Explorer Hernán Cortés was one of the many early Spaniards who aided in bringing the European slave trade to the Americas. In 1519, arriving in Mexico, he came across the Aztec Indians, whom he viewed as an inferior, devil-worshiping race. To rid them of this "evil," he believed that he would have to destroy their cities, convert them to Christianity, and turn them into slaves. Amid the inevitable mass destruction and slaughter that followed, Cortés crushed the Aztec Empire and ruthlessly enslaved thousands of the region's Native-Americans. While we certainly feel pity for his Indian victims, this must be balanced with the fact that the Aztecs had been wantonly and savagely enslaving one another for centuries prior to Cortés' arrival—yet another important item left out of our anti-West, liberally biased history books.

AFRICAN SLAVERY TODAY:
INCREASING & EXPANDING

WHAT YOU WERE TAUGHT: Just as racism is slowly disappearing from the world, slavery is also disappearing and will one day be completely extinct. African slavery in particular, both domestic and American, is now completely and forever abolished.

THE TRUTH: Since, as we have amply shown, race and slavery are not connected, this statement is nonsensical. More to the point, neither racism or slavery show any signs of declining, and never have. In fact, as both are inherited ancient survival mechanisms (the former an aspect of xenophobia, the latter an aspect of socioeconomics), we should not be surprised to learn that there is every indication that both are on the rise, concomitant with today's explosive growth in population worldwide.

Indeed, contrary to popular opinion, slavery did not die out after Lincoln's phony Emancipation Proclamation in 1863, or even following the Thirteenth Amendment in 1865. It continues to thrive and is universal in scope, involving and affecting all races: according to Britain's Anti-Slavery Society, the institution is still found all over the world, even in the U.S., though it continues to flourish most consistently in Africa, the Middle East, the Far East, and parts of South America.[1220]

Not only this, but studies reveal that the rate of slavery is actually increasing not decreasing, for *there are now more slaves in the world than at any other time in human history*.[1221] In 1933, for instance, 5 million slaves were estimated to exist around the globe.[1222] Yet, at the time of this writing, 2016, at least 30 million people are currently living under authentic slavery,[1223] while an additional 200 million people worldwide are suffering under one type of bondage or another.[1224] (Let us contrast these figures with the Old South, which never possessed more than 3.5 million servants,[1225] 86 percent of these, in 1860, which were American born.)[1226]

As for the U.S., according to a pre-2000 CIA study, 50,000 people (mostly women and children, some of them African-American) were enslaved in the U.S.[1227] At the time of this survey, this number was expected to rise—and indeed it has. As of 2013 there were 60,000 slaves in the U.S.[1228] Both these slaves and their enslavers come in every race and color, more proof that slavery—whether modern, Victorian, Medieval, ancient, or prehistoric—is not, and never has been, based on skin color.[1229]

Here in the conservative South we will continue our fight against racism and slavery, the same humanitarian movement that first began in Dixie over 300 years ago. As part of this campaign of racial unification we traditional Southerners, both white and black, are exposing the fake "race war" fabricated by the Left in its attempt to socially divide and politically conquer America. This book on African-Americans and the Civil War is just one small cog in that wheel. May its bright light shine out into the world, and expose the dark lies of the enemies of truth.

The End

In the 21st Century Africans continue to enslave one another in astonishing numbers. The black African master of these slaves is using them as porters to carry supplies from one village to another. As this early 20th-Century photo shows, African slavers spare no one, not even children.

African authorities, like this Susu chief and his staff, were responsible for the enslavement of thousands of fellow Africans, a reality now ignored by mainstream historians. If the inventors of what I call "The Great Yankee Coverup" had their way, no one would ever be exposed to the facts concerning indigenous African slavery, which has endured for thousands of years into the present. In 1908 pro-South author J. Clarence Stonebraker wrote: "[Yankee] slave dealers only obtained their slaves by one [African] tribe conquering another and delivering same into the hands of the slave dealers, or by the consent of parents, getting up their children and selling them. The very false stories that a [slave] vessel's crew could go into the jungles and drive out as many negroes as they wished is grossly vile, and was hatched along with many others by the unconscionable and incorrigible prejudice of [Northern] partisans, and for an equally vile purpose. Such things are still being taught and believed to an extent in the frigid [Yankee] section of our country." In essence, it was African chiefs who first enslaved other Africans, and it was African slave merchants, slave drivers known as *slattees*, who then forcibly marched them to the coast in chains and sold them to Arabs, Europeans, and eventually Yankees. In plain English, *up until at least 1820, "no free blacks ever came to America from Africa."* Will Africa ever acknowledge the fact that she greatly contributed to, eagerly helped maintain, and actually laid the groundwork for the Atlantic slave trade? Not if the supporters of The Great Yankee Coverup and other members of the anti-South movement have their way.

APPENDIX

Black Confederate Photo Gallery

Uncle Henry Lewis of the Second Louisiana Cavalry, with his medals and Confederate Flag, black Confederate soldier. (Photo courtesy Lani Burnette Rinkel, UDC.)

Confederate Veterans Reunion of Company A, Fourth and Eighth Tennessee Cavalry, 1892, with black Confederate soldier standing far right. (Photo courtesy Lani Burnette Rinkel, UDC.)

A group of black Confederate soldiers at the Tampa, Florida, United Confederate Veterans Reunion in 1927. (Photo courtesy Lani Burnette Rinkel, UDC.)

1905 Confederate Reunion of Terry's Texas Rangers, Austin, Texas, with several black Confederates on the right. (Photo courtesy Lani Burnette Rinkel, UDC.)

A Confederate Reunion in Mississippi, at Dean's Church near Blue Mountain, 1900, with several black Confederates on the right. (Photo courtesy Lani Burnette Rinkel, UDC.)

A United Confederate Veterans Reunion, Russell Co., Virginia, circa 1912, with numerous black Confederates on the left. (Photo courtesy Lani Burnette Rinkel, UDC.)

Martin Marble of Greenville, Mississippi. Though not formally enlisted in the Confederate army, due to his "many [wartime] acts of loyalty, honor, fidelity, and personal devotion to the white people he knew," at the request of his many European-American friends, he was later made an official Confederate soldier, with all of the accompanying rights and privileges, including a military pension. Private Marble died at the age of 86, his funeral and burial generously paid for by members of the United Daughters of the Confederacy. According to an old newspaper article, "the homage paid Martin Marble, a penniless old colored man, is but living evidence that true worth is appreciated and honored" in the traditional South. (Photo courtesy Lani Burnette Rinkel, UDC.)

Reuben Patterson, black Confederate soldier, with Mary Gardner Patterson, 1924. (Photo courtesy Lani Burnette Rinkel, UDC.)

Steve Everhart, from Georgia, black Confederate soldier. According to Private Everhart: "If it wasn't for the Southern white man, my ancestors would still be in the jungles of Africa, ignorant as wild beasts; but he brought me over here and made a human out of me!" (Photo courtesy Lani Burnette Rinkel, UDC.)

Black Confederate soldiers at a Tampa, Florida, United Confederate Veterans Reunion in 1927. (Photo courtesy Lani Burnette Rinkel, UDC.)

NOTES

1. See Jones, TDMV, pp. 144, 200-201, 273.

2. See Seabrook, TAHSR, passim. See also Stephens, ACVOTLW, Vol. 1, pp. 10, 12, 148, 150-151, 157-158, 161, 170, 192, 206, 210, 215, 219, 221-222, 238-240, 258-260, 288, 355, 360, 370, 382-384, 516, 575-576, 583, 587; Vol. 2, pp. 28-30, 32-33, 88, 206, 258, 631, 648; Pollard, LC, p. 178; J. H. Franklin, pp. 101, 111, 130, 149; Nicolay and Hay, ALCW, Vol. 1, p. 627.

3. Fitzhugh, p. 81.

4. See e.g., Seabrook, TQJD, pp. 30, 38, 76.

5. Seabrook, EYWTATCWIW, p. 13.

6. See e.g., *Confederate Veteran*, January-December 1910, Vol. 18, pp. 7, 57, 58, 65, 66, 101, 105, 113, 116, 129, 160, 180, 184, 231, 242, 251-253, 266, 269, 298, 322, 344, 374, 375, 387, 405, 409, 417, 419, 428, 478, 481, 516, 517, 563, 577. This same year (1910), the editors of *Confederate Veteran* placed the following note on their masthead: "The *civil* war was too long ago to be called the *late* war, and when correspondents use that term, 'War between the States' will be substituted. The terms 'New South' and 'lost cause' are objectionable to the Veteran."

7. Dunn and Dobzhansky, p. 105. For a late 19th-Century view on this topic, see W. T. Alexander, pp. 21-24.

8. Montague, TCOR, p. 11.

9. Acts 17:24, 26. Jesus also disregarded race, as he illustrated when he met the woman of Samaria at Jacob's Well in Sychar. The Samaritans were of "mixed race" and Jews were forbidden to associate with them. See John 4:5-10.

10. See Dunn and Dobzhansky, pp. 6-7.

11. W. T. Alexander, pp. 21-23.

12. See Dunn and Dobzhansky, pp. 16-17. It is interesting to note here that motor ability and emotional balance tests reveal that 50 percent of the differences between twins are due to environmental factors; less than half are due to heredity. Dunn and Dobzhansky, p. 22.

13. Montague, MMDM, p. 44.

14. Montague, TCOR, p. xiii.

15. Montague, SOR, pp. 150-151.

16. Dunn and Dobzhansky, p. 14.

17. The word racism appears to have been first coined by Union officer Richard Henry Pratt of New York, during a short speech at the "Proceedings of the Twentieth Annual Meeting of the Lake Mohonk Conference of Friends of the Indian" in New York in 1902. See Barrow, p. 134.

18. Montague, TCOR, pp. 17, 23.

19. See Mead, SATCOR, passim. See also Dahlberg, passim. For an early 20th-Century discussion on the falsity of "race," see Beard, pp. 229-263.

20. Alland, p. 128.

21. Speech to the United Nations General Assembly, 42nd General Assembly.

22. E. McPherson, PHUSAGR, p. 281.

23. B. Davidson, TAST, p. 30.

24. G. Bancroft, TLOWHS, Vol. 1, p. 122. Emphasis added.

25. Estes, p. 81. My paraphrasal.

26. G. Bancroft, TLOWHS, Vol. 1, p. 123.

27. Coughlan, pp. 80, 83-84, 85.

28. Craig, Graham, Kagan, Ozment, and Turner, p. 252.

29. Blake, p. 95.

30. Penrose, p. 49; F. R. Willis, pp. 687-688; J. H. Parry, p. 27; Herring, p. 104; Burne, p. 424.

31. Coughlan, p. 86; Rodriguez, THEOWS, Vol. 1, s.v. "Africa."

32. Crane, Feinberg, Berman, and Hall, p. 152.

33. U. B. Phillips, ANS, p. 9.

34. Moore and Dunbar, pp. 103, 106; Durant and Durant, pp. 31-32; Seabrook, EYWTAASIW, p. 65.

35. See Moore and Dunbar, pp. 112-116.

36. Coughlan, p. 80. I am dating this period from the arrival of the Portugese in Africa in 1441, to the ratification of America's Thirteenth Amendment in 1865.

37. Du Bois, D, p. 172; Seabrook, EYWTAASIW, p. 279.

38. Palmer and Colton, p. 231.

39. Furnas, p. 115.

40. Drescher and Engerman, p. 44.

41. Drescher and Engerman, p. 30.

42. Coughlan, pp. 82-83.

43. Blake, p. 102.

44. Blassingame, p.14.

45. Hacker, p. 18.

46. Blake, p. 101.

47. Shillington, pp. 174, 175.

48. Kishlansky, Geary, and O'Brien, p. 530.

49. Stonebraker, pp. 50-51. Emphasis added.

50. Blake, p. 455. Emphasis added.

51. Crane, Feinberg, Berman, and Hall, p. 120.

52. C. Morris, WCE, s.v. "Slave Coast."

53. B. Mayer, p. 327.

54. Garraty, HV, p. 77; Crane, Feinberg, Berman, and Hall, p. 70.

55. Blake, p. 103.

56. J. Thornton, p. 307.

57. Blake, p. 441.

58. Blake, p. 442.

59. Coughlan, p. 84.

60. Blake, p. 95.

61. Easton, TWH, p. 679.

62. T. Bourne, pp. 68-71.

63. G. Bourne, p. 69.

64. B. Davidson, TBMB, p. 26.

65. Seabrook, EYWTAASIW, pp. 87-88, 94-96.

66. Estes, pp. 133-134.

67. Sumner, WSITBS, p. 12.

68. T. A. Bailey, ADHOTAP, p. 215.

69. B. Mayer, p. v.

70. Rodriguez, THEOWS, Vol. 1, s.v. "Africa."

71. Drescher and Engerman, p. 1.

72. Nevinson, p. 110; Seabrook, EYWTAASIW, pp. 62-64.

73. Drescher and Engerman, p. 34.

74. U. B. Phillips, ANS, p. 37.

75. Seabrook, EYWTAASIW, pp. 96-108.

76. See e.g., Meltzer, Vol. 2, pp. 60, 61, 62, 63, 64; Drescher and Engerman, p. 371; Vaillant, pp. 124, 126, 133, 200, 220, 221, 225-226, 255, 258; Johnson and Earle, p. 267.

77. See e.g., Drescher and Engerman, p. 389; MacQuarrie, pp. 21-23, 31, 58, 201, 209-210, 229-230, 311, 353-356; Howells, p. 298.

78. See e.g., Meltzer, Vol. 2, pp. 61, 62, 64; Drescher and Engerman, pp. 147-148; R. S. Phillips, s.v. "Slavery"; Hendelson, s.v. "slavery."

79. Garraty and McCaughey, p. 7; Leonard, p. 102.

80. Meltzer, Vol. 2, p. 4.

81. Durant, pp. 125, 159, 229, 275, 293, 337-338; Meltzer, Vol. 1, pp. 9-201; Nye, p. 46; McKenzie, s.v. "Slave, slavery"; Hartman and Saunders, pp. 54, 62, 70, 383, 446; Kramer, pp. 81-83; Eban, p. 20; Westermann, p. 90; Breasted, AT, pp. 83, 153, 218, 220; Magoffin and Duncalf, pp. 76, 100, 112, 113; Becker and Duncalf, pp. 41-42, 50; McKay, Hill, and Buckler, Vol. 1, pp. 30, 44, 67; Swain, p. 47; Jones and Pennick, p. 184; Warnock and Anderson, p. 94; Wells, Vol. 1, p. 186; Childe, p. 163; Andrewes, p. 26; Hayes, Baldwin, and Cole, p. 15; Johnson and Earle, p. 248; Breasted, TCOC, p. 75; Cappelluti and

Grossman, pp. 94-96; Craig, Graham, Kagan, Ozment, and Turner, pp. 11-12; Estes, pp. 13-30.
82. Drescher and Engerman, p. 77.
83. British and Foreign Anti-Slavery Society, p. iv.
84. Rayfield, p. 180.
85. Montefiore, p. 643.
86. I. L. Gordon, p. 362.
87. Note: Contrary to popular thought, the swastika (from the Sanskrit "amen") was not invented by the Nazis. It is an ancient religious symbol that originated in prehistoric times. One was found, for example, on a cave wall containing Stone Age art that dates back 10,000 years. This truly universal emblem appeared not only in ancient India, Persia, Japan, Libya, Greece, Rome, Britain, and Scandinavia, but it was also used in Medieval Christian church design, art, and heraldry, where it was known as the gamma cross. Swastikas with clockwise pointing arms represent the Sun and the Masculine Principle. Counterclockwise pointing arms signify the Moon and the Feminine Principle. B. G. Walker, TWDOSASO, pp. 61-62.
88. Meltzer, Vol. 2, pp. 270-277.
89. Speer, pp. 472-474.
90. Shirer, pp. 946-951. For more on the Nazi enslavement of Jews specifically, see Parkes, pp. 189-235.
91. Drescher and Engerman, p. 289.
92. Shirer, pp. 946-951.
93. Seabrook, EYWTAASIW, pp. 125-153.
94. B. Holmes, p. 5. Emphasis added.
95. Sumner, WSITBS, p. 45.
96. E. T. Clough, p. 89.
97. Mostert, p. 285; Jamieson, p. 17.
98. Milton, p. 271.
99. Löwenheim, p. 11.
100. Muehlbauer and Ulbrich, pp. 124-125.
101. Jamieson, p. 229. See also Fremont-Barnes, passim; Boyde, passim.
102. Osler, pp. 294-325; Seabrook, EYWTAASIW, pp. 155-163.
103. Barnard and Spencer, s.v. "Slavery"; Rodriguez, THEOWS, Vol. 1, s.v. "Historiography, African."
104. Encyc. Brit., s.v. "slavery."
105. Dormon and Jones, p. 64.
106. Lovejoy, TIS, p. 15.
107. Mbiti, p. 60.
108. Estes, p. 53.
109. U. B. Phillips, ANS, pp. 7-8.
110. Moore and Dunbar, p. 129.
111. Estes, p. 105.
112. U. B. Phillips, ANS, p. 6. Emphasis added.
113. Herskovits, p. 42.
114. Doubleday's Encyc., s.v. "slavery."
115. Haines and Walsh, p. 875.
116. Dowley, pp. 564-565.
117. Easton, TWH, pp. 683-684.
118. Madden was born in Ireland, but later worked on behalf of the British government, particularly on the problem of African abolition.
119. Blake, p. 103. Emphasis added.
120. Crane, Feinberg, Berman, and Hall, p. 120.
121. Garraty, TAN, p. 42.
122. Nieboer, p. 142.
123. U. B. Phillips, ANS, p. 29.
124. B. Mayer, pp. 383-386.
125. J. Thornton, pp. 304, 306.
126. U. B. Phillips, ANS, p. 45. Emphasis added.
127. See J. Thornton, pp. 72-74.
128. Doubleday's Encyc., s.v. "slavery."

129. Coughlan, p. 80.

130. Chadwick, p. 243.

131. Website: www.infoplease.com/spot/slavery1.html. For more information on modern day slavery, see Website: www.antislavery.org/english/slavery_today/default.aspx.

132. Braddy, s.v. "Slave"; Drescher and Engerman, pp. 5, 163-168.

133. Rodriguez, THEOWS, Vol. 1, s.v. "American Anti-Slavery Group."

134. Seabrook, L, p. 349.

135. Website: www.infoplease.com/spot/slavery1.html.

136. See Fox, p. 48.

137. McKissack and McKissack, p. 119. See Fitzhugh, passim.

138. Seabrook, EYWTAASIW, p. 86.

139. Drescher and Engerman, p. 239.

140. Stampp, p. 16.

141. Drescher and Engerman, p. 239.

142. Garraty and McCaughey, p. 26.

143. Wilson and Ferris, s.v. "Plantations." Many Northern whites, like Yankee judge Samuel Sewall, disliked blacks so much that they advocated using white slaves instead. See Sewall, Vol. 2, pp. 17-18.

144. Brackett, p. 25.

145. J. T. Adams, p. 53.

146. Roger's wife, Anne Phoebe Charlton Key, was a sister of Francis Scott Key, who wrote the U.S. National Anthem, *The Star Spangled Banner*. Like Abraham Lincoln, lawyer-poet Francis Scott Key detested abolitionists and the abolition movement. Indeed, he was a co-founder of the American Colonization Society (ACS), a Yankee organization dedicated to the idea of deporting all freed American blacks out of the country, preferably to Liberia, Africa—a colony set up in 1822 by the ACS for this express purpose. Lincoln mentioned Liberia many times in his speeches and writings as the best solution to the "race problem." See Seabrook, L, pp. 584-633.

147. Furnas, p. 108.

148. Bennett, BTM, p. 50.

149. Morison and Commager, Vol. 1, p. 51.

150. Carman and Syrett, p. 39.

151. E. J. McManus, BBITN, p. 57.

152. Goodwyn, p. 72.

153. Hacker, pp. 17-18.

154. Bedford and Colbourn, p. 13.

155. DeGregorio, s.v. "James Madison" (pp. 55-56).

156. H. B. Adams, Vol. 14, pp. 243-247.

157. Bennett, BTM, p. 443.

158. Brackett, p. 25; Wilson and Ferris, s.v. "Plantations"; Seabrook, EYWTAASIW, pp. 108-114.

159. Lyell, Vol. 2, p. 57.

160. *The North British Review*, p. 240.

161. See Nicolay and Hay, ALCW, Vol. 2, pp. 237-238.

162. Tocqueville, Vol. 1, pp. 357-358. Emphasis added.

163. Seabrook, EYWTAASIW, pp. 659-660.

164. Lyell, Vol. 2, p. 162.

165. L. Abbott, p. 157.

166. Lyell, Vol. 2, pp. 98-99.

167. Buckingham, TSSOA, Vol. 2, p. 112.

168. Hawthorne, Vol. 2, pp. 109-110. Emphasis added.

169. Martineau, ROWT, Vol. 1, p. 191. Emphasis added.

170. E. K. Barnard, p. 111.

171. Sturge, p. 40. Emphasis added.

172. Dicey, Vol. 1, pp. 70-72. Emphasis added.

173. Lyell, Vol. 2, p. 99.

174. Lyell, Vol. 2, pp. 100-101. Emphasis added.

175. See Fogel and Engerman, pp. 179-180.

176. Olmsted, CK, Vol. 1, p. 39. Emphasis added.
177. Seabrook, EYWTAASIW, pp. 61-68.
178. Chesnut, DD, p. 226.
179. Seabrook, TMOCP, p. 162.
180. According to the FBI the top ten states where the most hate crimes occur are all *outside the South*, except for one. In order of percentage of hate crimes (beginning with the highest number to the lowest), these ten states are: 1) Washington, D.C.; 2) Massachusetts; 3) New Jersey; 4) Oregon; 5) Kentucky; 6) Maine; 7) North Dakota; 8) Connecticut; 9) Colorado; 10) Minnesota. Website: www.fbi.gov.
181. As I explain in Chapter 76, the modern KKK is not in any way connected to the KKK of the Reconstruction period.
182. Newton, p. 259.
183. One of the fastest growing KKK areas is Long Island, New York. See Website: http://www.nbcnewyork.com/news/local/kkk-hate-crimes-long-island-swastikas-police-302964991.html.
184. Lott, pp. 35-60.
185. Ashe, p. 10.
186. Seabrook, TCOTCSOAE, passim; Stonebraker, p. 46.
187. U. B. Phillips, ANS, p. 41.
188. de la Rochefoucauld Liancourt, Vol. 2, pp. 461-462. Emphasis added.
189. Flint, Vol.1 , p. 106.
190. Chace, p. 7.
191. Lott, pp. 65-68.
192. B. F. Riley, p. 30.
193. B. F. Riley, p. 30. Emphasis added.
194. Blake, pp. 440-441. Emphasis added.
195. Dunbar, Vol. 1, p. 218.
196. See Estes, p. 229.
197. W. H. Collins, p. 60.
198. Dodd, TCK, pp. 29-30. Emphasis added.
199. W. H. Collins, pp. 19-20.
200. Helper, COTICOTS, pp. 12-13. Emphasis added.
201. U. B. Phillips, ANS, pp. 34-35. Emphasis added.
202. Ahlstrom, p. 649.
203. Rosenbaum and Brinkley, s.v. "Slavery"; Crane, Feinberg, Berman, and Hall, p. 73; Coughlan, p. 84.
204. G. H. Moore, p. 5; Blake, p. 370; R. S. Phillips, s.v. "Slavery"; Bennett, BTM, p. 443. Massachusetts was also the first state to ban interracial marriage. See Wilson and Ferris, s.v. "Miscegenation"; K. C. Davis, p. 9.
205. McKissack and McKissack, p. 3.
206. Du Bois, TSOTAST, pp. 162-167. Emphasis added.
207. Ahlstrom, p. 649.
208. J. T. Adams, p. 253.
209. R. S. Phillips, s.v. "Slavery."
210. G. Bancroft, TLOWHS, Vol. 1, p. 293.
211. Hildreth, THOTUSOA, Vol. 1, pp. 251, 492.
212. Meltzer, Vol. 2, p. 139. Also see Cartmell, p. 26.
213. Norwood, p. 31.
214. G. H. Moore, p. 5; Blake, p. 370; R. S. Phillips, s.v. "Slavery"; Bennett, BTM, p. 443.
215. E. J. McManus, BBITN, pp. 9, 10, 11.
216. U. B. Phillips, ASN, p. 103.
217. H. U. Faulkner, p. 58.
218. U. B. Phillips, ASN, p. 103.
219. Bowen, p. 217.
220. Wertenbaker, TPO, p. 198.
221. Bennett, BTM, p. 50.
222. G. H. Moore, pp. 130-132.
223. E. J. McManus, BBITN, p. 146.
224. U. B. Phillips, ANS, p. 104. Emphasis added.

225. See B. C. Steiner, passim.
226. Hildreth, THOTUSOA, Vol. 1, pp. 371-372; Blake, p. 371.
227. U. B. Phillips, ANS, p. 105.
228. Seabrook, TMOCP, p. 173.
229. E. J. McManus, BBITN, p. 59.
230. For more on the history of the New England slavery system, see Greene, passim.
231. Goodell, p. 106.
232. For more on the topic of slavery in Rhode Island, as well as in other New England states, see Website: www.boston.com/bostonglobe/ideas/articles/2010/09/26/new_englands_hidden_history/?page=1.
233. The Massachusetts Historical Society maintains numerous examples of these letters in their "Collections." U. B. Phillips, ANS, p. 28.
234. D. B. Davis, p. 135.
235. Pendleton, p. 56; Coughlan, p. 84.
236. U. B. Phillips, ANS, p. 138.
237. Blake, p. 445.
238. Johnston, p. 18.
239. U. B. Phillips, ASN, p. 106.
240. Ahlstrom, p. 649; Zilversmit, pp. 4-7.
241. E. Channing, pp. 6, 12.
242. E. J. McManus, BBITN, pp. 6-7.
243. Kishlansky, Geary, and O'Brien, p. 530.
244. E. J. McManus, BBITN, p. 60.
245. K. C. Davis, pp. 20, 23.
246. See DeWolf, passim; C. M. Johnson, passim.
247. Meltzer, Vol. 2, pp. 145, 148; C. Johnson, TPIGTTS, pp. 125-126.
248. The Royall's original home and slave quarters have been turned into a museum located in Medford, MA. See Website: www.royallhouse.org.
249. A. T. Rice, TNAR, p. 607.
250. Francie Latour, "New England's Hidden History," The Boston Globe, September 26, 2010.
251. See Lemire, passim.
252. Farrow, Lang, and Frank, pp. 179-191.
253. Boston Female Anti-Slavery Society, p. 5, passim.
254. E. J. McManus, BBITN, p. 156.
255. Blake, p. 481.
256. Dowley, p. 547.
257. Nye, pp. 30, 49.
258. W. B. Garrison, LNOK, p. 186.
259. J. M. McPherson, NCW, pp. 78-79.
260. H. U. Faulkner, p. 318.
261. Smelser, DR, p. 44.
262. E. J. McManus, BBITN, p. 183.
263. J. M. Burns, p. 393.
264. Garraty and McCaughey, p. 146.
265. Garraty, TAN, p. 83.
266. J. T. Adams, p. 53.
267. E. J. McManus, BBITN, pp. 67-68.
268. J. M. Burns, p. 392.
269. Genovese, p. 451.
270. F. Douglass, NLFD, p. 116.
271. M. B. Davidson, Vol. 2, p. 340.
272. Derry, p. 67.
273. Seabrook, S101, p. 30.
274. W. H. Collins, p. 84.
275. Seabrook, TQJD, p. 68.
276. Blake, p. 379.

277. U. B. Phillips, ANS, pp. 132, 138-139.

278. U. B. Phillips, ANS, p. 202.

279. W. H. Collins, pp. 84-85.

280. Seabrook, TMOCP, p. 185.

281. W. H. Collins, p. 9.

282. E. A. Andrews, p. 176.

283. Featherstonhaugh, Vol. 1, pp. 126-127. Emphasis added.

284. U. B. Phillips, ANS, pp. 133-134. Emphasis added.

285. Ahlstrom, p. 650.

286. U. B. Phillips, ANS, p. 286.

287. Nell, p. 218.

288. Beard and Beard, Vol. 1, pp. 652-653.

289. U. B. Phillips, ANS, p. 123.

290. Blake, p. 389.

291. Child, p. 11.

292. Brodnax, p. 10.

293. Child, p. 6.

294. Derry, p. 67.

295. U. B. Phillips, ANS, p. 75.

296. Burne, pp. 740, 741.

297. Garraty and McCaughey, p. 81.

298. See U. B. Phillips, ASN, pp. 104-105.

299. Adams and Sanders, p. 118.

300. See Kolchin, pp. 78, 81, 89-90, 94, 128.

301. Drescher and Engerman, p. 213.

302. Seabrook, EYWTACWW, p. 158. Also see Ransom, pp. 214-215; Bennett, BTM, p. 87; W. J. Cooper, JDA, p. 378; Quarles, TNITCW, p. xiii; Stephenson, ALU, p. 168.

303. J. H. Russell, pp. 9, 12-13.

304. U. B. Phillips, ANS, p. 426.

305. U. B. Phillips, ANS, pp. 426-427.

306. Child, p. 5.

307. McLoughlin, p. 205. See also Levy, passim; L. Morton, passim.

308. Schoepf, Vol. 1, p. 149.

309. Grimké, p. 10.

310. W. Wilson, DR, pp. 113-114.

311. Blake, p. 389.

312. L. Abbott, p. 149.

313. U. B. Phillips, ANS, p. 113.

314. Manegold, pp. 132-134.

315. Seabrook, EYWTAASIW, p. 197.

316. Bennett, BTM, p. 37.

317. Wise, p. 286; *The Outlook*, p. 109.

318. C. Johnson, TPIGTTS, pp. 81-84.

319. Bennett, BTM, pp. 37-38.

320. Durant, pp. 125, 159, 229, 275, 293, 337-338; Meltzer, Vol. 1, pp. 9-201; Nye, p. 46; McKenzie, s.v. "Slave, slavery"; Hartman and Saunders, pp. 54, 62, 70, 383, 446; Kramer, pp. 81-83; Eban, p. 20; Westermann, p. 90; Breasted, AT, pp. 83, 153, 218, 220; Magoffin and Duncalf, pp. 76, 100, 112, 113; Becker and Duncalf, pp. 41-42, 50; McKay, Hill, and Buckler, Vol. 1, pp. 30, 44, 67; Swain, p. 47; Jones and Pennick, p. 184; Warnock and Anderson, p. 94; Wells, Vol. 1, p. 186; Childe, p. 163; Andrewes, p. 26; Hayes, Baldwin, and Cole, p. 15; Johnson and Earle, p. 248; Breasted, TCOC, p. 75; Cappelluti and Grossman, pp. 94-96; Craig, Graham, Kagan, Ozment, and Turner, pp. 11-12; Estes, pp. 13-30.

321. G. Bancroft, TLOWHS, Vol. 1, p. 119.

322. W. T. Alexander, pp. 119-120. Emphasis added.

323. R. S. Phillips, s.v. "Slavery."

324. For a discussion of the authentic history of prostitution, see Seabrook, *Aphrodite's Trade*, passim.

325. Encyc. Brit., "slavery"; Meltzer, Vol. 1, p. 2.
326. B. Mayer, p. vi.
327. Cartmell, p. 26; Norwood, p. 31; Meltzer, Vol. 2, p. 139.
328. G. H. Moore, p. 5; R. S. Phillips, s.v. "Slavery."
329. See Cottrol, passim.
330. Seabrook, S101, p. 11.
331. Rodriguez, THEOWS, Vol. 1, p. xiii.
332. Stimpson, p. 29.
333. C. Morris, WCE, s.v. "Slavery."
334. Blake, p. 17.
335. Braddy, s.v. "Slave."
336. Estes, p. 121.
337. See Meltzer, passim.
338. Encyc. Brit., "slavery." My paraphrasal.
339. Durant, p. 20.
340. McKitrick, p. 13.
341. J. Campbell, pp. 212-213.
342. R. S. Phillips, s.v. "Slavery."
343. Meltzer, Vol. 1, pp. 1-6. The one early people who seem to have completely eschewed slavery were the Minoans of ancient Crete. For more on the fascinating world of the Minoans, see Gimbutas, passim. Some believe that the Australian aborigines did not engage in slavery (see e.g., Nieboer, pp. 85-87), but this is debatable.
344. Seabrook, S101, p. 13.
345. Mish, s.v. "slave."
346. Rosenbaum, s.v. "Slavs"; "Slavonic Languages."
347. Gwatkin and Whitney, Vol. 2, pp. 421, 430.
348. Meltzer, Vol. 1, p. 3.
349. Montefiore, p. 643.
350. The American South had a population of 3.5 million black servants in 1860.
351. I. L. Gordon, p. 362.
352. Note: Contrary to popular thought, the swastika (from the Sanskrit "amen") was not invented by the Nazis. It is an ancient religious symbol that originated in prehistoric times. One was found, for example, on a cave wall containing Stone Age art that dates back 10,000 years. This truly universal emblem appeared not only in ancient India, Persia, Japan, Libya, Greece, Rome, Britain, and Scandinavia, but it was also used in Medieval Christian church design, art, and heraldry, where it was known as the gamma cross. Swastikas with clockwise pointing arms represent the Sun and the Masculine Principle. Counterclockwise pointing arms signify the Moon and the Feminine Principle. B. G. Walker, TWDOSASO, pp. 61-62.
353. Meltzer, Vol. 2, pp. 270-277.
354. Drescher and Engerman, p. 289.
355. Seabrook, EYWTAASIW, p. 152.
356. U. B. Phillips, ANS, p. 107.
357. Hurd, Vol. 1, pp. 277-278.
358. Seabrook, EYWTAASIW, pp. 215-216.
359. Heston, p. 40.
360. T. W. Foote, pp. 36-37.
361. Blake, p. 371.
362. U. B. Phillips, ANS, pp. 108-109.
363. Ripley and Dana, Vol. 12, p. 371.
364. Williams-Meyers, pp. 22, 54. See also pp. 87-93.
365. Website: www.sites.google.com/site/tenbroeckmansion/Home.
366. Website: www.historiccherryhill.org.
367. Website: www.nysparks.state.ny.us/historic-sites/33/details.aspx.
368. Blake, p. 373.
369. Commissioners of Statutory Revision, p. 18.
370. Seabrook, TMOCP, pp. 174-175.

371. Stewart, p. xxvi.
372. McKissack and McKissack, p. 3. Strangely, while Sewall had understandable sympathy for enslaved blacks, he had absolutely none for the free whites who were hanged (or crushed under rock) for witchcraft, due, in great part, to his judicial support of the accusations. To his credit Sewall later expressed remorse over his actions, even asking his church congregation for forgiveness. This is small solace, however, to the living descendants and relations of his victims.
373. E. J. McManus, BBITN, p. 62.
374. Greene, pp. 172-173.
375. Such ploys were not always successful. See E. J. McManus, BBITN, p. 149.
376. Blake, p. 381.
377. E. J. McManus, BBITN, pp. 16, 17.
378. D. B. Davis, p. 135.
379. Countryman, p. 11.
380. Blake, p. 406.
381. W. H. Collins, pp. 19-20.
382. Farrow, Lang, and Frank, pp. 82-90.
383. Farrow, Lang, and Frank, pp. 4-5.
384. Dimont, p. 359.
385. Seabrook, EYWTAASIW, pp. 172, 216-219.
386. Hacker, p. 525.
387. Ellis, FB, p. 103.
388. A. J. Northrup, pp. 246-247.
389. Wallechinsky and Wallace, p. 427.
390. Seabrook, EYWTAASIW, pp. 220-222, 441.
391. Seabrook, EYWTAASIW, p. 420.
392. Eaton, HSC, p. 93; Hinkle, p. 125.
393. W. J. Cooper, JDA, p. 378; Quarles, TNITCW, p. xiii.
394. E. J. McManus, BBITN, p. 5.
395. Fogel, pp. 203-204.
396. M. M. Smith, pp. 4-5.
397. Seabrook, EYWTAASIW, p. 273.
398. Seabrook, EYWTAASIW, p. 426.
399. U. B. Phillips, ANS, p. 101.
400. U. B. Phillips, ANS, p. 112.
401. E. J. McManus, BBITN, p. 61.
402. H. A. White, p. 63; Seabrook, EYWTAASIW, pp. 270, 425-426.
403. U. B. Phillips, ANS, p. 110.
404. A. J. Northrup, pp. 267-268.
405. Garraty, TAN, p. 84.
406. Garraty, TAN, p. 84.
407. Blake, p. 379.
408. E. J. McManus, BBITN, pp. 129-130. My paraphrasal.
409. U. B. Phillips, ANS, p. 418; Seabrook, EYWTAASIW, pp. 459-460.
410. U. B. Phillips, ANS, p. 328.
411. H. A. White, p. 63.
412. See e.g., Seabrook, TMOCP, pp. 145-146.
413. Lincoln called his "Emancipation Proclamation" exactly what it was: not a civil rights emancipation, but a "military emancipation." In other words, its true purpose was to "liberate" black servants, not so they could be free, but so the liberal Yankee president could use them in his armies. See e.g., Seabrook, L, p. 647.
414. H. A. White, pp. 63-64. Emphasis added.
415. Thornton and Ekelund, p. 96.
416. Drescher and Engerman, p. 302.
417. Paulding, pp. 225-226. Emphasis added.
418. *Confederate Veteran*, March 1912, Vol. 20, No. 3, p. 105. Emphasis added.
419. Blake, p. 829.

420. Lyell, Vol. 1, p. 353. Emphasis added.

421. Fogel and Engerman, pp. 127, 128.

422. M. M. Smith, p. 189. Also see Berlin and Morgan, passim.

423. Fogel and Engerman, pp. 151, 241.

424. U. B. Phillips, ANS, p. 268.

425. Sitterson, p. 97; J. G. Taylor, p. 33.

426. Smedes, ASP, p. 71. Emphasis added.

427. Genovese, pp. 531, 535-536, 557.

428. Smedes, ASP, p. 106.

429. Thomson, pp. 183-184. Emphasis added.

430. Schoepf, Vol. 1, p. 221. Emphasis added.

431. C. S. Davis, p. 4; U. B. Phillips, LALITOS, p. 5.

432. For more on the hunting and fishing activities of Southern servants, see Genovese, pp. 486-488.

433. Sitterson, p. 97; J. G. Taylor, p. 33; U. B. Phillips, ANS, p. 268.

434. U. B. Phillips, ANS, p. 113.

435. Genovese, p. 566.

436. Rosenbaum and Brinkley, s.v. "Slavery"; M. M. Smith, p. 189.

437. W. H. Russell, Vol. 1, p. 140; Genovese, p. 569; J. G. Taylor, p. 128.

438. Bennett, BTM, p. 104.

439. Drescher and Engerman, p. 36.

440. U. B. Phillips, ANS, p. 268.

441. Rosenbaum and Brinkley, s.v. "Slavery"; M. M. Smith, p. 189.

442. See e.g., S. A. Hill, p. 21; Perlman, pp. 60-61.

443. Seabrook, EYWTAASIW, pp. 304-316, 321-322, 442, 668, 674, 796, 823.

444. Seabrook, EYWTAASIW, pp. 347-350.

445. Rodriguez, THEOWS, Vol. 1, s.v. "Antiliteracy Laws."

446. Chesnut, MCCW, p. 263.

447. See e.g., Starr, pp. 210-211.

448. Lyell, Vol. 1, pp. 360-361. Emphasis added.

449. Buckley, p. 62; Dumond, pp. 59-60; *Acts and Resolves Passed by the General Assembly of the State of Rhode Island and Providence Plantations*, January Session, 1911, p. 299.

450. Garrison and Garrison, Vol. 1, p. 323.

451. Bedford and Colbourn, p. 187.

452. Rosenbaum and Brinkley, s.v. "Jim Crow Laws"; C. Johnson, TPIGTTS, pp. 206-207; Seabrook, EYWTAASIW, pp. 647-648.

453. Rosenbaum and Brinkley, s.v. "Free Blacks."

454. Lincoln conceded that the Emancipation Proclamation had "no constitutional or legal justification, except as a military measure." D. Donald, LR, p. 203.

455. H. C. Bailey, p. 155; DiLorenzo, RL, pp. 26-27, 257-258.

456. Seabrook, EYWTAASIW, pp. 647-648.

457. Blake, p. 372. Emphasis added.

458. Fogel, p. 194.

459. Seabrook, EYWTAASIW, pp. 208, 252-254.

460. Genovese, p. 445.

461. Yetman, pp. 21, 35, 59, 112, 182.

462. Rubin, p. 159.

463. Genovese, pp. 448-449.

464. U. B. Phillips, ANS, p. 439.

465. Barrow, p. 134. Yankee Pratt, a Union officer during Lincoln's War, was the originator of the word "racism" in 1902.

466. Rosenbaum and Brinkley, s.v. "Jim Crow Laws."

467. C. Johnson, TPIGTTS, pp. 206-207.

468. O. Williams, pp. 48, 70.

469. U. B. Phillips, ANS, pp. 438-439.

470. U. B. Phillips, ANS, p. 111.

471. E. A. Andrews, p. 51.
472. M. Hall, pp. 137, 138.
473. E. A. Andrews, p. 167.
474. See e.g., Fox, p. 36; Seabrook, EYWTAASIW, pp. 654-655.
475. Pollard, SHW, Vol. 2, p. 296.
476. Pollard, SHW, Vol. 2, p. 202. Emphasis added.
477. See U. B. Phillips, ANS, p. 74.
478. Ransom, p. 41.
479. Burne, p. 581.
480. W. J. Cooper, JDA, p. 666. For an example of Davis using the word servitude, see J. D. Richardson, ACOTMAPOTC, Vol. 1, p. 494.
481. Grissom, p. 128.
482. Meine, s.v. "Slavery."
483. Bruford, p. 107.
484. Stampp, p. 192.
485. Fogel and Engerman, pp. 151-152, 241; M. M. Smith, pp. 184-185.
486. Fogel, p. 194.
487. Nye, pp. 146-147. Douglass' independence was purchased by British sympathizers.
488. Garraty and McCaughey, p. 159; Rosenbaum, s.v. "Vesey, Denmark"; Bowman, CWDD, s.v. "May 1822." Vesey bought his freedom in 1800 using money he had won in a lottery.
489. K. C. Davis, p. 23.
490. C. Johnson, TPIGTTS, pp. 131, 188-189; Quarles, TNITCW, p. 128.
491. Bruford, p. 107.
492. Fogel, p. 194.
493. Traupman, s.v. "slave."
494. M. M. Smith, pp. 4-5.
495. Seabrook, EYWTATCWIW, p. 160.
496. Seabrook, EYWTAASIW, pp. 106, 108, 251-252.
497. Estes, pp. 229-230.
498. There were Southerners who did not like the fact that Yankee abolitionists intended to destroy slavery in the North. However, these Southerners did not send 75,000 troops into the region with the order to annihilate everything in their path, they did not seek to overturn the Constitution, nor did they kill hundreds of thousands of innocent civilians and non-combatants. Lincoln did do all of this, however, and yet it is the South who is still blamed for the War.
499. The Northwest Ordinance, issued in 1787 and inspired by Southerner Thomas Jefferson, banned slavery throughout the Northwest Territory, an area that included what would soon become the Midwestern states of Illinois, Wisconsin, Ohio, Michigan, and Indiana.
500. U. B. Phillips, ANS, p. 120.
501. Wallechinsky and Wallace, p. 427.
502. Blake, pp. 405-406.
503. For more on gradual emancipation in New England, see Melish, passim.
504. See Seabrook, TUAL, p. 40; Seabrook, EYWTATCWIW, p. 46.
505. Seabrook, EYWTAASIW, pp. 242-243.
506. For more on the Southern Confederacy, see Seabrook, C101, passim.
507. Seabrook, EYWTAASIW, p. 602.
508. Wallechinsky and Wallace, p. 425.
509. Seabrook, EYWTAASIW, pp. 599, 612.
510. Crane, Feinberg, Berman, and Hall, p. 120.
511. W. T. Alexander, p. 240; Bedford and Colbourn, p. 85; P. M. Roberts, p. 198; Garraty and McCaughey, p. 81; Rosenbaum and Brinkley, s.v. "Slavery"; "Slave States."
512. Meltzer, Vol. 2, pp. 141-142; Roche, pp. 14-15; J. B. Gordon, pp. 18-19.
513. Behrens, p. 147.
514. Furnas, pp. 119, 121.
515. U. B. Phillips, ANS, p. 131. Emphasis added.
516. Collections of the Massachusetts Historical Society, Vol. 3, 5th Series, p. 402. Emphasis added.

517. Litwack, NS, pp. 4, 6.

518. Nicolay and Hay, ALCW, Vol. 1, pp. 231-232.

519. Seabrook, EYWTAASIW, pp. 236-239, 745-754.

520. Derry, p. 67.

521. Seabrook, S101, p. 30.

522. Cash, p. 63.

523. McDannald, s.v. "Slavery."

524. H. C. Bailey, p. 197.

525. Oates, AF, p. 29; M. Perry, passim.

526. See Grimké, passim.

527. D. D. Wallace, p. 446. Emphasis added.

528. See my nine books on Forrest: 1) *A Rebel Born: A Defense of Nathan Bedford Forrest - Confederate General, American Legend*; 2) *Nathan Bedford Forrest: Southern Hero, American Patriot - Honoring a Confederate Icon and the Old South*; 3) *The Quotable Nathan Bedford Forrest: Selections From the Writings and Speeches of the Confederacy's Most Brilliant Cavalryman*; 4) *Give 'Em Hell Boys! The Complete Military Correspondence of Nathan Bedford Forrest*; 5) *Forrest! 99 Reasons to Love Nathan Bedford Forrest*; 6) *Saddle, Sword, and Gun: A Biography of Nathan Bedford Forrest*; 7) *Nathan Bedford Forrest and the Battle of Fort Pillow: Yankee Myth, Confederate Fact*; 8) *Nathan Bedford Forrest and African-Americans: Yankee Myth, Confederate Fact*; 9) *Nathan Bedford Forrest and the Ku Klux Klan: Yankee Myth, Confederate Fact.*

529. See my two books on Lee: 1) *The Quotable Robert E. Lee: Selections From the Writings and Speeches of the South's Most Beloved Civil War General*; 2) *The Old Rebel: Robert E. Lee As He Was Seen By His Contemporaries.*

530. Seabrook, EYWTAASIW, pp. 220, 571-572, 596, 622.

531. See Seabrook, C101, passim.

532. Foley, pp. 811-812.

533. Seabrook, EYWTATCWIW, pp. 33-37.

534. McKissack and McKissack, p. 3.

535. Seabrook, TQJD, p. 68.

536. Seabrook, EYWTAASIW, pp. 230-231, 541, 549, 571.

537. See Johnston, p. 19; E. J. McManus, BBITN, pp. 196, 199.

538. Drescher and Engerman, p. 215.

539. Rodriguez, THEOWS, Vol. 1, s.v. "Black Slaveowners."

540. Greenberg and Waugh, p. 376.

541. See Foner, FSFLFM, pp. 87-88. See also Hacker, p. 581; Quarles, TNITCW, p. xiii; Weintraub, p. 70; W. J. Cooper, JDA, p. 378; Rosenbaum and Brinkley, s.v. "Civil War"; C. Eaton, HSC, p. 93; Hinkle, p. 125.

542. Wiley, SN, pp. 106, 148.

543. See Website: www.nps.gov/timu/historyculture/kp.htm.

544. Greenberg and Waugh, pp. 392-393.

545. M. M. Smith, p. 205. In 1860 a male slave could bring as much as $1,800, or about $56,000 in today's currency. Coughlan, p. 84.

546. In the 1850s prime field slaves could fetch up to $1,800, about $51,000 in today's money. Garraty and McCaughey, p. 214.

547. Greenberg and Waugh, p. 393; Seabrook, EYWTATCWIW, pp. 85-86.

548. U. B. Phillips, ANS, pp. 433-436. Emphasis added.

549. Grissom, pp. 131, 182; Stonebraker, p. 46; J. C. Perry, pp. 96, 99, 101, 174; Rosenbaum and Brinkley, s.v. "Five Civilized Tribes"; M. Perry, p. 183; Simmons, s.v. "Stand Watie"; "Indians, in the War"; Jahoda, pp. 85, 148, 154, 225, 241, 246, 247, 249.

550. C. Eaton, HSC, p. 49.

551. Gragg, p. 84; DiLorenzo, LU, p. 174.

552. J. C. Perry, p. 101.

553. For more on black slave owners, see Johnson and Roark, passim; Koger, passim.

554. L. Donald, passim; Ruby, passim.

555. Robinson, pp. 56-57.

556. Seabrook, EYWTAASIW, pp. 244-249.

557. See Chapter 1.

558. J. Campbell, pp. 212-213.

559. R. S. Phillips, s.v. "Slavery."

560. de la Vega, pp. 192, 355.

561. Mendelssohn, p. 173. For more on the Aztec religion, see Gardner, pp. 284-305.

562. Meltzer, Vol. 2, pp. 61-73.

563. Nieboer, pp. 47-86.

564. Nieboer, pp. 70-71. Emphasis added.

565. Rosenbaum and Brinkley, s.v. "Five Civilized Tribes."

566. Simmons, s.v. "Indians, in the War."

567. Nieboer, pp. 67-68.

568. Rodriguez, THEOWS, Vol. 1, s.v. "Amerindian Slavery, General."

569. "Hispanics" here is used to indicate those born in, or deriving ancestry, from Spain or Portugal. "Latinos" refers to those of Latin-American origin; that is, those of mixed European (that is, Caucasian) heritage and Native-American (that is, Asian) heritage. Hispanics were responsible for bringing *European* slavery to the New World (it already existed among Native-Americans), while Latinos were responsible for expanding it across the Americas. For more on the history of Hispanic slavery, see Rodriguez, THEOWS, Vol. 1, s.v. "Historiography, Latin American."

570. Stimpson, p. 30.

571. C. Morris, WCE, s.v. "Slavery."

572. Lott, p. 18.

573. See Burne, p. 453. For more on Cuban slavery, see Blake, pp. 356-357.

574. Crane, Feinberg, Berman, and Hall, p. 71.

575. Garraty and McCaughey, p. 25.

576. Greer, p. 216.

577. Meltzer, Vol. 2, p. 4.

578. Drescher and Engerman, p. 371.

579. Stimpson, p. 30.

580. Burne, p. 449.

581. McKissack and McKissack, p. 3.

582. Rutherford, FA, p. 38; Wallechinsky, Wallace, and Wallace, p. 11; Woods, p. 67.

583. E. B. Andrews, p. 73.

584. Furnas, p. 27; Meltzer, Vol. 2, p. 127

585. U. B. Phillips, ANS, p. 16.

586. Bertrand, pp. 185-186, 188; Albrecht-Carrié, p. 44.

587. Diamond, p. 210.

588. Bennett, BTM, p. 34; Swain, p. 730.

589. Coughlan, p. 82; Blake, p. 99.

590. Blake, p. 100.

591. Palmer and Colton, p. 92.

592. C. F. Adams, Vol. 4, p. 355.

593. Albrecht-Carrié, p. 44.

594. It is said that Spain murdered, by burning and hanging, some 50 million Native-Americans between the 1500s and the 1600s alone. Lubasz, p. 52.

595. Kennedy, pp. 21-23.

596. McKissack and McKissack, p. 3.

597. Rutherford, FA, p. 38; Wallechinsky, Wallace, and Wallace, p. 11; Woods, p. 67.

598. G. H. Moore, p. 5; Blake, p. 370; R. S. Phillips, s.v. "Slavery"; Bennett, BTM, p. 443.

599. A. J. Northrup, pp. 246-247.

600. Seabrook, EYWTAASIW, p. 280.

601. S. Foote, Vol. 1, p. 537. Lincoln also refers to Captain Gordon, along with several other seized Yankee slave ships, in his First Annual Message to Congress. See Nicolay and Hay, ALCW, Vol. 2, p. 101.

602. Nicolay and Hay, ALCW, Vol. 2, pp. 121-122.

603. Farrow, Lang, and Frank, pp. 131-132.

604. Kennedy, pp. 104-105.

605. For more on the *Nightingale*, see A. H. Clark, pp. 164-165, 343.

606. See e.g., Chace, pp. 11-12.

607. Boller and Story, p. 180.
608. Seabrook, EYWTAASIW, pp. 240-242.
609. Estes, pp. 229-230.
610. J. Williams, pp. 27-50; Encyc. Brit., s.v. "slavery."
611. E. J. McManus, BBITN, p. 148.
612. J. T. Adams, p. 199.
613. C. Adams, pp. 4, 58.
614. Curti, Thorpe, and Baker, p. 572; Rosenbaum and Brinkley, s.v. "Slavery."
615. Zinn, p. 185.
616. Chace, pp. 11-12. Emphasis added.
617. Boller and Story, p. 166.
618. J. T. Adams, p. 255.
619. Nicolay and Hay, ALCW, Vol. 2, pp. 1-2; Seabrook, GTBTAY, p. 48; Nicolay and Hay, ALCW, Vol. 2, p. 6; Beard and Beard, Vol. 2, p. 65; DiLorenzo, LU, pp. 24, 25.
620. Findlay and Findlay, p. 227; Fogel, p. 207.
621. For more on New England's so-called "abolition" of slavery, see Melish, passim.
622. F. Moore, Vol. 1, p. 45. I have slightly altered the text for modern readers.
623. Nicolay and Hay, ALCW, Vol. 1, p. 272. Emphasis added.
624. Nicolay and Hay, ALCW, Vol. 1, p. 539. Emphasis added.
625. See e.g., Nicolay and Hay, ALCW, Vol. 1, pp. 257, 259, 449, 469.
626. Kennedy, pp. 191, 233.
627. Nicolay and Hay, ALCW, Vol. 1, p. 231. Emphasis added.
628. For more on Stephens and his genuine attitude toward African-Americans, see Seabrook, TAHSR, passim; and Seabrook, TQAHS, passim.
629. C. Adams, p. 4.
630. Seabrook, TAHSR, p. 205. Emphasis added.
631. Seabrook, TQAHS, pp. 328-329.
632. Seabrook, S101, p. 67.
633. Seabrook, TQAHS, p. 329. Emphasis added.
634. Seabrook, EYWTAASIW, pp. 260-264.
635. E. J. McManus, BBITN, pp. 6-7.
636. C. Adams, pp. 4, 58.
637. Nicolay and Hay, ALCW, Vol. 2, p. 1.
638. See Spooner, NT, No. 6, p. 54; J. R. Graham, BM, passim.
639. Shenkman, p. 124.
640. J. M. Burns, p. 393.
641. Rosenbaum and Brinkley, s.v. "Underground Railroad."
642. See Foner, GTF, passim.
643. Gragg, pp. 191-192.
644. See Still, passim.
645. Siebert, p. 220.
646. Drescher and Engerman, pp. 106-107. See also Winks, passim.
647. U. B. Phillips, ANS, p. 110.
648. J. M. Burns, p. 393.
649. See e.g., Dormon and Jones, p. 160.
650. Seabrook, TMOCP, p. 141.
651. Fogel and Engerman, pp. 23-24.
652. Scott and Stowe, p. 321. Dr. Washington's expectation was fulfilled. He was buried in Tuskegee, Alabama, on November 17, 1915.
653. Seabrook, EYWTAASIW, pp. 335-336.
654. M. M. Smith, pp. 4-5.
655. Gragg, p. 84; DiLorenzo, LU, p. 174.
656. Parker, p. 343; Seabrook, EYWTAASIW, p. 273.
657. Fogel and Engerman, p. 240. My paraphrasal. Emphasis added.
658. Fogel and Engerman, pp. 232, 238-239, 240.

659. U. B. Phillips, ANS, p. 270.
660. Smedes, MOASP, p. 191.
661. Flint, Vol. 1, p. 248.
662. Stampp, pp. 178, 179.
663. U. B. Phillips, ANS, p. 328.
664. Estes, p. 131. Emphasis added.
665. Paulding, p. 223. Emphasis added.
666. Jervey, p. 68.
667. W. Wilson, DR, p. 127. Emphasis added.
668. Stroud, p. 50; Goodell, p. 46; U. B. Phillips, ANS, p. 493.
669. Library of Congress. Emphasis added.
670. See my book of the same name.
671. In other words, it cost Americans ten times more to fight and kill each other for four years than if they would have simply ended slavery (more proof that Lincoln's War was not over slavery). Rutland, p. 226. See also C. Johnson, p. 200.
672. J. Davis, RFCG, Vol. 1, p. 80.
673. Cleveland, p. 820.
674. Cleveland, p. 828.
675. Seabrook, EYWTAASIW, p. 1013.
676. Nicolay and Hay, ALCW, Vol. 2, p. 1.
677. Lester, pp. 359-360.
678. Nicolay and Hay, ALCW, Vol. 2, pp. 227-228.
679. Seabrook, TUAL, p. 40.
680. Seabrook, GTBTAY, p. 48; Nicolay and Hay, ALCW, Vol. 2, p. 6; Beard and Beard, Vol. 2, p. 65; DiLorenzo, LU, pp. 24, 25.
681. E. McPherson, PHUSAGR, p. 286. Emphasis added.
682. Seabrook, S101, pp. 74-79.
683. J. B. Gordon, pp. 18-19.
684. J. Davis, RFCG, Vol. 2, p. 764.
685. Seabrook, C101, p. 89.
686. J. Davis, RFCG, Vol. 2, p. 763.
687. See e.g., Nicolay and Hay, ALCW, Vol. 2, p. 568.
688. Seabrook, AL, pp. 47-49.
689. Nicolay and Hay, ALCW, Vol. 1, p. 299.
690. Seabrook, AL, pp. 47-49.
691. Like all liberals, Lincoln liked the idea of the government bailing out mismanaged, bankrupt, and corrupt businesses, an idea then known as "internal improvements," but which we now more honestly refer to as "corporate welfare." See e.g., Lincoln's comment on, and support of, the internal improvement idea in Nicolay and Hay, ALCW, Vol. 1, p. 8.
692. Simpson, p. 75.
693. Rosenbaum and Brinkley, s.v. "American System."
694. Weintraub, pp. 48-49.
695. Today we would refer to the Federalists and Hamiltonians as Democrats; in other words, liberals.
696. Woods, p. 34.
697. A. Cooke, ACA, p. 140.
698. Seabrook, AL, pp. 47-48.
699. For current news on the conservative fight against the big government that Lincoln helped install, see Website: www.breitbart.com.
700. Foley, p. 684; Weintraub, p. 44.
701. See Benson and Kennedy, passim.
702. Seabrook, HJDA, p. 68.
703. See McCarty, passim.
704. See Browder, passim.
705. Seabrook, TGYC, p. 60.
706. See DiLorenzo, LU, pp. 149-155.

707. Napolitano, p. 76.

708. Seabrook, S101, pp. 80-81.

709. See Stephens, ACVOTLW, Vol. 1, pp. 10, 12, 148, 150-151, 157-158, 161, 170, 192, 206, 210, 215, 219, 221-222, 238-240, 258-260, 288, 355, 360, 370, 382-384, 516, 575-576, 583, 587; Vol. 2, pp. 28-30, 32-33, 88, 206, 258, 631, 648.

710. Stephens, ACVOTLWBTS, Vol. 2, pp. 9-10. Emphasis added.

711. Seabrook, C101, p. 90.

712. For more on this topic see Seabrook, TQJD, passim; Seabrook, TAHSR, passim; Seabrook, TQAHS, passim.

713. For more on this topic, see Seabrook, C101, passim; Seabrook, TGYC, passim.

714. Seabrook, AL, pp. 76-77.

715. Burns, Peltason, Cronin, Magleby, and O'Brien, p. 151.

716. Seabrook, L, pp. 84-85. Emphasis added.

717. Shillington, p. 178.

718. Weintraub, p. 54.

719. Wertenbaker, TPO, p. 198.

720. Crane, Feinberg, Berman, and Hall, p. 120.

721. Garraty, TAN, p. 65.

722. For more on the Cotton and Slave Triangles, see Farrow, Lang, and Frank, pp. 48-49, 50.

723. Garraty, TAN, p. 80.

724. Seabrook, TCOTCSOAE, p. 65.

725. Stonebraker, p. 81.

726. Nicolay and Hay, ALCW, Vol. 2, p. 1. See also Boller and Story, pp. 166 (the Republican Party Platform of 1860, paragraph 4), 180; J. T. Adams, p. 255.

727. Spooner, NT, No. 6, p. 54. See also J. R. Graham, BM, passim; Melish, passim.

728. See Spooner, NT, No. 6, p. 54; Pollard, LC, p. 154; J. R. Graham, BM, passim; Seabrook, EYWTAASIW, p. 220.

729. Seabrook, ARB, p. 259.

730. Segars and Barrow, pp. 28-29.

731. Eaton, HSC, p. 93.

732. Barrow, Segars, and Rosenburg, BC, p. 97; Hinkle, p. 106; *The United Daughters of the Confederacy Magazine*, Vols. 54-55, 1991, p. 32. If we utilize Yankee General August Valentine Kautz's definition of a "soldier," then as many as 1 million Southern blacks served in one capacity or another in the Confederate military. See Kautz, p. 11.

733. Hinkle, p. 108. See also Quintero, Gonzales, and Velazquez, passim.

734. Lonn, p. 218.

735. Rosen, p. 161.

736. Hinkle, p. 108; Blackerby, passim.

737. Seabrook, C101, p. 102.

738. As I discuss, inexplicably, Union soldiers were also well-known to burn down schools, universities, laboratories, libraries, and even hospitals. In some cases they even dug up the graves of Southern men, women, and children in an effort to find valuable personal belongings that may have been hidden by Confederate families. See e.g., The Weekly News and Courier, pp. 116-127; Gragg, passim.

739. Let us note here that "uncle" was a common soldier's prefix, a term of endearment that was applied to both whites and blacks. See e.g., W. B. Smith, p. 77.

740. *Confederate Veteran*, September 1915, Vol. 23, No. 9, p. 425. Emphasis added.

741. *Confederate Veteran*, September 1900, Vol. 8, No. 9, p. 399. Emphasis added.

742. *Confederate Veteran*, September 1900, Vol. 8, No. 9, pp. 399-400. Emphasis added.

743. *Confederate Veteran*, June 1910, Vol. 18, No. 6, p. 294. Emphasis added.

744. *Confederate Veteran*, September 1903, Vol. 8, No. 9, p. 422. Emphasis added.

745. *Confederate Veteran*, September 1903, Vol. 8, No. 9, pp. 422-423. Emphasis added.

746. *Confederate Veteran*, September 1903, Vol. 8, No. 9, p. 423. Emphasis added.

747. *Confederate Veteran*, September 1903, Vol. 8, No. 9, p. 422. Emphasis added.

748. See Seabrook, EYWTATCWIW, passim.

749. Much of the information on black Confederates in this section came from the personal military collection of Ronny Mangrum—Adjutant for Roderick, Forrest's War Horse Camp 2072, Sons of Confederate Veterans—to whom I am indebted.

750. Seabrook, CFF, p. 208.

751. W. J. Cooper, JDA, p. 378; Quarles, TNITCW, p. xiii.

752. Berkin and Wood, p. 31.

753. Current, LNK, p. 228. See also Barney, p. 141.

754. Gragg, p. 88.

755. Current, LNK, p. 228.

756. B. F. Riley, pp. 63-64. Emphasis added.

757. L. H. Johnson, p. 180.

758. Seabrook, AL, p. 330; Quarles, TNITCW, p. 37; Greenberg and Waugh, pp. 372-373.

759. Barrow, Segars, and Rosenburg, BC, pp. 8, 25.

760. E. M. Thomas, p. 236; Fleming, p. 208; Quarles, TNITCW, pp. xiii, 48.

761. Genovese, p. 541.

762. *Confederate Veteran*, June 1896, Vol. 4, No. 6, p. 178. Emphasis added.

763. *Confederate Veteran*, May 1896, Vol. 4, No. 5, p. 153. Emphasis added.

764. *Confederate Veteran*, September 1915, Vol. 23, No. 9, p. 411. Emphasis added.

765. *Confederate Veteran*, September 1912, Vol. 20, No. 9, p. 410. Emphasis added.

766. *Confederate Veteran*, September 1912, Vol. 20, No. 9, p. 410. Emphasis added.

767. *Confederate Veteran*, September 1912, Vol. 20, No. 9, p. 410. Emphasis added.

768. *Confederate Veteran*, February 1913, Vol. 21, No. 2, p. 71. Emphasis added.

769. *Confederate Veteran*, September 1904, Vol. 12, No. 9, p. 443. Emphasis added.

770. *Confederate Veteran*, August 1894, Vol. 2, No. 8, p. 233. Emphasis added.

771. Shurter, pp. 28-29. Emphasis added.

772. C. Morris, TOSATN, p. 372. Emphasis added.

773. C. Morris, TOSATN, p. 372. Emphasis added.

774. Gay, pp. 100-103. Emphasis added.

775. *Confederate Veteran*, February 1904, Vol. 12, No. 2, p. 68. Emphasis added.

776. Washington is wrong here. Nearly a year before the War ended the Confederacy had announced that it was planning on full abolition. See Quarles, TNITCW, p. 280.

777. B. T. Washington, pp. 12-15. Emphasis added.

778. *Confederate Veteran*, June 1912, Vol. 20, No. 6, p. 293. Emphasis added.

779. *Confederate Veteran*, June 1912, Vol. 20, No. 6, p. 293. Emphasis added.

780. *Confederate Veteran*, March 1912, Vol. 20, No. 3, p. 105. Emphasis added.

781. There were some 182,000 free blacks in the eleven states of the Confederacy (Quarles, TNITCW, p. 35), nearly all who sided with Dixie. In addition, most traditional Southern historians believe that between 100,000 and 300,000 Southern slaves fought for Dixie. See Barrow, Segars, and Rosenburg, BC, p. 97; *The United Daughters of the Confederacy Magazine*, Vols. 54-55, 1991, p. 32; Hinkle, p. 106; R. M. Brown, p. xiv; Shenkman and Reiger, p. 106.

782. See e.g., Barrow, Segars, and Rosenburg, BC, p. 19; Greenberg and Waugh, p. 385.

783. See Kautz, p. 11.

784. These numbers do not include the other three "races," yellow, brown, and red, that sided with and fought for the Confederacy. See C. Johnson, TPIGTTS, pp. 169-197.

785. Using Kautz' definition and these numbers, 200,000 blacks fought for the Union, 1 million blacks for the Confederacy. Thus, five times, or 500 percent, more blacks wore Rebel gray than wore Yankee blue.

786. Seabrook, EYWTAASIW, pp. 689-690.

787. Derry, p. 114. Emphasis added.

788. Quarles, TNITCW, p. 273.

789. E. M. Thomas, p. 236.

790. See Barrow, Segars, and Rosenburg, BC and FC, passim; also see Segars and Barrow, BSCA, passim.

791. Kennedy and Kennedy, SWR, p. 89.

792. Gragg, pp. 191-192.

793. L. W. Hopkins, pp. 203-205. Emphasis added.

794. Long and Wright, pp. 319-320. Emphasis added.

795. See e.g., Barrow, Segars, and Rosenburg, p. 161.

796. Sorrel, p. 65. Emphasis added.

797. Seabrook, L, p. 916; Nicolay and Hay, ALCW, Vol. 2, p. 662. Emphasis added.

798. ORA, Ser. 3, Vol. 2, p. 809. Emphasis added.

799. ORA, Ser. 3, Vol. 2, p. 809.

800. White, Foscue, and McKnight, p. 212. It should be pointed out that there were also white sharecroppers. See Wilson and Ferris, s.v. "Plantations."

801. R. Taylor, pp. 279-280. Emphasis added.

802. L. W. Hopkins, pp. 136-137. Emphasis added.

803. Chesnut, DD, p. 403.

804. Seabrook, EYWTATCWIW, pp. 161-165.

805. Cornish, p. 15; Segars and Barrow, p. 134.

806. E. L. Jordan, pp. 218, 266.

807. ORA, Ser. 4, Vol. 1, p. 409.

808. Greeley, AC, Vol. 2, p. 522.

809. Seabrook, AL, pp. 335-336.

810. ORA, Ser. 1, Vol. 15, pp. 556-557.

811. J. M. McPherson, NCW, p. 165. See also Seabrook, AL, p. 376.

812. Seabrook, EYWTAASIW, pp. 817-818.

813. ORA, Ser. 3, Vol. 1, p. 184. The Union opinion of America's "savages" was aptly expressed by Yankee General Philip H. Sheridan, who said of them, "they are bound to be exterminated." Latham, p. 155.

814. Seabrook, S101, p. 83.

815. See e.g., Wiley, SN, pp. 241, 309-310, 317.

816. C. Johnson, p. 170.

817. Eaton, HSC, p. 93; Hinkle, p. 125.

818. Mullen, p. 33; Rosenbaum and Brinkley, s.v. "Forty Acres and a Mule."

819. J. H. Franklin, p. 37.

820. Grissom, p. 162.

821. C. Adams, p. 49.

822. W. B. Garrison, CWC, p. 220.

823. J. Davis, RFCG, Vol. 1, p. 439.

824. Spooner, NT, No. 6, p. 55.

825. See C. Adams, p. 36.

826. M. Davis, p. 80.

827. W. J. Cooper, JDA, p. 551. For more on this topic, see Seabrook, AL, pp. 453-467.

828. Confederate, p. 83. Emphasis added.

829. R. E. Lee, Jr., p. 100.

830. Barrow, Segars, and Rosenburg, BC, p. 97; *The United Daughters of the Confederacy Magazine*, Vols. 54-55, 1991, p. 32. See also Hinkle, p. 106.

831. Kautz, p. 11. Emphasis added.

832. Current, LNK, p. 228. See also Barney, p. 141.

833. Seabrook, AL, pp. 335-336.

834. Seabrook, EYWTAASIW, pp. 784-785.

835. For a European's view of the severity of Northern white racism (as compared to Southern white racism) in the early 1800s, see Tocqueville, Vol. 1, pp. 357-358. See also Seabrook, AL, pp. 189-240.

836. Greenberg and Waugh, p. 385.

837. Seabrook, TMOCP, p. 109.

838. L. H. Steiner, pp. 19-20.

839. Heysinger, p. 123.

840. Paradis, p. 25.

841. ORA, Ser. 2, Vol. 8, p. 324.

842. See Seabrook, L, pp. 883-917.

843. *Douglass' Monthly*, September, 1861, Vol. 4, p. 516. Emphasis added.

844. W. B. Garrison, LNOK, p. 186; DiLorenzo, LU, p. 28.

845. Seabrook, TUAL, p. 81.

846. See DiLorenzo, LU, p. 101.

847. Barrow, Segars, and Rosenburg, BC, p. 4; Mullen, p. 31.

848. L. Johnson, p. 134.

849. *ORA*, Ser. 3, Vol. 3, p. 252.

850. Cornish, p. 46.

851. Wiley, SN, pp. 322-323; Mullen, p. 25.

852. See Cornish, pp. 181-196.

853. Douglass, LTFD, p. 303.

854. Barney, pp. 146-147.

855. S. K. Taylor, p. 51.

856. Quarles, TNITCW, pp. 200-201.

857. Page Smith, p. 308.

858. Though 5,000 white Union officers eventually commanded all-black troops, only "about one hundred" blacks ever held Union officer commissions during Lincoln's War, and this despite the apathy, protests, and even outright opposition of Lincoln and his War Department. Cornish, pp. 214-215.

859. Alotta, p. 27. Lincoln paid his black soldiers $7 a month; he paid his white soldiers $13 a month. Quarles, TNITCW, p. 200.

860. E. M. Thomas, p. 297.

861. Seabrook, S101, p. 84.

862. Tocqueville, Vol. 1, pp. 383-385.

863. Seabrook, EYWTATCWIW, p. 171.

864. See Nicolay and Hay, CWAL, Vol. 11, pp. 105-106; Nicolay and Hay, ALCW, Vol. 1, p. 483; Holzer, pp. 22-23, 67, 318, 361.

865. Seabrook, TUAL, p. 81.

866. Seabrook, EYWTAASIW, p. 836.

867. Seabrook, AL, pp. 437-438.

868. At first Lincoln also refused to allow Native-Americans to serve in the Union army. Secretary of War Cameron was speaking for Lincoln when he said that the conflict "forbids the use of savages." ORA, Ser. 3, Vol. 1, p. 184.

869. Nicolay and Hay, ALCW, Vol. 2, p. 235.

870. Seabrook, TMOCP, p. 292; Page Smith, p. 308.

871. Henderson, Vol. 2, p. 411; C. Adams, p. 134.

872. Page Smith, p. 308. My paraphrasal.

873. Foote, Vol. 2, p. 393; Katcher, CWSB, p. 159.

874. Eaton, HSC, p. 263.

875. Catton, Vol. 3, p. 24.

876. Garrison, CWC, p. 105.

877. Simmons, s.v. "Negro Troops."

878. Seabrook, AL, p. 365; Page Smith, p. 309.

879. ORA, Ser. 3, Vol. 4, p. 1029; Katcher, CWSB, pp. 128, 158-159.

880. Gragg, p. 192.

881. Seabrook, AL, p. 294; Pollard, SHW, Vol. 2, pp. 196-198.

882. Wiley, SN, pp. 241, 309-310, 317.

883. Seabrook, AL, p. 349; Henry, ATSF, p. 248.

884. Eaton, HSC, p. 30.

885. Cornish, pp. 87, 269.

886. Nicolay and Hay, ALCW, Vol. 2, p. 398.

887. Seabrook, L, p. 656.

888. Furnas, p. 750.

889. Simmons, s.v. "Negro Troops."

890. Wiley, SN, p. 321.

891. Seabrook, TMOCP, p. 295; Buckley, p. 82.

892. Seabrook, L, p. 641; Nicolay and Hay, ALCW, Vol. 2, p. 288.

893. Wiley, SN, pp. 201-202, 212-213.

894. Leech, p. 293.

895. Quarles, TNITCW, p. 60.
896. Wiley, SN, p. 175.
897. Rhodes, Vol. 3, p. 466.
898. See e.g., Nicolay and Hay, ALCW, Vol. 1, p. 539; Nicolay and Hay, ALCW, Vol. 2, pp. 257, 289, 369-370, 433.
899. See e.g., Nicolay and Hay, ALCW, Vol. 2, pp. 257, 449, 469.
900. Garrison, LNOK, p. 176.
901. J. M. McPherson, BCF, pp. 788-789.
902. Mullen, p. 25.
903. Channing, p. 23.
904. Seabrook, AL, p. 225; Wiley, SN, pp. 322-323.
905. Current, TC, s.v. "African-Americans in the Confederacy."
906. Cartmell, pp. 144, 145.
907. Wiley, SN, pp. 323-324.
908. Seabrook, AL, p. 361.
909. Alotta, pp. 26-28.
910. Seabrook, L, pp. 918-938; Christian, p. 7; Meriwether, pp. 54-55; Oates, AL, pp. 5, 40, 53; Current, LNK, pp. 58, 60-61; Kane, p. 163; Southern Review, January 1873, Vol. 12, No. 25, p. 364; Lamon, LAL, pp. 488, 489, 493; W. B. Garrison, LNOK, p. 265; Barton, p. 146; DeGregorio, s.v. "Abraham Lincoln."
911. Channing, p. 129.
912. Seabrook, TMOCP, p. 297.
913. Jimerson, p. 81; Swint, p. 61; Jaquette, p. 37. My paraphrasal.
914. Simmons, s.v. "Negro Troops."
915. Durden, p. 269.
916. McKissack and McKissack, pp. 138-139.
917. N. A. Hamilton, p. 120; Förster and Nagler, p. 207; Masur, p. 110; J. M. McPherson, NCW, p. 163. My paraphrasal.
918. Nicolay and Hay, ALCW, Vol. 2, p. 1.
919. DiLorenzo, RL, p. 21.
920. L. Johnson, p. 135.
921. Pollard, SHW, Vol. 2, p. 198.
922. Wiley, SN, p. 202.
923. Page Smith, pp. 362-363.
924. Quarles, TNITCW, pp. 46-47. See also Seabrook, TMOCP, pp. 289-290, 300.
925. Seabrook, TMOCP, pp. 289, 300.
926. Chesnut, DD, p. 227.
927. Chesnut, MCCW, p. 798. My paraphrasal.
928. G. H. Moore, pp. 5, 11, 17-19.
929. Foote, Vol. 1, p. 537.
930. Seabrook, L, p. 281; Truth, p. 254.
931. De Angelis, pp. 12-18; Lott, p. 65.
932. De Angelis, p. 49.
933. McKissack and McKissack, pp. 142, 143, 144.
934. See Nicolay and Hay, CWAL, Vol. 11, pp. 105-106; Nicolay and Hay, ALCW, Vol. 1, p. 483; Holzer, pp. 22-23, 67, 318, 361.
935. See e.g., Nicolay and Hay, ALCW, Vol. 1, pp. 257, 259, 449, 469.
936. Horwitz, p. 204.
937. McFeely, G, pp. 22, 62, 69.
938. Meriwether, p. 219.
939. C. Johnson, p. 167.
940. Tragically, refugeeing slaves sometimes meant the breakup of black families as well as plantation communities themselves, a rich social network of white and black relationships, many of them tender, loving, and lifelong. E. M. Thomas, p. 240. In this way, among many others, Lincoln actually damaged race relations in the South, one of his goals to begin with.

941. Seabrook, TQREL, p. 106. See my two books on Lee: 1) *The Quotable Robert E. Lee: Selections From the Writings and Speeches of the South's Most Beloved Civil War General*; 2) *The Old Rebel: Robert E. Lee As He Was Seen By His Contemporaries*.
942. Kennedy, p. 91.
943. Smelser, DR, p. 42; Buckley, p. 37.
944. Foley, p. 970.
945. Farrow, Lang, and Frank, pp. 82-90, 179-191; Meltzer, Vol. 2, pp. 139, 145, 148; E. J. McManus, BBITN, pp. 6-7, 9, 10, 11; Bowen, p. 217; C. Johnson, TPIGTTS, pp. 125-126.
946. Derry, p. 428; Seabrook, CFF, passim.
947. ORA, Ser. 4, Vol. 1, p. 1020.
948. J. T. Wilson, p. 481. Emphasis added.
949. Seabrook, CPGS, p. 56; McDonough and Connelly, pp. 137-138.
950. Warner, GG, s.v. "Patrick Ronayne Cleburne."
951. Nicolay and Hay, ALCW, Vol. 2, pp. 508-509.
952. Durden, pp. 245, 215; Quarles, TNITCW, p. 280; Seabrook, EYWTAASIW, pp. 799-802.
953. McElroy, p. 357.
954. McFeely, G, p. 71.
955. A. D. Richardson, p. 95.
956. A. D. Richardson, p. 152.
957. McFeely, G, pp. 22, 62, 69.
958. Website: www.understandingprejudice.org/slavery/presinfo.php?president=18. See also Simon, Vol. 2, p. 22.
959. Cramer, p. 85.
960. S. Foote, Vol. 2, p. 638. Grant uttered this remark in a letter to Elihu B. Washburne, August 30, 1863.
961. U. S. Grant, Vol. 1, p. 215.
962. As Daugherty writes of the Emancipation Proclamation: Lincoln "had played his trump card, and nothing had happened." Daugherty, p. 169.
963. Rutherford, FA, p. 38; Wallechinsky, Wallace, and Wallace, p. 11; Woods, p. 67.
964. T. N. Page, p. 57; R. H. McKim, p. 31.
965. Rutherford, FA, p. 38.
966. McFeely, G, p. 439.
967. Seabrook, EYWTAASIW, pp. 524, 860-863.
968. M. M. Smith, pp. 4-5.
969. Seabrook, C101, p. 98.
970. Seabrook, EYWTAASIW, pp. 167-229.
971. Seabrook, EYWTAASIW, p. 225.
972. Seabrook, C101, p. 99.
973. See Seabrook, TGYC, passim.
974. Quarles, TNITCW, p. 280.
975. Seabrook, EYWTAASIW, p. 243.
976. Seabrook, EYWTAASIW, p. 602.
977. Seabrook, EYWTAASIW, pp. 549-646.
978. Seabrook, TQREL, p. 106.
979. Durden, pp. 245, 215; Quarles, TNITCW, p. 280; Seabrook, EYWTAASIW, pp. 799-802.
980. Seabrook, C101, p. 100.
981. Hacker, p. 584.
982. Quarles, TNITCW, pp. 146-147.
983. For the full text see Nicolay and Hay, ALCW, Vol. 2, pp. 222-225. See also W. P. Pickett, pp. 317-323.
984. Nicolay and Hay, ALCW, Vol. 2, p. 223.
985. Nicolay and Hay, ALCW, Vol. 2, p. 223.
986. Nicolay and Hay, ALCW, Vol. 2, p. 224.
987. See R. L. Riley, p. 109.
988. Quarles, TNITCW, p. 148.
989. Oates, AL, p. 103. See also Janessa Hoyte, "Taking Another Look at Abraham Lincoln," *The Crisis*, November/December 2000, pp. 52-54.

990. *Douglass' Monthly*, September 1862, Vol. 5, pp. 707-708. Emphasis added.

991. See the *National Anti-Slavery Standard*, September 6, 1862.

992. Fogel, pp. 31-32.

993. Meltzer, Vol. 2, p. 127.

994. Fogel and Engerman, pp. 23-24. Contrary to Northern mythology, of the South's 3,500,000 black servants, only 14 percent (or about 500,000 individuals) were imported from Africa between the settling of Jamestown, Virginia, and 1861. The other 3,000,000 (86 percent), all American-born, were the result of natural reproduction. Garraty and McCaughey, p. 214.

995. Blight, p. 141.

996. *An Appeal*, pp. 4, 7-8.

997. W. W. Brown, pp. 258-259. Emphasis added.

998. Buckley, p. 65.

999. Hacker, p. 580; Rosenbaum and Brinkley, s.v. "Lincoln and Douglas"; L. Johnson, p. 54; DeGregorio, s.v. "Abraham Lincoln"; C. Adams, p. 159; Litwack, p. 276; W. C. Wade, p. 39. See Bennett, passim. See also Nicolay and Hay, ALCW, Vol. 1, p. 284; Basler, ALSW, pp. 400, 402, 403-404; Stern, pp. 492-493; Holzer, pp. 189, 251.

1000. Garraty and McCaughey, p. 253; Hacker, p. 584; Grissom, p. 127.

1001. Findlay and Findlay, p. 227; Fogel, p. 207.

1002. Long and Long, pp. 593-594.

1003. J. D. Richardson, Vol. 1, p. 494.

1004. Quarles, TNITCW, p. 280.

1005. Seabrook, C101, p. 100; Seabrook, EYWTATCWIW, p. 110.

1006. See C. Johnson, pp. 187-188.

1007. J. Davis, RFCG, Vol. 2, p. 701.

1008. Hinkle, p. 108.

1009. See e.g., Greenberg and Waugh, pp. 351-358.

1010. Seabrook, TUAL, p. 80.

1011. Seabrook, TUAL, p. 81.

1012. Seabrook, ARB, p. 12.

1013. J. Davis, RFCG, Vol. 2, p. 701.

1014. Shenkman and Reiger, p. 124.

1015. J. Davis, RFCG, Vol. 1, p. 518.

1016. Seabrook, EYWTATCWIW, pp. 109-115.

1017. Seabrook, TQSJ, pp. 17, 373-374.

1018. Seabrook, TQSJ, p. 88.

1019. The issuance of Lincoln's several emancipations proceeded this way: the first, a draft submitted privately to his cabinet on July 22, 1862; the second, the Preliminary one released publicly on September 22, 1862; the third, a draft of the Final proclamation submitted to his cabinet on December 30, 1862; and the fourth, the Final version issued on January 1, 1863. See Nicolay and Hay, ALCW, Vol. 2, p. 213; Nicolay and Hay, ALCW, Vol. 2, pp. 237-238; Nicolay and Hay, ALCW, Vol. 2, p. 285; Nicolay and Hay, ALCW, Vol. 2, pp. 287-288.

1020. D. H. Donald, L, p. 374.

1021. Nicolay and Hay, ALCW, Vol. 2, p. 237.

1022. Seabrook, L, p. 642.

1023. Nicolay and Hay, ALCW, Vol. 2, p. 274.

1024. Cornish, p. 95.

1025. G. Alexander, p. 557.

1026. Nicolay and Hay, ALCW, Vol. 2, p. 271.

1027. D. H. Donald, L, p. 355.

1028. See e.g., Tocqueville, Vol. 1, pp. 357-358.

1029. Unger, Vol. 2, p. 442. See also Brodie, passim.

1030. Rhodes, Vol. 1, pp. 307, 309.

1031. Shufeldt, p. 115. Emphasis added.

1032. E. J. McManus, BBITN, p. 66.

1033. Seligmann, p. 9.

1034. See Darwin, p. 91.

1035. Bailyn, Dallek, Davis, Donald, Thomas, and Wood, p. 29.

1036. By "authentic abolitionists" I mean antislavery advocates who were both for abolition *and* for welcoming blacks into American society as full-fledged citizens with complete equal rights. Very few individuals, even the so-called most vociferous abolitionists, fell into this category. In fact, authentic abolitionists were so rare at the time that they could almost be counted on one hand. Even William Lloyd Garrison (the founder of the *Northern* abolition movement), Horace Greeley (abolitionist founder of the New York *Tribune*), and Harriet Beecher Stowe (abolitionist author of *Uncle Tom's Cabin*), at one time supported black colonization: the deportation of all free African-Americans. Fogel, p. 254; Burlingame, p. 50.

1037. Nicolay and Hay, ALCW, Vol. 1, p. 539. Emphasis added.

1038. Fox, p. 52.

1039. Fox, p. 54.

1040. Blake, p. 359.

1041. Fox, p. 42.

1042. See e.g., Lincoln's plea for black colonization in his Preliminary Emancipation Proclamation, issued September 22, 1862, Nicolay and Hay, ALCW, Vol. 2, p. 237.

1043. B. F. Butler, p. 903. See also W. P. Pickett, p. 326; M. Davis, pp. 147-148; Adams and Sanders, p. 192.

1044. Seabrook, AL, p. 256; B. F. Butler, p. 903. Emphasis added. See also W. P. Pickett, pp. 326-327; Woodson, p. 20.

1045. Seabrook, AL, p. 256; B. F. Butler, p. 907.

1046. J. G. de R. Hamilton, p. 157. Emphasis added.

1047. Woodson, p. 21.

1048. W. P. Pickett, pp. 328, 330.

1049. Lincoln's death in April 1865, at Booth's hands, allowed the Radicals (abolitionists) in his party to take over the government, after which they pushed through the Thirteenth Amendment in December 1865. It was this bill, not Lincoln's Emancipation Proclamation, that finally ended slavery across the entire U.S. In this sense then Booth was the "Great Emancipator," not Lincoln. See Seabrook, EYWTAASIW, pp. 734-779.

1050. See Foote, Vol. 1, pp. 536-537.

1051. See Nicolay and Hay, ALCW, Vol. 1, pp. 433, 451, 468.

1052. Nicolay and Hay, ALCW, Vol. 1, p. 659. For Stephens' response, see Seabrook, TQAHS, pp. 98-101.

1053. Liberal Lincoln was promoting anti-South Yankee propaganda here. The Conservative South never once demanded that "slavery ought to be extended." She only asked that individuals be given the choice as to whether or not they practiced slavery in the new Western Territories. After all, the institution was still legal under the Constitution at the time. As always, the South's main interest was the preservation of individual and states' rights, not the preservation of slavery.

1054. Nicolay and Hay, ALCW, Vol. 1, p. 197. Emphasis added.

1055. Seabrook, L, pp. 420-421; Nicolay and Hay, ALCW, Vol. 1, p. 508. Emphasis added.

1056. Seabrook, EYWTATCWIW, p. 148.

1057. Nicolay and Hay, ALCW, Vol. 1, p. 234. Emphasis added.

1058. Nicolay and Hay, ALCW, Vol. 1, p. 556.

1059. Seabrook, L, pp. 353-475; Ransom, p. 173.

1060. Nicolay and Hay, ALCW, Vol. 1, p. 257.

1061. W. Wilson, DR, pp. 130-131.

1062. DiLorenzo, LU, p. 101.

1063. *The Congressional Globe*, 36th Congress, 1st Session, p. 58; Carey, p. 181. See also Seabrook, EYWTAASIW, pp. 772-776.

1064. Nicolay and Hay, ALCW, Vol. 1, p. 669.

1065. Nicolay and Hay, ALCW, Vol. 2, pp. 1-2; Seabrook, GTBTAY, p. 48.

1066. Seabrook, AL, pp. 372-373.

1067. Long and Long, s.v. "February 25, 1862."

1068. Boller and Story, p. 180.

1069. R. S. Phillips, s.v. "Emancipation Proclamation."

1070. Encyc. Brit., s.v. "slavery."

1071. Woods, p. 67; Rutherford, FA, p. 38; Wallechinsky, Wallace, and Wallace, p. 11. Grant did not free his slaves until he was forced to by the passage of the Thirteenth Amendment on December 6, 1865, eight months after Lincoln's War ended.

1072. Seabrook, AL, p. 315; Nicolay and Hay, ALCW, Vol. 2, pp. 287-288.

1073. T. A. Baily, p. 341.

1074. Seabrook, L, p. 647.

1075. Sandburg, SOL, p. 152.

1076. Seabrook, EYWTAASIW, pp. 609, 611, 686-688, 694.

1077. Lincoln's procrastination toward issuing the Emancipation Proclamation earned him numerous unflattering titles from fellow Republicans, such as "the tortoise president" and "the slow coach at Washington." Seabrook, EYWTAASIW, p. 696.

1078. C. Adams, p. 135; DiLorenzo, GC, p. 255; Johannsen, p. 55.

1079. Nicolay and Hay, ALCW, Vol. 3, p. 33.

1080. Nicolay and Hay, CWAL, Vol. 1, p. 15.

1081. McKissack and McKissack, pp. 134, 135.

1082. Seabrook, L, p. 647.

1083. W. B. Garrison, LNOK, p. 186; DiLorenzo, LU, p. 28.

1084. De Angelis, pp. 12-18; Lott, p. 65; J. J. Holland, passim.

1085. Garrison, LNOK, p. 176; J. M. McPherson, BCF, pp. 788-789.

1086. See Spooner, NT, No. 6, p. 54; Pollard, LC, p. 154; Graham, BM, passim.

1087. See Nicolay and Hay, CWAL, Vol. 11, pp. 105-106; Nicolay and Hay, ALCW, Vol. 1, p. 483; Holzer, pp. 22-23, 67, 318, 361.

1088. Current, LNK, pp. 242-246; W. C. Davis, AHD, p. 164; Garrison, LNOK, p. 181; Weintraub, p. 73.

1089. B. F. Butler, p. 903. See also W. P. Pickett, pp. 326-327.

1090. Current, LNK, pp. 218-219; W. B. Garrison, LNOK, pp. 35-37; Greenberg and Waugh, p. 355.

1091. Seabrook, GTBTAY, p. 48; Nicolay and Hay, ALCW, Vol. 2, p. 6; Beard and Beard, Vol. 2, p. 65; DiLorenzo, LU, pp. 24, 25.

1092. M. Davis, p. 83. See also Seabrook, AL, passim.

1093. See e.g., T. A. Bailey, TAS, pp. 468-469.

1094. Seabrook, EYWTAASIW, pp. 686-694, 732, 764.

1095. Nicolay and Hay, ALCW, Vol. 2, pp. 508-509.

1096. Seabrook, EYWTAASIW, pp. 718-719.

1097. Seabrook, EYWTAASIW, p. 722.

1098. Fogel and Engerman, p. 261.

1099. Billingsley, p. 69.

1100. Hurmence, p. 102. My paraphrasal.

1101. To his credit, Lincoln had at first crusaded for gradual compensated emancipation. But the Radicals (that is, abolitionists) in his party wanted complete, immediate, unconditional, and non-compensated emancipation. Under pressure to secure votes for his 1864 reelection campaign, Lincoln caved into the abolitionists and issued his disastrous and illegal Final Emancipation Proclamation on January 1, 1863.

1102. Seabrook, EYWTAASIW, p. 35.

1103. Seabrook, EYWTAASIW, pp. 716-717.

1104. Thornton and Ekelund, p. 96.

1105. Wilson and Ferris, s.v. "Cotton Culture."

1106. Latham, pp. 269-270; Billingsley, p. 69.

1107. Buckley, p. 116. My paraphrasal.

1108. Website: www.archives.gov/nae/news/featured-programs/lincoln/080920Lincoln02Transcript.pdf. Emphasis added.

1109. Keckley, pp. 140-141. Emphasis added.

1110. Seabrook, EYWTAASIW, pp. 722-726, 810.

1111. See e.g., Nicolay and Hay, CWAL, Vol. 11, pp. 105-106; Nicolay and Hay, ALCW, Vol. 1, p. 483; Nicolay and Hay, ALCW, Vol. 2, p. 237; Holzer, pp. 22-23, 67, 318, 361.

1112. *Douglass' Monthly*, September 1862, Vol. 5, pp. 707-708.

1113. Schwartz, p. 86. My paraphrasal.

1114. F. Douglass, LTFD, p. 872. Emphasis added.

1115. Seabrook, EYWTAASIW, pp. 730-731.

1116. Nicolay and Hay, ALCW, Vol. 1, p. 659. Lincoln made this statement in a "strictly confidential" letter to North Carolinian John A. Gilmer, on December 15, 1860. The president-elect was interested in appointing Gilmer secretary of the treasury. Desperate to have a Southerner in his cabinet, in his letter Lincoln laid out his position on slavery, hoping to allay any fears Gilmer might have about the future of the institution. Gilmer saw through it and the ploy failed. New Englander Salmon P. Chase became Lincoln's first secretary of the treasury.

1117. Seabrook, EYWTAASIW, p. 696.

1118. Shotwell, p. 436.

1119. Cromwell, pp. 121-122.

1120. Though earlier in his presidency Lincoln had promised that he would never interfere with slavery in Washington, D.C., as usual, when it benefitted him he changed his mind. In this case, he needed the abolitionist vote for his upcoming bid for reelection. Additionally, freeing Washington's slaves allowed him to press Congress harder for black deportation and colonization.

1121. J. C. Perry, p. 191. This did not end segregation, of course. If anything it exasperated the problem of Northern white racism. Indeed, total integration was not achieved in Washington, D.C. until 1956. See Weintraub, p. 147.

1122. The National Almanac (1863), p. 250.

1123. Nicolay and Hay, ALCW, Vol. 2, p. 144.

1124. Lincoln and the abolitionists, Caucasian Washingtonians declared, were determined to make the city "a hell on earth for the white man." Leech, pp. 295, 298.

1125. Buckley, p. 86; Leech, p. 298.

1126. Truth, p. 254. See also McKissack and McKissack, pp. 142, 143, 144.

1127. See Greenberg and Waugh, pp. 351-358.

1128. See, e.g., Chesnut, MCCW, p. 435. We will note that in the South "aunty" (and "uncle" for men) was considered a term of endearment by both whites and blacks, particularly when applied to one's own servants.

1129. McKissack and McKissack, p. 146; Coffin, p. 457.

1130. Findlay and Findlay, p. 227; Fogel, p. 207.

1131. Garraty and McCaughey, p. 254.

1132. Nicolay and Hay, ALCW, Vol. 1, p. 231.

1133. Nicolay and Hay, ALCW, Vol. 1, p. 234. See also Reuter, pp. 120-122; Fogel and Engerman, pp. 130-136.

1134. Warren, WSFTN, p. 262.

1135. M. Davis, pp. 154-155.

1136. See Bennett, FIG, passim

1137. W. Wilson, DR, p. 125.

1138. Nicolay and Hay, ALCW, Vol. 1, p. 218.

1139. Seabrook, AL, pp. 421-422.

1140. Fleming, p. 665.

1141. Seabrook, NBF, p. 56.

1142. Hurst, p. 305; Lester and Wilson, p. 26; Rogers, KKS, p. 34.

1143. W. Jones, p. 75.

1144. Seabrook, ARB, p. 441; Horn, IE, pp. 362-363. We will note that at one time (1920s-1930s) even the modern KKK—though it has no connection with the Reconstruction KKK that arose shortly after Lincoln's War—possessed African-American members, and treated both whites and blacks the same. Terkel, p. 239. In Indiana, for example, white Klansmen decided to broaden their racial base by organizing a "colored division" whose uniform was comprised of white capes, blue masks, and red robes. Blee, p. 169.

1145. S. E. F. Rose, pp. 55-59; Seabrook, NBFATKKK, p. 104.

1146. Few things were worse to traditional Southerners than the scallywag. Known widely across the South as "vile, vindictive, unprincipled," and "scaly, scabby runts in a herd of cattle" (J. H. Franklin, pp. 98, 101), Wade Hampton referred to them as "the mean, lousy and filthy kind that are not fit for butchers or dogs." Harrell, Gaustad, Boles, Griffith, Miller, and Woods, p. 525. Known by Southern conservatives as "the lepers of the community," scallywags were hated even more than carpetbaggers. A former governor of North Carolina said: "We have no problem with Northerners per se, even those who fought against us in Lincoln's War. What we can't and won't abide is one of our own here in the South turning against us. Such a man will never get respect and will never be trusted." (My paraphrasal.) Foner, R, p. 297. To this day, revulsion toward the scallywag is a sentiment still very much alive across the South.

1147. Horn, IE, pp. 124, 169, 264-265; Simpson, p. 62.

1148. C. Adams, p. 153; Weintraub, p. 75.

1149. *Index to Reports of the Committees of the House of Representatives for the Second Session of the Forty-Third Congress, 1874-1875*, p. 344.

1150. See J. H. Franklin, pp. 38-39.

1151. Seabrook, AL, p. 530. My paraphrasal.

1152. C. Adams, pp. 153-155.

1153. Seabrook, ARB, p. 443; Lytle, p. 385; Morton, p. 345; Hurst, p. 327.

1154. Butler and Watson, p. 293.

1155. See Seabrook, NBFATKKK, passim.

1156. See W. C. Wade, passim.

1157. December 17, 2000, "Sunday Morning News," CNN.

1158. Seabrook, NBFATKKK, passim.

1159. S. E. F. Rose, pp. 18-19.

1160. S. E. F. Rose, pp. 34, 69. Emphasis added.

1161. Seabrook, NBFATKKK, pp. 42-43.

1162. C. Adams, p. 151.

1163. W. C. Wade, p. 39.

1164. Weintraub, p. 89.

1165. W. C. Wade, p. 39. As noted earlier, Lincoln's Republican Party was what we would now call the Democratic Party (i.e., Liberals), while the Democratic Party of the mid 1800s was what we would now refer to as the Republican Party (i.e., Conservatives). Thus, though Lincoln was a Republican, today he would be considered a Democrat.

1166. Henry, FWMF, p. 443.

1167. Seabrook, ARB, pp. 446-447; Lester and Wilson, pp. 19-21.

1168. For more on the facts about Forrest and his life, see my books: 1) *Nathan Bedford Forrest: Southern Hero, American Patriot*; 2) *A Rebel Born: A Defense of Nathan Bedford Forrest*; 3) *Forrest! 99 Reasons to Love Nathan Bedford Forrest*; 4) *The Quotable Nathan Bedford Forrest*; 5) *Give 'Em Hell Boys: The Complete Military Correspondence of Nathan Bedford Forrest*; 6) *Saddle, Sword, and Gun: A Biography of Nathan Bedford Forrest For Teens*; 7) *Nathan Bedford Forrest and the Battle of Fort Pillow: Yankee Myth, Confederate Fact*; 8) *Nathan Bedford Forrest and African-Americans: Yankee Myth, Confederate Fact*; 9) *Nathan Bedford Forrest and the Ku Klux Klan: Yankee Myth, Confederate Fact*; and my screenplay, *A Rebel Born* (based on the book of the same name).

1169. Seabrook, F, p. 86.

1170. According to the Reconstruction KKK's *Prescript*: "Any member who shall reveal or betray the secrets of this Order, shall suffer the extreme penalty of the law" (Article 10, Clause 10). Burton, p. 37.

1171. Wills, p. 336.

1172. Seabrook, ARB, p. 448. Gordon was one of the unlucky 702 Rebels captured at the Battle of Franklin II, November 30, 1864.

1173. Seabrook, NBFAAA, p. 35.

1174. See Seabrook, EYWTAASIW, pp. 860-863.

1175. Seabrook, NBFAAA, p. 35.

1176. Seabrook, ARB, p. 220.

1177. Seabrook, ARB, p. 220.

1178. Seabrook, NBFAAA, p. 37.

1179. Seabrook, ARB, p. 214.

1180. Seabrook, NBFAAA, pp. 38-39.

1181. Seabrook, ARB, pp. 214-215.

1182. Seabrook, NBFAAA, p. 39.

1183. Seabrook, ARB, p. 215.

1184. Seabrook, ARB, p. 221. Emphasis added.

1185. Henry, FWMF, p. 14.

1186. *Report of the Joint Select Committee to Inquire into the Condition of Affairs in the Late Insurrectionary States*, p. 20. Emphasis added.

1187. Wyeth, TDF, p. xxi.

1188. Seabrook, ARB, pp. 26, 144; Seabrook, NBFAAA, p. 44.

1189. *Confederate Veteran*, May 1901, Vol. 9, No. 5, pp. 218-219. Emphasis added.

1190. Cincinnati *Commercial*, August 28, 1868.

1191. Segars and Barrow, p. 155.

1192. Seabrook, ARB, p. 35.

1193. For more on the General's life, see my nine Forrest books and Forrest screenplay.

1194. Seabrook, TQNBF, pp. 114-116. Emphasis added.

1195. Seabrook, ARB, pp. 547-548. My paraphrasal.

1196. Seabrook, ARB, p. 213.

1197. See e.g., B. F. Butler, p. 903. Many other famous Northerners also did not believe in abolition or equality of the races, such as General William T. Sherman. See e.g., Seabrook, EYWTACWW, p. 175.

1198. Seabrook, ARB, p. 548.

1199. Seabrook, ARB, pp. 26, 466-467.

1200. Seabrook, ARB, pp. 466-467.

1201. Strangely, most black Southerners today do not express shame for their ancestral involvement in black slavery, nor have they ever apologized for it. As far as I am aware, neither have Native-Americans or Latin-Americans.

1202. Meltzer, Vol. 2, p. 139. Also see Cartmell, p. 26; Norwood, p. 31.

1203. Lott, pp. 35-60.

1204. G. H. Moore, pp. 5, 11, 17-19; Blake, p. 370.

1205. Drescher and Engerman, p. 372.

1206. W. T. Alexander, p. 240; Bedford and Colbourn, p. 85; Rosenbaum and Brinkley, s.v. "Slavery"; Melish, passim.

1207. L. Abbott, p. 155.

1208. L. Abbott, p. 149. Emphasis added. Note: this text is a paraphrasal by Beecher's editor Lyman Abbott.

1209. Seabrook, AL, pp. 161-165.

1210. Fogel, p. 207.

1211. G. H. Moore, pp. 5, 11, 17-19.

1212. R. S. Phillips, s.v. "Slavery."

1213. Greenberg and Waugh, p. 376; Grissom, pp. 131, 182; Stonebraker, p. 46; J. C. Perry, pp. 96, 99, 101, 174.

1214. Kennedy and Kennedy, SWR, p. 83; M. M. Smith, pp. 4-5.

1215. Meltzer, Vol. 2, p. 4.

1216. Encyc. Brit., s.v. "slavery."

1217. M. Perry, p. 49.

1218. Lott, p. 18; Furnas, p. 27; Garraty and McCaughey, p. 25; Garraty, HV, p. 77.

1219. Furnas, p. 108.

1220. Chadwick, p. 243; The World Book Encyc., s.v. "slavery."

1221. Website: www.foreignpolicy.com/articles/2008/02/19/a_world_enslaved.

1222. McDannald, s.v. "Slavery."

1223. Website: www.csmonitor.com/2004/0901/p16s01-wogi.html.

1224. Website: www.pbs.org/newshour/bb/law/jan-june01/slavery_3-8.html.

1225. W. J. Cooper, JDA, p. 378; Quarles, TNITCW, p. xiii.

1226. Garraty and McCaughey, p. 214. See also Fogel and Engerman, pp. 23-24.

1227. Website: www.pbs.org/newshour/bb/law/jan-june01/slavery_3-8.html.

1228. Website: www.nytimes.com/2013/11/07/opinion/slavery-isnt-a-thing-of-the-past.html?_r=0.

1229. Seabrook, EYWTAASIW, pp. 164-165.

BIBLIOGRAPHY

Abbott, John Stevens Cabot. *The Life of General Ulysses S. Grant.* Boston, MA: B. B. Russell, 1868.

Abbott, Lyman. *Henry Ward Beecher.* Boston, MA: Houghton, Mifflin and Co., 1903.

Abel, Annie Heloise. *The American Indian as Slaveholder and Secessionist.* Cleveland, OH: Arthur H. Clarke Co., 1915.

——. *The American Indian as Participant in the Civil War.* Cleveland, Ohio: Arthur H. Clark, 1919.

Adams, Charles. *When in the Course of Human Events: Arguing the Case for Southern Secession.* Lanham, MD: Rowman and Littlefield, 2000.

Adams, Charles Francis (ed.). *Memoirs of John Quincy Adams, Comprising Portions of His Diary From 1795 to 1848.* 4 vols. Philadelphia, PA: J. B. Lippincott and Co., 1875.

Adams, Francis D., and Barry Sanders. *Alienable Rights: The Exclusion of African Americans in a White Man's Land, 1619-2000.* 2003. New York, NY: Perennial, 2004 ed.

Adams, H. (ed.). *South Africa: Sociological Perspectives.* New York, NY: Oxford University press, 1971.

Adams, Henry (ed.). *Documents Relating to New-England Federalism, 1800-1815.* Boston, MA: Little, Brown, and Co., 1877.

Adams, Herbert Baxter. *Baltimore, Slavery, and Constitutional History* (Vol. 14). Baltimore, MD: Johns Hopkins Press, 1896.

Adams, James Truslow. *The Epic of America.* Boston, MA: Little, Brown, and Co., 1931.

Adams, Nehemiah. *A South-side View of Slavery: Three Months at the South in 1854.* Boston, MA: T. R. Marvin, 1855.

Adams, William Henry Davenport. *Shore and Sea; Or, Stories of Great Vikings and Sea Captains.* London, UK: Hodder and Stoughton, 1883.

Adeuyan, Jacob Oluwatayo. *The Return of the Tidal Flow of the Middle Passage.* Bloomington, IN: AuthorHouse, 2011.

Agorsah, E. Kofi (ed.). *Maroon Heritage: Archaeological, Ethnographic and Historical Perspectives.* Kingston, Jamaica: Canoe Press, 1994.

Ahlstrom, Sydney E. *A Religious History of the American People.* New Haven, CT: Yale University Press, 1972.

Albrecht-Carrié, René. *Europe, 1500-1848.* 1953. Patterson, NJ: Littlefield, Adams, and Co., 1962 ed.

Alexander, Edward Porter. *Military Memoirs of a Confederate: A Critical Narrative.* New York, NY: Charles Scribner's Sons, 1907.

Alexander, Gross (ed.). *The Methodist Review Quarterly,* July 1909. Nashville, TN: Methodist Episcopal Church, 1909.

Alexander, William T. *History of the Colored Race in America.* Kansas City, MO: Palmetto Publishing Co., 1899.

Alfriend, Frank H. *The Life of Jefferson Davis.* Cincinnati, OH: Caxton Publishing House, 1868.

Alland, Alexander, Jr. *Human Diversity.* Garden City, NY: Anchor Books, 1973.

Allen, Gardner Weld. *Our Navy and the Barbary Corsairs.* Boston, MA: Houghton, Mifflin and Co., 1905.

Alotta, Robert I. *Civil War Justice: Union Army Executions Under Lincoln.* Shippensburg, PA: White Mane, 1989.

American Colonization Society. *Forty-fourth Annual Report of the American Colonization Society.* Washington, D.C.: American Colonization Society, 1861.

Ames, Mary. *From a New England Woman's Diary in 1865.* Norwood, MA: The Plimpton Press, 1906.

An Appeal From the Colored Men of Philadelphia to the President of the United States. Philadelphia, PA, 1862.

Anderson, John Q. (ed.). *Brokenburn: The Journal of Kate Stone, 1861-1868.* 1955. Baton Rouge, LA: Louisiana State University Press, 1995 ed.

Andrewes, Antony. *The Greeks.* 1967. New York, NY: W. W. Norton and Co., 1978 ed.

Andrews, E. Benjamin. *History of the United States: From the Earliest Discovery of America to the End of 1902.* 2 vols. New York, NY: Charles Scribner's Sons, 1904.

Andrews, Ethan Allen. *Slavery and the Domestic Slave Trade in the United States.* Boston, MA: Light and Stearns, 1836.

Andrews, Sidney. *The South Since the War: As Shown by Fourteen Weeks of Travel and Observation.* Boston, MA: Ticknor and Fields, 1866.

Ashe, Captain Samuel A'Court. *A Southern View of the Invasion of the Southern States and War of 1861-1865.* 1935. Crawfordville, GA: Ruffin Flag Co., 1938 ed.

Ashworth, John. *Slavery, Capitalism, and Politics in the Antebellum Republic.* 2 vols. New York, NY: Cambridge University Press, 2007.

Astor, Gerald. *The Right to Fight: A History of African Americans in the Military*. Cambridge, MA: Da Capo, 2001.

Ayers, Edward. *The Promise of the New South*. Oxford, UK: Oxford University Press, 1992.

Baepler, Paul (ed.). *White Slaves, African Masters: An Anthology of American Barbary Captivity Narratives*. Chicago, IL: University of Chicago Press, 1999.

Baigent, Michael, Richard Leigh, and Henry Lincoln. *Holy Blood, Holy Grail*. New York, NY: Dell, 1983.

——. *The Messianic Legacy*. New York, NY: Dell, 1986.

Bailey, Anne C. *African Voices of the Atlantic Slave Trade: Beyond the Silence and the Shame*. Boston, MA: Beacon Press, 2005.

Bailey, Hugh C. *Hinton Rowan Helper: Abolitionist-Racist*. Tuscaloosa, AL: University of Alabama Press, 1965.

Bailey, Thomas A. *A Diplomatic History of the American People*. 1940. New York, NY: Appleton-Century-Crofts, 1970 ed.

——. *The American Spirit: United States History as Seen by Contemporaries*. Boston, MA: D. C. Heath and Co., 1963.

Bailyn, Bernard, Robert Dallek, David Brion Davis, David Herbert Donald, John L. Thomas, and Gordon S. Wood. *The Great Republic: A History of the American People*. 1977. Lexington, MA: D. C. Heath and Co., 1992 ed.

Baker, George E. (ed.). *The Works of William H. Seward*. 5 vols. 1861. Boston, MA: Houghton, Mifflin and Co., 1888 ed.

Baker, Ray Stannard. *Following the Color Line: An Account of Negro Citizenship in the American Democracy*. New York, NY: Doubleday, Page and Co., 1908.

Baldwin, James. *The Fire Next Time*. New York, NY: The Dial Press, 1963.

Ball, Charles. *Slavery in the United States: A Narrative of the Life and Adventures of Charles Ball, a Black Man*. New York, NY: John S. Taylor, 1837.

Ballagh, James Curtis. *White Servitude in the Colony of Virginia: A Study of the System of Indentured Servitude in the American Colonies*. Whitefish, MT: Kessinger Publishing, 2004.

Bancroft, Frederic. *The Life of William H. Seward*. 2 vols. New York, NY: Harper and Brothers, 1900.

——. *Slave-Trading in the Old South*. Baltimore, MD: J. H. Furst, 1931.

Bancroft, Frederic, and William A. Dunning (eds.). *The Reminiscences of Carl Schurz*. 3 vols. New York, NY: McClure Co., 1909.

Bancroft, George. *History of the United States of America, From the Discovery of the Continent*. 10 vols. New York, NY: D. Appleton and Co., 1886.

Barnard, Alan, and Jonathan Spencer. *Encyclopedia of Social and Cultural Anthropology*. 1996. London, UK: Routledge, 2002 ed.

Barnard, Ella Kent. *Dorothy Payne, Quakeress: A Side-light Upon the Career of "Dolly" Madison*. Philadelphia, PA: Ferris and Leach, 1909.

Barnes, Albert. *An Inquiry into the Scriptural Views of Slavery*. 1846. Philadelphia, PA: Parry and McMillan, 1855 ed.

Barnes, Gilbert H. *The Antislavery Impulse, 1830-1844*. New York, NY: Harbinger, 1964.

Barnes, Gilbert H., and Dwight L. Dumond (eds.). *Letters of Theodore Dwight Weld, Angelina Grimké Weld and Sarah Grimké, 1822-1844*. 2 vols. New York, NY: D. Appleton-Century Co., 1934.

Barney, William L. *Flawed Victory: A New Perspective on the Civil War*. New York, NY: Praeger Publishers, 1975.

Barraclough, Geoffrey. *The Times Atlas of World History*. 1978. Maplewood, NJ: Hammond, 1989 ed.

Barringer, Paul Brandon. *The American Negro: His Past and Future*. Raleigh, NC: Edwards and Broughton, 1900.

Barrow, Charles Kelly, J. H. Segars, and R. B. Rosenburg (eds.). *Black Confederates*. 1995. Gretna, LA: Pelican Publishing Co., 2001 ed.

——. *Forgotten Confederates: An Anthology About Black Southerners*. Saint Petersburg, FL: Southern Heritage Press, 1997.

Barrow, Isabel C. (ed.). *Proceedings of the Twentieth Annual Meeting of the Lake Mohonk Conference of Friends of the Indian, 1902*. New York: The Lake Mohonk Conference, 1903.

Barton, William E. *The Soul of Abraham Lincoln*. New York, NY: George H. Doran, 1920.

Bascom, Henry Bidleman. *Methodism and Slavery: With Other Matters in Controversy Between the North and the South*. Frankfort, KY: Henry Bidleman Bascom, 1845.

Basler, Roy Prentice (ed.). *Abraham Lincoln: His Speeches and Writings*. 1946. New York, NY: Da Capo Press, 2001 ed.

—— (ed.). *The Collected Works of Abraham Lincoln*. 9 vols. New Brunswick, NJ: Rutgers University Press, 1953.

Bateman, William O. *Political and Constitutional Law of the United States of America*. St. Louis, MO: G. I. Jones and Co., 1876.

Baughman, Emmett E. *Black Americans: A Psychological Analysis*. New York, NY: Academic Press, 1971.

Baxter, Maurice G. *Henry Clay and the American System*. Lexington, KY: University Press of Kentucky, 2004.

Beard, Charles A. (ed.). *Whither Mankind: A Panorama of Modern Civilization*. New York, NY: Longmans, Green and Co., 1928.

Beard, Charles A., and Birl E. Schultz. *Documents on the State-Wide Initiative, Referendum and Recall*. New York, NY: Macmillan, 1912.

Beard, Charles A., and Mary R. Beard. *The Rise of American Civilization*. 1927. New York, NY: MacMillan, 1930 ed.

Beaumont, Alexander. *The History of Spain, From the Earliest Authentic Accounts to the Present Times*. London, UK: S. A. and H. Oddy, 1809.

Becker, Carl L., and Frederic Duncalf. *Story of Civilization*. 1938. New York, NY: Silver Burdett Co., 1944 ed.

Beckles, Hilary, and Verene Shepherd. *Caribbean Slave Society and Economy: A Student Reader*. Kingston, Jamaica: Ian Randle, 1994.

Bede, Saint. *A History of the English Church and People*. (Original work written in 731.) 1955. Harmondsworth, UK: Penguin, 1974 ed.

Bedford, Henry F., and Trevor Colbourn. *The Americans: A Brief History*. 1972. New York, NY: Harcourt Brace Jovanovich, 1980 ed.

Behrens, C. B. A. *The Ancien Régime*. New York, NY: Harcourt, Brace and World, 1967.

Bekkaoui, Khalid. *White Women Captives in North Africa: Narratives of Enslavement, 1735-1830*. New York, NY: Macmillan, 2011.

Bellagamba, Alice, Sandra E. Greene, and Martin A. Klein (eds). *African Voices on Slavery and the Slave Trade*. Cambridge, UK: Cambridge University Press, 2013.

Benedict, S. W., and Isaac Knapp (eds.). *The American Anti-Slavery Almanac for 1839 and 1840*. New York, NY: American Anti-Slavery Society, 1840.

Bennett, Lerone, Jr. *Before the Mayflower: A History of Black America*. 1961. Harmondsworth, UK: Penguin, 1993 ed.

——. *Forced Into Glory: Abraham Lincoln's White Dream*. Chicago, IL: Johnson Publishing Co., 2000.

Benson, Al, Jr., and Walter Donald Kennedy. *Lincoln's Marxists*. Gretna, LA: Pelican Publishing, 2011.

Benton, Thomas Hart. *Thirty Years View; or A History of the Working of the American Government for Thirty Years, From 1820 to 1850*. 2 vols. New York, NY: D. Appleton and Co., 1854.

Bergh, Albert Ellery (ed.). *The Writings of Thomas Jefferson*. 20 vols. Washington, D.C.: Thomas Jefferson Memorial Association of the U.S., 1905.

Berkin, Carol, and Leonard Wood. *Land of Promise: A History of the United States From 1865*. Glenview, IL: Scott, Foresman and Co., 1983.

Berlin, Ira, and Philip D. Morgan (eds.). *The Slaves' Economy: Independent Production by Slaves in the Americas*. London, UK: Frank Cass, 1991.

Bernard, Jessie. *Marriage and Family Among Negroes*. Englewood Cliffs, NJ: Prentice-Hall, 1966.

Bernhard, Winfred E. A. (ed.). *Political Parties in American History* (Vol. 1, 1789-1828). New York, NY: G. P. Putnams' Sons, 1973.

Berry, Wendell. *The Unsettling of America: Culture and Agriculture*. San Francisco, CA: Sierra Club Books, 1996.

Bertrand, Louis. *The History of Spain*. New York, NY: Collier, 1971.

Berwanger, Eugene H. *The Frontier Against Slavery: Western Anti-Negro Prejudice and the Slavery Extension Controversy*. 1967. Urbana, IL: University of Illinois Press, 1971 ed.

Bevan, William Latham. *The Student's Manual of Ancient Geography*. London, UK: John Murray, 1875.

Billingsley, Andrew. *Black Families in White America*. Englewood Cliffs, NJ: Prentice-Hall, 1968.

Birney, James Gillespie. *The American Churches, the Bulwarks of American Slavery*. Concord, NH: Parker Pillsbury, 1885.

Birney, William. *James G. Birney and His Times: The Genesis of the Republican Party With Some Account of Abolition Movements in the South Before 1828*. New York, NY: D. Appleton and Co., 1890.

Black, Chauncey F. *Essays and Speeches of Jeremiah S. Black*. New York, NY: D. Appleton and Co., 1886.

Blake, William O. *The History of Slavery and the Slave Trade, Ancient and Modern*. Columbus, OH: H. Miller, 1861.

Blanchard, Jonathan, and Nathan Lewis Rice. *A Debate on Slavery: Held in the City of Cincinnati, on the First, Second, Third, and Sixth Days of October, 1845*. Cincinnati, OH: William H. Moore, 1846.

Blanchard, Peter. *Slavery and Abolition in Early Republican Peru*. Wilmington, DE: Scholarly Resources, 1992.

Blassingame, John W. *The Slave Community: Plantation Life in the Antebellum South*. 1972. New York, NY: Oxford University Press, 1974 ed.

Bledsoe, Albert Taylor. *An Essay on Liberty and Slavery.* Philadelphia, PA: J. B. Lippincott and Co., 1856.

——. *A Theodicy; or a Vindication of the Divine Glory, as Manifested in the Constitution and Government of the Moral World.* New York, NY: Carlton and Porter, 1856.

——. *Is Davis a Traitor; or Was Secession a Constitutional Right Previous to the War of 1861?* Richmond, VA: Hermitage Press, 1907.

Blee, Kathleen M. *Women of the Klan: Racism and Gender in the 1920s.* 1991. Berkeley, CA: University of California Press, 1992 ed.

Blight, David W. *Frederick Douglass' Civil War: Keeping Faith in Jubilee.* 1989. Baton Rouge, LA: Louisiana State University Press, 1991 ed.

Bliss, William Dwight Porter (ed.). *The Encyclopedia of Social Reform.* New York, NY: Funk and Wagnalls, 1897.

Boller, Paul F., Jr., and Ronald Story. *A More Perfect Union: Documents in U.S. History - Vol. 1: to 1877.* Boston, MA: Houghton Mifflin Co., 1984.

Booth, Mary Louise. *History of the City of New York, From its Earliest Settlement to the Present Time.* New York, NY: W. R. C. Clark and Co., 1860.

Boston Female Anti-Slavery Society. *Annual Report of the Boston Female Anti-Slavery Society.* Boston, MA: Isaac Knapp, 1837.

Botkin, Benjamin Albert (ed.). *Lay My Burden Down: A Folk History of Slavery.* 1945. Chicago, IL: University of Chicago Press, 1969 ed.

Botume, Elizabeth Hyde. *First Days Amongst the Contrabands.* Boston, MA: Lee and Shepard, 1893.

Bourne, George. *Picture of Slavery in the United States of America.* Middletown, CT: Edwin Hunt, 1834.

Bourne, Theodore. *Rev. George Bourne: The Pioneer of American Antislavery.* Methodist Church (article from the *Methodist Quarterly Review*, January 1882).

Bowen, Catherine Drinker. *John Adams and the American Revolution.* 1949. New York, NY: Grosset and Dunlap, 1977 ed.

Bowman, John S. (ed.). *The Civil War Day by Day: An Illustrated Almanac of America's Bloodiest War.* 1989. New York, NY: Dorset Press, 1990 ed.

——. *Encyclopedia of the Civil War* (ed.). 1992. North Dighton, MA: JG Press, 2001 ed.

Bowser, Frederick P. *The African Slave in Colonial Peru, 1524-1650.* Stanford, CA: Stanford University Press, 1974.

Boxer, Charles R. *Race Relations in the Portuguese Colonial Empire, 1415-1825.* Oxford, UK: Clarendon Press, 1963.

Boyde, Henry. *Several Voyages to Barbary: Containing an Historical and Geographical Account of the Country, With the Hardships, Sufferings, and Manner of Redeeming Christian Slaves.* London, UK: Olive Payne, 1736.

Brackett, Jeffrey Richardson. *The Negro in Maryland: A Study of the Institution of Slavery.* Baltimore, MD: Johns Hopkins University, 1889.

Braddy, Nella (ed.). *The New Concise Illustrated Encyclopedia.* 1934. Cleveland, OH: World Publishing Co., 1943 ed.

Bradford, James C. (ed.). *Atlas of American Military History.* New York, NY: Oxford University Press, 2003.

Breasted, James Henry. *Ancient Times: A History of the Early World.* 1916. Boston, MA: Ginn and Co., 1944 ed.

——. *The Conquest of Civilization.* New York, NY: Harper and Brothers, 1926.

British and Foreign Anti-Slavery Society. *Slavery and the Slave Trade in British India; With Notices of the Existence of These Evils in the Islands of Ceylon, Malacca, and Penang, Drawn from Official Documents.* London, UK: Thomas Ward, 1841.

Brockett, Linus Pierpont. *The Life and Times of Abraham Lincoln, Sixteenth President of the United States.* Philadelphia, PA: Bradley and Co., 1865.

Brodie, Fawn McKay. *Thaddeus Stevens: Scourge of the South.* New York, NY: W. W. Norton, 1966.

Brodnax, William H. *The Speech of William H. Brodnax, in the House of Delegates of Virginia, on the Policy of the State With Respect to its Colored Population.* Richmond, VA: William H. Brodnax, 1832.

Bronowski, J., and Bruce Mazlish. *The Western Intellectual Tradition: From Leonardo to Hegel.* 1960. New York, NY: Harper and Row, 1975 ed.

Browder, Earl. *Lincoln and the Communists.* New York, NY: Workers Library Publishers, Inc., 1936.

Brown, Dee. *Bury My Heart at Wounded Knee: An Indian History of the American West.* 1970. New York, NY: Owl Books, 1991 ed.

Brown, James. *American Slavery in its Moral and Political Aspects, Comprehensively Examined.* New York, NY: James Brown, 1840.

Brown, Rita Mae. *High Hearts.* New York, NY: Bantam, 1987.

Brown, William Montgomery. *The Crucial Question, or Where and How Shall the Color Line Be Drawn*. Little Rock, AR: The Arkansas Churchman's Publishing Co., 1907.

Brown, William Wells. *The Black Man: His Antecedents, His Genius, and His Achievements*. New York, NY: Thomas Hamilton, 1863.

Browne, Ray B., and Lawrence A. Kreiser, Jr. *The Civil War and Reconstruction*. Westport, CT: Greenwood Publishing, 2003.

Bruce, Henry Clay. *The New Man: Twenty-nine Years a Slave, Twenty-nine Years a Free Man*. York, PA: P. Anstadt and Sons, 1895.

Bruce, Philip Alexander. *The Plantation Negro As a Freeman*. New York, NY: G. P. Putnam's Sons, 1889.

Bruford, W. H. *Germany in the Eighteenth Century: The Social Background of the Literary Revival*. 1935. Cambridge, UK: Cambridge University Press, 1965 ed.

Brunner, Borgna (ed.). *The Time Almanac* (1999 ed.). Boston, MA: Information Please, 1998.

Bruns, Roger (ed.). *Am I Not a Man and a Brother: The Antislavery Crusade of Revolutionary America 1688-1788*. New York, NY: Chelsea House, 1977.

Buckingham, James Silk. *Travels in Mesopotamia*. 2 vols. London, UK: Henry Colburn, 1827.

——. *The Slave States of America*. 2 vols. London, UK: Fisher, Son, and Co., 1842.

Buckland, William Warwick. *The Roman Law of Slavery: The Condition of the Slave in Private Law From Augustus to Justinian*. Cambridge, UK: Cambridge University Press, 1908.

Buckley, Gail. *American Patriots: The Story of Blacks in the Military From the Revolution to Desert Storm*. New York, NY: Random House, 2001.

Bullock, Alan. *Hitler: A Study in Tyranny*. 1962. New York, NY: Perennial Library, 1971 abridged ed.

Bultman, Bethany. *Redneck Heaven: Portrait of a Vanishing Culture*. New York, NY: Bantam, 1996.

Bunson, Matthew. *Encyclopedia of the Roman Empire*. New York, NY: Facts On File, 1994.

Burckhardt, John Lewis. *Travels in Nubia*. London, UK: John Murray, 1819.

Burin, Eric. *Slavery and the Peculiar Solution: A History of the American Colonization Society*. Gainesville, FL: University of Florida Press, 2008.

Burlingame, Michael. *The Inner World of Abraham Lincoln*. Champaign, IL: University of Illinois Press, 1997.

Burn, Andrew Robert. *The Pelican History of Greece*. 1965. Harmondsworth, UK: Penguin, 1968 ed.

Burke, James. *Connections*. Boston, MA: Little, Brown and Co., 1978.

Burn, Andrew Robert. *The Pelican History of Greece*. 1965. Harmondsworth, UK: Penguin, 1968 ed.

Burne, Jerome (ed.). *Chronicle of the World*. 1989. Mount Kisco, NY: Ecam, 1990 ed.

Burns, James MacGregor. *The Vineyard of Liberty*. New York, NY: Knopf, 1982.

Burns, James MacGregor, and Jack Walter Peltason. *Government by the People: The Dynamics of American National, State, and Local Government*. 1952. Englewood Cliffs, NJ: Prentice-Hall, 1964 ed.

Burns, James MacGregor, Jack Walter Peltason, Thomas E. Cronin, David B. Magleby, and David M. O'Brien. *Government by the People* (National Version). 1952. Upper Saddle River, NJ: Prentice Hall, 2001-2002 ed.

Burrell, Sidney A. *Handbook of Western Civilization: Beginnings to 1700*. 1965. New York, NY: John Wiley and Sons, 1972 ed.

Burton, Annie Cooper. *The Ku Klux Klan*. Los Angeles, CA: Warren T. Potter, 1916.

Bush, Barbara. *Slave Women in Caribbean Society, 1650-1838*. Kingston, Jamaica: Heinemann Caribbean, 1990.

Bushnell, Horace. *The Census and Slavery, Thanksgiving Discourse, Delivered in the Chapel at Clifton Springs, New York, November 29, 1860*. Hartford, CT: L. E. Hunt, 1860.

Butler, Benjamin Franklin. *Butler's Book (Autobiography and Personal Reminiscences of Major-General Benjamin F. Butler: A Review of His Legal, Political, and Military Career)*. Boston, MA: A. M. Thayer and Co., 1892.

Butler, Lindley S., and Alan D. Watson (eds.). *The North Carolina Experience: An Interpretive and Documentary History*. Chapel Hill, NC: University of North Carolina Press, 1984.

Butler, Trent C. (ed.). *Holman Bible Dictionary*. Nashville, TN: Holman Bible Publishers,1991.

Buxton, Thomas Fowell. *The African Slave Trade and the Remedy For It*. Edinburgh, Scotland: Ballantine and Co., 1840.

Cahill, Thomas. *How the Irish Saved Civilization: The Untold Story of Ireland's Heroic Role From the Fall of Rome to the Rise of Medieval Europe*. New York, NY: Doubleday, 1995.

Caldwell, Arthur Bunyan (ed.). *History of the American Negro and His Institutions*. Atlanta, GA: A. B. Caldwell, 1917.

Cameron, Rondo. *A Concise Economic History of the World: From Paleolithic Times to the Present*. 1989. Oxford, UK: Oxford University Press, 2003 ed.

Campbell, Bernard G. (ed.). *Humankind Emerging*. Boston, MA: Little, Brown and Co., 1976.

Campbell, Gwyn, Suzanne Miers, and Joseph C. Miller (eds.). *Women and Slavery*. 2 vols. Athens, OH: Ohio University Press, 2007.

Campbell, Joseph. *The Masks of God: Primitive Mythology*. 1959. New York, NY: Arkana, 1991 ed.

Cannon, Devereaux D., Jr. *The Flags of the Confederacy: An Illustrated History*. Memphis, TN: St. Lukes Press, 1988.

Cantor, Milton (ed.). *Black Labor in America*. Westport, CT: Negro Universities Press, 1969.

Cantor, Norman F. *Inventing the Middle Ages: The Lives, Works, and Ideas of the Great Medievalists of the Twentieth Century*. New York, NY: William Morrow and Co., 1991.

Cappelluti, Frank J., and Ruth H. Grossman. *The Human Adventure: A History of Our World*. San Francisco, CA: Field Educational Publications, 1970.

Carman, Harry J., and Harold C. Syrett. *A History of the American People - Vol. 1: To 1865*. 1952. New York, NY: Alfred A. Knopf, 1958 ed.

Carpenter, Stephen D. *Logic of History: Five Hundred Political Texts, Being Concentrated Extracts of Abolitionism*. Madison, WI: Stephen D. Carpenter, 1864.

Cartmell, Donald. *Civil War 101*. New York, NY: Gramercy, 2001.

Cash, W. J. *The Mind of the South*. 1941. New York, NY: Vintage, 1969 ed.

Catterall, Helen T. (ed.). *Judicial Cases Concerning American Slavery and the Negro*. 5 vols. Washington, D.C.: Carnegie Institute, 1926-1937.

Catton, Bruce. *The Coming Fury* (Vol. 1). 1961. New York, NY: Washington Square Press, 1967 ed.

——. *Terrible Swift Sword* (Vol. 2). 1963. New York, NY: Pocket Books, 1967 ed.

——. *A Stillness at Appomattox* (Vol. 3). 1953. New York, NY: Pocket Books, 1966 ed.

Chace, Elizabeth Buffum. *Anti-Slavery Reminiscences*. Central Falls, RI: E. L. Freeman and Son, 1891.

Chadwick, Owen. *A History of Christianity*. New York, NY: St. Martin's Griffin, 1998.

Chamberlain, Nathan Henry. *Samuel Sewall and the World He Lived In*. Boston, MA: De Wolfe, Fiske and Co., 1898.

Chan, Alexandra. *Slavery in the Age of Reason: Archaeology at a New England Farm*. Knoxville, TN: University of Tennessee Press, 2007.

Channing, Edward. *The Narragansett Planters: A Study of Causes*. Baltimore, MD: Johns Hopkins University, 1886.

Channing, Steven A. *Confederate Ordeal: The Southern Home Front*. 1984. Morristown, NJ: Time-Life Books, 1989 ed.

Channing, William Ellery. *Slavery*. Boston, MA: James Munroe and Co., 1835.

Chayanov, A. V. *The Theory of Peasant Economy*. Madison, WI: University of Wisconsin Press, 1986.

Chesnut, Mary. *A Diary From Dixie: As Written by Mary Boykin Chesnut, Wife of James Chesnut, Jr., United States Senator from South Carolina, 1859-1861, and Afterward an Aide to Jefferson Davis and a Brigadier-General in the Confederate Army*. (Isabella D. Martin and Myrta Lockett Avary, eds.). New York, NY: D. Appleton and Co., 1905 ed.

——. *Mary Chesnut's Civil War*. 1860-1865 (Woodward, Comer Vann, ed.). New Haven, CT: Yale University Press, 1981 ed.

Child, Lydia Maria. *The Evils of Slavery, and the Cure of Slavery. The First Proved by Southerners Themselves, the Last Shown by Historical Evidence*. Newburyport, MA: Charles Whipple, 1836.

Childe, Gordon. *What Happened in History*. 1942. Harmondsworth, UK: Penguin, 1964 ed.

Chirichigno, Gregory C. *Debt-Slavery in Israel and the Ancient Near East*. Sheffield, UK: JSOT Press, 1993.

Chodes, John. *Destroying the Republic: Jabez Curry and the Re-Education of the Old South*. New York, NY: Algora, 2005.

Christian, George L. *Abraham Lincoln: An Address Delivered Before R. E. Lee Camp, No. 1 Confederate Veterans at Richmond, VA, October 29, 1909*. Richmond, VA: L. H. Jenkins, 1909.

Church, Thomas. *The History of the Great Indian War of 1675 and 1676, Commonly Called Philip's War*. New York, NY: H. Dayton, 1845.

Cisco, Walter Brian. *War Crimes Against Southern Civilians*. Gretna, LA: Pelican Publishing Co., 2007.

Civil War Book of Lists. 1993. Edison, NJ: Castle Books, 2004 ed.

Civil War Society, The. *Civil War Battles: An Illustrated Encyclopedia*. 1997. New York, NY: Gramercy, 1999 ed.

——. *The Civil War Society's Encyclopedia of the Civil War*. New York, NY: Wings Books, 1997.

Clarence-Smith, William Gervase (ed.). *The Economics of the Indian Ocean Slave Trade in the Nineteenth Century*. London, UK: Frank Cass, 1989.

Clark, Arthur Hamilton. *The Clipper Ship Era: An Epitome of Famous American and British Clipper Ships, Their Owners, Builders, Commanders, and Crews, 1843-1869*. New York, NY: G. P. Putnam's Sons, 1912.

Clark, Kenneth. *Civilisation: A Personal View*. New York, NY: Harper and Row, 1969.

Clarke, James W. *The Lineaments of Wrath: Race, Violent Crime, and American Culture*. 1998. New Brunswick, NJ: Transaction, 2001 ed.

Clarkson, Thomas. *An Essay on the Slavery and Commerce of the Human Species, Particularly the African*. London, UK: Thomas Clarkson, 1787.

Cleveland, Henry. *Alexander H. Stephens in Public and Private*. Philadelphia, PA: National Publishing Co., 1866.

Clough, Ethlyn T. (ed.). *Africa: An Account of Past and Contemporary Conditions and Progress*. Detroit, MI: Bay View Reading Club, 1911.

Clough, Shepard B. *The Rise and Fall of Civilization: An Inquiry Into the Relationship Between Economic Development and Civilization*. 1951. New York, NY: Columbia University Press, 1957 ed.

Clough, Shepard B., Nina G. Garsoian, and David L. Hicks. *A History of the Western World: Ancient and Medieval*. Boston, MA: D. C. Heath and Co., 1964.

Coffin, Charles Carleton. *Abraham Lincoln*. New York, NY: Harper and Brothers, 1893.

Cohen, David W., and Jack P. Greene (eds.). *Neither Slave nor Free: The Freedman of African Descent in the Slave Societies of the New World*. Baltimore, MD: Johns Hopkins University Press, 1972.

Coit, Margaret L. *John C. Calhoun: American Portrait*. Boston, MA: Sentry, 1950.

Coldham, Peter Wilson. *Emigrants in Chains, 1607-1776*. Baltimore, MD: Genealogical Publishing Co., 1992.

Collections of the Massachusetts Historical Society. Boston, MA: Massachusetts Historical Society, 1877.

Collier, Christopher, and James Lincoln Collier. *Decision in Philadelphia: The Constitutional Convention of 1787*. 1986. New York, NY: Ballantine, 1987 ed.

Collins, Elizabeth. *Memories of the Southern States*. Taunton, UK: J. Barnicott, 1865.

Collins, John A. (ed.). *The Anti-Slavery Picknick: A Collection of Speeches, Poems, Dialogues and Songs Intended for Use in Schools and Anti-Slavery Meetings*. Boston, MA: H. W. Williams, 1842.

Collins, Winfield Hazlitt. *The Domestic Slave Trade of the Southern States*. New York, NY: Broadway Publishing, 1904.

Commissioners of Statutory Revision. *The Colonial Laws of New York From the Year 1664 to the Revolution*. 2 vols. Albany, NY: New York State, 1894.

Conrad, Robert. *The Destruction of Brazilian Slavery, 1850-1888*. Berkeley, CA: University of California Press, 1972.

Conway, Moncure Daniel. *Testimonies Concerning Slavery*. London, UK: Chapman and Hall, 1865.

Cooke, Alistair. *Alistair Cooke's America*. 1973. New York, NY: Knopf, 1984 ed.

Cooke, John Esten. *A Life of General Robert E. Lee*. New York, NY: D. Appleton and Co., 1871.

Cooley, Henry S. *A Study of Slavery in New Jersey*. Baltimore, MD: Johns Hopkins University Press, 1896.

Cooper, Frederick. *Plantation Slavery on the East Coast of Africa*. New Haven, CT: Yale University Press, 1977.

Cooper, William J., Jr. *Jefferson Davis, American*. New York, NY: Vintage, 2000.

——. (ed.). *Jefferson Davis: The Essential Writings*. New York, NY: Random House, 2003.

Copley, Esther. *A History of Slavery, and its Abolition*. London, UK: Houlston and Stoneman, 1839.

Cornish, Dudley Taylor. *The Sable Arm: Black Troops in the Union Army, 1861-1865*. 1956. Lawrence, KS: University Press of Kansas, 1987 ed.

Cottrol, Robert J. (ed.). *From African to Yankee: Narratives of Slavery and Freedom in Antebellum New England*. Armonk, NY: M. E. Sharpe, 1998.

Coughlan, Robert. *Tropical Africa*. New York, NY: Time, 1962.

Coughtry, Jay. *The Notorious Triangle: Rhode Island and the African Slave Trade, 1700-1807*. Philadelphia, PA: Temple Press, 1981.

Countryman, Edward. *The American Revolution*. 1985. New York, NY: Hill and Wang, 1993 ed.

Cox, Earnest Sevier. *White America: The American Racial Problem As Seen in a Worldwide Perspective and Lincoln's Negro Policy*. Richmond, VA: White America Society, 1923.

Craig, Albert M., William A. Graham, Donald Kagan, Steven Ozment, and Frank M. Turner. *The Heritage of World Civilizations - Vol.1: To 1600*. 1986. New York, NY: Macmillan College Publishing Co., 1994 ed.

Crallé, Richard Kenner. (ed.). *The Works of John C. Calhoun*. 6 vols. New York: NY: D. Appleton and Co., 1853-1888.

Cramer, Jesse Grant (ed.). *Letters of Ulysses S. Grant to His Father and His Youngest Sister, 1857-78*. New York, NY: G. P. Putnam's Sons, 1912.

Crane, Louise, Harvey Feinberg, Eleanor Berman, and Susan Hall. *Africa: History, Culture, Geography*.

Englewood Cliffs, NJ: Globe Book Co., 1989.

Cromwell, John Wesley. *The Negro in American History: Men and Women Eminent in the Evolution of the American of African Descent.* Washington, D.C.: American Negro Academy, 1914.

Cross, Samuel Creed. *The Negro and the Sunny South.* Martinsburg, WV: self-published, 1899.

Cummins, Joseph. *Anything For a Vote: Dirty Tricks, Cheap Shots, and October Surprises in U.S. Presidential Campaigns.* Philadelphia, PA: Quirk, 2007.

Current, Richard N. *The Lincoln Nobody Knows.* 1958. New York, NY: Hill and Wang, 1963 ed.

——. (ed.) *The Confederacy (Information Now Encyclopedia).* 1993. New York, NY: Macmillan, 1998 ed.

Curti, Merle, Willard Thorpe, and Carlos Baker (eds.). *American Issues: The Social Record.* 1941. Chicago, IL: J. B. Lippincott, 1960 ed.

Dabbs, James M. *The Southern Heritage.* New York, NY: Knopf, 1958.

Dabney, Robert Lewis. *A Defense of Virginia and the South.* Dahlonega, GA: Confederate Reprint Co., 1999.

Dahlberg, Gunnar. *Race, Reason and Rubbish: A Primer of Race Biology.* New York, NY: Columbia University Press, 1942.

Daniel, John M. *The Richmond Examiner During the War.* New York, NY: John M. Daniel, 1868.

Daniel, John W. *Life and Reminiscences of Jefferson Davis by Distinguished Men of His Time.* Baltimore, MD: R. H. Woodward and Co., 1890.

Darwin, Charles. *On the Origin of Species By Means of Natural Selection.* London, UK: John Murray, 1866.

Daugherty, James. *Abraham Lincoln.* 1943. New York, NY: Scholastic Book Services, 1966 ed.

d' Auvergne, Edmund B. *Human Livestock: An Account of the Share of the English-speaking Peoples in the Development, Maintenance and Suppression of Slavery and the Slave Trade.* London, UK: Grayson and Grayson, 1933.

Davidson, Basil. *The African Slave Trade.* 1961. Boston, MA: Back Bay Books, 1980 ed.

——. *The Black Man's Burden: Africa and the Curse of the Nation-State.* New York, NY: Times Books, 1992.

Davis, Charles S. *The Cotton Kingdom in Alabama.* Montgomery, AL: Alabama State Dept. of Archives and History, 1939.

Davis, Darién J. (ed.). *Slavery and Beyond: The African Impact on Latin America and the Caribbean.* Lanham, MD: SR Books, 1995.

Davis, David Brion. *The Problem of Slavery in Western Culture.* 1966. Ithaca, NY: Cornell University Press, 1969 ed.

Davis, Jefferson. *The Rise and Fall of the Confederate Government.* 2 vols. New York, NY: D. Appleton and Co., 1881.

——. *A Short History of the Confederate States of America.* New York, NY: Belford, 1890.

——. *Andersonville and Other War-Prisons.* New York, NY: Belford Co., 1890.

Davis, Kenneth C. *Don't Know Much About the Civil War: Everything You Need to Know About America's Greatest Conflict But Never Learned.* 1996. New York, NY: HarperCollins, 1997 ed.

Davis, Michael. *The Image of Lincoln in the South.* Knoxville, TN: University of Tennessee Press, 1971.

Davis, Robert C. *Christian Slaves, Muslim Masters: White Slavery in the Mediterranean, the Barbary Coast and Italy, 1500-1800.* New York, NY: Macmillan, 2004.

Davis, Simon. *Race Relations in Ancient Egypt: Greek, Egyptian, Hebrew, Roman.* London, UK: Methuen, 1953.

Davis, Varina. *Jefferson Davis: Ex-President of the Confederate States of America - A Memoir by His Wife.* 2 vols. New York, NY: Belford Co., 1890.

Davis, William C. *Jefferson Davis: The Man and His Hour.* New York, NY: HarperCollins, 1991.

——. *An Honorable Defeat: The Last Days of the Confederate Government.* New York, NY: Harcourt, 2001.

——. *Look Away: A History of the Confederate States of America.* 2002. New York, NY: Free Press, 2003 ed.

De Angelis, Gina. *It Happened in Washington, D.C.* Guilford, CT: Globe Pequot Press, 2004.

DeFord, Deborah H. *Life Under Slavery.* New York, NY: Chelsea House, 2006.

De Forest, John William. *A Volunteer's Adventures: A Union Captain's Record of the Civil War.* 1946. North Haven, CT: Archon, 1970 ed.

Degler, Carl N. *Neither Black Nor White: Slavery and Race Relations in Brazil and the United States.* New York, NY: Macmillan, 1971.

DeGregorio, William A. *The Complete Book of U.S. Presidents.* 1984. New York, NY: Barricade, 1993 ed.

De Kock, Victor. *Those in Bondage.* London, UK: George Allen and Unwin, 1950.

de la Rochefoucauld Liancourt, Duke. *Travels Through the United States of North America, the Country of the Iroquois, and Upper Canada, in the Years 1795, 1796, and 1797.* 2 vols. London, UK: R. Phillips, 1800.

de las Casas, Bartolomé. *The Tears of the Indians: Being an Historical and True Account of the Cruel Massacres and Slaughters of Above Twenty Millions of Innocent People; Committed by the Spaniards in the Islands of Hispaniola, Cuba, Jamaica, etc.; As also, in the Continent of Mexico, Peru, and Other Places of the West*

Indies, to the Total Destruction of Those Countries. London, UK: Nathaniel Brook, 1656.

de la Vega, Garcilaso. *The Incas.* New York, NY: Avon, 1961.

Derry, Joseph Tyrone. *Story of the Confederate States; or, History of the War for Southern Independence.* Richmond, VA: B. F. Johnson, 1895.

de Saint Croix, G. E. M. *The Class Struggle in the Ancient Greek World: From the Archaic Age to the Arab Conquests.* Ithaca, NY: Cornell University Press, 1980.

Devine, Edward T. (ed.). *The Negro in the Cities of the North.* New York, NY: The Charity Organization Society, 1905.

Dew, Charles B. *Bond of Iron: Master and Slave at Buffalo Forge.* New York, NY: W. W. Norton, 1994.

DeWolf, Thomas Norman. *Inheriting the Trade: A Northern Family Confronts Its Legacy as the Largest Slave-Trading Dynasty in U.S. History.* Boston, MA: Beacon Press, 2008.

Diamond, Jared. *Guns, Germs, and Steel: The Fate of Human Societies.* 1997. New York, NY: W. W. Norton, 1999 ed.

Dicey, Edward. *Six Months in the Federal States.* 2 vols. London, UK: Macmillan and Co., 1863.

Dick, Everett Newfon. *The Dixie Frontier: A Social History.* New York, NY: Knopf, 1948.

DiLorenzo, Thomas J. "The Great Centralizer: Abraham Lincoln and the War Between the States." *The Independent Review,* Vol. 3, No. 2, Fall 1998, pp. 243-271.

———. *The Real Lincoln: A New Look at Abraham Lincoln, His Agenda, and an Unnecessary War.* Three Rivers, MI: Three Rivers Press, 2003.

———. *Lincoln Unmasked: What You're Not Supposed to Know About Dishonest Abe.* New York, NY: Crown Forum, 2006.

———. *Hamilton's Curse: How Jefferson's Archenemy Betrayed the American Revolution—and What It Means for America Today.* New York, NY: Crown Forum, 2008.

Dimont, Max I. *Jews, God and History.* New York, NY: Signet, 1962.

Dinkins, James. *1861 to 1865: Personal Recollections and Experiences in the Confederate Army, by an "Old Johnnie."* Cincinnati, OH: Robert Clarke, 1897.

Dixon, Mrs. Archibald. *History of Missouri Compromise and Slavery in American Politics.* Cincinnati, OH: Robert Clarke, Co., 1903.

Dockés, Pierre. *Medieval Slavery and Liberation.* Chicago, IL: University of Chicago Press, 1982.

Dodd, William E. *Jefferson Davis.* Philadelphia, PA: George W. Jacobs and Co., 1907.

———. *The Cotton Kingdom: A Chronicle of the Old South.* New Haven, CT: Yale University Press, 1920.

Doddridge, Joseph. *Notes on the Settlement and Indian Wars of the Western Parts of Virginia and Pennsylvania, From 1763 to 1783, Inclusive.* Albany, NY: Joel Munsell, 1876.

Dodson, Howard. *Jubilee: The Emergence of African-American Culture.* New York, NY: National Geographic, 2003.

Donald, David Herbert. *Lincoln Reconsidered: Essays on the Civil War Era.* 1947. New York, NY: Vintage Press, 1989 ed.

———. (ed.). *Why the North Won the Civil War.* 1960. New York, NY: Collier, 1962 ed.

———. *Lincoln's Herndon.* New York, NY: Knopf, 1989.

———. *Lincoln.* New York, NY: Simon and Schuster, 1995.

Donald, Leland. *Aboriginal Slavery on the Northwest Coast of North America.* Berkeley, CA: University of California Press, 1997.

Donnan, Elizabeth (ed.). *Documents Illustrative of the History of the Slave Trade to America.* 3 vols. Washington, D.C.: Carnegie Institute, 1930-1935.

Dormon, James H., and Robert R. Jones. *The Afro-American Experience: A Cultural History Through Emancipation.* New York, NY: John Wiley and Sons, 1974.

Doubleday's Encyclopedia. 1931. New York, NY: Doubleday, Doran and Co., 1939 ed.

Douglas, Henry Kyd. *I Rode With Stonewall: The War Experiences of the Youngest Member of Jackson's Staff.* 1940. Chapel Hill, NC: University of North Carolina Press, 1968 ed.

Douglass, Frederick. *Narrative of the Life of Frederick Douglass: An American Slave.* 1845. New York, NY: Signet, 1997 ed.

———. *The Life and Times of Frederick Douglass, From 1817 to 1882.* London, UK: Christian Age Office, 1882.

Douglass, Harlan Paul. *Christian Reconstruction in the South.* Cambridge, MA: The University Press, 1909.

Dowd, Jerome. *The Negro in American Life.* New York, NY: Century, 1926.

Dowley, Tim (ed.). *The History of Christianity.* 1977. Oxford, UK: Lion, 1990 ed.

Doyle, Bertram W. *The Etiquette of Race Relations in the South: A Study in Social Control.* Chicago, IL: University of Chicago Press, 1937.

Drake, St. Clair, and Horace Clayton. *Black Metropolis: A Study of Negro Life in a Northern City*. New York, NY: Harcourt, Brace and Co., 1945.

Draper, John William. *History of the American Civil War*. 3 vols. New York, NY: Harper and Brothers, 1870.

Drescher, Seymour. *The Mighty Experiment: Free Labor Versus Slavery in British Emancipation*. New York, NY: Oxford University Press, 2002.

Drescher, Seymour, and Stanley L. Engerman (eds.). *A Historical Guide to World Slavery*. New York, NY: Oxford University Press, 1998.

Drew, Benjamin. *The Refugee: Or the Narratives of Fugitive Slaves in Canada*. Boston, MA: John P. Jewett and Co., 1856.

Du Bois, William Edward Burghardt. *The Suppression of the African Slave Trade to the United States of America, 1638-1870*. New York, NY: Longmans, Green, and Co., 1896.

——. *Darkwater: Voices From Within the Veil*. New York, NY: Harcourt, Brace and Howe, 1920.

——. *The Gift of Black Folk: The Negroes in the Making of America*. Boston, MA: Stratford, 1924.

——. *Black Reconstruction*. New York, NY: Harcourt, Brace, 1935.

Du Bois, William Edward Burghardt, and Augustus Granville Dill (eds.). *The Negro American Artisan*. Atlanta, GA: Atlanta University Press, 1912.

Dumond, Dwight Lowell. *Antislavery Origins of the Civil War in the United States*. 1939. Ann Arbor, MI: University of Michigan Press, 1960 ed.

Dunbar, Rowland (ed.). *Jefferson Davis, Constitutionalist: His Letters, Papers, and Speeches*. 10 vols. Jackson, MS: Mississippi Department of Archives and History, 1923.

Dunn, L. C., and Theodosius Dobzhansky. *Heredity, Race and Society: A Scientific Explanation of Human Differences*. 1946. New York, NY: Mentor, 1949 ed.

Dunn, Mary M., and Richard S. Dunn (eds.). *The Papers of William Penn*. 2 vols. Philadelphia, PA: University of Pennsylvania Press, 1986.

Dunn, Richard S. *Sugar and Slaves: The Rise of the Planter Class in the English West Indies*. Chapel Hill, NC: University of North Carolina Press, 1972.

Durant, Will. *Our Oriental Heritage*. 1935. New York, NY: Simon and Schuster, 1954 ed.

Durant, Will, and Ariel Durant. *The Age of Reason Begins: A History of European Civilization in the Period of Shakespeare, Bacon, Montaigne, Rembrandt, Galileo, and Descartes, 1558-1648*. New York, NY: Simon and Schuster, 1961.

Durden, Robert F. *The Gray and the Black: The Confederate Debate on Emancipation*. Baton Rouge, LA: Louisiana State University Press, 1972.

Easton, Stewart C. *The Heritage of the Past: From the Earliest Times to the Close of the Middle Ages*. 1955. New York, NY: Rinehart and Co., 1957 ed.

——. *The Western Heritage*. New York, NY: Holt, Rinehart and Winston, 1961.

Eaton, Clement. *A History of the Southern Confederacy*. 1945. New York, NY: Free Press, 1966 ed.

——. *Henry Clay and the Art of American Politics*. Chicago, IL: Scott Foresman and Co., 1957.

——. *Jefferson Davis*. New York, NY: Free Press, 1977.

Eaton, John, and Ethel Osgood Mason. *Grant, Lincoln and the Freedmen: Reminiscences of the Civil War, With Special Reference to the Work of the Contrabands and Freedmen of the Mississippi Valley*. New York, NY: Longmans, Green, and Co., 1907.

Eban, Abba. *Heritage: Civilization and the Jews*. New York, NY: Summit, 1984.

Ellis, Joseph J. *American Sphinx: The Character of Thomas Jefferson*. 1996. New York, NY: Vintage, 1998 ed.

——. *Founding Brothers: The Revolutionary Generation*. 2000. New York, NY: Vintage, 2002 ed.

Emerson, Bettie Adler Calhoun. *Historic Southern Monuments: Representative Memorials of the Heroic Dead of the Southern Confederacy*. New York, NY: Neale Publishing Co., 1911.

Encyclopedia Britannica: A New Survey of Universal Knowledge. 1768. Chicago, IL/London, UK: Encyclopedia Britannica, 1955 ed.

Estes, Matthew. *A Defence of Negro Slavery, as it Exists in the United States*. Montgomery, AL: Press of the *Alabama Journal*, 1846.

Farrow, Anne, Joel Lang, and Jennifer Frank. *Complicity: How the North Promoted, Prolonged, and Profited From Slavery*. New York, NY: Ballantine, 2005.

Faulkner, Harold Underwood. *American Political and Social History*. 1937. New York, NY: Appleton-Century-Crofts, 1948 ed.

Faulkner, William. *The Unvanquished*. 1934. New York, NY: Vintage, 1966 ed.

Faust, Patricia L. (ed.). *Historical Times Illustrated Encyclopedia of the Civil War*. New York, NY: Harper and Row, 1986.

Featherstonhaugh, George William. *Excursion Through the Slave States*. 2 vols. London, UK: John Murray, 1844.

Fehrenbacher, Don E. (ed.). *Abraham Lincoln: A Documentary Portrait Through His Speeches and Writings*. New York, NY: Signet, 1964.

——. *Lincoln in Text and Context: Collected Essays*. Stanford, CA: Stanford University Press, 1987.

——. (ed.) *Abraham Lincoln: Speeches and Writings, 1859-1865*. New York, NY: Library of America, 1989.

——. *The Slaveholding Republic: An Account of the United States Government's Relations to Slavery*. New York, NY: Oxford University Press, 2002.

Ferguson, Wallace K., and Geoffrey Bruun. *A Survey of European Civilization - Part 1: To 1660*. 1936. Boston, MA: Houghton Mifflin Co., 1947 ed.

——. *A Survey of European Civilization - Part 2: Since 1660*. 1936. Boston, MA: Houghton Mifflin Co., 1947 ed.

Ferris, Marcie Cohen, and Mark I. Greenberg (eds.). *Jewish Roots in Southern Soil: A New History*. Waltham, MA: Brandeis University Press, 2006.

Ferris, William Henry. *The African Abroad, or His Evolution in Western Civilization*. 2 vols. New Haven CT: The Tuttle, Morehouse and Taylor Press, 1913.

Findlay, Bruce, and Esther Findlay. *Your Rugged Constitution: How America's House of Freedom is Planned and Built*. 1950. Stanford, CA: Stanford University Press, 1951 ed.

Fite, Emerson David. *The Presidential Election of 1860*. New York, NY: MacMillan, 1911.

Fitts, Robert. K. *Inventing New England's Slave Paradise: Master / Slave Relations in Eighteenth-Century Narragansett, Rhode Island*. New York, NY: Garland, 1998.

Fitzhugh, George. *Sociology for the South, or the Failure of Free Society*. Richmond, VA: A. Morris, 1854.

Fleming, Walter Lynwood. *Civil War and Reconstruction in Alabama*. New York, NY: Macmillan, 1905.

Flint, Timothy. *The History and Geography of the Mississippi Valley*. 2 vols. Cincinnati, OH: E. H. Flint, 1833.

Flood, Charles Bracelen. *1864: Lincoln At the Gates of History*. New York, NY: Simon and Schuster, 2009.

Fogel, Robert William. *Without Consent or Contract: The Rise and Fall of American Slavery*. New York, NY: W. W. Norton, 1989.

Fogel, Robert William, and Stanley L. Engerman. *Time On the Cross: The Economics of American Negro Slavery*. Boston, MA: Little, Brown, and Co., 1974.

Foley, John P. (ed.). *The Jeffersonian Cyclopedia*. New York, NY: Funk and Wagnalls, 1900.

Foner, Eric. *Free Soil, Free Labor, Free Men: The Ideology of the Republican Party Before the Civil War*. New York, NY: Oxford University Press, 1970.

——. *Reconstruction: America's Unfinished Revolution, 1863-1877*. 1988. New York, NY: Harper and Row, 1989 ed.

——. *Gateway to Freedom: The Hidden History of the Underground Railroad*. New York, NY: W. W. Norton and Co., 2015.

Foote, Shelby. *The Civil War: A Narrative, Fort Sumter to Perryville, Vol. 1*. 1958. New York, NY: Vintage, 1986 ed.

——. *The Civil War: A Narrative, Fredericksburg to Meridian, Vol. 2*. 1963. New York, NY: Vintage, 1986 ed.

——. *The Civil War: A Narrative, Red River to Appomattox, Vol. 3*. 1974. New York, NY: Vintage, 1986 ed.

Foote, Thelma Wills. *Black and White Manhattan: The History of Racial Formation in Colonial New York City*. New York, NY: Oxford University Press, 2004.

Ford, Paul Leicester (ed.). *The Works of Thomas Jefferson*. 12 vols. New York, NY: G. P. Putnam's Sons, 1904.

Ford, Worthington Chauncey (ed.). *A Cycle of Adams Letters*. 2 vols. Boston, MA: Houghton Mifflin, 1920.

Forman, S. E. *The Life and Writings of Thomas Jefferson*. Indianapolis, IN: Bowen-Merrill, 1900.

Förster, Stig, and Jörg Nagler (eds.). *On the Road to Total War: The American Civil War and the German Wars of Unification, 1861-1871*. 1997. Cambridge, UK: Cambridge University Press, 2002 ed.

Fortune, Timothy T. *Black and White: Land, Labor, and Politics in the South*. New York, NY: Arno, 1968.

Foster, John W. *A Century of American Diplomacy*. Boston, MA: Houghton, Mifflin and Co., 1901.

Fowler, John D. *The Confederate Experience Reader: Selected Documents and Essays*. New York, NY: Routledge, 2007.

Fowler, William Chauncey. *The Sectional Controversy; or Passages in the Political History of the United States, Including the Causes of the War Between the Sections*. New York, NY: Charles Scribner, 1864.

Fox, Early Lee. *The American Colonization Society, 1817-1840*. Baltimore, MD: Johns Hopkins Press, 1919.

Fox-Genovese, Elizabeth. *Within the Plantation Household: Black and White Women of the Old South (Gender and American Culture)*. Chapel Hill, NC: University of North Carolina Press, 1988.

Franklin, John Hope. *Reconstruction After the Civil War*. Chicago, IL: University of Chicago Press, 1961.

Fremont-Barnes, Gregory. *The Wars of the Barbary Pirates: To the Shores of Tripoli - The Rise of the US Navy and*

Marines. Oxford, UK: Osprey, 2006.

French, A. M. *Slavery in South Carolina and the Ex-Slaves; Or the Port Royal Mission*. New York, NY: Winchell M. French, 1862.

Freyre, Gilberto. *The Masters and the Slaves*. New York, NY: Knopf, 1956.

Furnas, J. C. *The Americans: A Social History of the United States, 1587-1914*. New York, NY: G. P. Putnam's Sons, 1969.

Gardner, Joseph L. (ed.). *Mysteries of the Ancient Americas: The New World Before Columbus*. 1986. Pleasantville, NY: Reader's Digest, 1992 ed.

Garlan, Yvon. *Slavery in Ancient Greece*. Ithaca, NY: Cornell University Press, 1988.

Garland, Hugh A. *The Life of John Randolph of Roanoke*. New York, NY: D. Appleton and Co., 1874.

Garraty, John A. *The American Nation: A History of the United States to 1877*. 1966. New York, NY: Harper and Row, 1971 ed.

——. (ed.) *Historical Viewpoints: Notable Articles From American Heritage, Vol. One to 1877*. 1970. New York, NY: Harper and Row, 1979 ed.

Garraty, John A., and Robert A. McCaughey. *A Short History of the American Nation*. 1966. New York, NY: HarperCollins, 1989 ed.

Garrison, Webb B. *Civil War Trivia and Fact Book*. Nashville, TN: Rutledge Hill Press, 1992.

——. *The Lincoln No One Knows: The Mysterious Man Who Ran the Civil War*. Nashville, TN: Rutledge Hill Press, 1993.

——. *Civil War Curiosities: Strange Stories, Oddities, Events, and Coincidences*. Nashville, TN: Rutledge Hill Press, 1994.

——. *The Amazing Civil War*. Nashville, TN: Rutledge Hill Press, 1998.

Garrison, Wendell Phillips, and Francis Jackson Garrison. *William Lloyd Garrison, 1805-1879*. 4 vols. New York, NY: Century Co., 1889.

Garrison, William Lloyd. *Thoughts on African Colonization*. Boston, MA: Garrison and Knapp, 1832.

Gaspar, David Barry, and Darlene Clark Hine (eds.). *More Than Chattel: Black Women and Slavery in the Americas*. Bloomington, IN: Indiana University Press, 1996.

Gates, Henry Louis, Jr. (ed.) *The Classic Slave Narratives*. New York, NY: Mentor, 1987.

Gay, Mary Ann Harris. *Life in Dixie During the War*. Atlanta, GA: Constitution Job Office, 1892.

Gellman, David N. *Emancipating New York: The Politics of Slavery and Freedom 1777-1827*. Baton Rouge, LA: Louisiana State University Press, 2006.

Gemery, Henry A., and Jan S. Hogendorn (eds.). *The Uncommon Market: Essays in the Economic History of the Atlantic Slave Trade*. New York, NY: Academic Press, 1979.

Genovese, Eugene D. *Roll, Jordan, Roll: The World the Slaves Made*. New York, NY: Pantheon, 1974.

Gilliam, Edward Winslow. *Uncle Sam and the Negro in 1920*. Lynchburg, VA: J. P. Bell Co., 1906.

Gimbutas, Marija. *The Civilization of the Goddess: The World of Old Europe*. New York, NY: Harper Collins, 1991.

Golay, Michael. *A Ruined Land: The End of the Civil War*. New York, NY: John Wiley and Sons, 1999.

Goodell, William. *The American Slave Code in Theory and Practice*. New York, NY: The American and Foreign Anti-Slavery Society, 1853.

Goodloe, Daniel Reaves. *Inquiry Into the Causes Which Have Retarded the Accumulation of Wealth and Increase of Population in the Southern States: In Which the Question of Slavery is Considered in a Politico-Economical Point of View*. Washington, D.C.: W. Blanchard (printer), 1846.

Goodwyn, Lawrence. *The Populist Moment: A Short History of the Agrarian Revolt in America*. 1976. Oxford, UK: Oxford University Press, 1978 ed.

Gordon, Armistead Churchill. *Figures From American History: Jefferson Davis*. New York, NY: Charles Scribner's Sons, 1918.

Gordon, Irving L. *World History: Review Text*. 1965. New York, NY: Amsco School Publications, 1969 ed.

Gordon, John Brown. *Reminiscences of the Civil War*. New York, NY: Charles Scribner's Sons, 1903.

Gragg, Rod. *The Illustrated Confederate Reader: Extraordinary Eyewitness Accounts by the Civil War's Southern Soldiers and Civilians*. New York, NY: Gramercy Books, 1989.

Graham, John Remington. *A Constitutional History of Secession*. Gretna, LA: Pelican Publishing Co., 2003.

——. *Blood Money: The Civil War and the Federal Reserve*. Gretna, LA: Pelican Publishing Co., 2006.

Graham, Lloyd M. *Deceptions and Myths of the Bible*. 1975. New York, NY: Citadel Press, 1991 ed.

Graham, Stephen. *Children of the Slaves*. London, UK: Macmillan and Co., 1920.

Grant, Anne MacVicar. *Memoirs of an American Lady, With Sketches of Manners and Scenery in America as They Existed Previous to the Revolution*. 2 vols in 1. New York, NY: D. Appleton and Co., 1846.

Grant, Arthur James. *Greece in the Age of Pericles*. London, UK: John Murray, 1893.

Grant, Michael. *The World of Rome*. 1960. New York, NY: Mentor, 1964 ed.

——. *Constantine the Great: The Man and His Times*. New York, NY: Charles Scribner's Sons, 1993.

Grant, Ulysses Simpson. *Personal Memoirs of U. S. Grant*. 2 vols. 1885-1886. New York, NY: Charles L. Webster and Co., 1886.

Gray, Louis Herbert (ed.). *The Mythology of All Races*. 13 vols. Boston, MA: Marshall Jones, 1918.

Gray, Thomas R. *The Confessions of Nat Turner: The Leader of the Late Insurrection in Southampton, Virginia*. Richmond, VA: Thomas R. Gray, 1831.

Greeley, Horace (ed.). *The Writings of Cassius Marcellus Clay*. New York, NY: Harper and Brothers, 1848.

——. *A History of the Struggle for Slavery Extension or Restriction in the United States From the Declaration of Independence to the Present Day*. New York, NY: Dix, Edwards and Co., 1856.

——. *The American Conflict: A History of the Great Rebellion in the United States, 1861-1865*. 2 vols. Hartford, CT: O. D. Case and Co., 1867.

Green, Constance McLaughlin. *Eli Whitney and the Birth of American Technology*. Boston, MA: Little, Brown, and Co., 1956.

——. *Washington: A History of the Capital, 1800-1950*. 1962. Princeton, NJ: Princeton University Press, 1976 ed.

Green, John Richard. *A Short History of the English People*. 2 vols. London, UK: Macmillan and Co., 1892.

Green, William A. *British Slave Emancipation: The Sugar Colonies and the Great Experiment, 1830-1865*. Oxford, UK: Clarendon Press, 1976.

Greenberg, Martin H., and Charles G. Waugh (eds.). *The Price of Freedom: Slavery and the Civil War—Vol. 1, The Demise of Slavery*. Nashville, TN: Cumberland House, 2000.

Greene, Lorenzo Johnston. *The Negro in Colonial New England, 1620-1776*. New York, NY: Columbia University Press, 1942.

Greene, Sandra E. *West African Narratives of Slavery: Texts From Late Nineteenth- and Early Twentieth-Century Ghana*. Bloomington, IN: Indiana University Press, 2011.

Greenhow, Rose O'Neal. *My Imprisonment and the First Year of Abolition Rule at Washington*. London, UK: Richard Bentley, 1863.

Greer, Thomas H. *A Brief History of Western Man: To 1650*. New York, NY: Harcourt Brace Jovanovich, 1972.

Grey, Lewis Cecil. *History of Agriculture in the Southern United States to 1860*. 2 vols. Washington, DC: Carnegie Institution of Washington, 1933.

Grimké, Angelina Emily. *Letters to Catherine E. Beecher, in Reply to an Essay on Slavery and Abolitionism, Addressed to A. E. Grimké*. Boston, MA: Angelina Emily Grimké, 1838.

Grimsley, Mark. *The Hard Hand of War: Union Military Policy Toward Southern Civilians, 1861-1865*. 1995. Cambridge, UK: Cambridge University Press, 1997 ed.

Grissom, Michael Andrew. *Southern By the Grace of God*. 1988. Gretna, LA: Pelican Publishing Co., 1995 ed.

Gutman, Herbert G. *The Black Family in Slavery and Freedom, 1750-1925*. New York, NY: Pantheon, 1976.

Gwatkin, H. M., and J. P. Whitney (eds.). *The Cambridge Medieval History, Vol. 2: The Rise of the Saracens and the Foundation of the Western Empire*. New York, NY: Macmillan, 1913.

Hacker, Louis Morton. *The Shaping of the American Tradition*. New York, NY: Columbia University Press, 1947.

Hadas, Moses (ed.). *A History of Rome: From Its Origins to 259 A.D. as Told by Roman Historians*. Garden City, NY: Doubleday Anchor, 1956.

Haines, C. Grove, and Warren B. Walsh. *The Development of Western Civilization*. 2 vols. 1941. New York, NY: Henry Holt and Co., 1947 ed.

Hale, Will Thomas, and Dixon Lanier Merritt. *A History of Tennessee and Tennesseans*. 8 vols. Chicago, IL: Lewis Publishing Co., 1913.

Hall, B. C., and C. T. Wood. *The South: A Two-step Odyssey on the Backroads of the Enchanted Land*. New York, NY: Touchstone, 1996.

Hall, Basil. *Travels in North America, in the Years 1827 and 1828*. 3 vols. Edinburgh, Scotland: Cadell and Co., 1829.

Hall, Francis. *Travels in Canada, and the United States, in 1816 and 1817*. London, UK: Longman, Hurst, Rees, Orme, and Brown, 1818.

Hall, Gwendolyn M. *Africans in Colonial Louisiana: The Development of Afro-Creole Culture in the Eighteenth Century*. Baton Rouge, LA: Louisiana State University Press, 1992.

Hall, John (ed.). *Forty Years' Familiar Letters of James W. Alexander, D.D.* 2 vols. New York, NY: Charles Scribner, 1860.

Hall, Kermit L. (ed). *The Oxford Companion to the Supreme Court of the United States*. New York, NY: Oxford University Press, 1992.

Hall, Marshall. *The Two-Fold Slavery of the United States; With a Project of Self-Emancipation*. London, UK: Adam Scott, 1854.

Hall, Walter Phelps, Robert Greenhalgh Albion, and Jennie Barnes Pope. *A History of England and the Empire-Commonwealth*. 1937. Waltham, MA: Blaisdell, 1965 ed.

Hamblin, Ken. *Pick a Better Country: An Unassuming Colored Guy Speaks His Mind About America*. New York, NY: Touchstone, 1997.

Hamilton, J. G. de Roulhac (ed.). *Selections From the Writings of Abraham Lincoln*. Chicago, IL: Scott, Foresman and Co., 1922.

Hamilton, Neil A. *Rebels and Renegades: A Chronology of Social and Political Dissent in the United States*. New York, NY: Routledge, 2002.

Handler, Jerome S. *The Unappropriated People: Freedmen in the Slave Society of Barbados*. Baltimore, MD: Johns Hopkins University Press, 1974.

Handlin, Oscar (ed.). *Readings in American History: Vol. 1 - From Settlement to Reconstruction*. 1957. New York, NY: Knopf, 1970 ed.

Harper, William. *Memoir of Slavery, Read Before the Society for the Advancement of Learning, of South Carolina, at its Annual Meeting at Columbia*. Charleston, SC: James S. Burges, 1838.

Harper, William, James Henry Hammond, William Gilmore Simms, and Thomas Roderick Dew. *The Pro-Slavery Argument, As Maintained by the Most Distinguished Writers of the Southern States*. Charleston, SC: Walker, Richards and Co., 1852.

Harrell, David Edwin, Jr., Edwin S. Gaustad, John B. Boles, Sally Foreman Griffith, Randall M. Miller, and Randall B. Woods. *Unto a Good Land: A History of the American People*. Grand Rapids, MI: William B. Eerdmans, 2005.

Harris, Joel Chandler. *Stories of Georgia*. New York, NY: American Book Co., 1896.

Harris, Joseph E., Alusine Jalloh, Joseph E. Inikori, Colin A. Palmer, Douglas B. Chambers, and Dale T. Graden. *The African Diaspora*. Arlington, TX: Texas A&M University Press, 1996.

Harris, Leslie M. *In the Shadow of Slavery: African Americans in New York City, 1626-1863*. Chicago, IL: University of Chicago Press, 2004.

Harris, Marvin. *Our Kind: Who We Are, Where We Came From, Where We Are Going*. New York, NY: Harper and Row, 1989.

Harris, Norman Dwight. *The History of Negro Servitude in Illinois*. Chicago, IL: A. C. McClurg and Co., 1904.

Harrison, Peleg D. *The Stars and Stripes and Other American Flags*. 1906. Boston, MA: Little, Brown, and Co., 1908 ed.

Hart, Albert Busnell. *Slavery and Abolition*. New York, NY: Haskell House, 1906.

———. *The Southern South*. New York, NY: D. Appleton and Co., 1912.

Hartman, Gertrude, and Lucy S. Saunders. *Builders of the Old World*. 1946. Boston, MA: Little, Brown and Co., 1959 ed.

Hartzell, Josiah. *The Genesis of the Republican Party*. Canton, OH: n.p., 1890.

Harwell, Richard B. (ed.). *The Confederate Reader: How the South Saw the War*. 1957. Mineola, NY: Dover, 1989 ed.

Hawthorne, Julian (ed.). *Orations of American Orators*. 2 vols. New York, NY: Colonial Press, 1900.

Hawthorne, Julian, James Schouler, and Elisha Benjamin Andrews. *United States, From the Discovery of the North American Continent Up to the Present Time*. 9 vols. New York, NY: Co-operative Publication Society, 1894.

Hawthorne, Nathaniel. *The Works of Nathaniel Hawthorne*. 15 vols. 1850. Boston, MA: Houghton, Mifflin and Co., 1888 ed.

Hay, John H. Drummond. *Western Barbary: Its Wild Tribes and Savage Animals*. London, UK: John Murray, 1891.

Hayes, Carlton J. H., Marshall Whited Baldwin, and Charles Woolsey Cole. *History of Europe*. 1949. New York, NY: Macmillan Co., 1950 ed.

Haygood, Atticus G. *Our Brother in Black: His Freedom and His Future*. Nashville, TN: M. E. Church, 1896.

Hellie, Richard. *Slavery in Russia, 1450-1725*. Chicago, IL: University of Chicago Press, 1982.

Helper, Hinton Rowan. *Compendium of the Impending Crisis of the South*. New York, NY: A. B. Burdick, 1860.

———. *Miscegenation: The Theory of Blending of the Races, Applied to the American White Man and Negro*. Hamilton, NY: H. Dexter, 1864.

———. *Nojoque: A Question for a Continent*. New York, NY: George W. Carleton, 1867.

———. *The Negroes in Negroland: The Negroes in America; and Negroes Generally*. New York, NY: George W. Carlton, 1868.

———. *Oddments of Andean Diplomacy and Other Oddments*. St. Louis, MO: W. S. Bryan, 1879.

Hendelson, William H. (ed). *Funk and Wagnalls New Encyclopedia*. New York, NY: Funk and Wagnalls, 1973 ed.

Henderson, George Francis Robert. *Stonewall Jackson and the American Civil War*. 2 vols. London, UK: Longmans, Green, and Co., 1919.

Henry, Robert Selph (ed.). *The Story of the Confederacy*. 1931. New York, NY: Konecky and Konecky, 1999 ed.

——. *As They Saw Forrest: Some Recollections and Comments of Contemporaries*. 1956. Wilmington, NC: Broadfoot Publishing Co., 1991 ed.

——. *First With the Most: Forrest*. New York, NY: Konecky and Konecky, 1992.

Herring, Hubert. *A History of Latin America: From the Beginnings to the Present*. 1955. New York, NY: Alfred A. Knopf, 1968 ed.

Herskovits, Melville J. *The Myth of the Negro Past*. 1941. Boston, MA: Beacon Press, 1969 ed.

Hertz, Emanuel. *Abraham Lincoln: A New Portrait*. 2 Vols. New York, NY: H. Liveright, 1931.

——. *The Hidden Lincoln*. New York, NY: Blue Ribbon Works, 1940.

Hervey, Anthony. *Why I Wave the Confederate Flag, Written By a Black Man: The End of Niggerism and the Welfare State*. Oxford, UK: Trafford Publishing, 2006.

Heston, Alfred Miller. *Story of the Slave: Slavery and Servitude in New Jersey*. Camden, NJ: Sinnickson Chew and Sons Co., 1903.

Heuman, Gad J. *Between Black and White: Race, Politics, and the Free Coloreds in Jamaica, 1792-1865*. Westport, CT: Greenwood Press, 1981.

——. *Out of the House of Bondage, Runaways, Resistance and Maroonage in Africa and the New World*. London, UK: Frank Cass, 1986.

Heysinger, Issac Winter. *Antietam and the Maryland and Virginia Campaigns of 1862*. New York, NY: Neale Publishing Co., 1912.

Higman, Barry W. *Slave Populations of the British Caribbean, 1807-1834*. Baltimore, MD: Johns Hopkins University Press, 1984.

Hildreth, Richard. *The White Slave: Another Picture of Slave Life in America*. London, UK: George Rutledge and Co., 1852.

——. *The History of the United States*. 6 vols. New York, NY: Harper and Brothers, 1882.

Hill, George Birkbeck (ed.). *Colonel Gordon in Central Africa 1874-1879*. London, UK: Thomas de la Rue, 1881.

Hill, Shirley, A. *Families: A Social Class Perspective*. Thousand Oaks, CA: Sage, 2012.

Hinkle, Don. *Embattled Banner: A Reasonable Defense of the Confederate Battle Flag*. Paducah, KY: Turner Publishing Co., 1997.

Holmes, Burton. *Burton Holmes Travelogues: Cities of the Barbary Coast, Vol. 4*. New York, NY: McClure Co., 1908.

Holmes, Thomas Rice. *Caesar's Conquest of Gaul: An Historical Narrative*. London, UK: Macmillan and Co., 1903.

Holzer, Harold (ed.). *The Lincoln-Douglas Debates: The First Complete, Unexpurgated Text*. 1993. Bronx, NY: Fordham University Press, 2004 ed.

Homans, Isaac Smith. *Sketches of Boston, Past and Present, and of Some Few Places in its Vicinity*. Boston, MA: Phillips, Samson, and Co., 1851.

Hood, John Bell. *Advance and Retreat: Personal Experiences in the United States and Confederate States Armies*. New Orleans, LA: G. T. Beauregard, 1880.

Hopkins, John Henry. *The Bible View of American Slavery: A Letter From the Bishop of Vermont to the Bishop of Pennsylvania*. London, UK: Saunders, Otley, and Co., 1863.

Hopkins, Keith. *Conquerors and Slaves*. Cambridge, UK: Cambridge University Press, 1978.

Hopkins, Luther W. *From Bull Run to Appomattox: A Boy's View*. Baltimore, MD: Fleet-McGinley Co., 1908.

Horn, Stanley F. *Invisible Empire: The Story of the Ku Klux Klan, 1866-1871*. 1939. Montclair, NJ: Patterson Smith, 1969 ed.

——. *The Decisive Battle of Nashville*. 1956. Baton Rouge, LA: Louisiana State University Press, 1991 ed.

Horton, James A. B. (ed.). *Black Nationalism in Africa, 1867*. New York, NY: Africana Publishing, 1969.

Horwitz, Tony. *Confederates in the Attic: Dispatches From the Unfinished Civil War*. 1998. New York, NY: Vintage, 1999 ed.

Howard, Warren S. *American Slavers and the Federal Law, 1837-1862*. Berkeley, CA: University of California Press, 1963.

Howells, William. *Back of History: The Story of Our Own Origins*. 1954. Garden City, NY: Doubleday, 1963 ed.

Hudson, Larry E., Jr. *To Have and to Hold: Slave Work and Family Life in Antebellum South Carolina.* Athens, GA: University of Georgia Press, 1997.

Humphreys, Mary Gay. *Catherine Schuyler.* New York, NY: Charles Scribner's Sons, 1897.

Hundley, Daniel Robinson. *Social Relations in Our Southern States.* New York, NY: Henry B. Price, 1860.

Hunt, John Gabriel (ed.). *The Essential Abraham Lincoln.* Avenel, NJ: Portland House, 1993.

Hurd, John Codman. *The Law of Freedom and Bondage in the United States.* 2 vols. Boston, MA: Little, Brown and Co., 1862.

Hurmence, Belinda (ed.). *Before Freedom, When I Can Just Remember: Twenty-seven Oral Histories of Former South Carolina Slaves.* 1989. Winston-Salem, NC: John F. Blair, 2002 ed.

Hurst, Jack. *Nathan Bedford Forrest: A Biography.* 1993. New York, NY: Vintage, 1994 ed.

Illinois State Historical Society. *Transactions of the Illinois State Historical Society for the Year 1908.* (Pub. 13, Ninth Annual Meeting of the Society.) Springfield, IL: Illinois State Historical Society, 1909.

Ingersoll, Charles Jared. *African Slavery in America.* Philadelphia, PA: Charles Jared Ingersoll, 1856.

Ingersoll, Thomas G., and Robert E. O'Connor. *Politics and Structure: Essential of American National Government.* North Scituate, MA: Duxbury Press, 1979.

Ingraham, Joseph Holt. *The South-West.* 2 vols. New York, NY: Harper and Brothers, 1835.

Inikori, Joseph E., and Stanley L. Engerman (eds.). *The Atlantic Slave Trade: Effects on Economics, Societies, and Peoples in Africa, the Americas, and Europe.* Durham, NC: Duke University Press, 1992.

Isaacman, Allen F. *Mozambique: The Africanization of a European Institution: The Zambezi Prazos, 1750-1902.* Madison, WI: University of Wisconsin Press, 1972.

Isichei, Elizabeth. *A History of African Societies to 1870.* 1997. Cambridge, UK: Cambridge University Press, 2000 ed.

Jackson, G. A. *Algiers: Being a Complete Picture of the Barbary States; Their Government, Laws, Religion, and Natural Productions.* London, UK: R. Edwards, 1817.

Jacobs, Harriet Ann ("Linda Brent"). *Incidents in the Life of a Slave Girl.* Boston, MA: the author, 1861.

Jahoda, Gloria. *The Trail of Tears: The Story of the American Indian Removals, 1813-1855.* 1975. New York, NY: Wings Book, 1995 ed.

Jameson, J. Franklin (ed.). *Narratives of New Netherland, 1609-1664.* New York, NY: Charles Scribner's Sons, 1909.

Jamieson, Alan G. *Lords of the Sea: A History of the Barbary Corsairs.* London, UK: Reaktion, 2012.

Jaquette, Henrietta Stratton (ed.). *South After Gettysburg: Letters of Cornelia Hancock, 1863-1868.* Philadelphia, PA: University of Pennsylvania Press, 1937.

Jervey, Theodore D. *Robert Y. Hayne and His Times.* New York, NY: Macmillan, 1909.

Jimerson, Randall C. *The Private Civil War: Popular Thought During the Sectional Conflict.* Baton Rouge, LA: Louisiana State University Press, 1988.

Johannsen, Robert Walter. *Lincoln, the South, and Slavery: The Political Dimension.* Baton Rouge, LA: Louisiana State University Press, 1991.

Johnsen, Julie E. *The Negro Problem.* New York, NY: H. W. Wilson Co., 1921.

Johnson, Adam Rankin. *The Partisan Rangers of the Confederate States Army.* Louisville, KY: George G. Fetter, 1904.

Johnson, Allen W., and Timothy Earle. *The Evolution of Human Societies: From Foraging Group to Agrarian State.* Stanford, CA: Stanford University Press, 1987.

Johnson, Benjamin Heber. *Making of the American West: People and Perspectives.* Santa Barbara, CA: ABC-Clio, 2007.

Johnson, Clint. *The Politically Incorrect Guide to the South (and Why It Will Rise Again).* Washington, D.C.: Regnery, 2006.

——. *A Vast and Fiendish Plot: The Confederate Attack on New York City.* New York, NY: Kensington, 2010.

Johnson, Cynthia Mestad. *James DeWolf and the Rhode Island Slave Trade.* Charleston, SC: History Press, 2014.

Johnson, Ludwell H. *North Against South: The American Iliad, 1848-1877.* 1978. Columbia, SC: Foundation for American Education, 1993 ed.

Johnson, Michael, and James L. Roark. *Black Masters: A Free Family of Color in the Old South.* New York, NY: W.W. Norton, 1984.

Johnson, Oliver. *William Lloyd Garrison and His Times.* 1879. Boston, MA: Houghton Mifflin and Co., 1881 ed.

Johnson, Robert Underwood (ed.). *Battles and Leaders of the Civil War.* 4 vols. New York, NY: The Century Co., 1884-1888.

Johnson, Thomas Cary. *The Life and Letters of Robert Lewis Dabney.* Richmond, VA: Presbyterian Committee of Publication, 1903.

Johnston, William D. *Slavery in Rhode Island, 1755-1776*. Providence, RI: Rhode Island Historical Society, 1894.

Johnstone, Huger William. *Truth of War Conspiracy, 1861*. Idylwild, GA: H. W. Johnstone, 1921.

Jones, Charles Colcock. *The Religious Instruction of the Negroes in the United States*. Savannah, GA: Thomas Purse, 1842.

Jones, Gwyn. *A History of the Vikings*. 1968. Oxford, UK: Oxford University Press, 1984 ed.

Jones, Jacqueline. *Labor of Love, Labor of Sorrow: Black Women and the Family From Slavery to the Present*. New York, NY: Basic Books, 1985.

Jones, John Beauchamp. *A Rebel War Clerk's Diary at the Confederate States Capital*. 2 vols. in 1. Philadelphia, PA: J. B. Lippincott and Co., 1866.

Jones, John William. *Personal Reminiscences, Anecdotes, and Letters of Gen. Robert E. Lee*. New York, NY: D. Appleton and Co., 1874.

——. *The Davis Memorial Volume; Or Our Dead President, Jefferson Davis and the World's Tribute to His Memory*. Atlanta, GA: B. F. Johnson and Co., 1889.

Jones, Norrece T., Jr. *Born a Child of Freedom, Yet a Slave: Mechanisms of Control and Strategies of Resistance in Antebellum South Carolina*. Hanover, NH: Wesleyan University Press, 1990.

Jones, Prudence, and Nigel Pennick. *A History of Pagan Europe*. London, UK: Routledge, 1995.

Jones, Wilmer L. *Generals in Blue and Gray*. 2 vols. Westport, CT: Praeger, 2004.

Jordan, Don, and Michael Walsh. *White Cargo: The Forgotten History of Britain's White Slaves in America*. New York, NY: New York University Press, 2008.

Jordan, Ervin L. *Black Confederates and Afro-Yankees in Civil War Virginia*. Charlottesville, VA: University Press of Virginia, 1995.

Jordan, Thomas, and John P. Pryor. *The Campaigns of General Nathan Bedford Forrest and of Forrest's Cavalry*. New Orleans, LA: Blelock and Co., 1868.

Jordan, Winthrop D. *White Over Black: American Attitudes Toward the Negro 1550-1812*. Chapel Hill, NC: University of North Carolina Press, 1968.

Kamble, N. D. *Bonded Labor in India*. New Delhi, India: Uppal, 1982.

Kane, Joseph Nathan. *Facts About the Presidents: A Compilation of Biographical and Historical Data*. 1959. New York, NY: Ace, 1976 ed.

Karasch, Mary. *Slave Life in Rio de Janeiro*. Princeton, NJ: Princeton University Press, 1987.

Katcher, Philip. *The Civil War Source Book*. 1992. New York, NY: Facts on File, 1995 ed.

——. *Brassey's Almanac: The American Civil War*. London, UK: Brassey's, 2003.

Katz, William Loren. *Black Indians: A Hidden Heritage*. New York, NY: Simon and Schuster, 2012.

Kautz, August Valentine. *Customs of Service for Non-Commissioned Officers and Soldiers (as Derived from Law and Regulations and Practised in the Army of the United States)*. Philadelphia, PA: J. B. Lippincott and Co., 1864.

Keckley, Elizabeth. *Behind the Scenes, or Thirty Years a Slave, and Four Years in the White House*. New York, NY: G. W. Carlton and Co., 1868.

Kemble, Frances Anne. *Journal of a Residence on a Georgian Plantation in 1838-1839*. New York, NY: Harper and Brothers, 1864.

Kennedy, James Ronald, and Walter Donald Kennedy. *The South Was Right!* Gretna, LA: Pelican Publishing Co., 1994.

——. *Why Not Freedom!: America's Revolt Against Big Government*. Gretna, LA: Pelican Publishing Co., 2005.

——. *Nullifying Tyranny: Creating Moral Communities in an Immoral Society*. Gretna, LA: Pelican Publishing Co., 2010.

Kennedy, Walter Donald. *Myths of American Slavery*. Gretna, LA: Pelican Publishing Co., 2003.

Kishlansky, Mark, Patrick Geary, and Patricia O'Brien. *Civilization in the West - Vol. 2: Since 1555*. New York, NY: Harper Collins, 1995.

Klein, Herbert S. *Slavery in the Americas: A Comparative Study of Virginia and Cuba*. Chicago, IL: University of Chicago Press, 1967.

——. *The Middle Passage: Comparative Studies in the Atlantic Slave Trade*. Princeton, NJ: Princeton University Press, 1978.

——. *African Slavery in Latin America and the Caribbean*. New York, NY: Oxford University Press, 1986.

Klein, Martin A. (ed.). *Breaking the Chains: Slavery, Bondage and Emancipation in Africa and Asia*. Madison, WI: University of Wisconsin Press, 1993.

——. *Historical Dictionary of Slavery and Abolition*. Lanham, MD: Scarecrow Press, 2002.

Knox, Thomas Wallace. *Camp-Fire and Cotton-Field: Southern Adventure in Time of War - Life With the Union Armies, and Residence on a Louisiana Plantation*. New York, NY: Blelock and Co., 1865.

Koger, Larry. *Black Slaveowners: Free Black Slave Masters in South Carolina, 1790-1860*. Columbia, SC: University of South Carolina Press, 1995.

Kolchin, Peter. *American Slavery, 1619-1877*. 1993. New York, NY: Hill and Wang, 2003 ed.

Kousser, J. Morgan. *The Shaping of Southern Politics*. New Haven, CT: Yale University Press, 1974.

Kramer, Samuel Noah. *Cradle of Civilization*. New York, NY: Time-Life Books, 1967.

Lamon, Ward Hill. *The Life of Abraham Lincoln: From His Birth to His Inauguration as President*. Boston, MA: James R. Osgood and Co., 1872.

——. *Recollections of Abraham Lincoln: 1847-1865*. Chicago, IL: A. C. McClurg and Co., 1895.

Lanning, Michael Lee. *The African-American Soldier: From Crispus Attucks to Colin Powell*. 1997. New York, NY: Citadel Press, 2004 ed.

Latham, Henry. *Black and White: A Journal of a Three Months' Tour in the United States*. Philadelphia, PA: Lippincott, 1867.

Lauber, Almon Wheeler. *Indian Slavery in Colonial Times Within the Present Limits of the United States*. 1913. New York, NY: AMS Press, 1969 ed.

Lawrence, William. *Life of Amos A. Lawrence*. Boston, MA: Houghton, Mifflin, and Co., 1899.

Lee, Robert E., Jr. *Recollections and Letters of General Robert E. Lee*. New York, NY: Doubleday, Page and Co., 1904.

Leech, Margaret. *Reveille in Washington, 1860-1865*. 1941. Alexandria, VA: Time-Life Books, 1980 ed.

Leigh, Frances Butler. *Ten Years on a Georgia Plantation Since the War*. London, UK: Richard Bentley and Son, 1883.

Lemire, Elise. *Black Walden: Slavery and Its Aftermath in Concord, Massachusetts*. Philadelphia, PA: University of Pennsylvania Press, 2009.

Leonard, Jonathan Norton. *Ancient America*. New York, NY: Time, 1967.

Lester, Charles Edwards. *Life and Public Services of Charles Sumner*. New York, NY: U.S. Publishing Co., 1874.

Lester, John C., and D. L. Wilson. *Ku Klux Klan: Its Origin, Growth, and Disbandment*. 1884. New York, NY: Neale Publishing, 1905 ed.

Levine, Lawrence. *Black Culture and Black Consciousness: Afro-American Folk Thought From Slavery to Freedom*. New York, NY: Oxford University Press, 1977.

Lewis, Bernard. *Race and Slavery in the Middle-East*. New York, NY: Oxford University Press, 1990.

Lewis, Lloyd. *Myths After Lincoln*. 1929. New York, NY: The Press of the Reader's Club, 1941 ed.

Lewis, Ronald L. *Coal, Iron, and Slaves: Industrial Slavery in Maryland and Virginia, 1715-1865*. Westport, CT: Greenwood Press, 1979.

LeVert, Suzanne (ed.). *The Civil War Society's Encyclopedia of the Civil War*. New York, NY: Wings Books, 1997.

Levy, Andrew. *The First Emancipator: Slavery, Religion, and the Quiet Revolution of Robert Carter*. New York, NY: Random House, 2005.

Libby, David J. *Slavery and Frontier Mississippi, 1720-1835*. Jackson, MS: University of Mississippi Press, 2004.

Liddell, Henry George. *A History of Rome: From the Earliest Times to the Establishment of the Empire*. 2 vols. London, UK: John Murray, 1855.

Litwack, Leon F. *North of Slavery: The Negro in the Free States, 1790-1860*. Chicago, IL: University of Chicago Press, 1961.

——. *Been in the Storm So Long: The Aftermath of Slavery*. New York, NY: Vintage, 1980.

Livermore, Thomas L. *Numbers and Losses in the Civil War in America, 1861-65*. 1900. Carlisle, PA: John Kallmann, 1996 ed.

Long, Armistead Lindsay, and Marcus J. Wright. *Memoirs of Robert E. Lee: His Military and Personal History*. New York, NY: J. M. Stoddart and Co., 1887.

Long, Everette Beach, and Barbara Long. *The Civil War Day by Day: An Almanac, 1861-1865*. 1971. New York, NY: Da Capo Press, 1985 ed.

Longstreet, James. *From Manassas to Appomattox: Memoirs of the Civil War in America*. Philadelphia, PA: J. B. Lippincott 1908.

Lonn, Ella. *Foreigners in the Confederacy*. 1940. Chapel Hill, NC: University of North Carolina Press, 2002 ed.

Lott, Stanley K. *The Truth About American Slavery*. 2004. Clearwater, SC: Eastern Digital Resources, 2005 ed.

Lovejoy, Paul E. *Transformations in Slavery: A History of Slavery in Africa*. Cambridge, UK: Cambridge University Press, 1983.

Lovejoy, Paul E., and Jan S. Hogendorn. *Slow Death for Slavery: The Course of Abolition in Northern Nigeria, 1897-1936*. Cambridge, UK: Cambridge University Press, 1993.

Löwenheim, Oded. *Predators and Parasites: Persistent Agents of Transnational Harm and Great Power Authority*. Ann

Arbor, MI: University of Michigan Press, 2007.

Lubasz, Heinz (ed.). *Revolutions in Modern European History*. New York, NY: Macmillan, 1966.

Luna, Francisco Vidal, and Herbert S. Klein. *Slavery and the Economy of São Paulo,1750-1850*. Stanford, CA: Stanford University Press, 2003.

Lyell, Charles. *A Second Visit to the United States of North America*. 2 vols. London, UK: John Murray, 1850.

Lytle, Andrew Nelson. *Bedford Forrest and His Critter Company*. New York, NY: G. P. Putnam's Sons, 1931.

Macaulay, Zachary. *Negro Slavery; Or a View of Some of the More Prominent Features of That State of Society, as it Exists in the United States of America and in the Colonies of the West Indies, Especially in Jamaica*. London, UK: Hatchard and Son, 1823.

Mackay, Charles. *Life and Liberty in America, or Sketches of a Tour in the United States and Canada in 1857-58*. New York, NY: Harper and Brothers, 1859.

MacQuarrie, Kim. *The Last Days of the Incas*. New York, NY: Simon and Schuster, 2007.

Magoffin, Ralph V. D., and Frederic Duncalf. *Ancient and Medieval History: The Rise of Classical Culture and the Development of Medieval Civilization*. Morristown, NJ: Silver Burdett Co., 1959.

Mallard, Robert Q. *Plantation Life Before Emancipation*. Richmond, VA: Whittet and Shepperson, 1892.

Malone, Ann Patton. *Sweet Chariot: Slave Family and Household Structure in Nineteenth-Century Louisiana*. Chapel Hill, NC: University of North Carolina Press, 1992.

Mancall, Peter C. (ed.). *The Atlantic World and Virginia, 1550-1624*. Chapel Hill, NC: University of North Carolina Press, 2007.

Mandel, Bernard. *Labor, Free and Slave: Workingmen and the Anti-Slavery Movement in the United States*. New York, NY: Associated Authors, 1955.

Manegold, C. S. *Ten Hills Farm: The Forgotten History of Slavery in the North*. Princeton, NJ: Princeton University Press, 2010.

Mann, Horace. *Slavery and the Slave-Trade in the District of Columbia*. Speech delivered in the House of Representatives of the United States, February 23, 1849. Philadelphia, PA: Merrihew and Thompson (printers), 1849.

Mann, Kristin. *Slavery and the Birth of an African City: Lagos, 1760-1900*. Bloomington, IN: Indiana University Press, 2007.

Manning, Patrick. *Slavery and African Life: Occidental, Oriental, and African Slave Traders*. Cambridge, UK: Cambridge University Press, 1990.

Manning, Timothy D., Sr. (ed.) *Lincoln Reconsidered: Conference Reader*. High Point, NC: Heritage Foundation Press, 2006.

Mannix, Daniel Pratt. *Black Cargoes: A History of the Atlantic Slave Trade, 1518-1865*. New York, NY: Viking, 1962.

Marsh, Edward G. (ed.). *Account of the Slavery of Friends in the Barbary States, Towards the Close of the Seventeenth Century*. London, UK: Edward G. Marsh, 1848.

Martin, Kingsley. *French Liberal Thought in the Eighteenth Century: A Study of Political Ideas From Bayle to Condorcet*. 1929. New York, NY: Harper and Row, 1963 ed.

Martineau, Harriet. *Society in America*. 3 vols. London, UK: Saunders and Otley, 1837.

——. *Retrospect of Western Travel*. 2 vols. London, UK: Saunders and Otley, 1838.

Masur, Louis P. *The Real War Will Never Get In the Books: Selections From Writers During the Civil War*. New York, NY: Oxford University Press, 1993.

Mathes, Capt. J. Harvey. *General Forrest*. New York, NY: D. Appleton and Co., 1902.

Maude, H. E. *Slavers in Paradise: The Peruvian Slave Trade in Polynesia, 1862-1864*. Stanford, CT: Stanford University Press, 1981.

Maury, Dabney Herndon. *Recollections of a Virginian in the Mexican, Indian, and Civil Wars*. New York, NY: Charles Scribner's Sons, 1894.

Mayer, Brantz (ed.). *Captain Canot; or, Twenty Years of an African Slaver*. New York, NY: D. Appleton and Co., 1854.

Mayer, David N. *The Constitutional Thought of Thomas Jefferson*. Charlottesville, VA: University of Virginia Press, 1995.

Mayer, Henry. *All on Fire: William Lloyd Garrison and the Abolition of Slavery*. New York, NY: St. Martin's Press, 1998.

Mbiti, John S. *African Religions and Philosophy*. 1969. Nairobi, Kenya: Heinemann Kenya Limited, 1988 ed.

McCarty, Burke (ed.). *Little Sermons In Socialism by Abraham Lincoln*. Chicago, IL: The Chicago Daily Socialist, 1910.

McCusker, John J., and Russell R. Menard. *The Economy of British America, 1607-1789*. Chapel Hill, NC:

University of North Carolina Press, 1985.

McDannald, A. H. (ed.). *The Modern Encyclopedia.* 1 vol. New York, NY: William H. Wise and Co., 1933.

McDonald, Forrest. *States' Rights and the Union: Imperium in Imperio, 1776-1876.* Lawrence, KS: University Press of Kansas, 2000.

McDonough, James Lee, and Thomas L. Connelly. *Five Tragic Hours: The Battle of Franklin.* 1983. Knoxville, TN: University of Tennessee Press, 2001 ed.

McElroy, Robert. *Jefferson Davis: The Unreal and the Real.* 1937. New York, NY: Smithmark, 1995 ed.

McEnnis, John T. *The White Slaves of Free America: Being an Account of the Sufferings, Privations and Hardships of the Weary Toilers in Our Great Cities.* Chicago, IL: R. S. Peale and Co., 1888.

McFeely, William S. *Yankee Stepfather: General O. O. Howard and the Freedmen - The Story of a Civil War Promise to Former Slaves Made—and Broken.* 1968. New York, NY: W. W. Norton, 1994 ed.

——. *Grant: A Biography.* 1981. New York, NY: W. W. Norton, 1982 ed.

McKay, John P., Bennett D. Hill, and John Buckler. *A History of Western Society - Vol. 1: From Antiquity to the Enlightenment.* Boston, MA: Houghton Mifflin, 1987.

——. *A History of Western Society - Vol. 2: Since 1500.* Boston, MA: Houghton Mifflin, 1988.

McKenzie, John L. *Dictionary of the Bible.* New York, NY: Collier, 1965.

McKim, Randolph H. *The Soul of Lee.* New York, NY: Longmans, Green and Co., 1918.

McKissack, Patricia C., and Frederick McKissack. *Sojourner Truth: Ain't I a Woman?* New York: NY: Scholastic, 1992.

McKitrick, Eric (ed.). *Slavery Defended: The Views of the Old South.* Englewood Cliffs, NJ: Prentice-Hall, 1963.

McLoughlin, William G. *Isaac Backus and the American Pietistic Tradition.* Boston, MA: Little, Brown and Co., 1967.

McManus, Edgar J. *A History of Negro Slavery in New York.* Syracuse, NY: Syracuse University Press, 1966.

——. *Black Bondage in the North.* Syracuse, NY: Syracuse University Press, 1973.

McPherson, Edward. *The Political History of the United States of America, During the Great Rebellion (from November 6, 1860, to July 4, 1864).* Washington, D.C.: Philp and Solomons, 1864.

——. *The Political History of the United States of America, During the Period of Reconstruction, (from April 15, 1865, to July 15, 1870,) Including a Classified Summary of the Legislation of the Thirty-ninth, Fortieth, and Forty-first Congresses.* Washington, D.C.: Solomons and Chapman, 1875.

McPherson, James M. *The Struggle for Equality: Abolitionists and the Negro in the Civil War and Reconstruction.* 1964. Princeton, NJ: Princeton University Press, 1992 ed.

——. *The Negro's Civil War: How American Negroes Felt and Acted During the War for the Union.* 1965. Chicago, IL: University of Illinois Press, 1982 ed.

——. *Battle Cry of Freedom: The Civil War Era.* Oxford, UK: Oxford University Press, 2003.

——. *The Atlas of the Civil War.* Philadelphia, PA: Courage Books, 2005.

McPherson, James M., and the staff of the *New York Times. The Most Fearful Ordeal: Original Coverage of the Civil War by Writers and Reporters of the New York Times.* New York, NY: St. Martin's Press, 2004.

Mead, Margaret. *Male and Female: A Study of the Sexes in a Changing World.* 1949. New York, NY: Mentor, 1959 ed.

——. *Science and the Concept of Race.* New York, NY: Columbia University Press, 1968.

Meillassoux, Claude. *The Anthropology of Slavery: The Womb of Iron and Gold.* Chicago, IL: University of Chicago Press, 1991.

Meine, Franklin J. (ed.). *The Consolidated-Webster Encyclopedic Reference Dictionary.* 1940. Chicago, IL: Consolidated Book Publishers, 1947 ed.

Melden, Charles Manly. *From Slave to Citizen.* New York, NY: Methodist Book Concern, 1921.

Melick, Charles Wesley. *Some Phases of the Negro Question.* Mt. Rainier, MD: David H. Deloe, 1908.

Melish, Joanne Pope. *Disowning Slavery: Gradual Emancipation and "Race" in New England 1780-1860.* Ithaca, NY: Cornell University Press, 1998.

Mellafe, Rolando. *Negro Slavery in Latin America.* Berkeley, CA: University of California Press, 1975.

Meltzer, Milton. *Slavery: A World History.* 2 vols. in 1. 1971. New York, NY: Da Capo Press, 1993 ed.

Mendelsohn, I. *Slavery in the Ancient Near East: A Comparative Study of Slavery in Babylonia, Assyria, Syria, Palestine, from the Middle of the Third Millennium.* New York, NY: Oxford University Press, 1949.

Meriwether, Elizabeth Avery. *Facts and Falsehoods Concerning the War on the South, 1861-1865.* (Originally written under the pseudonym "George Edmonds.") Memphis, TN: A. R. Taylor, 1904.

Milton, Giles. *White Gold: The Extraordinary Story of Thomas Pellow and Islam's One Million White Slaves.* New York, NY: Farrar, Straus, and Giroux, 2005.

Min, Pyong Gap (ed.). *Encyclopedia of Racism in the United States.* 3 vols. Westport, CT: Greenwood Press,

2005.

Minges, Patrick N. *Slavery in the Cherokee Nation: The Keetoowah Society and the Defining of a People, 1855-1867.* New York, NY: Routledge, 2003.

Minor, Charles Landon Carter. *The Real Lincoln: From the Testimony of His Contemporaries.* Richmond, VA: Everett Waddey Co., 1904.

Mish, Frederick C. (ed.). *Webster's Ninth New Collegiate Dictionary.* 1984. Springfield, MA: Merriam-Webster.

Mitchell, J. (ed.). *Race Riots in Black and White.* Englewood Cliffs, NJ: Prentice-Hall, 1970.

Montague, Ashley. *Man's Most Dangerous Myth: The Fallacy of Race.* 1942. Walnut Creek, CA: AltaMira Press, 1997 ed.

——. *Statement on Race.* 1951. New York, NY: Oxford University Press, 1972 ed.

——. (ed.) *The Concept of Race.* 1964. London, UK: Collier Books, 1969 ed.

Montefiore, Simon Sebag. *Stalin: The Court of the Red Star.* 2003. New York, NY: Vintage, 2004 ed.

Moore, Clark D., and Ann Dunbar (eds.). *Africa Yesterday and Today.* 1968. New York, NY: 1970 ed.

Moore, George Henry. *Notes on the History of Slavery in Massachusetts.* New York, NY: D. Appleton and Co., 1866.

Moorhead, James H. *American Apocalypse: Yankee Protestants and the Civil War, 1860-1869.* New Haven, CT: Yale University Press, 1971.

Morel, Edmund D. *The Congo Slave State: A Protest Against the New African Slavery.* Liverpool, UK: John Richardson and Sons, 1903.

Morey, William Carey. *Outlines of Greek History With a Survey of Ancient Oriental Nations.* New York, NY: American Book Co., 1903.

Morgan, Edmund. *American Slavery, American Freedom: The Ordeal of Colonial Virginia.* New York, NY: W. W. Norton, 1975.

Morgan, Joseph. *A Compleat History of the Piratical States of Barbary.* London, UK: R. Griffiths, 1750.

Morison, Samuel Eliot, and Henry Steele Commager. *The Growth of the American Republic.* 2 vols. 1930. New York, NY: Oxford University Press, 1965 ed.

Morel, Edmund Dene. *Affairs of West Africa.* London, UK: William Heinemann, 1902.

——. *The Congo Slave State.* Liverpool, UK: William Heinemann, 1903.

Mörner, Magnus. *Race Mixture in the History of Latin America.* Boston, MA: Little, Brown and Co., 1967.

Morris, Charles. *The Old South and the New.* Philadelphia, PA: n.p., 1907.

——. (ed.). *Winston's Cumulative Encyclopedia.* Philadelphia, PA: John C. Winston Co., 1912.

Morris, Richard B. *Government and Labor in Early America.* New York, NY: Columbia University Press, 1947.

Morris, Thomas D. *Free Men All: The Personal Liberty Laws of the North, 1780-1861.* Baltimore, MD: Johns Hopkins University Press, 1974.

——. *Southern Slavery and the Law, 1619-1860.* Chapel Hill, NC: University of North Carolina Press, 1996.

Morrissey, Marietta. *Slave Women in the New World: Gender Stratification in the Caribbean.* Lawrence, KS: University Press of Kansas, 1989.

Morton, Fred. *Children of Ham: Freed Slaves and Fugitive Slaves on the Kenya Coast, 1873 to 1907.* Boulder, CO: Westview, 1990.

Morton, John Watson. *The Artillery of Nathan Bedford Forrest's Cavalry.* Nashville, TN: The M. E. Church, 1909.

Morton, Louis. *Robert Carter of Nomini Hall: A Virginia Tobacco Planter of the Eighteenth Century.* Charlottesville, VA: University Press of Virginia, 1969.

Morton, Patricia. *Disfigured Images: The Historical Assault on Afro-American Women.* New York, NY: Greenwood Press, 1991.

Moss, Richard Shannon. *Slavery on Long Island: A Study in Local Institutional and Early African-American Communal Life.* New York, NY: Garland, 1993.

Mostert, Noel. *The Line Upon the Wind: The Great War at Sea, 1793-1815.* New York, NY: W. W. Norton, 2008.

Muehlbauer, Matthew S., and David J. Ulbrich. *Ways of War: American Military History From the Colonial Era to the Twenty-First Century.* New York, NY: Routledge, 2014.

Mullen, Robert W. *Blacks in America's Wars: The Shift in Attitudes From the Revolutionary War to Vietnam.* 1973. New York, NY: Pathfinder, 1991 ed.

Muller, Herbert J. *The Uses of the Past: Profiles of Former Societies.* 1954. New York, NY: Mentor, 1960 ed.

Munford, Beverly Bland. *Virginia's Attitude Toward Slavery and Secession.* 1909. Richmond, VA: L. H. Jenkins, 1914 ed.

Napolitano, Andrew P. *The Constitution in Exile: How the Federal Government Has Seized Power by Rewriting the Supreme Law of the Land.* Nashville, TN: Nelson Current, 2006.

Nash, Gary B. *The Urban Crucible: The Northern Seaports and the Origins of the American Revolution.* Cambridge, MA: Harvard University Press, 1986.

Nash, Gary B., and Jean R. Soderlund. *Freedom By Degrees: Emancipation in Pennsylvania and Its Aftermath.* Oxford, UK: Oxford University Press, 1991.

Naylor, Celia E. *African Cherokees in Indian Territory: From Chattel to Citizens.* Chapel Hill, NC: University of North Carolina Press, 2008.

Neely, Mark E., Jr. *The Fate of Liberty: Abraham Lincoln and Civil Liberties.* New York, NY: Oxford University Press, 1991.

Neilson, William Allan (ed.). *Webster's Biographical Dictionary.* Springfield, MA: G. and C. Merriam Co., 1943.

Nell, William Cooper. *The Colored Patriots of the American Revolution, With Sketches of Several Distinguished Colored Persons to Which is Added a Brief Survey of the Condition and Prospects of Colored Americas.* Boston, MA: Robert F. Wallcut, 1855.

Nellis, Eric G. *Shaping the New World: African Slavery in the Americas, 1500-1888.* North York, Canada: University of Toronto Press, 2013.

Nevinson, Henry W. *A Modern Slavery.* London, UK: Harper and Brothers, 1906.

Newton, Michael. *White Robes and Burning Crosses: A History of the Ku Klux Klan from 1866.* Jefferson, NC: McFarland & Co., 2014.

Nichols, James Lawrence, and William Henry Crogman. *Progress of a Race, or the Remarkable Advancement of the American Negro.* Naperville, IL: J. L. Nichols and Co., 1920.

Nicolay, John G., and John Hay (eds.). *Abraham Lincoln: A History.* 10 vols. New York, NY: The Century Co., 1890.

———. *Complete Works of Abraham Lincoln.* 12 vols. 1894. New York, NY: Francis D. Tandy Co., 1905 ed.

———. *Abraham Lincoln: Complete Works.* 12 vols. 1894. New York, NY: The Century Co., 1907 ed.

Nieboer, Herman Jeremias. *Slavery as an Industrial System: Ethnological Researches.* The Hague, Netherlands: Martinus Nijhoff, 1900.

Noble, Frederic Perry. *The Redemption of Africa: A Story of Civilization.* 2 vols. Chicago, IL: Fleming H. Revell Co., 1899.

Noel, Donald L. (ed.). *The Origins of American Slavery and Racism.* Columbus, OH: Charles E. Merrill, 1972.

Nolen, Claude H. *African American Southerners in Slavery, Civil War and Reconstruction.* Jefferson, NC: McFarland and Co., 2001.

Norris, Robert. *A Short Account of the African Slave Trade.* London, UK: W. Lowndes, 1789.

Northrup, Ansel Judd. *Slavery in New York.* (Article from the *State Library Bulletin,* "History," No. 4, May 1900.) New York, NY: University of the State of New York, 1900.

Northrup, David. *Indentured Labor in the Age of Imperialism, 1834-1922.* Cambridge, UK: Cambridge University Press, 1995.

Northup, Solomon. *Twelve Years a Slave: Narrative of Solomon Northup, a Citizen of New-York, Kidnapped in Washington City in 1841, and Rescued in 1853, From a Cotton Plantation Near the Red River, in Louisiana.* New York, NY: Miller, Orton, and Mulligan, 1855.

Norwood, Thomas Manson. *A True Vindication of the South.* Savannah, GA: Citizens and Southern Bank, 1917.

Nuñez, Benjamin. *Dictionary of Afro-Latin American Civilization.* Westport, CT: Greenwood Press, 1980.

Nye, Russel B. *William Lloyd Garrison and the Humanitarian Reformers.* Boston, MA: Little, Brown and Co., 1955.

Oakes, James. *The Ruling Race: A History of American Slaveholders.* New York, NY: Knopf, 1982.

———. *Slavery and Freedom: An Interpretation of the Old South.* New York, NY: Knopf, 1990.

Oates, Stephen B. *Abraham Lincoln: The Man Behind the Myths.* New York, NY: Meridian, 1984.

———. *The Approaching Fury: Voices of the Storm, 1820-1861.* New York, NY: Harper Perennial, 1998.

O'Callaghan, Edward Bailey. *Voyage of the Slavers St. John and Arms of Amsterdam.* Albany, NY: Munsell, 1967.

Oglesby, Thaddeus K. *Some Truths of History: A Vindication of the South Against the Encyclopedia Britannica and Other Maligners.* Atlanta, GA: Byrd Printing, 1903.

Ohaegbulam, Festus Ugboaja. *Towards an Understanding of the African Experience From Historical and Contemporary Perspectives.* Lanham, MD: University Press of America, 1990.

Oliver, Edmund Henry. *Roman Economic Conditions to the Close of the Republic.* Toronto, CAN: University of Toronto Library, 1907.

Olmsted, Frederick Law. *A Journey in the Seaboard Slave States, With Remarks on Their Economy.* New York, NY: Dix and Edwards, 1856.

———. *A Journey Through Texas; or a Saddle-Trip on the Western Frontier.* New York, NY: Dix and Edwards, 1857.

———. *A Journey in the Back Country.* New York, NY: Mason Brothers, 1860.

———. *The Cotton Kingdom: A Traveler's Observations on Cotton and Slavery in the American Slave States.* 2 vols.

London, UK: Sampson Low, Son, and Co., 1862.

Olson, Ted (ed.). *CrossRoads: A Southern Culture Annual*. Macon, GA: Mercer University Press, 2004.

Oostindie, Gert (ed.). *Fifty Years Later: Antislavery, Capitalism and Modernity in the Dutch Orbit*. Pittsburgh, PA: University of Pittsburgh Press, 1996.

ORA (full title: *The War of the Rebellion: A Compilation of the Official Records of the Union and Confederate Armies*. (Multiple volumes.) Washington, D.C.: Government Printing Office, 1880.

ORN (full title: *Official Records of the Union and Confederate Navies in the War of the Rebellion*). (Multiple volumes.) Washington, D.C.: Government Printing Office, 1894.

Osler, Edward. *The Life of Admiral Viscount Exmouth*. London, UK: Smith, Elder and Co., 1841.

Owsley, Frank Lawrence. *King Cotton Diplomacy: Foreign Relations of the Confederate States of America*. 1931. Chicago, IL: University of Chicago Press, 1959 ed.

Page, Thomas Nelson. *Robert E. Lee: Man and Soldier*. New York, NY: Charles Scribner's Sons, 1911.

Palmer, Colin. *Human Cargoes: The British Slave Trade to Spanish America, 1700-1739*. Urbana, IL: University of Illinois Press, 1981.

Palmer, R. R., and Joel Colton. *A History of the Modern World*. 1950. New York, NY: Knopf, 1965 ed.

Palmié, Stephan (ed.). *Slave Cultures and the Cultures of Slavery*. Knoxville, TN: University of Tennessee Press, 1995.

Paquette, Robert L., and Mark M. Smith (eds.). *The Oxford Handbook of Slavery in the Americas*. Oxford, UK: Oxford University Press, 2010.

Paradis, James M. *African Americans and the Gettysburg Campaign*. Lanham, MD: Scarecrow Press, 2013.

Park, Mungo. *Travels in the Interior Districts of Africa, Performed in the Years 1795, 1796, and 1797*. 2 vols. London, UK: William Griffin, 1816.

Parker, Bowdoin S. (ed.). *What One Grand Army Post Has Accomplished: History of Edward W. Kinsley Post, No. 113*. Norwood, MA: Norwood Press, 1913.

Parkes, James. *A History of the Jewish People*. 1962. Harmondsworth, UK: Penguin, 1964 ed.

Parry, J. H. *The Establishment of the European Hegemony, 1415-1715: Trade and Exploration in the Age of the Renaissance*. 1949. New York, NY: Harper Torchbooks, 1966 ed.

Paulding, James Kirke. *Slavery in the United States*. New York, NY: Harper and Brothers, 1836.

Pendleton, Louis Beauregard. *Alexander H. Stephens*. Philadelphia, PA: George W. Jacobs and Co., 1907.

Penrose, Boies. *Travel and Discovery in the Renaissance, 1420-1620*. 1952. New York, NY: Atheneum, 1962 ed.

Perlman, Alan M. *What Went Wrong?* Bloomington, IN: CrossBooks, 2013.

Perry, James M. *Touched With Fire: Five Presidents and the Civil War Battles That Made Them*. New York, NY: Public Affairs, 2003.

Perry, John C. *Myths and Realities of American Slavery: The True History of Slavery in America*. Shippenburg, PA: Burd Street Press, 2002.

Perry, Mark. *Lift Up Thy Voice: The Grimké Family's Journey From Slaveholders to Civil Rights Leaders*. New York, NY: Penguin, 2001.

Perry, Marvin. *Western Civilization: A Brief Survey - Vol. 1: to 1789*. Boston, MA: Houghton Mifflin, 1990.

Phillips, Robert S. (ed.). *Funk and Wagnalls New Encyclopedia*. 1971. New York, NY: Funk and Wagnalls, 1979 ed.

Phillips, Ulrich Bonnell. *Plantation and Frontier Documents: 1649-1863 - Illustrative of Industrial History in the Colonial and Ante-Bellum South*. 2 vols. Cleveland, OH: Arthur H. Clark Co., 1909.

——. *American Negro Slavery: A Survey of the Supply, Employment and Control of Negro Labor as Determined by the Plantation Régime*. New York, NY: D. Appleton and Co., 1929.

——. *Life and Labor in the Old South*. Boston, MA: Little, Brown and Co., 1929.

Pickett, George E. *The Heart of a Soldier: As Revealed in the Intimate Letters of General George E. Pickett, CSA*. 1908. New York, NY: Seth Moyle, 1913 ed.

Pickett, William Passmore. *The Negro Problem: Abraham Lincoln's Solution*. New York, NY: G. P. Putnam's Sons, 1909.

Pierson, Donald. *Negroes in Brazil*. Carbondale, IL: Southern Illinois University Press, 1942.

Pike, James Shepherd. *The Prostrate State: South Carolina Under Negro Government*. New York, NY: D. Appleton and Co., 1874.

Pinkerton, John. *An Inquiry Into the History of Scotland Preceding the Reign of Malcolm III, or the Year 1056*. 2 vols. London, UK: George Nicol, 1789.

Pitman, Frank Wesley. *The Development of the British West Indies, 1700-1763*. 4 vols. New Haven, CT: Yale University Press, 1917.

Planter, Professional (pseudonym). *Practical Rules for the Management and Medical Treatment of Negro Slaves, in the*

Sugar Colonies. London, UK: Vernor and Hood, 1803.

Plumb, J. H. *The Italian Renaissance: A Concise Survey of Its History and Culture*. 1961. New York, NY: Harper and Row, 1965 ed.

Pollard, Edward A. *Black Diamonds Gathered in the Darkey Homes of the South*. New York, NY: Pudney and Russell, 1859.

——. *Southern History of the War*. 2 vols. in 1. New York, NY: Charles B. Richardson, 1866.

——. *The Lost Cause*. 1867. Chicago, IL: E. B. Treat, 1890 ed.

——. *The Lost Cause Regained*. New York, NY: G. W. Carlton and Co., 1868.

——. *Life of Jefferson Davis, With a Secret History of the Southern Confederacy, Gathered "Behind the Scenes in Richmond."* Philadelphia, PA: National Publishing Co., 1869.

Post, Lydia Minturn (ed.). *Soldiers' Letters, From Camp, Battlefield and Prison*. New York, NY: Bunce and Huntington, 1865.

Postma, Johannes. *The Dutch in the Atlantic Slave Trade, 1600-1815*. Cambridge, UK: Cambridge University Press, 1990.

Potter, David M. *The Impending Crisis: 1848-1861*. New York, NY: Harper and Row, 1976.

Powdermaker, Hortence. *After Freedom: A Cultural Study in the Deep South*. New York, NY: Atheneum, 1968.

Powell, Edward Payson. *Nullification and Secession in the United States: A History of the Six Attempts During the First Century of the Republic*. New York, NY: G. P. Putnam's Sons, 1897.

Quarles, Benjamin. *The Negro in the Civil War*. 1953. Cambridge, MA: Da Capo Press, 1988 ed.

——. *The Negro in the American Revolution*. Chapel Hill, NC: University of North Carolina Press, 1961.

——. *Black Abolitionists*. New York, NY: Oxford University Press, 1969.

Quillin, Frank Uriah. *The Color Line in Ohio: A History of Race Prejudice in a Typical Northern State*. Ann Arbor, MI: George Wahr, 1913.

Quintero, José Agustín, Ambrosio José Gonzales, and Loreta Janeta Velazquez (Phillip Thomas Tucker, ed.). *Cubans in the Confederacy*. Jefferson, NC: McFarland and Co., 2002.

Rabinowitz, Howard. *Race Relations in the Urban South, 1865-1890*. Urbana, IL: University of Illinois Press, 1980.

Rable, George C. *The Confederate Republic: A Revolution Against Politics*. Chapel Hill, NC: University of North Carolina Press, 1994.

Raboteau, Albert. *Slave Religion: The Invisible Institution in the Antebellum South*. New York, NY: Oxford University Press, 1978.

Ransom, Roger L. *Conflict and Compromise: The Political Economy of Slavery, Emancipation, and the American Civil War*. Cambridge, UK: Cambridge University Press, 1989.

Ransom, Roger L., and Richard Sutch. *One Kind of Freedom: The Economic Consequences of Emancipation*. Cambridge, UK: Cambridge University Press, 1977.

Rawick, George P. *The American Slave: A Composite Autobiography*. 10 vols. 1941. Westport, CT: Greenwood Publishing Co., 1972 ed.

Rawle, William. *A View of the Constitution of the United States of America*. Philadelphia, PA: Philip H. Nicklin, 1829.

Rawley, James A. *The Transatlantic Slave Trade: A History*. New York, NY: W. W. Norton, 1981.

Rayfield, Donald. *Stalin and His Hangmen: The Tyrant and Those Who Killed For Him*. New York, NY: Random House, 2004.

Report of the Joint Select Committee to Inquire into the Condition of Affairs in the Late Insurrectionary States. Washington, D.C.: Government Printing Office, 1872.

Reuter, Edward Byron. *The Mulatto in the United States*. Boston, MA: Gorham Press, 1918.

Rhodes, James Ford. *History of the United States from the Compromise of 1850 to the Final Restoration of Home Rule at the South in 1877*. 7 vols. 1895. New York, NY: Macmillan Co., 1907 ed.

Rhys, John. *Celtic Folklore: Welsh and Manx*. 2 vols. Oxford, UK: Clarendon Press, 1901.

——. *Celtic Britain*. London, UK: Society for Promoting Christian Knowledge, 1908.

Rice, Allen Thorndike (ed.). *The North American Review*, Vol. 227. New York, NY: D. Appleton and Co., 1879.

——. (ed.). *Reminiscences of Abraham Lincoln, by Distinguished Men of His Time*. New York, NY: North American Review, 1888.

Rice, David. *A Kentucky Protest Against Slavery*. New York, NY: The Rebellion Record, 1812.

Richardson, Albert Deane. *A Personal History of Ulysses S. Grant*. Hartford, CT: American Publishing Co., 1868.

Richardson, James Daniel (ed.). *A Compilation of the Messages and Papers of the Confederacy*. 2 vols. Nashville, TN: United States Publishing Co., 1905.

——. *A Compilation of the Messages and Papers of the Presidents, 1789-1908*. 11 vols. New York, NY: Bureau of National Literature and Art, 1909.

Richardson, John Anderson. *Richardson's Defense of the South*. Atlanta, GA: A. B. Caldwell, 1914.

Richburg, Keith B. *Out of America: A Black Man Confronts Africa*. New York, NY: Basic Books, 2009.

Rickard, J. A. *History of England*. 1933. New York, NY: Barnes and Noble, 1957 ed.

Riley, Benjamin F. *The White Man's Burden: A Discussion of the Interracial Question With Special Reference to the Responsibility of the White Race to the Negro Problem*. Birmingham, AL: B. F. Riley, 1910.

Riley, Franklin Lafayette (ed.). *Publications of the Mississippi Historical Society*. Oxford, MS: The Mississippi Historical Society, 1902.

——. *General Robert E. Lee After Appomattox*. New York, NY: MacMillan Co., 1922.

Riley, Russell Lowell. *The Presidency and the Politics of Racial Inequality*. New York, NY: Columbia University Press, 1999.

Ripley, George, and Charles Anderson Dana (eds.). *The American Cyclopedia: A Popular Dictionary of General Knowledge*. New York, NY: D. Appleton and Co., 1881.

Roberts, Andrew. *A History of the Bemba: Political Growth and Change in North-eastern Zambia Before 1900*. Madison, WI: University of Wisconsin Press, 1973.

Roberts, Paul M. *United States History: Review Text*. 1966. New York, NY: Amsco School Publications, Inc., 1970 ed.

Roberts, R. Philip. *Mormonism Unmasked: Confronting the Contradictions Between Mormon Beliefs and True Christianity*. Nashville, TN: Broadman and Holman, 1998.

Roberts, Sam. *Who We Are: A Portrait of America Based on the Latest U.S. Census*. New York, NY: Time, 1994.

Robertson, Claire, and Martin A. Klein (eds.). *Women and Slavery in Africa*. Madison, WI: University of Wisconsin Press, 1983.

Robertson, James I., Jr. *Soldiers Blue and Gray*. 1988. Columbia, SC: University of South Carolina Press, 1998 ed.

Robinson, Thomas H., and Others. *Men, Groups, and the Community: A Survey in the Social Sciences*. New York, NY: Harper and Brothers, 1940.

Roche, Emma Langdon. *Historic Sketches of the South*. New York, NY: The Knickerbocker Press, 1914.

Rodriguez, Junius P. (ed.). *The Historical Encyclopedia of World Slavery*. 2 vols. Santa Barbara, CA: ABC-CLIO, 1997.

——. (ed.) *Slavery in the United States: A Social, Political, and Historical Encyclopedia*. Santa Barbara, CA: ABC-CLIO, 2007.

——. (ed.) *Encyclopedia of Slave Resistance and Rebellion*. 2 vols. Westport, CT: Greenwood Press, 2007.

Rogers, Joel Augustus. *The Ku Klux Spirit*. 1923. Baltimore, MD: Black Classic Press, 1980 ed.

——. *Africa's Gift to America: The Afro-American in the Making and Saving of the United States*. St. Petersburg, FL: Helga M. Rogers, 1961.

Roman, Charles Victor. *American Civilization and the Negro: The Afro-American in Relation to National Progress*. Philadelphia, PA: F. A. Davis Co., 1916.

Rose, S. E. F. *The Ku Klux Klan or Invisible Empire*. New Orleans, LA: L. Graham Co., 1914.

Rose, Willie Lee. *Rehearsal for Reconstruction: The Port Royal Experiment*. Indianapolis, IN: Bobbs-Merrill, 1964.

——. *A Documentary History of Slavery in North America*. New York, NY: Oxford University Press, 1976.

Rosen, Robert N. *The Jewish Confederates*. Columbia, SC: University of South Carolina Press, 2000.

Rosenbaum, Robert A. (ed). *The New American Desk Encyclopedia*. 1977. New York, NY: Signet, 1989 ed.

Rosenbaum, Robert A., and Douglas Brinkley (eds.). *The Penguin Encyclopedia of American History*. New York, NY: Viking, 2003.

Ross, Fitzgerald. *A Visit to the Cities and Camps of the Confederate States*. Edinburgh, Scotland: William Blackwood and Sons, 1865.

Ross, Frederick Augustus. *Slavery Ordained of God*. Philadelphia, PA: J. B. Lippincott and Co., 1857.

Rubin, Morton. *Plantation County*. Chapel Hill, NC: University of North Carolina Press, 1951.

Ruby, Robert. H. *Indian Slavery in the Pacific Northwest*. Glendale, CA: Arthur H. Clark, 1993.

Ruffin, Edmund. *The Diary of Edmund Ruffin: Toward Independence: October 1856-April 1861*. Baton Rouge, LA: Louisiana State University Press, 1972.

Russell, Bertrand. *A History of Western Philosophy*. 1945. New York, NY: Touchstone, 1972 ed.

Russell, John Henderson. *The Free Negro in Virginia, 1619-1865*. Baltimore, MD: Johns Hopkins Press, 1913.

Russell, Michael. *History and Present Condition of the Barbary States*. New York, NY: Harper and Brothers, 1854.

Russell, Robert. *North America, Its Agriculture and Culture*. Edinburgh, Scotland: Adam and Charles Black, 1857.

Russell, William Howard. *My Diary North and South*. 2 vols. London, UK: Bradbury and Evans, 1863.

Rutherford, Mildred Lewis. *Four Addresses*. Birmingham, AL: The Mildred Rutherford Historical Circle, 1916.
——. *A True Estimate of Abraham Lincoln and Vindication of the South*. N.p., n.d.
——. *Truths of History: A Historical Perspective of the Civil War From the Southern Viewpoint*. Confederate Reprint Co., 1920.
——. *The South Must Have Her Rightful Place In History*. Athens, GA, 1923.
Rutland, Robert Allen. *The Birth of the Bill of Rights, 1776-1791*. 1955. Boston, MA: Northeastern University Press, 1991 ed.
Sachsman, David B., S. Kittrell Rushing, and Roy Morris, Jr. (eds.). *Words at War: The Civil War and American Journalism*. West Lafayette, IN: Purdue University Press, 2008.
Salley, Alexander Samuel, Jr. *South Carolina Troops in Confederate Service*. 2 vols. Columbia, SC: R. L. Bryan, 1913 and 1914.
Salzberger, Ronald P., and Mary C. Turck (eds.). *Reparations For Slavery: A Reader*. Lanham, MD: Rowman and Littlefield, 2004.
Sam, Dickey. *Liverpool and Slavery: An Historical Account of the Liverpool-Africa Slave Trade*. Liverpool, UK: A. Bowker and Son, 1884.
Samuel, Bunford. *Secession and Constitutional Liberty*. 2 vols. New York, NY: Neale Publishing, 1920.
Sancho, Ignatius. *Letters of the Late Ignatius Sancho, an African*. 1782. New York, NY: Cosimo Classics, 2005 ed.
Sandburg, Carl. *Abraham Lincoln: The War Years*. 4 vols. New York, NY: Harcourt, Brace and World, 1939.
——. *Storm Over the Land: A Profile of the Civil War*. 1939. Old Saybrook, CT: Konecky and Konecky, 1942 ed.
Schwartz, Philip J. *Slave Laws in Virginia*. Athens, GA: University of Georgia Press, 1996.
Scott, Alexander Maccallum. *Barbary: The Romance of the Nearest East*. New York, NY: Dodd, Mead and Co., 1921.
Scott, Emmett J., and Lyman Beecher Stowe. *Booker T. Washington: Builder of a Civilization*. Garden City, NY: Doubleday, Page, and Co., 1916.
Shea, George. *Jefferson Davis: A Statement Concerning the Imputed Special Causes of His Long Imprisonment by the Government of the United States, and His Tardy Release by Due Process of Law*. London, UK: Edward Stanford, 1877.
Shell, Robert Carl-Heinz. *Children of Bondage: A Social History of the Slave Society at the Cape of Good Hope, 1652-1838*. Hanover, NH: University Press of New England, 1994.
Shenkman, Richard. *Legends, Lies and Cherished Myths of American History*. New York, NY: Perennial, 1988.
Shenkman, Richard, and Kurt Edward Reiger. *One-Night Stands with American History: Odd, Amusing, and Little-Known Incidents*. 1980. New York, NY: Perennial, 2003 ed.
Sherman, William A. *Forced Native Labor in Sixteenth-Century Central America*. Lincoln, NE: University of Nebraska Press, 1979.
Schlüter, Herman. *Lincoln, Labor and Slavery: A Chapter From the Social History of America*. New York, NY: Socialist Literature Co., 1913.
Schoepf, Johann David. *Travels in the Confederation, 1783-1784*. 2 vols. (Alfred J. Morrison, trans. and ed.) 1788. Philadelphia, PA: William J. Campbell, 1911 ed.
Seabrook, Lochlainn. *Aphrodite's Trade: The Hidden History of Prostitution Unveiled*. 1993. Franklin, TN: Sea Raven Press, 2011 ed.
——. *Britannia Rules: Goddess-Worship in Ancient Anglo-Celtic Society - An Academic Look at the United Kingdom's Matricentric Spiritual Past*. 1999. Franklin, TN: Sea Raven Press, 2007 ed.
——. *The Caudills: An Etymological, Ethnological, and Genealogical Study - Exploring the Name and National Origins of a European-American Family*. 2003. Franklin, TN: Sea Raven Press, 2010 ed.
——. *Carnton Plantation Ghost Stories: True Tales of the Unexplained From Tennessee's Most Haunted Civil War House!* 2005. Franklin, TN: Sea Raven Press, 2010 ed.
——. *Nathan Bedford Forrest: Southern Hero, American Patriot: Honoring a Confederate Hero and the Old South*. 2007. Franklin, TN: Sea Raven Press, 2010 ed.
——. *Abraham Lincoln: The Southern View*. 2007. Franklin, TN: Sea Raven Press, 2013 ed.
——. *The McGavocks of Carnton Plantation: A Southern History - Celebrating One of Dixie's Most Noble Confederate Families and Their Tennessee Home*. 2008. Franklin, TN: Sea Raven Press, 2011 ed.
——. *A Rebel Born: A Defense of Nathan Bedford Forrest*. 2010. Franklin, TN: Sea Raven Press, 2011 ed.
——. *A Rebel Born: The Movie* (screenplay). Franklin, TN: Sea Raven Press, unpublished.
——. *Everything You Were Taught About the Civil War is Wrong, Ask a Southerner!* 2010. Franklin, TN: Sea Raven Press, revised 2014 ed.
——. *The Quotable Jefferson Davis: Selections From the Writings and Speeches of the Confederacy's First President*.

Franklin, TN: Sea Raven Press, 2011.
——. *Lincolnology: The Real Abraham Lincoln Revealed In His Own Words.* Franklin, TN: Sea Raven Press, 2011.
——. *The Unquotable Abraham Lincoln: The President's Quotes They Don't Want You To Know!* Franklin, TN: Sea Raven Press, 2011.
——. *The Quotable Robert E. Lee: Selections From the Writings and Speeches of the South's Most Beloved Civil War General.* 2011. Franklin, TN: Sea Raven Press, 2014 ed.
——. *The Constitution of the Confederate States of America Explained: A Clause-by-Clause Study of the South's Magna Carta.* Franklin, TN: Sea Raven Press, 2012.
——. *The Old Rebel: Robert E. Lee As He Was Seen By His Contemporaries.* Franklin, TN: Sea Raven Press, 2012.
——. *The Quotable Stonewall Jackson: Selections From the Writings and Speeches of the South's Most Famous General.* Franklin, TN: Sea Raven Press, 2012.
——. *Honest Jeff and Dishonest Abe: A Southern Children's Guide to the Civil War.* Franklin, TN: Sea Raven Press, 2012.
——. *Give 'Em Hell Boys! The Complete Military Correspondence of Nathan Bedford Forrest.* Franklin, TN: Sea Raven Press, 2012 Sesquicentennial Civil War Edition.
——. *The Great Impersonator: 99 Reasons to Dislike Abraham Lincoln.* Franklin, TN: Sea Raven Press, 2012.
——. *Forrest! 99 Reasons to Love Nathan Bedford Forrest.* Franklin, TN: Sea Raven Press, 2012 Sesquicentennial Civil War Edition.
——. *The Quotable Nathan Bedford Forrest: Selections From the Writings and Speeches of the Confederacy's Most Brilliant Cavalryman.* Franklin, TN: Sea Raven Press, 2012 Sesquicentennial Civil War Edition.
——. *Encyclopedia of the Battle of Franklin: A Comprehensive Guide to the Conflict That Changed the Civil War.* Franklin, TN: Sea Raven Press, 2012 Sesquicentennial Civil War Edition.
——. *The Quotable Alexander H. Stephens: Selections From the Writings and Speeches of the Confederacy's First Vice President.* Franklin, TN: Sea Raven Press, 2013.
——. *The Alexander H. Stephens Reader: Excerpts From the Works of a Confederate Founding Father.* Franklin, TN: Sea Raven Press, 2013.
——. *Saddle, Sword, and Gun: A Biography of Nathan Bedford Forrest For Teens.* Franklin, TN: Sea Raven Press, 2013 Sesquicentennial Civil War Edition.
——. *Jesus and the Law of Attraction: The Bible-Based Guide to Creating Perfect Health, Wealth, and Happiness Following Christ's Simple Formula.* Franklin, TN: Sea Raven Press, 2013.
——. *The Articles of Confederation Explained: A Clause-by-Clause Study of America's First Constitution.* Franklin, TN: Sea Raven Press, 2014.
——. *Give This Book to a Yankee: A Southern Guide to the Civil War For Northerners.* Franklin, TN: Sea Raven Press, 2014.
——. *Confederacy 101: Amazing Facts You Never Knew About America's Oldest Political Tradition.* Franklin, TN: Sea Raven Press, 2015.
——. *The Great Yankee Coverup: What the North Doesn't Want You to Know About Lincoln's War!* Franklin, TN: Sea Raven Press, 2015.
——. *Confederate Blood and Treasure: An Interview With Lochlainn Seabrook.* Franklin, TN: Sea Raven Press, 2015.
——. *Everything You Were Taught About American Slavery War is Wrong, Ask a Southerner!* Franklin, TN: Sea Raven Press, 2015.
——. *Slavery 101: Amazing Facts You Never Knew About American's "Peculiar Institution."* Franklin, TN: Sea Raven Press, 2015.
——. *Confederacy 101: Amazing Facts You Never Knew About America's Oldest Political Tradition.* Franklin, TN: Sea Raven Press, 2015.
——. *The Great Yankee Coverup: What the North Doesn't Want You to Know About Lincoln's War!* Franklin, TN: Sea Raven Press, 2015.
——. *Confederate Flag Facts: What Every American Should Know About Dixie's Southern Cross.* Franklin, TN: Sea Raven Press, 2015.
——. *Nathan Bedford Forrest and the Battle of Fort Pillow: Yankee Myth, Confederate Fact.* Franklin, TN: Sea Raven Press, 2015.
——. *Nathan Bedford Forrest and the Ku Klux Klan: Yankee Myth, Confederate Fact.* Franklin, TN: Sea Raven Press, 2015.
——. *Nathan Bedford Forrest and African-Americans: Yankee Myth, Confederate Fact.* Franklin, TN: Sea Raven Press, 2016.
Segars, J. H., and Charles Kelly Barrow. *Black Southerners in Confederate Armies: A Collection of Historical Accounts.* Atlanta, GA: Southern Lion Books, 2001.

Seligmann, Herbert J. *The Negro Faces America*. New York, NY: Harper and Brothers, 1920.
Sellers, James Benson. *Slavery in Alabama*. Tuscaloosa, AL: University of Alabama Press, 1950.
Semmes, Admiral Ralph. *Service Afloat, or the Remarkable Career of the Confederate Cruisers Sumter and Alabama During the War Between the States*. London, UK: Sampson Low, Marston, Searle, and Rivington, 1887.
SenGupta, Gunja. *From Slavery to Poverty: The Racial Origins of Welfare in New York, 1840-1918*. New York, NY: New York University, 2009.
Sewall, Samuel. *Diary of Samuel Sewall*. 3 vols. Boston, MA: The Society, 1879.
Sherwood, Marika. *After Abolition: Britain and the Slave Trade Since 1807*. London, UK: I. B. Tauris, 2007.
Shillington, Kevin. *History of Africa*. 1989. New York, NY: St. Martin's Press, 1994 ed.
Shirer, William L. *The Rise and Fall of the Third Reich: A History of Nazi Germany*. New York, NY: Simon and Schuster, 1960.
Shotwell, Walter G. *Life of Charles Sumner*. New York, NY: Thomas Y. Crowell and Co., 1910.
Shufeldt, Robert Wilson. *The Negro: A Menace to American Civilization*. Boston, MA: Richard G. Badger, 1907.
Shuffleton, Frank (ed.). *A Mixed Race: Ethnicity in America*. New York, NY: Oxford University Press, 1993.
Shurter, Edwin DuBois (ed.). *The Complete Orations and Speeches of Henry W. Grady*. New York, NY: Hinds, Noble and Eldredge, 1910.
Siebert, Wilbur H. *The Underground Railroad: From Slavery to Freedom*. New York, NY: Macmillan, 1898.
Siepel, Kevin H. *Rebel: The Life and Times of John Singleton Mosby*. New York, NY: St. Martin's Press, 1983.
Sikainga, Ahmad Alawad. *Slaves Into Workers: Emancipation and Labor in Colonial Sudan*. Austin, TX: University of Texas Press, 1996.
Simmons, Henry E. *A Concise Encyclopedia of the Civil War*. New York, NY: Bonanza Books, 1965.
Simon, John Y. (ed.). *The Papers of Ulysses S. Grant*. 2 vols. Carbondale, IL: Southern Illinois University Press, 1969.
Simons, Gerald. *Barbarian Europe*. 1968. New York, NY: Time-Life Books, 1975 ed.
Simpson, Lewis P. (ed.). *I'll Take My Stand: The South and the Agrarian Tradition*. 1930. Baton Rouge, LA: University of Louisiana Press, 1977 ed.
Sinha, Manisha. *The Counterrevolution of Slavery: Politics and Ideology in Antebellum South Carolina*. Chapel Hill, NC: University of North Carolina Press, 2000.
Sitterson, J. Carlyle. *Sugar Country: The Cane Sugar Industry in the South, 1753-1950*. Lexington, KY: University of Kentucky Press, 1953.
Smallwood, Stephanie E. *Saltwater Slavery: A Middle Passage from Africa to American Diaspora*. Cambridge, MA: Harvard University Press, 2009.
Smedes, Susan Dabney. *A Southern Planter: Social Life in the Old South*. 1887. New York, NY: James Pott and Co., 1900 ed.
——. *Memorials of a Southern Planter*. Baltimore, MD: Cushings and Bailey, 1888.
Smedley, Audrey. *Race in North America: Origin and Evolution of a World View*. Boulder, CO: Westview Press, 1993.
Smelser, Marshall. *American Colonial and Revolutionary History*. 1950. New York, NY: Barnes and Noble, 1966 ed.
——. *The Democratic Republic, 1801-1815*. New York, NY: Harper and Row, 1968.
Smith, Abbot Emerson. *Colonists in Bondage: White Servitude and Convict Labor in America, 1607-1776*. Chapel Hill, NC: University of North Carolina Press, 1947.
Smith, Emma Peters, David Saville Muzzey, and Minnie Lloyd. *World History: The Struggle for Civilization*. Boston, MA: Ginn and Co., 1946.
Smith, Hedrick. *Reagan: The Man, The President*. Oxford, UK: Pergamon Press, 1980.
Smith, John David (ed.). *Black Soldiers in Blue: African American Troops in the Civil War Era*. Chapel Hill, NC: University of North Carolina Press, 2002.
Smith, Joseph. *The Pearl of Great Price*. Salt Lake City, UT: George Q. Cannon and Sons, 1891.
Smith, Lacey Baldwin. *This Realm of England: 1399 to 1688*. 1966. Lexington, MA: D. C. Heath and Co., 1983 ed.
Smith, Mark M. (ed.). *The Old South*. Oxford, UK: Blackwell Publishers, 2001.
Smith, Page. *A People's History of the United States*. 8 vols. New York, NY: McGraw-Hill, 1976-1987.
Smith, Philip. *A History of the World: From the Creation to the Fall of the Western Roman Empire*. 3 vols. New York, NY: D. Appleton and Co., 1885.
Smith, Philip D., Jr. *Tartan for Me!: Suggested Tartan for 13,695 Scottish, Scotch-Irish, Irish and North American Names with Lists of Clan, Family, and District Tartans*. Bruceton, WV: Scotpress, 1990.

Smith, Robert Edwin. *Christianity and the Race Problem*. New York, NY: Fleming H. Revell Co., 1922.

Sorrel, Gilbert Moxley. *Recollections of a Confederate Staff Officer*. New York, NY: Neale Publishing, 1905.

Speer, Albert. *Inside the Third Reich*. 1969. New York, NY: Avon, 1971 ed.

Spence, James. *On the Recognition of the Southern Confederation*. Ithaca, NY: Cornell University Library, 1862.

Spero, Sterling D., and Abram L. Harris. *The Black Worker: A Study of the Negro and the Labor Movement*. New York, NY: Columbia University Press, 1931.

Spooner, Lysander. *No Treason* (only Numbers 1, 2, and 6 were published). Boston, MA: Lysander Spooner, 1867-1870.

Stampp, Kenneth M. *The Peculiar Institution: Slavery in the Antebellum South*. New York, NY: Vintage, 1956.

Stanford, Peter Thomas. *The Tragedy of the Negro in America*. Boston, MA: Peter Thomas Stanford, 1898.

Stanley, Henry Morton. *The Autobiography of Sir Henry Morton Stanley*. Boston, MA: Houghton Mifflin Co., 1909.

Starobin, Robert S. *Industrial Slavery in the Old South*. New York, NY: Oxford University Press, 1970.

Starr, Chester G. *Civilization and the Caesars: The Intellectual Revolution in the Roman Empire*. 1954. New York, NY: W. W. Norton and Co., 1965 ed.

Staudenraus, P. J. *The African Colonization Movement, 1816-1865*. New York, NY: Columbia University Press, 1961.

Steiner, Bernard Christian. *History of Slavery in Connecticut*. Baltimore, MD: Johns Hopkins University Press, 1893.

Steiner, Lewis Henry. *Report of Lewis H. Steiner: Inspector of the Sanitary Commission, Containing a Diary Kept During the Rebel Occupation of Frederick, MD, September, 1862*. New York, NY: Anson D. F. Randolph, 1862.

Steinfeld, Robert J. *The Invention of Free Labor: The Employment Relation in English and American Law and Culture, 1350-1870*. Chapel Hill, NC: University of North Carolina Press, 1991.

Stephen, James. *The Slavery of the British West India Colonies Delineated, As it Exists in Both Law and Practice*. 2 vols. London, UK: Joseph Butterworth and Son, 1824.

Stephens, Alexander H. *A Constitutional View of the Late War Between the States; Its Causes, Character, Conduct and Results*. 2 vols. Philadelphia, PA: National Publishing, Co., 1870.

——. *Recollections of Alexander H. Stephens: His Diary Kept When a Prisoner at Fort Warren, Boston Harbour, 1865*. New York, NY: Doubleday, Page, and Co., 1910.

Stephenson, Nathaniel Wright. *Lincoln: An Account of His Personal Life, Especially of Its Springs of Action as Revealed and Deepened by the Ordeal of War*. Indianapolis, IN: Bobbs-Merrill, 1922.

Sterling, Dorothy (ed.). *Speak Out in Thunder Tones: Letters and Other Writings by Black Northerners, 1787-1865*. 1973. Cambridge, MA: Da Capo, 1998 ed.

Stern, Philip Van Doren (ed.). *The Life and Writings of Abraham Lincoln*. 1940. New York, NY: Modern Library, 2000 ed.

Stevenson, Brenda E. *Life in Black and White: Family and Community in the Slave South*. New York, NY: Oxford University Press, 1996.

Steward, Austin. *Twenty-two Years a Slave, and Forty Years a Freeman*. Canandaigua, NY: the author, 1867.

Stewart, James Brewer. *Holy Warriors: The Abolitionists and American Slavery*. New York, NY: Hill and Wang, 1976.

Stewart, L. Lloyd. *A Far Cry From Freedom: Gradual Abolition (1799-1827): New York State's Crime Against Humanity*. Bloomington, IN: AuthorHouse, 2005.

Stiles, Robert. *Four Years Under Marse Robert*. New York, NY: Neal Publishing Co., 1910.

Still, William. *The Underground Railroad: A Record of Facts, Authentic Narratives, Letters, Etc*. Philadelphia, PA: Porter and Coates, 1872.

Stimpson, George. *A Book About American History*. 1956. New York, NY: Premier Books, 1960 ed.

Stirling, James. *Letters From the Slave States*. London, UK: John W. Parker and Son, 1857.

Stone, Alfred Holt. *Studies in the American Race Problem*. New York, NY: Doubleday, Page and Co., 1908.

Stone, Kate. *Brokenburn: The Journal of Kate Stone, 1861-1868*. (John Q. Anderson, ed.). Baton Rouge, LA: Louisiana State University Press, 1955.

Stonebraker, J. Clarence. *The Unwritten South: Cause, Progress and Results of the Civil War - Relics of Hidden Truth After Forty Years*. Seventh ed., n.p., 1908.

Storke, Elliot G., and Linus Pierpoint Brockett. *A Complete History of the Great Rebellion, Embracing Its Causes, Events and Consequences*. 3 vols. Auburn, NY: The Auburn Publishing Co., 1865.

Strode, Hudson. *Jefferson Davis: American Patriot*. 3 vols. New York, NY: Harcourt, Brace and World, 1955, 1959, 1964.

Stroud, George M. *A Sketch of the Laws in Relation to Slavery in the United States of America*. Philadelphia, PA: Kimber and Sharpless, 1827.

Stuckey, Sterling. *Slave Culture: Nationalist Theory and the Foundation of Black America*. Oxford, UK: Oxford University Press, 1987.

Sturge, Joseph. *A Visit to the United States in 1841*. London, UK: Hamilton, Adams, and Co., 1842.

Sumner, Charles. *White Slavery in the Barbary States: A Lecture Before the Boston Mercantile Library Association, Feb. 17, 1847*. Boston, MA: William D. Ticknor and Co., 1847.

——. *The Crime Against Kansas: The Apologies for the Crime - The True Remedy*. Boston, MA: John P. Jewett, 1856.

Swain, Joseph Ward. *The Harper History of Civilization*. New York, NY: Harper and Brothers, 1958.

Swint, Henry L. (ed.) *Dear Ones at Home: Letters From Contraband Camps*. Nashville, TN: Vanderbilt University Press, 1966.

Taylor, Joe Gray. *Negro Slavery in Louisiana*. New York, NY: Negro Universities Press, 1969.

Taylor, Richard. *Destruction and Reconstruction: Personal Experiences of the Late War in the United States*. New York, NY: D. Appleton, 1879.

Taylor, Susie King. *Reminiscences of My Life in Camp With the 33rd United States Colored Troops Late 1st S. C. Volunteers*. Boston, MA: Susie King Taylor, 1902.

The National Almanac and Annual Record for the Year 1863. Philadelphia, PA: George W. Childs, 1863.

The North British Review. February-May 1862, Vol. 36. Edinburgh, Scotland: T. and T. Clark, 1862.

The Outlook. September 4, 1909. New York, NY: The Outlook Company, 1909.

The Weekly News and Courier. *Our Women in the War: The Lives They Lived; The Deaths They Died*. Charleston, SC: The Weekly News and Courier Book Presses, 1885.

The World Book Encyclopedia. 1928. Chicago, IL: Field Enterprises Educational Corp., 1966 ed.

Thomas, Emory M. *The Confederate Nation: 1861-1865*. New York, NY: Harper and Row, 1979.

Thomas, Gabriel. *An Account of Pennsylvania and West New Jersey*. 1698. Cleveland, OH: Burrows Brothers Co., 1903 ed.

Thomas, Hugh. *The Slave Trade: The History of the Atlantic Slave Trade, 1440-1870*. New York, NY: Simon and Schuster, 1999.

Thomas, William Hannibal. *The American Negro: What He Was, What He Is, and What He May Become*. New York, NY: Macmillan Co., 1901.

Thome, James A., and J. Horace Kimball. *Emancipation in the West Indies: A Six Month's Tour in Antigua, Barbadoes, and Jamaica, in the Year 1837*. New York, NY: The American Anti-Slavery Society, 1838.

Thompson, Edward Palmer. *The Making of the English Working Class*. London, UK: Victor Gollancz, 1963.

Thompson, Frank Charles (ed.). *The Thompson Chain Reference Bible* (King James Version). 1908. Indianapolis, IN: B. B. Kirkbride Bible Co., 1964 ed.

Thompson, Jack H., and Robert D. Reischauer (eds.). *Modernization of the Arab World*. Princeton, NJ: D. Van Nostrand Co., 1966.

Thompson, James Westfall, and Edgar Nathaniel Johnson. *An Introduction to Medieval Europe: 300-1500*. New York, NY: W. W. Norton and Co., 1937.

Thompson, Neal. *Driving With the Devil: Southern Moonshine, Detroit Wheels, and the Birth of NASCAR*. Three Rivers, MI: Three Rivers Press, 2006.

Thompson, Robert Means, and Richard Wainwright (eds.). *Confidential Correspondence of Gustavus Vasa Fox, Assistant Secretary of the Navy, 1861-1865*. 2 vols. 1918. New York, NY: Naval History Society, 1920 ed.

Thomson, William. *A Tradesman's Travels in the United States and Canada, in the Year 1840, 40, and 42*. Edinburgh, Scotland: Oliver and Boyd, 1842.

Thornton, Brian. *101 Things You Didn't Know About Lincoln: Loves and Losses, Political Power Plays, White House Hauntings*. Avon, MA: Adams Media, 2006.

Thornton, Gordon. *The Southern Nation: The New Rise of the Old South*. Gretna, LA: Pelican Publishing Co., 2000.

Thornton, John. *Africa and Africans in the Making of the Atlantic World, 1400-1800*. 1992. Cambridge, UK: Cambridge University Press, 1999 ed.

Thornton, Mark, and Robert B. Ekelund, Jr. *Tariffs, Blockades, and Inflation: The Economics of the Civil War*. Wilmington, DE: Scholarly Resources, 2004.

Thornton, Willis, and James Daugherty. *Almanac for Americans*. 1941. New York, NY: Greenberg, 1954 ed.

Thwaites, Reuben Gold (ed.). *Early Western Travels, 1748-1846* (Vol. 12). Cleveland, OH: Arthur H. Clark Co., 1905.

Tibbles, Anthony (ed.). *Transatlantic Slavery: Against Human Dignity*. 1995. Liverpool, UK: Liverpool

University Press, 2005 ed.

Tilley, John Shipley. *Lincoln Takes Command.* 1941. Nashville, TN: Bill Coats Limited, 1991 ed.

——. *Facts the Historians Leave Out: A Confederate Primer.* 1951. Nashville, TN: Bill Coats Limited, 1999 ed.

Tinker, Hugh. *A New System of Slavery: The Export of Indian Labour Overseas, 1830-1920.* London, UK: Oxford University Press, 1974.

Tocqueville, Alexis de. *Democracy in America.* 2 vols. (Translated by Henry Reeve.) New York, NY: George Adlard, 1839.

Traupman, John C. *The New College Latin and English Dictionary.* 1966. New York, NY: Bantam, 1988 ed.

Trevelyan, George Macaulay. *History of England.* 2 vols. 1926. Garden City, NY: Doubleday Anchor, 1952 ed.

Trexler, Harrison Anthony. *Slavery in Missouri, 1804-1865.* Baltimore, MD: Johns Hopkins Press, 1914.

Trumbull, Lyman. *Speech of Honorable Lyman Trumbull, of Illinois, at a Mass Meeting in Chicago, August 7, 1858.* Washington, D.C.: Buell and Blanchard, 1858.

Truth, Sojourner. *Sojourner Truth's Narrative and Book of Life.* 1850. Battle Creek, MI: Sojourner Truth, 1881 ed.

Tuchman, Barbara W. *A Distant Mirror: The Calamitous 14th Century.* New York, NY: Knopf, 1978.

Tucker, St. George. *On the State of Slavery in Virginia, in View of the Constitution of the United States, With Selected Writings.* Indianapolis, IN: Liberty Fund, 1999.

Turner, Edward Raymond. *The Negro in Pennsylvania: Slavery, Servitude, Freedom, 1639-1861.* Washington, D.C.: American Historical Association, 1911.

——. *Slavery in Pennsylvania: A Dissertation.* Baltimore, MD: The Lord Baltimore Press, 1911.

Tushnet, Mark. *The American Law of Slavery, 1810-1860.* Princeton, NJ: Princeton University Press, 1981.

Tyler, Lyon Gardiner. *The Letters and Times of the Tylers.* 3 vols. Williamsburg, VA: n.p., 1896.

——. *Propaganda in History.* Richmond, VA: Richmond Press, 1920.

——. *The Gray Book: A Confederate Catechism.* Columbia, TN: Gray Book Committee, SCV, 1935.

Unger, Irwin. *These United States: The Question of Our Past - Vol. 2: Since 1865.* 1978. Englewood Cliffs, NJ: Prentice Hall, 1992 ed.

Upshur, Abel Parker. *A Brief Enquiry Into the True Nature and Character of Our Federal Government.* Philadelphia, PA: John Campbell, 1863.

Vaillant, George C. *The Aztecs of Mexico: Origin, Rise and Fall of the Aztec Nation.* 1944. Harmondsworth, UK: Penguin, 1960 ed.

Voegeli, Victor Jacque. *Free But Not Equal: The Midwest and the Negro During the Civil War.* Chicago, IL: University of Chicago Press, 1967.

Volk, Ernest. *The Archaeology of the Delaware Valley.* Cambridge, MA: Peabody Museum of American Archeology and Ethnology, 1911.

Wade, Richard C. *Slavery in the Cities: The South 1820-1860.* New York, NY: Oxford University Press, 1964.

Wade, Wyn Craig. *The Fiery Cross: The Ku Klux Klan in America.* 1987. New York, NY: Touchstone, 1988 ed.

Walker, Barbara G. *The Woman's Encyclopedia of Myths and Secrets.* New York, NY: Harper and Row, 1983.

——. *The Woman's Dictionary of Symbols and Sacred Objects.* New York, NY: Harper and Row, 1988.

Walker, Moses Fleetwood. *Our Home Colony: A Treatise on the Past, Present and Future of the Negro Race in America.* Steubenville, OH: M. F. Walker, 1908.

Walker, Sheila S. (ed.). *African Roots/American Cultures: Africa in the Creation of the Americas.* Lanham, MD: Rowman and Littlefield, 2001.

Wallace, David Duncan. *The Life of Henry Laurens.* New York, NY: G. P. Putnam's Sons, 1915.

Wallechinsky, David, and Irving Wallace. *The People's Almanac #2.* New York, NY: William Morrow and Co., 1978.

Wallechinsky, David, Irving Wallace, and Amy Wallace. *The People's Almanac Presents The Book of Lists.* New York, NY: William Morrow and Co., 1977.

Ware, Camilla. *Slavery In Vermont, and in Other Parts of the United States.* Woodstock, VT: Davis and Greene, 1858.

Waring, George Edward, Jr. *Whip and Spur.* New York, NY: Doubleday and McClure, 1897.

Warner, Ezra J. *Generals in Gray: Lives of the Confederate Commanders.* 1959. Baton Rouge, LA: Louisiana State University Press, 1989 ed.

——. *Generals in Blue: Lives of the Union Commanders.* 1964. Baton Rouge, LA: Louisiana State University Press, 2006 ed.

Warnock, Robert, and George K. Anderson. *The Ancient Foundations.* 1950. Glenview, IL: Scott, Foresman and Co., 1967 ed.

Warren, Robert Penn. *John Brown: The Making of a Martyr*. New York, NY: Payson and Clarke, 1929.

——. *Who Speaks for the Negro?* New York, NY: Random House, 1965.

Washington, Booker T. *Up From Slavery: An Autobiography*. 1900. New York, NY: A. L. Burt Co., 1901 ed.

Washington, Henry Augustine. *The Writings of Thomas Jefferson*. 9 vols. New York, NY: H. W. Derby, 1861.

Watkins, Samuel Rush. *"Company Aytch," Maury Grays, First Tennessee Regiment; or, A Side Show of the Big Show*. 1882. Chattanooga, TN: Times Printing Co., 1900 ed.

Watson, Alan. *Roman Slave Law*. Baltimore, MD: Johns Hopkins University Press, 1987.

——. *Slave Law in the Americas*. Athens, GA: University of Georgia Press, 1989.

Watson, Harry L. *Andrew Jackson vs. Henry Clay: Democracy and Development in Antebellum America*. New York, NY: St. Martin's Press, 1998.

Watson, James L. (ed.). *Asian and African Systems of Slavery*. Oxford, UK: Basil Blackwood, 1980.

Watts, Peter. *A Dictionary of the Old West*. 1977. New York, NY: Promontory Press, 1987 ed.

Waugh, John C. *Surviving the Confederacy: Rebellion, Ruin, and Recovery - Roger and Sara Pryor During the Civil War*. New York, NY: Harcourt, 2002.

Weatherford, Willis D., and Charles S. Johnson. *Race Relations: Adjustment of Whites and Negroes in the United States*. Boston, MA: Heath, 1934.

Webster, Daniel. *Webster's Speeches: Reply to Hayne - The Constitution and the Union*. Boston, MA: Ginn and Co., 1897.

Weeks, Stephen Beauregard. *Southern Quakers and Slavery: A Study in Institutional History*. Baltimore, MD: Johns Hopkins Press, 1896.

Weiner, Marli F. *Mistresses and Slaves: Plantation Women in South Carolina, 1830-1880*. Urbana, IL: University of Illinois Press, 1997.

Weintraub, Max. *The Blue Book of American History*. New York, NY: Regents Publishing Co., 1960.

Welby, Adlard. *A Visit to North America and the English Settlements in Illinois, With a Winter Residence at Philadelphia*. London, UK: J. Drury, 1821.

Weld, Theodore D. (ed.). *American Slavery As It Is: Testimony of a Thousand Witnesses*. New York, NY: American Anti-Slavery Society, 1839.

Welles, Gideon. *Diary of Gideon Welles, Secretary of the Navy Under Lincoln and Johnson* (Vol. 1). Boston, MA: Houghton Mifflin, 1911.

Welling, James Clarke. *Slavery in the Territories*. Washington, D.C.: U.S. Government Printing Office, 1892.

Wells, H. G. *The Outline of History: Being a Plain History of Life and Mankind*. 2 vols. 1920. Garden City, NY: Garden City Books, 1961 ed.

Westermann, William L. *The Story of Ancient Nations*. New York, NY: D. Appleton and Co., 1912.

Wertenbaker, Thomas Jefferson. *The Puritan Oligarchy: The Founding of American Civilization*. New York, NY: Grosset's Universal Library, 1947.

——. *The Shaping of Colonial Virginia: The Planters of Colonial Virginia*. New York, NY: Russell and Russell, 1958.

Westermann, William L. *The Story of Ancient Nations*. New York, NY: D. Appleton and Co., 1912.

Wheeler, Jacob D. *Practical Treatise on the Law of Slavery*. New York, NY: Allan Pollock, Jr., 1837.

White, Charles Langdon, Edwin Jay Foscue, and Tom Lee McKnight. *Regional Geography of Anglo-America*. 1943. Englewood Cliffs, NJ: Prentice-Hall, 1985 ed.

White, Deborah Gray. *Ar'n't I a Woman? Female Slaves in the Plantation South*. New York, NY: W. W. Norton, 1985.

White, Henry Alexander. *Robert E. Lee and the Southern Confederacy, 1807-1870*. 1897. New York, NY: G. P. Putnam's Sons, 1900 ed.

White, Jon Manchip. *Everyday Life in Ancient Egypt*. 1963. New York, NY: Perigee, 1980 ed.

Wiley, Bell Irvin. *Southern Negroes: 1861-1865*. 1938. New Haven, CT: Yale University Press, 1969 ed.

——. *The Life of Johnny Reb: The Common Soldier of the Confederacy*. 1943. Baton Rouge, LA: Louisiana State University Press, 1978 ed.

——. *The Life of Billy Yank: The Common Soldier of the Union*. 1952. Baton Rouge, LA: Louisiana State University Press, 2001 ed.

Wilkens, J. Steven. *America: The First 350 Years*. Monroe, LA: Covenant Publications, 1998.

Williams, Charles Richard. *The Life of Rutherford Birchard Hayes, Nineteenth President of the United States*. 2 vols. Boston, MA: Houghton Mifflin Co., 1914.

Williams, Eric. *Capitalism and Slavery*. Chapel Hill, NC: University of North Carolina, 1944.

Williams, George Washington. *History of the Negro Race in America: From 1619 to 1880, Negroes as Slaves, as Soldiers, and as Citizens*. 2 vols. New York, NY: G. P. Putnam's Sons, 1883.

——. *A History of the Negro Troops in the War of the Rebellion 1861-1865*. New York, NY: Harper and Brothers,

1888.

Williams, Henry Smith (ed.). *The Historians' History of the World*. 25 vols. London, UK: Hooper and Jackson, 1908.

Williams, James. *The South Vindicated*. London, UK: Longman, Green, Longman, Roberts, and Green, 1862.

Williams-Meyers, A. J. *Long Hammering: Essays on the Forging of an African American Presence in the Hudson River Valley to the Early Twentieth Century*. Trenton, NJ: Africa World Press, 1994.

Williams, Oscar. *African Americans and Colonial Legislation in the Middle Colonies*. New York, NY: Garland Publishing, 1998.

Williams, William H. *Slavery and Freedom in Delaware, 1639-1865*. Wilmington, DE: Scholarly Resources, 1996.

Willis, F. Roy. *World Civilizations - Vol. 1: From Ancient Times Through the Sixteenth Century*. 1982. Lexington, MA: D. C. Heath and Co., 1986 ed.

Wilson, Charles Reagan, and William Ferris. *Encyclopedia of Southern Culture* (Vol. 1). New York, NY: Anchor, 1989.

Wilson, Clyde N. *Why the South Will Survive: Fifteen Southerners Look at Their Region a Half Century After I'll Take My Stand*. Athens, GA: University of Georgia Press, 1981.

——. *A Defender of Southern Conservatism: M.E. Bradford and His Achievements*. Columbia, MO: University of Missouri Press, 1999.

——. *From Union to Empire: Essays in the Jeffersonian Tradition*. Columbia, SC: The Foundation for American Education, 2003.

——. *Defending Dixie: Essays in Southern History and Culture*. Columbia, SC: The Foundation for American Education, 2005.

Wilson, E. O. *Sociobiology: The New Synthesis*. Cambridge, MA: Belknap Press, 1975.

Wilson, Henry. *History of the Rise and Fall of the Slave Power in America*. 3 vols. Boston, MA: James R. Osgood and Co., 1877.

Wilson, Joseph Thomas. *The Black Phalanx: A History of the Negro Soldiers of the United States in the Wars of 1775-1812, 1861-'65*. Hartford, CT: American Publishing Co., 1890.

Wilson, Theodore B. *The Black Codes of the South*. Tuscaloosa, AL: University of Alabama Press, 1965.

Wilson, Woodrow. *Division and Reunion: 1829-1889*. 1893. New York, NY: Longmans, Green, and Co., 1908 ed.

——. *A History of the American People*. 5 vols. 1902. New York, NY: Harper and Brothers, 1918 ed.

Winks, Robin W. *The Blacks in Canada: A History*. New Haven, CT: Yale University Press, 1971.

Wise, Jennings Cropper. *Ye Kingdome of Accawmacke or the Eastern Shore of Virginia in the Seventeenth Century*. Richmond, VA: The Bell Book Stationary Co., 1911.

Wish, Harvey (ed.). *The Negro Since Emancipation*. Englewood Cliffs, NJ: Prentice-Hall, 1964.

Wood, Betty. *The Origins of American Slavery: Freedom and Bondage in the English Colonies*. New York, NY: Hill and Wang, 1998.

Woodard, Komozi. *A Nation Within a Nation: Amiri Baraka (LeRoi Jones) and Black Power Politics*. Chapel Hill, NC: University of North Carolina Press, 1999.

Woods, Thomas E., Jr. *The Politically Incorrect Guide to American History*. Washington, D.C.: Regnery, 2004.

Woodson, Carter G. (ed.). *The Journal of Negro History* (Vol. 4). Lancaster, PA: Association for the Study of Negro Life and History, 1919.

Yetman, Norman R. *Life Under the "Peculiar Institution": Selections from the Slave Narrative Collection*. New York, NY: Holt McDougal, 1970.

Zilversmit, Arthur. *The First Emancipation: The Abolition of Slavery in the North*. Chicago, IL: University of Chicago Press, 1967.

Zinn, Howard. *A People's History of the United States: 1492-Present*. 1980. New York, NY: HarperCollins, 1995.

INDEX

MEET THE AUTHOR

LOCHLAINN SEABROOK, winner of the prestigious Jefferson Davis Historical Gold Medal for his "masterpiece," *A Rebel Born: A Defense of Nathan Bedford Forrest*, is an unreconstructed Southern historian, award-winning author, Civil War scholar, and traditional Southern Agrarian of Scottish, English, Irish, Dutch, Welsh, German, and Italian extraction. An encyclopedist, lexicographer, musician, artist, graphic designer, genealogist, and photographer, as well as an award-winning poet, songwriter, and screenwriter, he has a 40 year background in historical nonfiction writing and is a member of the Sons of Confederate Veterans, the Civil War Trust, and the National Grange.

Due to similarities in their writing styles, ideas, and literary works, Seabrook is often referred to as the "new Shelby Foote," the "Southern Joseph Campbell," and the "American Robert Graves" (his English cousin).

The grandson of an Appalachian coal-mining family, Seabrook is a seventh-generation Kentuckian, co-chair of the Jent/Gent Family Committee (Kentucky), founder and director of the Blakeney Family Tree Project, and a board member of the Friends of Colonel Benjamin E. Caudill.

COPYRIGHT ©
SEA RAVEN PRESS

Lochlainn Seabrook, award-winning Civil War scholar and unreconstructed Southern historian, is America's most popular, well-respected, and prolific pro-South author.

Seabrook's literary works have been endorsed by leading authorities, museum curators, award-winning historians, bestselling authors, celebrities, noted scientists, well respected educators, TV show hosts and producers, renowned military artists, esteemed Southern organizations, and distinguished academicians from around the world.

Seabrook has authored over 45 popular adult books on the American Civil War, American and international slavery, the U.S. Confederacy (1781), the Southern Confederacy (1861), religion, theology and thealogy, Jesus, the Bible, the Apocrypha, the Law of Attraction, alternative health, spirituality, ghost stories, the paranormal, ufology, social issues, and cross-cultural studies of the family and marriage. His Confederate biographies, pro-South studies, genealogical monographs, family histories, military encyclopedias, self-help guides, and etymological dictionaries have received wide acclaim.

Seabrook's eight children's books include a Southern guide to the Civil War, a biography of Nathan Bedford Forrest, a dictionary of religion and myth, a rewriting of the King Arthur legend (which reinstates the original pre-Christian motifs), two bedtime stories for preschoolers, a naturalist's guidebook to owls, a worldwide look at the family, and an examination of the Near-Death Experience.

Of blue-blooded Southern stock through his Kentucky, Tennessee, Virginia, West Virginia, and North Carolina ancestors, he is a direct descendant of European royalty via his 6th great-grandfather, the Earl of Oxford, after which London's famous Harley Street is named. Among his celebrated male Celtic ancestors is Robert the Bruce, King of Scotland, Seabrook's 22nd great-grandfather. The 21st great-grandson of Edward I "Longshanks" Plantagenet), King of England, Seabrook is a thirteenth-generation Southerner through his descent from the colonists of Jamestown, Virginia (1607).

The 2nd, 3rd, and 4th great-grandson of dozens of Confederate soldiers, one of his closest connections to Lincoln's War is through his 3rd great-grandfather, Elias Jent, Sr., who fought for the Confederacy in the Thirteenth Cavalry Kentucky under Seabrook's 2nd cousin, Colonel Benjamin E.

Caudill. The Thirteenth, also known as "Caudill's Army," fought in numerous conflicts, including the Battles of Saltville, Gladsville, Mill Cliff, Poor Fork, Whitesburg, and Leatherwood.

Seabrook is a direct descendant of the families of Alexander H. Stephens, John Singleton Mosby, William Giles Harding, and Edmund Winchester Rucker, and is related to the following Confederates and other 18th- and 19th-Century luminaries: Robert E. Lee, Stephen Dill Lee, Stonewall Jackson, Nathan Bedford Forrest, James Longstreet, John Hunt Morgan, Jeb Stuart, Pierre G. T. Beauregard (approved the Confederate Battle Flag design), George W. Gordon, John Bell Hood, Alexander Peter Stewart, Arthur M. Manigault, Joseph Manigault, Charles Scott Venable, Thornton A. Washington, John A. Washington, Abraham Buford, Edmund W. Pettus, Theodrick "Tod" Carter, John B. Womack, John H. Winder, Gideon J. Pillow, States Rights Gist, Henry R. Jackson, John Lawton Seabrook, John C. Breckinridge, Leonidas Polk, Zachary Taylor, Sarah Knox Taylor (first wife of Jefferson Davis), Richard Taylor, Davy Crockett, Daniel Boone, Meriwether Lewis (of the Lewis and Clark Expedition) Andrew Jackson, James K. Polk, Abram Poindexter Maury (founder of Franklin, TN), Zebulon Vance, Thomas Jefferson, Edmund Jennings Randolph, George Wythe Randolph (grandson of Jefferson), Felix K. Zollicoffer, Fitzhugh Lee, Nathaniel F. Cheairs, Jesse James, Frank James, Robert Brank Vance, Charles Sidney Winder, John W. McGavock, Caroline E. (Winder) McGavock, David Harding McGavock, Lysander McGavock, James Randal McGavock, Randal William McGavock, Francis McGavock, Emily McGavock, William Henry F. Lee, Lucius E. Polk, Minor Meriwether (husband of noted pro-South author Elizabeth Avery Meriwether), Ellen Bourne Tynes (wife of Forrest's chief of artillery, Captain John W. Morton), South Carolina Senators Preston Smith Brooks and Andrew Pickens Butler, and famed South Carolina diarist Mary Chesnut.

Seabrook's modern day cousins include: Patrick J. Buchanan (conservative author), Cindy Crawford (model), Shelby Lee Adams (Letcher Co., Kentucky, photographer), Bertram Thomas Combs (Kentucky's 50th governor), Edith Bolling (wife of President Woodrow Wilson), and actors Andy Griffith, George C. Scott, Robert Duvall, Reese Witherspoon, Lee Marvin, Rebecca Gayheart, and Tom Cruise.

Seabrook's screenplay, *A Rebel Born*, based on his book of the same name, has been signed with acclaimed filmmaker Christopher Forbes (of Forbes Film). It is now in pre-production, and is set for release in 2016 as a full-length feature film. This will be the first movie ever made of Nathan Bedford Forrest's life story, and as a historically accurate project written from the Southern perspective, is destined to be one of the most talked about Civil War films of all time.

Born with music in his blood, Seabrook is an award-winning, multi-genre, BMI-Nashville songwriter and lyricist who has composed some 3,000 songs (250 albums), and whose original music has been heard in film (*A Rebel Born, Cowgirls 'n Angels, Confederate Cavalry, Billy the Kid: Showdown in Lincoln County, Vengeance Without Mercy, Last Step, County Line, The Mark*) and on TV and radio worldwide. A musician, producer, multi-instrumentalist, and renown performer—whose keyboard work has been variously compared to pianists from Hargus Robbins and Vince Guaraldi to Elton John and Leonard Bernstein—Seabrook has opened for groups such as the Earl Scruggs Review, Ted Nugent, and Bob Seger, and has performed privately for such public figures as President Ronald Reagan, Burt Reynolds, Loni Anderson, and Senator Edward W. Brooke. Seabrook's cousins in the music business include: Johnny Cash, Elvis Presley, Billy Ray and Miley Cyrus, Patty Loveless, Tim McGraw, Lee Ann Womack, Dolly Parton, Pat Boone, Naomi, Wynonna, and Ashley Judd, Ricky Skaggs, the Sunshine Sisters, Martha Carson, and Chet Atkins.

Seabrook, a libertarian, lives with his wife and family in historic Middle Tennessee, the heart of Forrest country and the Confederacy, where his conservative Southern ancestors fought valiantly against Liberal Lincoln and the progressive North in defense of Jeffersonianism, constitutional government, and personal liberty.

LochlainnSeabrook.com

In December 1927 U.S. President Calvin Coolidge, a Yankee from Vermont, took time from his busy schedule to meet with a group of Confederate veterans, then pose for this photograph in front of the White House. The Confederate Battle Flag is prominently displayed while the president looks on reverently. Unlike today's misguided anti-South bigots, Coolidge understood that Confederate soldiers were patriotic Americans and, as such, should be treated with the same dignity as Union soldiers. The U.S. Congress agreed, and in the first half of the 20th Century it passed numerous laws defining *all* Confederate service personnel, whether white, black, red, brown, or yellow, as U.S. military veterans.

MEET THE FOREWORD WRITER

GREGORY NEWSON was born in New York City. He is an author, educator, and artist with over 100 works of art to his credit. His literary works include the novels, *The Chandler Boys*, *CSA Buried Treasures*, a young adult book *Uncle T and the Uppity Spy*, and a comic book entitled *The Adventures of Rank Johnson*.

His artistic styles range from realism and abstraction to surrealistic and portraits. As a youngster he won numerous art shows and later received a scholarship from the Famous Artist School in Westport, Connecticut. He eventually ended up working as an assistant art director at Viking Press, and as of 2016 has not only illustrated his own books, but four children's books as well. His Civil War painting, *The Rescue*, was used on the cover of the paperback edition of award-winning author Lochlainn Seabrook's book, *Everything You Were Taught About African-Americans and the Civil War is Wrong, Ask a Southerner!* (Sea Raven Press), for which he also wrote the foreword.

Mr. Newson owns three companies: Green Beans Solutions, It's About Time Advertising, and Newson Publishing. He has two children and is currently working on his autobiography entitled, *I Get High Watching Paint Dry*. Through his writings and artwork he is dedicated to teaching the world the truth about African-Americans and the American Civil War, and in particular black Confederates.

NewsonPublishing.com

If you enjoyed this book you will be interested in Mr. Seabrook's other popular related titles:

☛ EVERYTHING YOU WERE TAUGHT ABOUT THE CIVIL WAR IS WRONG, ASK A SOUTHERNER!
☛ EVERYTHING YOU WERE TAUGHT ABOUT AMERICAN SLAVERY IS WRONG, ASK A SOUTHERNER!
☛ CONFEDERATE FLAG FACTS: WHAT EVERY AMERICAN SHOULD KNOW ABOUT DIXIE'S SOUTHERN CROSS
☛ CONFEDERACY 101: AMAZING FACTS YOU NEVER KNEW ABOUT AMERICA'S OLDEST POLITICAL TRADITION

Available from Sea Raven Press and wherever fine books are sold

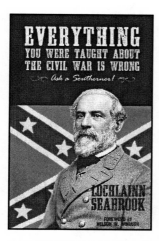

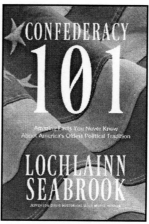

ALL OF OUR BOOK COVERS ARE AVAILABLE AS 11" X 17" POSTERS, SUITABLE FOR FRAMING

SeaRavenPress.com • NathanBedfordForrestBooks.com